Technical Analysis Explained

Technical Analysis Explained

The Successful Investor's Guide to Spotting Investment Trends and Turning Points

Fourth Edition

Martin J. Pring

McGraw-Hill
New York   Chicago   San Francisco
Lisbon   London   Madrid   Mexico City   Milan
New Delhi   San Juan   Seoul   Singapore
Sydney   Toronto

Library of Congress Cataloging-in-Publication Data

Pring, Martin J.
　　Technical analysis explained / the successful investor's guide to spotting
investment trends and turning points / by Martin Pring.—4th ed.
　　　　p.　　cm.
　　ISBN 0-07-138193-7
　　1. Investment analysis. I. Title

HG4529 .P75 2002
332.63'22—dc21   2001044981

McGraw-Hill

A Division of The McGraw·Hill Companies

ISBN: 0-07-138193-7

The sponsoring editor for this book was Stephen Isaacs and the production super-
visor was Clare Stanley. It was set in New Baskerville by MacAllister Publishing
Services, LLC.

Printed and bound by R. R. Donnelley & Sons Company.

This publication is designed to provide accurate and authoritative information in
regard to the subject matter covered. It is sold with the understanding that neither
the author nor the publisher is engaged in rendering legal, accounting, or other
professional service. If legal advice or other expert assistance is required, the services of a competent professional person should be sought.

　　　　　　　　　　　　　　–From a Declaration of Principles jointly adopted
　　　　　　　　　　　　　　　　　　by a Committee of the American Bar
　　　　　　　　　　　　　　　　Association and a Committee of Publishers

McGraw-Hill books are available at special quantity discounts to use as premiums
and sales promotions, or for use in corporate training programs. For more information, please write to the Director of Special Sales, Professional Publishing,
McGraw-Hill, Two Penn Plaza, New York, NY 10121-2298. Or contact your local
bookstore.

　This book is printed on recycled, acid-free paper containing a minimum of
　　　　50% recycled de-inked fiber.

To my son, Thomas William Pring

Contents

Preface

There is no reason why anyone cannot make a substantial amount of money in the financial markets, but there are many reasons why many people will not. As with most endeavors in life, the key to success is knowledge and action. This book has been written in an attempt to shed some light on the internal workings of the markets and to help expand the *knowledge* component, leaving the *action* to the patience, discipline, and objectivity of the individual investor.

The mid- to late 1980s saw the expansion of investment and trading opportunities to a global scale, in terms of both the cash and the futures markets. In the 1990s, innovations in the communications industry enabled anyone to plot data on an intraday basis for relatively little cost. Today, numerous charting sites have sprung up on the Internet, so virtually anyone now has the ability to practice technical analysis. As a consequence of the technological revolution, time horizons have been greatly shortened. I am not sure that this is a good thing because short-term trends experience more random noise than longer-term ones. This means that the technical indicators are not as effective. The fourth edition of *Technical Analysis Explained* has been expanded and totally revised to keep abreast of many of these changes, and to include some technical innovations and evolvement in my own thinking since the publication of the third edition.

Every chapter has been thoroughly reworked and expanded. In the interest of efficiency, some have been dropped and others substituted. Considerable attention continues to be focused on the U.S. equity market, but many of the marketplace examples feature international stock indexes, currencies, commodities, and precious metals. Special chapters also feature technical analysis of the credit markets and global equities. In most cases, the marketplace examples have been updated, but some older ones from previous editions have been left in deliberately to give the book some historical perspective. These historical examples also underscore the point that nothing has really changed in the last 100 years. The same true and tried principles are as relevant today as they always were. I have no doubt whatsoever that this will continue to be so in the future.

Thus, technical analysis could be applied in New York in 1850, in Tokyo in 1950, and in Moscow in 2150. This is true because price action in financial markets is a reflection of human nature, and human nature remains more or less constant. Technical principles can also be applied to any freely traded entity in any time frame. A trend reversal signal on a 5-minute bar chart is based on the same indicators as one on a monthly chart; only the significance is different. Shorter time frames reflect shorter trends and are therefore less significant.

Several new chapters have been added in this edition. One of the areas I become more impressed with the more I study it is the concept of one- and two-bar price reversals. They are also relevant for intraday and swing traders. Consequently, a brand new chapter on this subject has been introduced in this edition. In view of their growing popularity, candlesticks, previously relegated to an Appendix, now receive full treatment. A third chapter has been added to the momentum section so that material on the Directional Movement System, the Chaunde Momentum Oscillator, the Relative Momentum Index, and the parabolic (not a true momentum indicator, but valuable nonetheless) could be included. In addition, the expansion of the momentum section has left room for some of my own new ideas concerning momentum interpretation, such as extreme swings, mega-overboughts and mega-oversolds, and so on. The volume section also includes an additional chapter so that indicators such as the Demand Index and Chaikin Money Flow could be covered. Greater emphasis is also placed on volume momentum. The concept of relative strength is a very important and underappreciated arm of technical analysis. It too has been upgraded to full chapter status. Finally, a new chapter on applying technical analysis to contrary opinion theory expands our coverage of the psychological aspects of trading and investing.

Since the 1970s, the time horizon of virtually all market participants has shrunk considerably. As a result, technical analysis has become very popular for implementing short-term timing strategies. This use may lead to great disappointment: In my experience, there is a rough correlation between the reliability of the technical indicators and the time span being monitored. This is why most of the discussion here has been oriented toward intermediate and long-term trends. Even short-term traders with a 1- to 3-week time horizon need to have some understanding of the direction and maturity of the main or primary trend. This is because mistakes are usually made by taking on positions that go against the direction of the main trend. If a whipsaw is going to develop, it will usually arise from a contratrend signal.

To be successful, technical analysis should be regarded as the art of assessing the technical position of a particular security with the aid of several scientifically researched indicators. Although many of the mechanistic techniques described in this book offer reliable indications of changing market conditions, all suffer from the common characteristic that they can, and often do, fail to operate satisfactorily. This attribute presents no problem to the consciously disciplined investor or trader, since a good working knowledge of the principles underlying major price movements in financial markets and a balanced view of the overall technical position offer a superior framework within which to operate.

There is, after all, no substitute for independent thought. The action of the technical indicators illustrates the underlying characteristics of any market, and it is up to the analyst to put the pieces of the jigsaw puzzle together and develop a working hypothesis.

The task is by no means easy, as initial success can lead to overconfidence and arrogance. Charles H. Dow, the father of technical analysis, once wrote words to the effect that "Pride of opinion caused the downfall of more men on Wall Street than all the other opinions put together." This is true because markets are essentially a reflection of people in action. Normally, such activity develops on a reasonably predictable path. Since people can —and do—change their minds, price trends in the market can deviate unexpectedly from their anticipated course. To avoid serious trouble, investors, and especially traders, must adjust their attitudes as changes in the technical position emerge.

In addition to pecuniary rewards, a study of the market can also reveal much about human nature, both from observing other people in action and from the aspect of self-development. As investors react to the constant struggle through which the market will undoubtedly put them, they will also learn a little about their own makeup. Washington Irving might well have been referring to this challenge of the markets when he wrote, "Little minds are taxed and subdued by misfortune but great minds rise above it."

Martin J. Pring

Acknowledgments

This book has evolved over the last 20 years and has grown from a text of under 250 pages in the first edition to over 600 in the current one.

The material for the fourth edition of this book has been gathered from a substantial number of sources, and I am deeply indebted to the many organizations that have given their permission to reproduce charts and figures without which this book would not have been possible. Special thnks go to Tim Hayes and Ned Davis at Ned Davis research for providing many of the charts on sentiment and flow of funds indicators.

Appreciation also goes to Danny Pring who came up with the title for the first edition of this book. It's a great title and has followed it ever since.

Thanks also to my colleagues at Pring Research including Jimmie Sigsway whose efficiency and dedication allowed my writing to progress in a serene atmosphere uninterrupted by the construction going on around us. Anyone who has experienced the rebuilding of a home/office complex will know what I mean. She is also a grat mother in law!

Above all thanks go to my wife Lisa, who tirelessly reconstructed most of the charts and figures from my pathetic PowerPoint illustrations while simultaneously running a home, taking care of our son Thomas, maintaining our web site (pring.com) and managing a major house renovation.

Introduction

To investors willing to buy and hold common stocks for the long term, the stock market has offered excellent rewards over the years in terms of both dividend growth and capital appreciation. The market is even more challenging, fulfilling, and rewarding to resourceful investors willing to learn the art of market timing through a study of technical analysis.

The advantages of this approach over the buy-and-hold approach were particularly marked between 1966 and 1982. The market made no headway at all, as measured by the Dow Jones Industrial Average (DJIA), in the 16 years between 1966 and 1982. Yet there were some substantial price fluctuations. Although the DJIA failed to record a net advance between 1966 and 1982, the period included five major advances totaling over 1500 Dow points. The potential rewards of market timing were therefore significant.

A long-term investor fortunate enough to sell at the five tops in 1966, 1968, 1973, 1979, and 1981 and to reinvest the money at the troughs of 1966, 1970, 1974, 1980, and 1982 would have seen the total investment (excluding transactions costs and capital gains tax) grow from a theoretical $1000 (that is, $1 for every Dow point) in 1966 to over $10,000 by October 1983. In contrast, an investor following a buy-and-hold approach would have realized a mere $250 gain over the same period. Even during the spectacular rise that began in August 1982, technical analysis would have proved useful, since that period witnessed a considerable variation in performance between different industry groups.

A bull market, such as the one that occurred in the 1980s and 1990s, is a once-in-a-generation affair. In fact, it was a record in 200 years of recorded U.S. stock market history. This implies that the opening decade of the twenty-first century will be a more difficult and challenging period, and that market timing will prove to be of crucial importance.

In practice, of course, it is impossible to buy and sell consistently at exact turning points, but the enormous potential of this approach still leaves plenty of room for error, even when commission costs and taxes are included in the calculation. The rewards for identifying major market junctures and taking the appropriate action can be substantial.

Originally, technical analysis was applied principally in the equity market, but its popularity has gradually expanded to embrace commodities, debt instruments, currencies, and other international markets. In the days of the old market, participants had a fairly long time horizon, stretching over months or years. There have always been short-term traders and scalpers, but the technological revolution in communications has shortened the time horizon of just about everyone involved in markets. When holding periods are lengthy, it is possible to indulge in the luxury of fundamental analysis, but when time is short, timing is everything. In such an environment, technical analysis really comes into its own.

To be successful, the technical approach involves taking a position contrary to the expectations of the crowd. This requires the patience, objectivity, and discipline to acquire a financial asset at a time of depression and gloom, and liquidate it in an environment of euphoria and excessive optimism. The level of pessimism or optimism will depend on the turning point. Short-term peaks and troughs are associated with more moderate extremes in sentiment than longer-term ones. The aim of this book is to explain the technical characteristics to be expected at all of these market turning points, particularly major ones, and to help to assess them objectively.

Technical Analysis Defined

During the course of the book when it is time to emphasize a specific but important point, it will be highlighted in the following way:

> **Major Technical Principle**   Technical analysis deals in probabilities, never certainties.

The technical approach to investment is essentially a reflection of the idea that prices move in trends that are determined by the changing attitudes of investors toward a variety of economic, monetary, political, and psychological forces. The art of technical analysis, for it is an art, is to *identify a trend reversal at a relatively early stage and ride on that trend until the weight of the evidence shows or proves that the trend has reversed*. The evidence in this case is represented by the numerous *scientifically* derived indicators described in this book.

Human nature remains more or less constant and tends to react to similar situations in consistent ways. By studying the nature of previous market turning points, it is possible to develop some characteristics that can help to identify market tops and bottoms. Therefore, *technical analysis is based on the assumption that people will continue to make the same mistakes they have made in the past*. Human relationships are extremely complex and never repeat in identical combinations. The markets, which are a reflection of people in action, never duplicate their performance exactly, but the recurrence of similar characteristics is sufficient to enable technicians to identify juncture points. Since no single indicator has signaled, or indeed could signal, every top or bottom, technical analysts have developed an arsenal of tools to help isolate these points.

Three Branches of Technical Analysis

Technical analysis can be broken down into three essential areas: sentiment, flow-of-funds, and market structure indicators. Data and indicators for all three areas are available for the U.S. stock market. For other financial markets, the statistics are more or less confined to the market structure indicators. The major exceptions are futures markets based in the United States, for which short-term sentiment data are available. The following comments on sentiment and flow-of-funds indicators relate to the U.S. stock market.

Sentiment Indicators

Sentiment or expectational indicators monitor the actions of different market participants, such as insiders, mutual funds managers and investors, and floor specialists. Just as the pendulum of a clock continually moves from one extreme to another, so the sentiment indexes (which monitor the emotions of investors) move from one extreme at a bear market bottom to another at a bull market top. The assumption on which these indicators are based is that different groups of investors are consistent in their actions at major market turning points. For example, insiders (that is, key employees or major stockholders of a company) and New York Stock Exchange (NYSE) members as a group have a tendency to be correct at market turning points; in aggregate, their transactions are on the buy side toward market bottoms and on the sell side toward tops.

Conversely, advisory services as a group are often wrong at market turning points, since they consistently become bullish at market tops and bearish at market troughs. Indexes derived from such data show that certain readings have historically corresponded to market tops, while others have been associated with market bottoms. Since the consensus or majority opinion is normally wrong at market turning points, these indicators of market psychology are a useful basis from which to form a contrary opinion.

Flow-of-Funds Indicators

The area of technical analysis that involves what are loosely termed flow-of-funds indicators analyzes the financial position of various investor groups in an attempt to measure their potential capacity for buying or selling stocks. Since there has to be a purchase for each sale, the *ex post*, or actual dollar balance between supply and demand for stock, must always be equal. The price at which a stock transaction takes place has to be the same for the buyer and the seller, so naturally the amount of money flowing out of the market must equal that put in. The flow-of-funds approach is therefore concerned with the before-the-fact balance between supply and demand, known as the *ex ante relationship*. If at a given price there is a preponderance of buyers over sellers on an ex ante basis, it follows that the actual (ex post) price will have to rise to bring buyers and sellers into balance.

Flow-of-funds analysis is concerned, for example, with trends in mutual fund cash positions and those of other major institutions, such as pension funds, insurance companies, foreign investors, bank trust accounts, and customers' free balances, which are normally a source of cash on the buy side. On the supply side, flow-of-funds analysis is concerned with new equity offerings, secondary offerings, and margin debt.

This money flow analysis also suffers from disadvantages. Although the data measure the availability of money for the stock market (for example, mutual fund cash position or pension fund cash flow), they give no indication of the inclination of market participants to use this money for the purchase of stocks, or of their elasticity or willingness to sell at a given price on the sell side. The data for the major institutions and foreign investors are not sufficiently detailed to be of much use, and in addition they are reported well after the fact. In spite of these drawbacks, flow-of-funds statistics may be used as background material.

A superior approach to flow-of-funds analysis is derived from an examination of liquidity trends in the banking system, which measures financial pressure not only on the stock market, but on the economy as well.

Market Structure Indicators

This area of technical analysis is the main concern of this book, embracing *market structure* or the *character of the market indicators*. These indicators monitor the trend of various price indexes, market breadth, cycles, volume, and so on in order to evaluate the health of the prevailing trend.

Indicators that monitor the trend of a price include moving averages, peak-and-trough analysis, price patterns, and trendlines. Such techniques can also be applied to the sentiment and flow-of-funds indicators discussed previously. This is because these indicators also move in trends. When the trend of psychology, as reflected in these series, reverses, prices are also likely to change direction.

Most of the time, price and internal measures, such as market breadth, momentum, and volume, rise and fall together, but toward the end of market movements, the paths of many of these indicators diverge from the price. Such divergences offer signs of technical deterioration during advances, and technical strength following declines. Through judicious observation of these signs of latent strength and weakness, technically oriented investors are alerted to the possibility of a reversal in the trend of the market itself.

Since the technical approach is based on the theory that the price is a reflection of mass psychology, or the crowd in action, it attempts to forecast future price movements on the assumption that crowd psychology moves between panic, fear, and pessimism on one hand and confidence, excessive optimism, and greed on the other. As discussed here, the art of technical analysis is concerned with identifying these changes at an early phase, since these swings in emotion take time to accomplish. Studying these market trends enables technically oriented investors and traders to buy or sell with a degree of confidence in the principle that once a trend is set in motion, it will perpetuate itself.

Classification of Price Movements

Price movements may be classed as primary, intermediate, and short term. *Major movements*, sometimes called *primary* or *cyclical*, typically work themselves out in a period of 1 to 3 years and are a reflection of investors' attitudes toward the business cycle. *Intermediate movements* usually develop over a period of 6 weeks to as many months, sometimes longer. Although not of prime importance, they are nevertheless useful to identify. It is clearly important to distinguish between an intermediate reaction in a bull market and the first downleg of a bear market, for example. *Short-term movements*, which last less than 3 or 4 weeks, tend to be random in nature. Secular or very long term trends embracing several primary trend movements and intraday trends lasting a few minutes to a few hours round out the possibilities for price movements.

Discounting Mechanism of the Market

All price movements have one thing in common: *They are a reflection of the trend in the hopes, fears, knowledge, optimism, and greed of market participants.* The sum total of these emotions is expressed in the price level, which is, as Garfield Drew noted, "never what they [stocks] are worth, but what people think they are worth."[1]

This process of market evaluation was well expressed by an editorial in *The Wall Street Journal*:[2]

> The stock market consists of everyone who is "in the market" buying or selling shares at a given moment, plus everyone who is not "in the market," but might be if conditions were right. In this sense, the stock market is potentially everyone with any personal savings.
>
> It is this broad base of participation and potential participation that gives the market its strength as an economic indicator and as an allocator of scarce capital. Movements in and out of a stock, or in and out of the market, are made on the margin as each investor digests new information. This allows the market to incorporate all available information in a way that no one person could hope to. Since its judgments are the consensus of nearly everyone, it tends to outperform any single person or group. . . . [The market] mea-

---

[1]Garfield Drew, *New Methods for Profit in the Stock Market*, Metcalfe Press, Boston 1968, p. 18.
[2]The *Wall Street Journal*, Oct. 20, 1977. Reprinted by permission of the *Wall Street Journal*. Copyright Dow Jones & Co., Inc. 1977. All rights reserved.

> **Major Technical Principle** The market never discounts the same thing twice.

sures the after-tax profits of all the companies whose shares are listed in the market, and it measures these cumulative profits so far into the future one might as well say the horizon is infinite. This cumulative mass of after-tax profits is then, as the economists will say, "discounted back to present value" by the market. A man does the same thing when he pays more for one razor blade than another, figuring he'll get more or easier shaves in the future with the higher-priced one, and figuring its present value on that basis.

This future flow of earnings will ultimately be affected by business conditions everywhere on earth. Little bits of information are constantly flowing into the market from around the world as well as throughout the United States, and the market is much more efficient in reflecting these bits of news than are government statisticians. The market relates this information to how much American business can earn in the future. Roughly speaking, the general level of the market is the present value of the capital stock of the U.S.

This implies that investors and traders are looking ahead and taking action so that they can liquidate at a higher price when the anticipated news or development actually takes place. If expectations concerning the development are better or worse than originally thought, then investors sell either sooner or later through the market mechanism, depending on the particular circumstances. Thus, the familiar maxim *sell on good news* applies on when the *good* news is right on or below the market's (that is, the investors') expectations. If the news is good, but not as favorable as expected, a quick reassessment will take place, and the market (other things being equal) will fall. If the news is better than anticipated, the possibilities are obviously more favorable. The reverse will, of course, be true in a declining market. This process explains the paradox of equity markets peaking when economic conditions are strong, and forming a bottom when the outlook is most gloomy. The principle of discounting is not confined to equities alone, but can be applied to *any* freely traded entity.

The reaction of any market to news events can be most instructive because if the market, as reflected by price, ignores supposedly bullish news and sells off, it is certain that the event was well discounted, that is, already built into the price mechanism, and the reaction should therefore be viewed bearishly. If a market reacts more favorably to bad news than might be expected, this in turn should be interpreted as a positive sign. There is a good deal of wisdom in the saying, "A bear argument known is a bear argument understood."

The Financial Markets and the Business Cycle

The major movements in bond, stock, and commodity prices are caused by long-term trends in the emotions of the investing public. These emotions reflect the anticipated level and growth rate of future economic activity, and the attitude of investors toward that activity.

For example, there is a definite link between primary movements in the stock market and cyclical movements in the economy because trends in corporate profitability are an integral part of the business cycle. If basic economic forces alone influence the stock market, the task of determining the changes in primary movements would be relatively simple. In practice, it is not, and this is due to several factors.

First, changes in the direction of the economy can take some time to materialize. As the cycle unfolds, other psychological considerations, such as political developments or purely internal factors like a speculative buying wave or selling pressure from margin calls, can affect the equity market and result in misleading rallies and reactions of 5 to 10 percent or more.

Second, changes in the market usually precede changes in the economy by 6 to 9 months, but the lead time can sometimes be far shorter or longer. In 1921 and 1929, the economy turned before the market did.

Third, even when an economic recovery is in the middle of its cycle, doubts about its durability often arise. When these doubts coincide with political or other adverse developments, sharp and confusing counter-cyclical price movements usually develop.

Fourth, profits may increase, but investors' attitudes toward those profits may change. For example, in the spring of 1946 the DJIA stood at 22 times the price/earnings ratio. By 1948, the comparable ratio was 9.5 when measured against 1947 earnings. In this period, profits had almost doubled and price/earnings ratios had fallen, but stock prices were lower.

Changes in bond and commodity prices are linked much more directly to economic activity than are stock market prices, but even here, psycho-

Major Technical Principle These basic principles of technical analysis apply to all securities and time frames from 20-minute to 20-year trends.

logical influences on price are very important. Currencies do not fit well into business cycle analysis. Although data reported several months after the fact are very good at explaining currency movements, technical analysis has been most useful for timely forecasts and the identification of emerging trends.

Technical Analysis and Trend Determination

Since technical analysis involves a study of the action of markets, it is not concerned with the difficult and subjective tasks of forecasting trends in the economy, or assessing the attitudes of investors toward those changes. Technical analysis tries to identify turning points in the *market's* assessment of these factors.

Since technical analysis can be applied successfully to any freely traded entity such as stocks, market averages, commodities, bonds, currencies, and so on, I will frequently use the term *security* as a generic one embracing all of these entities, thereby avoiding unnecessary repetition.

The approach taken here differs from that found in standard presentations of technical analysis. The various techniques used to determine trends and identify their reversals will be examined in Part I, "Trend-Determining Techniques," which deals with price patterns, trendlines, moving averages (MAs), momentum, and so on.

Part II, "Market Structure," is principally concerned with analysis of the U.S. equity market, although examples using other securities are included to demonstrate that the principles are universally applicable. All that is required are the appropriate data. This section offers a more detailed explanation of the various indicators and indexes. It also shows how they can be combined to build a framework for determining the quality of the internal structure of the market. A study of market character is a cornerstone of technical analysis, since reversals of price trends in the major averages are almost always preceded by latent strength or weakness in the market structure. Just as a careful driver does not judge the performance of a car from the speedometer alone, so technical analysis looks further than the price trends of the popular averages. Trends of investor confidence are responsible for price movements, and this emotional aspect is examined from four viewpoints or dimensions, namely, price, time, volume, and breadth.

Changes in prices reflect changes in investor attitude, and *price,* the first dimension, indicates the level of that change.

Time, the second dimension, measures the recurrence and length of cycles in investor psychology. Changes in confidence go through distinct cycles, some long and some short, as investors swing from excesses of optimism toward deep pessimism. The degree of price movement in the market is usually a function of the time element. The longer it takes for investors to move from a bullish to a bearish extreme, the greater the ensuing price change is likely to be. The examples in the two chapters on time relate mainly to the U.S. stock market, but much of this material is equally valid for commodities, bonds, or currencies.

Volume, the third dimension, reflects the intensity of changes in investor attitudes. For example, the level of enthusiasm implied by a price rise on low volume is not nearly as strong as that implied by a similar price advance accompanied by very high volume.

The fourth dimension, *breadth,* measures the extent of the emotion. This is important because as long as stocks are advancing on a broad front, the trend in favorable emotion is dispersed among most stocks and industries, indicating a healthy and broad economic recovery and a widely favorable attitude toward stocks in particular. On the other hand, when interest has narrowed to a few blue-chip stocks, the quality of the trend has deteriorated, and a continuation of the bull market is highly suspect.

Technical analysis measures these psychological dimensions in a number of ways. Most indicators monitor two or more aspects simultaneously; for instance, a simple price chart measures both price (on the vertical axis) and time (on the horizontal axis). Similarly, an advance/decline line measures breadth and time.

Part III, "Other Aspects of Market Behavior," deals with more specialized aspects. These include interest rates and the stock market, sentiment, automated trading systems, individual stock selection, and technical analysis as applied to global markets.

Conclusion

Financial markets move in trends caused by the changing attitudes and expectations of investors with regard to the business cycle. Since investors continue to repeat the same type of behavior from cycle to cycle, an understanding of the historical relationships between certain price averages and market indicators can be used to identify turning points. No single indicator can ever be expected to signal all trend reversals, so it is essential to use a number of them together to build up a consensus.

This approach is by no means infallible, but a careful, patient, and objective use of the principles of technical analysis can put the odds of success very much in favor of the investor or trader who incorporates these principles into an overall strategy.

PART I
Trend-Determining Techniques

1
The Market Cycle Model

In the Introduction, technical analysis was defined as the art of identifying a trend reversal at a relatively early stage and riding on that trend until the weight of the evidence shows or proves that the trend has reversed. In order to identify a reversal, we must first know what a trend is. This chapter explains and categorizes the various trends, and concludes with a discussion of one of the basic trend-determining techniques, peak-and-trough progression. It is one of the simplest, and perhaps the most effective, trend-identification techniques used in technical analysis and forms a building block for many of the other techniques discussed later.

Three Important Trends

A *trend* is a time measurement of the direction in price levels covering different time spans. There are many trends, but the three that are most widely followed are primary, intermediate, and short term.

Primary

The primary trend generally lasts between 9 months and 2 years and is a reflection of investors' attitudes toward unfolding fundamentals in the business cycle. The business cycle extends statistically from trough to trough for approximately 3.6 years, so it follows that rising and falling primary trends (bull and bear markets) last for 1 to 2 years. Since building up takes longer than tearing down, bull markets generally last longer than bear markets.

The primary trend cycle is operative for bonds, equities, and commodities. Primary trends also apply to currencies, but since currencies reflect investors' attitudes toward the interrelationship of two different economies, an analysis of currency relationships does not fit neatly into the business cycle approach discussed in Chapter 2.

The primary trend is illustrated in Fig. 1-1 by the thickest line. In an idealized situation, the primary uptrend (bull market) is the same size as the primary downtrend (bear market), but in reality, of course, their magnitudes are different. Because it is very important to position both (short-term) trades and (long-term) investments in the direction of the main trend, a significant part of this book is concerned with identifying reversals in the primary trend.

Intermediate

Anyone who has looked at a price chart will notice that prices do not move in a straight line. A primary upswing is interrupted by several reactions along the way. These countercyclical trends within the confines of a primary bull market are known as *intermediate price movements*. They last anywhere from 6 weeks to as long as 9 months, sometimes even longer, but rarely shorter. Intermediate-term trends of the stock market are examined in greater detail in Chapter 4, and are shown as a thin solid line in Fig. 1-1.

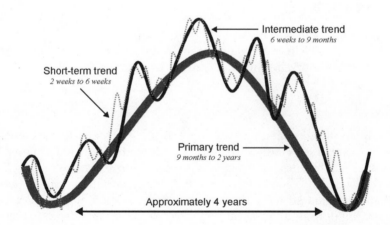

Figure 1-1   The market cycle model

It is important to have an idea of the direction and maturity of the primary trend, but an analysis of intermediate trends is also helpful for improving success rates in trading, as well as for determining when the primary movement may have run its course.

Short Term

Short-term trends typically last from 2 to 4 weeks, sometimes shorter and sometimes longer. They interrupt the course of the intermediate cycle, just as the intermediate-term trend interrupts primary price movements. Short-term trends are shown in the market cycle model (see Fig. 1-1) as a dotted line. They are usually influenced by random news events and are far more difficult to identify than their intermediate or primary counterparts.

The Market Cycle Model

It is apparent by now that the price level of any market is influenced simultaneously by several different trends, and it is important to understand which type is being monitored. For example, if a reversal in a short-term trend has just taken place, a much smaller price movement may be expected than if the primary trend had reversed.

Long-term investors are principally concerned with the direction of the primary trend, and thus it is important for them to have some perspective on the maturity of the prevailing bull or bear market. However, *long-term investors must also be aware of intermediate term and, to a lesser extent, short-term trends.* This is because an important step in the analysis is an examination and understanding of the relationship between short- and intermediate-term trends, and how they affect the primary trend. Also, if it is concluded that the long-term trend has just reversed to the upside, it may pay to wait before committing capital because the short-term trend is overextended on the upside. A lack of knowledge of the short-term trend's position by an investor could therefore prove costly at the margin.

Short-term traders are principally concerned with smaller movements in price, but they *also need to know the direction of the intermediate and primary trends.* This is because surprises occur on the upside in a bull market and

Major Technical Principle   As a general rule, the longer the time span of the trend, the easier it is to identify reversal.

on the downside in a bear market. In other words, rising short-term trends within the confines of a bull market are likely to be much greater in magnitude than short-term downtrends and vice versa. A trading loss usually happens because the trader is positioned in a countercyclical position against the main trend. In effect, *all market participants need to have some kind of working knowledge of all three trends,* although the emphasis will depend on whether their orientation comes from an investment or a short-term trading perspective.

Intraday Trends

In recent years, computers and real-time trading have enabled traders to identify hourly and even tick-by-tick movements. *The principles of technical analysis apply equally to these very short-term movements and are just as valid.* There are two main differences. First, reversals in the intraday charts have only a very short term implication and are not significant for longer-term price reversals. Second, extremely short-term price movements are much more influenced by psychology and instant reactions to news events than are longer-term ones. Decisions therefore have a tendency to be emotional, knee-jerk reactions. Intraday price action is also more susceptible to manipulation. As a consequence, price data used in very short-term charts are much more erratic and generally less reliable than those that appear in the longer-term charts.

The Secular Trend

The primary trend consists of several intermediate cycles, but the secular, or very long-term, trend is constructed from a number of primary trends. This super cycle, or long wave, extends over a substantially greater period, usually lasting well over 10 years, and often as long as 25 years. It is discussed more fully in Chapter 2. A diagram of the interrelationship between a secular and a primary trend is shown in Fig. 1-2.

It is certainly very helpful to understand the direction of the secular trend. Just as the primary trend influences the magnitude of the intermediate-term rally relative to the countercyclical reaction, so the secular trend influences the magnitude and duration of a primary trend rally or reaction. For example, in a rising secular trend, primary bull markets will be of greater magnitude than primary bear markets. In a secular downtrend, bear markets will be more powerful and will take longer to unfold than bull markets.

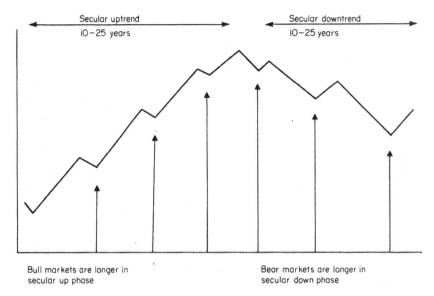

Secular uptrend
10 – 25 years

Secular downtrend
10 – 25 years

Bull markets are longer in
secular up phase

Bear markets are longer in
secular down phase

Figure 1-2 The relationship between the secular and primary trends.

Peak-and-Trough Progression

Technical analysis, as pointed out before, is the *art* of identifying a (price) trend reversal based on the weight of the evidence. As in a court of law, a trend is presumed innocent until proven guilty. The evidence is the objective element in technical analysis. It consists of a series of scientifically derived indicators or techniques that work well most of the time in the trend-identification process. The art consists of combining these indicators into an overall picture and recognizing when that picture resembles a market peak or trough.

Widespread use of computers has led to the development of some very sophisticated trend-identification techniques in market analysis. Some of these indicators work reasonably well, but most do not. The continual search for the "Holy Grail," or perfect indicator, will undoubtedly continue, but it is unlikely that such a technique will ever be discovered. Even if it were, news of its discovery would soon be disseminated and the indicator would gradually be discounted.

In the quest for sophisticated mathematical techniques, some of the simplest and most basic techniques of technical analysis are often overlooked. One simple, but basic technique that has been underused is peak-and-trough progression (see Chart 1-1), which relates to Charles Dow's original observation that a rising market moves in a series of waves, each rally and reaction being higher than its predecessor. When the series of rising peaks and troughs is interrupted, a trend reversal is signaled. To explain this approach, Dow used an analogy with the ripple effect of waves on a seashore. He pointed out that just as it was possible for someone on the beach to identify the turning of the tide by a reversal of receding wave action at low tide, so the same objective could be achieved in the market by observing the price action.

In Fig. 1-3, the price has been advancing in a series of waves, with each peak and trough reaching higher than its predecessors. Then, for the first time, a rally fails to move to a new high, and the subsequent reaction pushes it below the previous trough. This occurs at point X and gives a signal that the trend has reversed. Figure 1-4 shows a similar situation, but this time the trend reversal is from a downtrend to an uptrend.

The idea of the interruption of a series of peaks and troughs is the basic building block for both Dow theory (see Chapter 3) and price pattern analysis (see Chapter 5).

Chart 1-1 Moody's AAA bond yields and peak-and-trough analysis. The solid line above the yield corresponds to the primary bull and bear markets. The series of rising cyclical peaks and troughs extended from the end of World War II until 1981. This was a long period, even by secular standards. In 1981 the yield peaked and a new, downward secular trend began. Confirmation was given in 1985 as the series of rising peaks and troughs was reversed. The signal simply indicated a change in trend, but gave no indication as to magnitude. (*From Intermarket Review.*)

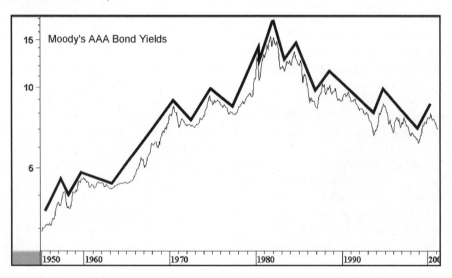

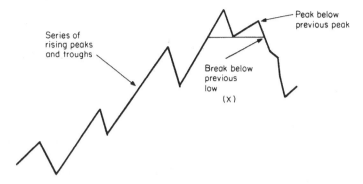

Figure 1-3 Reversal of rising peaks and troughs.

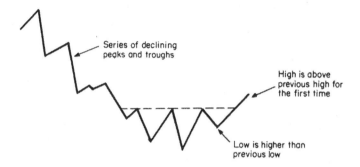

Figure 1-4 Reversal of falling peaks and troughs.

> **Major Technical Principle**   The significance of a peak-and-trough reversal is determined by the duration and magnitude of the rallies and reactions in question.

For example, if it takes 2 to 3 weeks to complete each wave in a series of rallies and reactions, the trend reversal will be an intermediate one, since intermediate price movements consist of a series of short-term (2- to 3-week) fluctuations. Similarly, the interruption of a series of falling intermediate peaks and troughs by a rising one signals a reversal from a primary bear to a primary bull market.

A Peak-and-Trough Dilemma

Occasionally, peak-and-trough progression becomes more complicated than the examples shown in Figs. 1-3 and 1-4. In Fig. 1-5(a), the market has been advancing in a series of rising peaks and troughs, but following the highest peak, the price declines at point X to a level that is below the previous low. At this juncture, the series of rising troughs has been broken, but *not* the series of rising peaks. In other words, at point X, only half a signal has been generated. The complete signal of a reversal of both rising peaks and troughs arises at point Y, when the price slips below the level previously reached at point X.

At point X, there is quite a dilemma because the trend should still be classified as positive, and yet the very fact that the series of rising troughs has been interrupted indicates underlying technical weakness. On the one hand, we are presented with half a bearish signal, while on the other hand, waiting for point Y would mean giving up a substantial amount of the profits earned during the bull market.

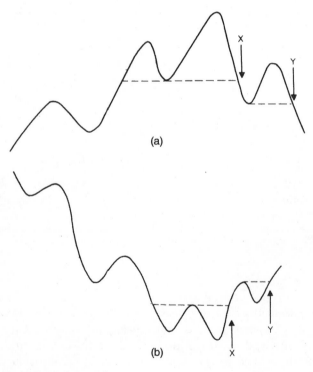

Figure 1-5   Half-signal reversals.

The dilemma is probably best dealt with by referring back to the second half of the definition of technical analysis given at the beginning of this chapter, "and riding that trend until the *weight of the evidence* shows or proves that it has been reversed."

In this case, if the "weight of the evidence" from other technical indicators, such as moving averages (MAs), volume, momentum, and breadth (discussed in later chapters), overwhelmingly indicates a trend reversal, it is probably safe to anticipate a change in trend, even though peak-and-trough progression has not completely confirmed the situation. It is still a wise policy, though, to view this signal with some degree of skepticism until the reversal is confirmed by an interruption in *both* series of rising peaks as well as troughs.

Figure 1-5(*b*) shows this type of situation for a reversal from a bear to bull trend. The same principles of interpretation apply at point *X*, as in Fig. 1-5(*a*). Occasionally, the determination of what constitutes a rally or reaction becomes a subjective process. One way around this problem is to choose an objective measure such as categorizing rallies greater than, say, 5 percent. This can be a tedious process, but some software programs (such as MetaStock with its zigzag tool) enable the user to establish such benchmarks almost instantly in a graphic format.

What Constitutes a Legitimate Peak and Trough?

Most of the time, the various rallies and reactions are self-evident, so it is easy to determine that these turning points are legitimate peaks and troughs. Technical lore has it that a reaction to the prevailing trend should retrace one-third to two-thirds of the previous move. Thus, in Fig. 1-6 the first rally from the trough low to the subsequent peak is 100 percent. The ensuing reaction appears to be just over a half or a 50 percent retracement of the previous move. Occasionally, the retracement can reach 100 percent. Technical analysis is far from precise, but if a retracement move is a good deal less than the minimum one-third, then the peak or trough in question is held to be suspect.

You can appreciate that a line is a fairly controlled period of profit taking or digestion of losses. The depth of the trading range can fall short of the minimum "approximate one-third retracement" requirement and, in such instances, the correction qualifies more on the basis of time than magnitude. A rule of thumb might be for the correction to last at least one-third to two-thirds of the time taken to achieve the previous advance or decline. In Fig. 1-7 the time distance between the low and the high for the move represents 100 percent. The consolidation prior to the breakout should constitute at least one-third to two-thirds of the time taken to achieve the advance, ample time to consolidate gains, and move on to a new high. It's possible for the consolidation to constitute more than 100 percent of the preceding price movement. In fact, the larger the consolidation, the greater the hustle between buyers and sellers and the more significant the upper and lower boundaries become.

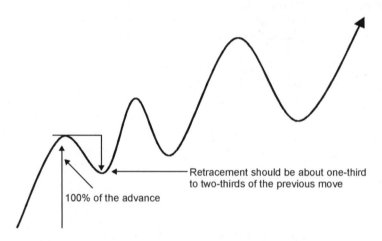

Figure 1-6 Identifying peaks and troughs (magnitude).

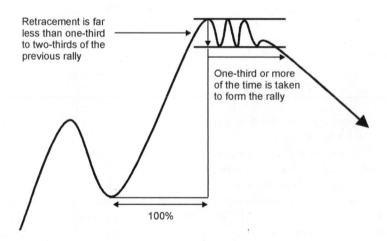

Figure 1-7 Identifying peaks and troughs (time).

These are only rough guidelines, and in the final analysis it is a judgment call based on experience, common sense, a bit of intuition, and, perhaps most important of all, a review of other factors such as volume, support, resistance principles, and so on. We have mainly been studying these concepts in a rising trend. However, the principles work exactly the same in a declining trend in that rallies should retrace one-third to two-thirds of the previous decline. Also, lines or consolidations should take at least one-third of the duration of the previous decline.

It is also important to categorize which kind of trend is being monitored. Obviously, a reversal derived from a series of rallies and reactions each lasting, say, 2 to 3 weeks would be an intermediate reversal. This is because the swings would be short term in nature. On the other hand, peak-and-trough reversals that develop in intraday charts are likely to have significance over a much shorter period. How short would depend on whether the swings were a reflection of hourly or, say, 5-minute bars.

Summary

- A number of different trends simultaneously influence the price level of any security.
- The three most important trends are primary, intermediate, and short term.
- The principles of technical analysis apply to intraday trends, but since they are more random in nature, the analysis is generally less reliable than for longer-term trends.
- Very long term, or secular, trends influence the magnitude of primary bull and bear trends.
- Peak-and-trough progression is the most basic trend-identification technique and is a basic building block of technical analysis.
- As a general rule, in order to qualify as a new legitimate peak or trough, the price should retrace between one-third and two-thirds of the previous move.
- Lines or consolidations also qualify as peaks and troughs where they form between one-third and two-thirds of the time taken to produce the previous advance or decline.

2

Financial Markets and the Business Cycle

Introduction

The basic concern of this book is the technical approach, but it is also important to understand that primary trends of stocks, bonds, and commodities are determined by the *attitude* of investors toward unfolding events in the business cycle. Each market has a tendency to peak and trough at different points during the business cycle in a consistent, chronological manner. An understanding of the interrelationship of debt, equity, and commodity markets provides a useful framework for identifying major reversals in each market.

The Discounting Mechanism of Financial Markets

The trend of all financial markets is essentially determined by investors' expectations of movements in the economy, the effect those changes are likely to have on the price of the asset in which a specific financial market deals, and the psychological attitude of investors toward these fundamental factors. Market participants typically anticipate future economic and financial developments and take action by buying or selling the appropriate assets, with the result that a market normally reaches a major turning point well ahead of the actual development.

An expanding level of economic activity is usually favorable for stock prices, a weak economy is bullish for bond prices, and a tight economy is favorable for industrial commodity prices. These three markets often move in different directions simultaneously because they are discounting different things.

An economy is rarely stable; generally, it is either expanding or contracting. As a result, financial markets are also in a continual state of flux. A hypothetical economy, as shown in Fig. 2-1, revolves around a point of balance known as *equilibrium*. Roughly speaking, equilibrium can be thought of as a period of zero growth in which the economy is neither expanding nor contracting. In practice, this state of affairs is rarely, if ever, attained, since an economy as a whole possesses tremendous momentum in either the expansionary or the contractionary phase, so that the turnaround rarely occurs at an equilibrium level.

In any event, the "economy" consists of a host of individual sectors, many of which are operating in different directions at the same time. Thus, at the beginning of the business cycle, leading economic indicators, such as housing starts, might be rising, while lagging indicators, such as capital spending or employment levels, could be falling. Investors in financial markets are not concerned with periods of extended stability or equilibrium, for such periods do not produce volatile price swings and opportunities to make quick profits. The ever-changing character of the economic cycle creates tremendous opportunities for investors and traders because it means that different industries are experiencing different economic conditions simultaneously. Since housing leads the economy, housing stocks do well at the start of the recovery, when capital-intensive stocks such as steel are still under pressure. Later in the cycle, the tables are turned and it's housing that peaks

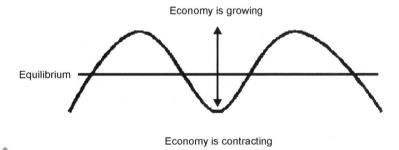

Economy is growing

Equilibrium

Economy is contracting

Figure 2-1 The idealized business cycle.

first. This situation gives rise to the group rotation process, which is discussed at length in Chapter 19.

Since the financial markets lead the economy, it follows that the greatest profits can be made just before the point of maximum economic distortion, or *disequilibrium*. Once investors realize that an economy is changing direction and returning toward the equilibrium level, they discount this development by buying or selling the appropriate asset. Obviously, the more dislocated and volatile an economy becomes, the greater is the potential for a return toward the equilibrium level, and also for a strong swing well beyond it to the other extreme. The risks are also greater if you are too early. Under such conditions, the possibilities for making money in financial markets are greater because they too will normally become subject to wider price fluctuations.

Market Movements and the Business Cycle

The major movements of interest rates, equities, and commodity prices are related to changes in the level of business activity. Please note that the term *commodity prices* refers to industrial prices that are sensitive to business conditions, as opposed to weather-driven commodities such as the grains. Figure 2-2 represents a business cycle, which ranges from 3 to 5 years between troughs. The horizontal line reflects a level of zero growth, above which are periods of expansion, and below which are periods of contraction. After the peak is experienced, the economy continues to grow, but at a declining rate, until the line crosses below the equilibrium level and contraction in economic activity takes place. The arrows in Fig. 2-2 show the idealized peaks and troughs of the financial markets as they relate to the business cycle.

Periods of expansion generally last longer than periods of contraction, because it takes longer to build something up than to tear it down. For this reason, bull markets for equities generally last longer than bear markets. The same could be said for interest rates and commodities, but in this case the magnitude and duration of a primary trend depend on the direction of the secular trend, as discussed in Chapter 1.

Figure 2-3 shows how the three markets of short-term interest rates, commodities, and equities also relate to the typical business cycle. In the example, interest rates have been plotted inversely to correspond with bond prices. A bull market for bonds is marked by a rising line and a bear market by a descending one.

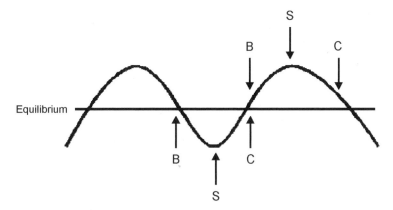

Figure 2-2 The idealized business cycle and financial market turning points. (B = Bonds; S = Stocks; C = Commodities)

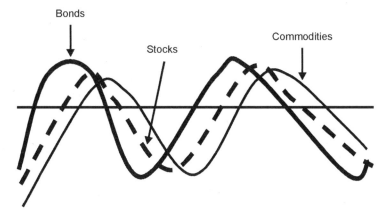

Figure 2-3 Idealized sine curves for three markets.

Referring back to Fig. 2-2, we can see that the bond market is the first financial market to begin a bull phase. This usually occurs after the growth rate in the economy has slowed down considerably from its peak rate and quite often is delayed until the initial stages of the recession. Generally speaking, the sharper the economic contraction, the greater the potential for a rise in bond prices (that is, a fall in interest rates). Alternatively, the stronger the period of expansion, the smaller the amount of economic and financial slack, and the greater the potential for a decline in bond prices (and a rise in interest rates).

Following the bear market low in bond prices, economic activity begins to contract more sharply. At this point, participants in the equity market are able to "look through" the valley in corporate profits, which are now declining sharply because of the recession, and begin accumulating stocks. Generally speaking, the longer the lead between the low in bonds and that of stocks, the greater the potential for the stock market to rally. This is because the lag implies a particularly weak recession in which extreme corporate belt tightening is able to drop break-even levels to a very low level. During the recovery, increases in revenue are therefore able to quickly move to the bottom line.

After the recovery has been under way for some time, capacity starts to tighten, resource-based companies feel some pricing power return, and commodity prices bottom. Occasionally after a commodity boom of unusual magnitude, industrial commodity prices reach their actual bottom during the recession due to severe margin liquidation on behalf of speculators. However, this bottom is often subsequently tested; a sustainable rally only begins after the recovery has been under way for a few months. At this point, all three financial markets are in a rising trend.

Gradually, the economic and financial slack, which developed as a result of the recession, is substantially absorbed, putting upward pressure on the price of credit, that is, interest rates. Since rising interest rates mean falling bond prices, the bond market peaks out and begins its bear phase. Because some excess plant and labor capacity still exists, rising business activity results in improved productivity and a continued positive outlook. The stock market discounts trends in corporate profits, so it remains in an uptrend until investors sense that the economy is becoming overheated and the potential for an improvement in profits is very low. At this point, there is less reason to hold equities, and they in turn enter into a bear phase. Later, the rise in interest rates takes its toll on the economy and commodity prices begin to slip.

Once this juncture has been reached, all three financial markets begin to fall. They will continue to decline until the credit markets bottom out. This final stage, which develops around the same time as the beginning of the recession, is usually associated with a free fall in prices in at least one of the financial markets. If a panic is to develop, this is one of the most likely points for it to take place.

Introducing the Six Stages

Since there are three financial markets and each has two turning points, it follows that there are conceptually six turning points in a typical cycle. I call these the *six stages* and they can be used as reference points for determining the current phase of the business cycle. The six stages are indicated in Fig. 2-4.

When identifying a stage, it is important to look at the long-term technical position of all three markets so that they can act as a cross-check on each other. The stages are also useful in that specific groups do well at particular times. For example, liquidity-driven or early-cycle leaders tend to outperform the market in Stages 1 and 2 when bond prices are rising and interest rates falling. On the other hand, earnings-driven or late-cycle leaders perform well in Stages 4 and 5 when commodity prices are rallying. These aspects are covered more fully in Chapter 19 on group rotation.

Longer Cycles

Some expansions encompass much longer periods, and they usually include at least one slowdown in the growth rate followed by a second round of economic expansion. This has the effect of splitting the overall expansion into two or three parts, each of which results in a complete cycle in the financial markets. I call this a *double cycle*. An example of this phenomenon is illustrated in Fig. 2-5.

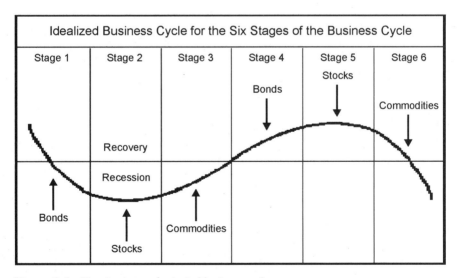

Figure 2-4 The six stages of a typical business cycle.

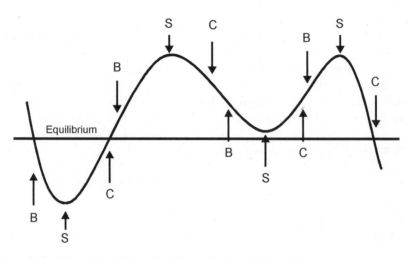

Figure 2-5   Financial market peaks and troughs in a double cycle.

A double cycle developed in the 1980s and another in the 1990s. In the mid-1980s, for example, commodity and industrial parts of the country were very badly affected, but the east and west coasts continued their expansions unabated. The strong areas more than offset the weaker ones and so the country as a whole avoided a recession. It is certainly true that the six-stage concept works well in many cycles, but it must be noted that there are exceptions. I believe, therefore, that it is best used as a conceptual framework rather than an ironclad discipline. For example, some of the worst exceptions in over 200 years of recorded history occurred in the 1990s when the U.S. equity market was experiencing an unprecedented equity rally, which fatally distorted the normal chronological sequence.

The Role of Technical Analysis

Technical analysis comes into play by helping to determine when the various markets have turned in a primary-sense way. This is achieved by applying the various techniques outlined in subsequent chapters, moving average crossovers, changes in the direction of long-term momentum, and so forth. Each market can then be used as a cross-check against the other two. For example, if the weight of the technical evidence suggests that bonds have bottomed but commodity prices remain in a bear market, the next thing to do would be to look for technical signs pointing to a stock market bottom.

Market Experience, 1966–2001

Chart 2-1 shows how peaks and troughs developed for the various markets between 1966 and 1977. Please note that inversely plotted short-term interest rates have been substituted for bond prices. This is because there is a much closer link between equity prices and short-term rates than with longer-term rates, due in part to the fact that corporations do more of their borrowing in the money markets than the bond markets. Also, market participants buy stocks on margin, the cost of which is determined by the level of short-term rates. Short-term rates are also more volatile than those at the end of the yield spectrum.

The peaks and troughs in Chart 2-1 turned out very much as expected. Although the chronological sequence was more or less perfect, the leads and lags in each cycle varied considerably, because of the different characteristics in each cycle. In 1966, for instance, bonds and stocks bottomed more or less simultaneously, whereas the lag for the commodity market bottom was well over a year.

Chart 2-2 shows the same markets, but this time we are looking at the 1980s. The two small, upward-pointing arrows in 1982 and 1990 reflect recessions. The series of three bottoms that developed between 1984 and 1986 reflects the mid-1980s growth recession. Generally speaking, the chronological sequence works satisfactorily until we get to the late 1980s where the

Chart 2-1 Three financial markets, 1966–1977. (*From Intermarket Review.*)

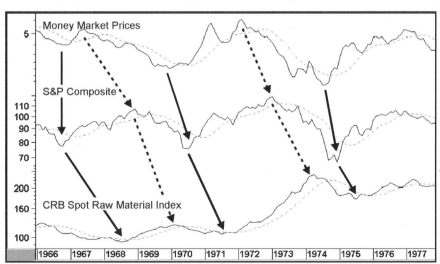

Chart 2-2   Three financial markets, 1980–1992. (*From Intermarket Review.*)

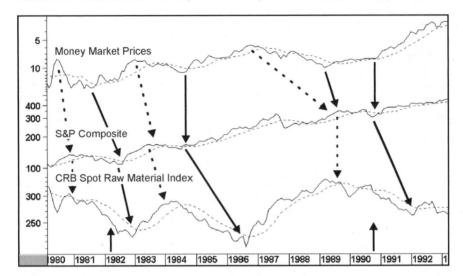

1989 bottom in rates is juxtaposed with the stock market peak. Unfortunately, these out-of-sequence events are a fact of life. Fortunately, in the 20 years I have studied these relationships, they represent the exception rather than the rule.

Chart 2-3 shows the closing years of the twentieth century. This is the most difficult period I have encountered because of the record performance by the stock market and the strong deflationary forces associated with the technological revolution. This had the effect of reducing the normal cyclical fluctuation in the equity market. Since the stock market boom was unprecedented, it is unlikely that the normal chronological sequences have been more than temporarily interrupted.

Summary

- A typical business cycle embraces three individual cycles for interest rates, equities, and commodities. All are influenced by the same economic and financial forces, but each responds differently.
- These markets undergo a chronological sequence, which repeats in most cycles.

Chart 2-3 Three financial markets, 1989–2001. (*From Intermarket Review.*)

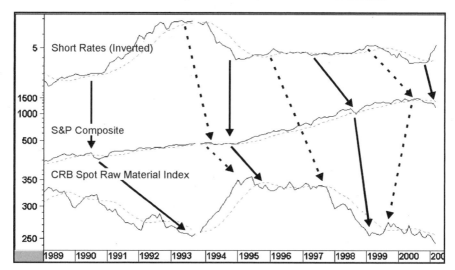

- Some cycles experience a slowdown in the growth rate and not an actual recession. Even so, the chronological sequence between the markets still appears to operate.
- The leads and lags vary from cycle to cycle and have little forecasting value.
- The chronological sequence of peaks and troughs in the various financial markets can be used as a framework for identifying the position of a specific market within its bull or bear market cycle.

3
Dow Theory

The Dow theory is the oldest and by far the most publicized method of identifying major trends in the stock market. An extensive account will not be necessary here, as there are many excellent books on the subject. A brief explanation, however, is in order because the basic principles of the Dow theory are used in other branches of technical analysis.

The goal of the theory is to determine changes in the primary or major movement of the market. Once a trend has been established, it is assumed to exist until a reversal is proved. Dow theory is concerned with the *direction* of a trend and has no forecasting value as to its ultimate *duration* or size.

Starting in 1897, an investor who purchased the stocks in the Dow Jones Industrial Average (DJIA) following each Dow theory buy signal, liquidated the position on sell signals, and reinvested the money on the next buy signal would have had his or her original investment of $44 in 1897 grow to about $51,268 by January 1990.[1] If, instead, the investor had held onto the original $44 investment throughout that period, the investment would also have grown, but only to about $2500. In reality, the substantial profit earned by following the Dow theory would have been trimmed by transaction costs and capital gains taxes. Even if a wide margin for error were allowed, and errors can certainly arise in the interpretation of the theory, the investment performance using this approach would still have been far superior to the results of a buy-and-hold strategy. The theory will still have done well in the period between 1990 and 2001. However, the spectacular bull market of the 1990s would not have made the comparison between the theory and the buy-and-hold approach particularly inspiring for Dow theorists.

---

[1]This assumes that the averages were available in 1897. Actually, Dow theory was first published in 1900.

It should be recognized that the theory does not always keep pace with events; it occasionally leaves the investor in doubt and is by no means infallible, since small losses are sometimes incurred. These points emphasize that, while mechanical devices can be useful for forecasting the stock market, there is no substitute for obtaining additional supportive analysis on which to base sound, balanced judgment. Remember, in our weight-of-the-evidence approach Dow theory is one piece of evidence.

The Dow theory evolved from the work of Charles H. Dow, who published a series of *The Wall Street Journal* editorials between 1900 and 1902 concerning market action. Dow used the behavior of the stock market as a barometer of business conditions rather than as a basis for forecasting stock prices themselves. His successor, William Peter Hamilton, developed Dow's principles and organized them into something approaching the theory as we know it today. These principles were outlined rather loosely in Hamilton's book *The Stock Market Barometer,* published in 1922. It was not until Robert Rhea published *Dow Theory* in 1932 that a more complete and formalized account of the principles finally became available.

The theory assumes that the majority of stocks follow the underlying trend of the market most of the time. In order to measure "the market," Dow constructed two indexes, which are now called the *Dow Jones Industrial Average* and the *Dow Jones Transportation Averages.* The Industrials were originally constructed from 12 (but now include 30) blue-chip stocks and the *Dow Jones Rail Average,* comprising 12 railroad stocks. Since the Rail Average was intended as a proxy for transportation stocks, the evolution of aviation and other forms of transportation has necessitated modifying the old Rail Average in order to incorporate additions to this industry. Consequently, the name of this index has been changed to *Transportation Average.*

Interpreting the Theory

In order to interpret the theory correctly, it is necessary to have a record of the daily closing[2] prices of the two averages and the total of daily transactions on the New York Stock Exchange (NYSE). The six basic tenets of the theory are as follows.

---

[2]It is important to use closing prices, since intraday fluctuations are more subject to manipulation.

1. The Averages Discount Everything

Changes in the daily closing prices reflect the aggregate judgment and emotions of all stock market participants, both current and potential. It is therefore assumed that this process discounts everything known and predictable that can affect the demand/supply relationship of stocks. Although acts of God are obviously unpredictable, their occurrence is quickly appraised and their implications are discounted.

2. The Market Has Three Movements

There are simultaneously three movements in the stock market.

Primary Movement   The most important is the *primary* or *major trend,* more generally known as a bull (rising) or bear (falling) market. Such movements last from less than 1 year to several years.

A *primary bear market* is a long decline interrupted by important rallies. It begins as the hopes on which the stocks were first purchased are abandoned. The second phase evolves as the levels of business activity and profits decline. The bear market reaches a climax when stocks are liquidated regardless of their underlying value (because of the depressing state of the news or because of forced liquidation caused, for example, by margin calls). This represents the third stage of the bear market.

A *primary bull market* is a broad upward movement, normally averaging at least 18 months, which is interrupted by secondary reactions. The bull market begins when the averages have discounted the worst possible news, and confidence about the future begins to revive. The second stage of the bull market is the response of equities to known improvements in business conditions, while the third and final phase evolves from overconfidence and speculation when stocks are advanced on projections that usually prove to be unfounded.

Secondary Reactions   A *secondary* or *intermediate reaction* is defined as "an important decline in a bull market or advance in a bear market, usually lasting from three weeks to as many months, during which interval, the movement generally retraces from 33 to 66 percent of the primary price change since the termination of the last preceding secondary reaction."[3] (My own view is that a secondary or intermediate move should last a minimum of 4 weeks.) This relationship is shown in Fig. 3-1 (*a*) for a rising market and in Fig. 3-1 (*b*) for a declining one.

Occasionally, a secondary reaction can retrace the whole of the previous primary movement, but normally the move falls in the one-half to two-thirds area, often at the 50 percent mark. As discussed in greater detail later in the chapter, the correct differentiation between the first leg of a new primary trend and a secondary movement within the existing trend provides Dow theorists with their most difficult problem.

Minor Movements   The *minor movement* lasts from a week or two up to as long as 6 weeks. It is important only in that it forms part of the primary or secondary moves; it has no forecasting value for longer-term investors. This is especially important since short-term movements can be manipulated to some extent, unlike the secondary or primary trends.

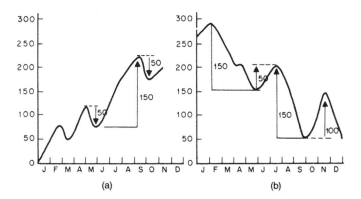

(a)   (b)

Figures 3-1   Secondary retracements.

[3]Rhea, Robert. *Dow Theory*. New York: Barron's, 1932.

3. Lines Indicate Movement

Rhea defined a line as "a price movement 2 to 3 weeks or longer, during which period, the price variation of both averages moves within a range of approximately 5 percent (of their mean average). Such a movement indicates either accumulation [*stock moving into strong and knowledgeable hands and therefore bullish*] or distribution [*stock moving into weak hands and therefore bearish*]."[4]

An advance above the limits of the line indicates accumulation and predicts higher prices, and vice versa. When a line occurs in the middle of a primary advance, it is really forming a horizontal secondary movement and should be treated as such.

My own view is that the formation of a legitimate line should probably take longer than 2 to 3 weeks with, say, a minimum of 4. After all, a line is really a substitute for an intermediate price trend and 2 to 3 weeks is the time for a short-term or minor price movement.

4. Price/Volume Relationships Provide Background

The normal relationship is for volume to expand on rallies and contract on declines. If volume becomes dull on a price advance and expands on a decline, a warning is given that the prevailing trend may soon be reversed. This principle should be used as background information only, since the conclusive evidence of trend reversals can be given only by the price of the respective averages.

5. Price Action Determines the Trend

Bullish indications are given when successive rallies penetrate peaks while the trough of an intervening decline is above the preceding trough. Conversely, bearish indications come from a series of declining peaks and troughs.

Figures 3-2(*a*)–(*d*) show a theoretical bull trend interrupted by a secondary reaction. In Fig. 3-2(*a*), the index makes a series of three peaks and troughs, each higher than its respective predecessor. The index rallies following the third decline, but is unable to surpass its third peak. The next

[4]Ibid.

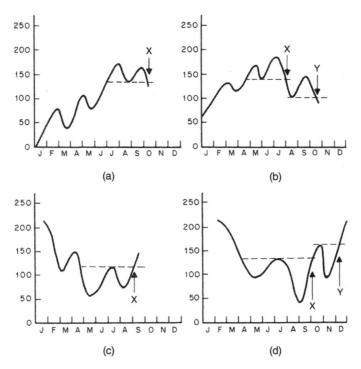

Figure 3-2 Primary trend reversals.

decline takes the average below its low point, confirming a bear market as it does so, at point *X*. In Fig. 3-2(*b*), following the third peak in the bull market, a bear market is indicated as the average falls below the previous secondary trough. In this instance, the preceding secondary is part of a bull market, not the first trough in a bear market, as shown in Fig. 3-2(*a*). Many Dow theorists do not consider penetration at point *X* in Fig. 3-2(*b*) to be a sufficient indication of a bear market. They prefer to take a more conservative position by waiting for a rally and a subsequent penetration of that previous trough marked as point *Y* in Fig. 3-2(*b*).

In such cases, it is wise to approach the interpretation with additional caution. If a bearish indication is given from the volume patterns and a clearly identifiable speculative stage for the bull market has already materialized, it is probably safe to assume that the bearish indication is valid. In the absence of such characteristics, it is wiser to give the bull market the benefit of the doubt and adopt a more conservative position. Remember, technical analysis is the art of identifying trend reversals based on the weight of the evidence. Dow theory is one piece of evidence, so if four or five other indicators are pointing to a trend reversal, it is usually a good idea to treat the half signal at point *X* as an indication that the trend has reversed. Figures 3-2(*c*) and (*d*) represent similar instances at the bottom of a bear market.

The examples in Figs. 3-3(*a*) and (*b*) show how the primary reversal would appear if the average had formed a line at its peak or trough. The importance of being able to distinguish between a valid secondary correction and the first leg of a new primary trend is now evident. This is perhaps the most difficult part of the theory to interpret, and unquestionably the most critical.

It is essential to establish that the secondary reaction has retraced at least one-third of the preceding primary movement, as measured from the termination of the preceding secondary. The secondary should also extend for at least 3 to 4 weeks.

Vital clues can also be obtained from volume characteristics and from an assessment of the maturity of the prevailing primary trend. The odds of a major reversal are much greater if the market has undergone its third phase, characterized by speculation and false hopes during a primary upswing or a bout of persistent liquidation and widespread pessimism during a major decline. A change in the primary trend can occur without a clearly identifiable third phase, but generally such reversals prove to be relatively short-

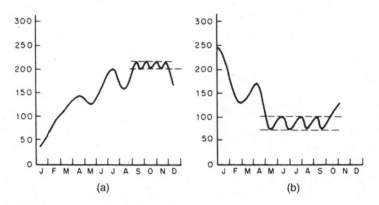

Figures 3-3 Lines being formed at a peak or trough.

lived. On the other hand, the largest primary swings usually develop when the characteristics of a third phase are especially marked during the preceding primary movement. Hence, the excessive bouts of speculation in 1919, 1929, 1968, and 2000 in the NASDAQ were followed by particularly sharp setbacks. Intermediate-term movements are discussed more extensively in Chapter 4.

6. The Averages Must Confirm

One of the most important principles of Dow theory is that the movement of the Industrial Average and the Transportation Average should always be considered together (that is, the two averages must confirm each other).

The need for confirming action by both averages would seem fundamentally logical, because if the market is truly a barometer of future business conditions, investors should be bidding up the prices both of companies that produce goods and of companies that transport them in an expanding economy. It is not possible to have a healthy economy in which goods are being manufactured but not sold (that is, shipped to market). This principle of confirmation is shown in Figs. 3-4(a) and (b).

In Fig. 3-4(a), the Industrial Average is the first to signal a bear trend (point A), but the actual bear market is not indicated until the Transportation Average confirms at point B. Figure 3-4(b) shows the beginning of a new bull market. Following a sharp decline, the Industrials make a new low. A rally then develops, but the next reaction holds above the pre-

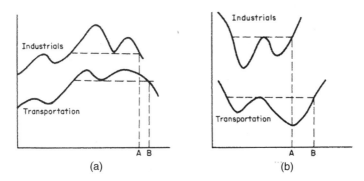

Figure 3-4 Dow Theory requires both averages to confirm.

vious low. When prices push above the preceding rally, a bull signal is given by the Industrials at point *A*. In the meantime, the Transportation Average makes a series of two succeeding lows. The question that arises is: Which average is correctly representing the prevailing trend? Since it is always assumed that a trend is in existence until a reversal is proved, the conclusion should be drawn at this point that the Transportation Average is indicating the correct outcome.

It is only when this average exceeds the peak of the preceding secondary at point *B* that a new bull market is confirmed by both averages, resulting in a Dow theory buy signal. The movement of one average unsupported by the other can often lead to a false and misleading conclusion, which is well illustrated in Fig. 3-5 by the following example from 1930.

The 1929–1932 bear market began in September 1929 and was confirmed by both averages in late October. In June 1930, both averages made a new low and then rallied and reacted in August. Following this correction, the Industrials surpassed their previous peak. Many observers believed that this signaled the end of a particularly sharp bear market and that it was only a matter of time before the Rails would follow suit. As it turned out, the action of the Industrials was totally misleading; the bear market still had another 2 years to run.

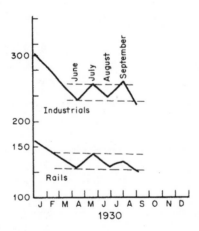

Figure 3-5   1930 example.

Additional Considerations

Dow theory does not specify a time period beyond which a confirmation of one average by the other becomes invalid. Generally, the closer the confirmation, the stronger the following move is likely to be. For example, confirmation of the 1929–1932 bear market was given by the Rail Average just 1 day after the Industrial Average. The sharp 1962 break was confirmed on the same day.

One of the major criticisms of Dow theory is that many of its signals have proved to be late, often 20 to 25 percent after a peak or trough in the averages has occurred. One rule of thumb that has enabled Dow theorists to anticipate probable reversals at an earlier date is to observe the dividend yield on the Industrials. When the yield on the Industrial Average has fallen to 3 percent or below, it has historically been a reliable indicator at market tops. Similarly, a yield of 6 percent has been a reliable indicator at market bottoms. Dow theorists would not necessarily use these levels as actual buying or selling points, but would probably consider altering the percentage of their equity exposure if a significant nonconfirmation developed between the Industrial Average and the Transportation Average when the yield on the Dow reached these extremes. This strategy would help to improve the investment return of the Dow theory, but would not always result in a superior performance. At the 1976 peak, for example, the yield on the Dow never reached the magic 3 percent level, and prices fell 20 percent before a mechanical signal was confirmed by both averages. In addition, the 3 percent top would have missed the mark by about 5 years in the late 1990s.

Over the years, many criticisms have been leveled at the theory on the basis that from time to time (as in periods of war) the Rails have been overregulated or that the new Transportation Average no longer reflects investors' expectations about the future movement of goods. The theory has stood the test of time, however, as Table 3-1 indicates. Indeed, criticism is perfectly healthy, for if the theory gained widespread acceptance and its signals were purely mechanistic instead of requiring experienced judgment, they would be instantly discounted, which would render the Dow theory useless for profitable investment.

Charts 3-1 to 3-4 show Dow theory signals between 1953 and 2001. These should not be taken as gospel since they represent my own interpretation that many could legitimately disagree with. They were also made with the benefit of hindsight. However, I tried to make them as conservative as

Table 3-1   Dow Theory Analysis

	Buy signals*			Sell signals*	
Date of Signal	Price of Dow	Percentage gain from sell signal when short	Date of Signal	Price of Dow	Percentage gain from buy signal
Jul. 1897	44		Dec. 1899	63	43
Oct. 1900	59	6	Jun. 1903	59	0
Jul. 1904	51	14	Apr. 1906	92	80
Apr. 1908	70	24	May 1910	85	21
Oct. 1910	82	4	Jan. 1913	85	3
Apr. 1915	65	24	Aug. 1917	86	32
May 1918	82	5	Feb. 1920	99	22
Feb. 1922	84	16	Jun. 1923	91	8
Dec. 1923	94	(loss) 3	Oct. 1929	306	226
May 1933	84	73	Sep. 1937	164	95
Jun. 1938	127	23	Mar. 1939	136	7
Jul. 1939	143	5	May 1940	138	(loss) 7
Feb. 1943	126	8	Aug. 1946	191	52
Apr. 1948	184	4	Nov. 1948	173	(loss) 6
Oct. 1950	229	(loss)32	Apr. 1953	280	22
Jan. 1954	288	(loss) 3	Oct. 1956	468	63
Apr. 1958	450	4	Mar. 1960	612	36
Nov. 1960	602	2	Apr. 1962	683	13
Nov. 1962	625	8	May 1966	900	43
Jan. 1967	823	9	Jun. 1969	900	9
Dec. 1970	823	9	Apr. 1973	921	12
Jan. 1975	680	26	Oct. 1977	801	18
Apr. 1978	780	3	Jul. 1981	960	23
Aug. 1982	840	13	Feb. 1984	1186	41
Jan. 1985	1261	(loss) 6	Oct. 1989	2510	104
Dec. 1990	2610	(loss) 1	Aug 1998	8490	225
Average of all cycles 10%			Average all cycles 46%		

*When considering the results, note that these signals are the result of my interpretation, in some cases with the benefit of hindsight. Some Dow theorists would disagree with my interpretation, but none would dispute the fact that, in general, the theory works.

Chart 3-1 Dow theory signals, 1953–1968.

Chart 3-2 Dow theory signals, 1968–1990.

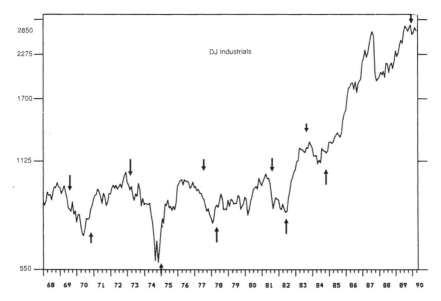

Chart 3-3   Dow theory signals, 1989–1997. A sell signal was given in October of 1989 (at the dashed vertical line) as the Industrials and Transports broke down from double tops (line formations). It may be pushing it a bit because the second Industrial peak was slightly higher than the first. Even though the Industrials went on to register a new high, the Transports never confirmed. Had they broken above the mid-1990 trading range, this would have constituted a confirmation, but this did not happen. The ensuing buy signal (at the solid vertical line) was also triggered with a couple of lines in the same manner in December 1990. The arrow at *A* shows that the Industrials broke down from a line but this was not confirmed by the Transports, so the bull trend remained intact. In 1994 the Transports broke down from a line, but this time it was the Industrials that refused to confirm.

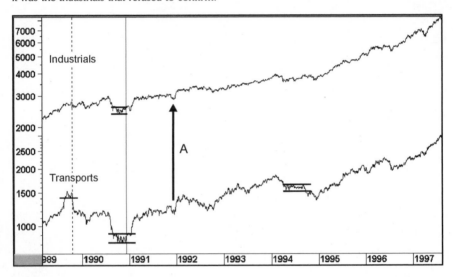

possible. Charts 3-3 and 3-4 feature both averages. The half-signals described at the end of Chapter 1 have not been allowed.

There is no question that interpretation of the theory can, at times, be very subjective. All the more reason to treat the signals as one witness in the weight of the evidence "pie."

Chart 3-4 Dow theory signals, 1997–2001. The 1990 bull signal remained in force until August 1998 when both series made new lows following an intermediate rally. The sell signal for the Industrials (at the dotted vertical line) is a bit controversial because this average actually made a marginal new high as it had done in 1989. However, if the price action of the spring/summer of 1998 is treated as a line formation, the signal is valid. The NYSE A/D line also crossed below its 200-day moving average around this time. After this, there was no period in which both series traced out a series of rising intermediate peaks and troughs. The new all-time high in the Industrials set in January 2000 would have been a bull signal, but the Transports were unable to confirm. True, they did make a new high in the spring of 1999, but there was no line or intermediate test of the 1998 low. After the start of 2000, the Industrials were never able to extend their rising peaks and troughs. The two horizontal lines in 2001 indicate the points at which both series would confirm for a new bull market.

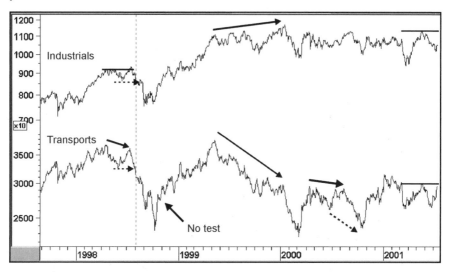

Summary

- Dow theory is concerned with determining the direction of the primary trend of the market, not the ultimate duration or size of the trend. Once confirmed by both averages, the new trend is assumed to be in existence until an offsetting confirmation by both averages takes place.
- Major bull and bear markets each have three distinct phases. Both the identification of these phases and the appearance of any divergence in the normal volume/price relationship offer useful indications that a reversal in the major trend is about to take place. Such supplementary evidence is particularly useful when the action of the price averages themselves is inconclusive.

4

Typical Parameters for Intermediate Trends

Some Basic Observations

The two previous chapters discussed the main or primary trend (that is, the price movement that corresponds to changes in economic activity over the course of a typical 3- to 4-year business cycle). Though it is clearly important to have an idea of the direction and maturity of the primary trend, it is also helpful to have some understanding of the typical character and duration of the intermediate trend for the purpose of improving success rates in trading, and also in assessing when the primary movement may have run its course.

A successful analysis of intermediate trends for any market or stock offers the following advantages:

- Changes in intermediate trends aid in the identification of turning points in the primary trend.
- Intermediate-term trading involves fewer transactions than trading of minor price movements and therefore results in lower commission costs.
- Intermediate-trend reversal points occur several times a year and can, if properly interpreted, enable a relatively high and quick return on capital.

Intermediate Cycles Defined

A primary trend typically consists of five intermediate trends, three of which form part of the prevailing trend, while the remaining two run counter to that trend. In a bull market, the intermediate countertrends are represented by price declines; in a bear market, they form rallies that separate the three intermediate downwaves, as shown in Fig. 4-1.

It is apparent from the previous discussion that there are essentially two types of intermediate price movements. The first, which goes in the direction of the primary trend, may be called a *primary intermediate price movement.* The second is an important price movement that lasts from 4 weeks to 3 months, occasionally longer. It normally retraces between one-third and two-thirds of the preceding primary intermediate trend. This price movement, which runs counter to the main trend, is called a *secondary movement* or *reaction.* Since a primary intermediate price movement operates in the same direction as the primary or main market trend, it almost always lasts longer than its secondary counterpart. Its price magnitude is normally much greater as well.

These countertrends or reactions against the main trend are notoriously difficult to forecast in terms of character, magnitude, and duration. Therefore, they should generally be avoided from a trading point of view, as they will almost invariably be subject to confusing whipsaws. By their very nature, they tend to fool the majority and are usually extremely treacherous. It is possible to design successful mechanized systems based on

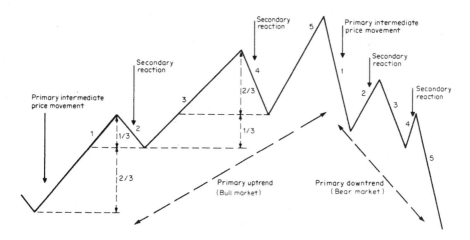

Figure 4-1 Intermediate cycles in a primary trend.

intermediate price movements, but poor or losing signals usually come from secondary market movements that occur against the main trend. Intermediate-term trends that move in the same direction as the primary trend generally are easier to profit from. Traders who do not have the patience to invest for the longer term will find that a successful analysis of intermediate movements offers superior results, especially as the day-to-day or minor swings are, to a large degree, random in nature and therefore even more difficult to capitalize on. This tendency has been most pronounced in recent years when increasingly sharp price movements have resulted from emotional knee-jerk reactions to the release of unexpected economic data.

A secondary reaction does not have to be a decline in a bull market or a bear market rally. It can also take the form of a sideways movement or consolidation, under the same idea as Charles Dow's line formation (see the discussion in Chapter 3).

Intermediate-Term Cycles

Intermediate movements can either go with or against the main trend, which means that there is an intermediate cycle, just as there is a primary one. An intermediate cycle consists of a primary intermediate price movement and a secondary reaction. It extends from the low of one intermediate trend to the low of the other, as shown in Fig. 4-2.

In a bull market, the up phase of the cycle should be longer in time and greater in magnitude. The low on the secondary reaction should be higher

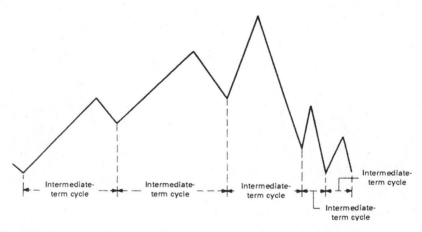

Figure 4-2 Intermediate-term cycles.

than its predecessor. In a bear market, the reverse conditions hold true (that is, declines are longer and greater while rallies are short and sharp, but of less magnitude). Accordingly, technicians are alerted first to the possibility of a reversal in the primary trend when a third intermediate cycle is nearing completion. It is also important to note whether the overall technical structure looks weak (strong in a bear market) as the previous intermediate low (high) is approached and, finally, to note whether that level is decisively broken on the downside (upside).

This does not mean that primary movements can never encompass more or fewer than three primary intermediate price movements, for often they do. Expect three as a normal event, but do not be caught off guard if there are fewer or more.

Causes of Secondary Reactions

Since the primary trend of stock prices is determined by the *attitudes* of investors to the future flow of profits, which are in turn determined to a large degree by the course of the business cycle, it would seem illogical at first to expect longer-term movements to be interrupted by what often prove to be very uncomfortable reactions (or in the case of a bear market, very deceptive rallies).

History shows that secondary reactions occur because of technical distortions, which arise in the market as a result of overoptimism (or excess pessimism), and also because new factors emerge suggesting that business conditions are not going to be as extreme as was originally anticipated, or even that they are going to materialize in the opposite direction. For example, after the first intermediate-term rally in a bull market for equities, a reaction may develop because investors, who had discounted a strong recovery, now see some chinks appearing that might even forecast an actual decline in business conditions. Such fears eventually prove ungrounded, but are sufficient to cause a countercyclical intermediate reaction. Another possibility might be fear of rising interest rates, which could choke off the recovery. Since prices had discounted a strong recovery, this change in perception causes investors to pull back and prices to fall accordingly. At the same time, many investors get carried away during the rally phase and leverage themselves up. As prices begin to fall, this causes their equity to shrink and forces them to liquidate, which adds further fuel to the price decline.

A bear market rally for stocks generally takes place because of an improved outlook for business conditions over what was anticipated. A bear

> **Major Technical Principle**   At any one time, there are four influ-
> ences on prices. They are psychological, technical, economic, and
> monetary.

market rally for bonds develops under the opposite set of conditions.
Corrections in commodity and currency markets all have their roots in a
changed but incorrect perception of the underlying (primary) economic
trend. The catalyst for the rally is the rush by traders and investors to cover
their short positions (for a definition and explanation of short selling, see
the Glossary). It should be added that the *apparent* motivating force for the
correction need not necessarily be directly linked to the outlook for business or interest rates.

Any of these influences could be the excuse for a countercyclical intermediate price movement. It could be linked to the anticipated resolution
or worsening of a political or military problem, for example. Essentially,
the change in anticipated conditions combined with the unwinding of the
technical distortions of the previous primary intermediate trend and its
associated sharp price movement is sufficient to confuse the majority. Only
when business conditions are correctly expected to change from recovery
to recession (or vice versa) is the primary trend of equities likely to
reverse.

In his excellent book *Profits in the Stock Market,* H. M. Gartley[1] pointed out
that in the 40 years ending in 1935, two-thirds of all bull market corrections
in the U.S. stock market developed in two waves of liquidation separated by
a minor rally that retraced between one-third and two-thirds of the first
decline. An observation of such corrections since 1935 also bears out the
finding that most intermediate corrections consist of two, rather than one
or three, phases of liquidation. Unfortunately, intermediate corrections
within a bear market cannot be so easily categorized since some are
one-move affairs or consist of a rally out of a small base, while still others
unfold as a very volatile sideways movement. Even though Gartley's observations are concerned with equities, this form of correction applies to all
financial markets.

[1]Lambert Gann Publishing, Pomeroy, Washington, 1981.

Relationship between Primary Intermediate Moves and Subsequent Reactions

In *Profits in the Stock Market*, Gartley published a series of diagrams using the classification of intermediate trends established by Robert Rhea. Gartley's conclusion was that *the smaller in magnitude the primary intermediate-term movement was, the larger the retracement tended to be, and vice versa.* He noted that this was just as valid for bull market reactions as for bear market rallies. Observations of the period since 1933 for virtually all markets appear to support this hypothesis.

For example, the rally off the 1962 stock market low was only 18 percent compared to the mean average of 30 percent between 1933 and 1982. This represented part of a double bottom formation and therefore the first primary intermediate rally. This relatively small advance was followed by a somewhat larger 71 percent retracement. However, the ensuing rally from late 1962 until mid-1963 was 32 percent and was followed by a small 25 percent retracement of the gain. Interested readers may wish to be satisfied that what goes up does not necessarily come down, and vice versa.

The 1976–1980 gold bull market was very powerful, but the intermediate corrections were quite brief. On the other hand, the rallies between 1982 and 1990 were far less strong, but were followed by corrections of much greater magnitude proportionally.

Using Intermediate Cycles to Identify Primary Reversals

Number of Intermediate Cycles

A primary movement may normally be expected to encompass two and a half intermediate cycles (see Fig. 4-1). Unfortunately, not all primary movements correspond to the norm; an occasional primary movement may consist of one, two, three, or even four intermediate cycles. Furthermore, these intermediate cycles may be of very unequal lengths or magnitude, making their classification and identification possible only after the event. Even so, intermediate cycle analysis can still be used as a basis for identifying the maturity of the primary trend in most cases.

Whenever prices are well advanced in a primary intermediate trend following the completion of two intermediate cycles, technicians should be alerted to the fact that a reversal of the primary trend itself may be about to take place. Again, if only one intermediate cycle has been completed, the chances of prices reaching higher levels (lower levels in a bear market) are quite high.

Characteristics of a Final Intermediate Cycle in a Primary Trend

In addition to actually counting the number of intermediate cycles, it is also possible to compare the characteristics of a particular cycle with those of a primary trend's typical pivotal or reversal cycle. These characteristics are discussed in the following section.

Reversal from Bull to Bear Market   Since volume leads price, the failure of volume to increase above the levels of the previous intermediate cycle up phase is a bearish sign. Alternatively, if over a period of 3 to 4 weeks volume expands on the intermediate rally close to the previous peak in volume but fails to move prices significantly, it represents churning and should also be treated bearishly. Coincidence of either of these characteristics with a downward crossover of a 40-week moving average (see Chapter 9) or a divergence in an intermediate-term momentum indicator (see Chapter 10) would be an additional reason for caution.

There are essentially two broad characteristics that suggest that the downward phase of an intermediate cycle could be the first downleg of a bear market. The first is a substantial increase in volume during the price decline. The second is a cancellation or retracement of 80 percent or more of the up phase of that same intermediate cycle. The greater the retracement, the greater the probability that the basic trend has reversed, especially because a retracement in excess of 100 percent means that any series of rising troughs has been broken, thereby placing the probabilities in favor of a change in the primary trend.

Other signs would include the observation of a mega-oversold or an extreme swing (see Chapter 10 on momentum for a full explanation of these terms).

Reversal from Bear to Bull Market   The first intermediate up phase of a bull market is usually accompanied by a substantial expansion in volume that is significantly greater than those of previous intermediate up phases (see Fig. 4-3). In other words, the first upleg in a bull market attracts noticeably more volume than any of the intermediate rallies in the previ-

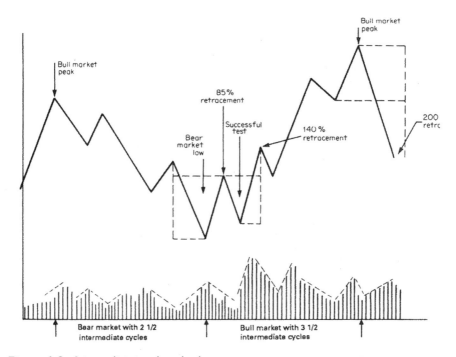

Figure 4-3 Intermediate trends and volume.

ous bear market. Another sign of a basic reversal occurs when prices retrace at least 80 percent of the previous decline. Again, the greater the proportion of retracement, the greater the odds of a reversal in the basic trend. If the retracement is greater than 100 percent, the odds clearly indicate that a reversal in the downward trend is likely because the series of declining peaks will have broken down.

Since volume normally expands substantially as the intermediate down phase during a bear market reaches a low, a shrinkage in volume during an intermediate decline could well be a warning that the bear market has run its course. This is especially true if the price does not reach a new low during this intermediate decline, since the series of declining intermediate cyclical lows, which is a characteristic of a bear market, may no longer be intact.

An example of this is shown in Chart 5-10, where the overall peak in volume was seen in the June 1962 decline rather than the August to October sell-off. Chart 5-7 shows no perceptible slackening of volume at the lows, but the volume expansion during the January rally, combined with the bettering of the October to November high (a 100 percent retracement), offered a valuable clue that the bear market was over. The final decline in October represented the down phase of the third intermediate cycle in the bear market, which should have warned of its probable maturity. A final sign might include a mega-overbought condition or an extreme swing. Again, please refer to Chapter 10 for an explanation of these concepts.

Intermediate Trends in the U.S. Stock Market, 1897–1982

Amplitude and Duration of Primary Intermediate Upmoves

Between 1897 and 1933, Robert Rhea, the author of *Dow Theory*, classified 53 intermediate-trend advances within a primary bull market, which ranged in magnitude from 7 to 117 percent, as shown in Table 4-1.

I have classified 35 intermediate-term moves between 1933 and 1982, and the median averaged 22 percent from low to high. The results are shown in Table 4-2.

Table 4-1 Primary Intermediate Upmoves, 1897–1933

Porportion of intermediate moves	Price magnitude
25	7–14
50	15–28
25	28–117
‾‾‾	
100	
Median 20	

Table 4-2 Primary Intermediate Upmoves, 1933–1982

	Swings from low to high, percent	Duration, weeks
Mean average	30	22
Median	22	24
Range	10–105	3–137

The median average primary intermediate advance since 1897 appears to be around 20 to 22 percent. The median primary intermediate upmove in the 1933–1982 period does not differ from that of the earlier period classified by Rhea. However, the median duration appears to have increased considerably from 13 weeks in the 1897–1933 period to 24 weeks in the 1933–1982 period.

Amplitude and Duration of Primary Intermediate Downmoves

Using Rhea's classification, 39 cases of a primary intermediate decline developed between 1900 and 1932, as summarized in Table 4-3.

My research shows that between 1932 and 1982 there were 35 primary intermediate declines, with a median of 16 percent (the decline was measured as a percentage from the high). The results are summarized in Table 4-4.

The results in the 1932–1982 period did not differ appreciably from those in the 1897–1933 period. Rhea's median average swing was 18 percent, as compared to the more recent 16 percent, whereas the median duration in the earlier period was 13 weeks, as compared to 14 weeks in the 1932–1982 period.

Table 4-3 Primary Intermediate Downmoves, 1900–1932

Proportion of intermediate moves	Price magnitude
25	3–12
50	13–27
25	28–54
Median 18	

Table 4-4 Primary Intermediate Downmoves, 1932–1982

	Swings from high	Duration (weeks)
Mean average	18	17
Median	16	14
Range	7–40	3–43

Amplitude and Duration of Bull Market Secondary Reactions

Between 1898 and 1933, Rhea classified 43 cases of bull market secondaries. In terms of retracement of the previous primary intermediate upmove, they ranged from 12.4 to 180 percent, with a median of 56 percent. This compared with a range in the 1933–1982 period from 25 to 148 percent, with a median of 51 percent. The duration of the median in the earlier period was 5 weeks, as compared to 8 weeks between 1933 and 1982. The median percentage loss from the previous primary intermediate peak was 12 percent (the mean average was 13 percent) between 1933 and 1982.

Amplitude and Duration of Bear Market Rallies

Rhea estimated that the median bear market rally retraced 52 percent of the previous decline, which is comparable to my own median estimate of 61 percent in the 1932–1982 period. The two ranges were 30 and 116 percent and 26 and 99 percent, respectively. Median durations were 6 weeks in 1898–1933 and 7 weeks in 1932–1982. Rallies off the low averaged 12 and 10 percent for mean and median, respectively, for the 1933–1982 period.

Intermediate Trends in the U.S. Stock Market Since 1982

Charts 4-1 and 4-2 show the Standard & Poor's (S&P) Composite between the end of 1982 and the opening of the twenty-first century. The thick vertical lines approximate intermediate rally peaks and the thin ones intermediate troughs. The lower panel contains an intermediate oscillator, the intermediate KST (see Chapter 12 for an explanation), which roughly reflects the turning points. This period encompassed the secular bull market that began in 1982 and ended at the turn of the century. The classification of intermediate trends was particularly difficult compared to previous periods. I tried (as much as possible) to make the intermediate trends fit the swings in the oscillator. Because oscillators have a tendency to lead in bull markets, the actual peaks in the intermediate rallies usually lag those in the KST. The two charts show that the classification of these trends is far from a precise task and confirms earlier research between 1897 and 1982 that the range of intermediate trends varies tremendously. In the period

Chart 4-1   S&P Composite, 1982–1991, and an intermediate KST. (*From www.pring.com.*)

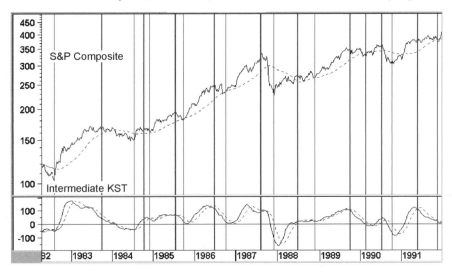

Chart 4-2   S&P Composite, 1991–2001, and an intermediate KST. (*From www.pring.com.*)

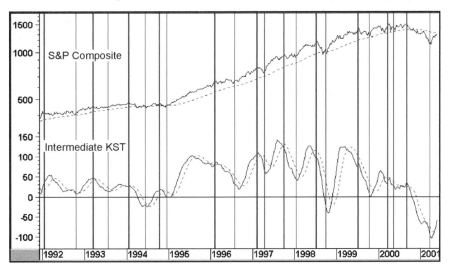

covered by Chart 4-1, for instance, the first intermediate rally in the bull market lasted well over a year from August 1982 to October 1983. Even if I had taken the July 1983 top as a reference point, the rally would still have lasted for almost a year. Moreover, the whole year of 1995 was consumed by one complete intermediate advance.

Summary

- The typical primary trend can be divided into two one-half primary intermediate cycles, each consisting of an upmove and a downmove. In a bull market, each successive upwave should reach a new cyclical high, and in a bear market, each successive downwave of the intermediate cycle should reach a new low. Breaking the pattern of rising lows and falling peaks is an important, but *not* unequivocal, warning of a reversal in the primary trend. For more conclusive proof, technicians should derive a similar conclusion from a *consensus* of indicators.
- A secondary movement or reaction is that part of an intermediate cycle that runs counter to the main trend, a downward reaction in a bull market or a rally in a bear market. Secondary intermediate movements typically last from 4 weeks to 3 months and retrace between one-third and two-thirds of the previous primary intermediate price movement. Secondary price movements may also take the form of a line or horizontal trading pattern.
- The character of intermediate cycles can be used to help identify primary trend reversals.
- As an approximate rule, the stronger an intermediate rally, the less the retracement is likely to be, and vice versa for primary bear markets.

5

Price Patterns

Basic Concepts

The techniques discussed in this chapter and in Chapters 6 through16 are concerned with analysis of any price trend that has been determined by the interaction of buyers and sellers in a free market.

The concept of price patterns is demonstrated in Figs. 5-1 and 5-2. Figure 5-1 represents a typical price cycle in which there are three trends: up, sideways, and down. The sideways trend is essentially a horizontal or transitional one, which separates the two major market movements. Sometimes

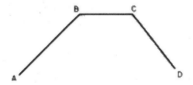

Figure 5-1   Normal reversal.

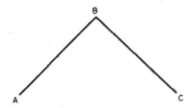

Figure 5-2   V-type reversal.

a highly emotional market can change without warning, as in Fig. 5-2, but this rarely happens. Consider a fast-moving train, which takes a long time to slow down and then go into reverse; the same is normally true of financial markets.

To the market technician, the transitional phase has great significance because it marks the turning point between a rising and a falling market. If prices have been advancing, the enthusiasm of the buyers has outweighed the pessimism of sellers up to this point, and prices have risen accordingly. During the transition phase, the balance becomes more or less even until finally, for one reason or another, it is tipped in a new direction as the relative weight of selling pushes the trend (of prices) down. At the termination of a bear market, the reverse process occurs.

These transition phases are almost invariably signaled by clearly definable price patterns or formations. The successful completion of such patterns or formations alerts the technician to the fact that a reversal in trend has taken place. This phenomenon is illustrated in Fig. 5-3, which shows the price action at the end of a long rising trend. As soon as the price rises above line *BB,* it is in the transitional area, although this is apparent only some time after the picture has developed.

Once into the area, the price rises to line *AA,* which is technically termed a *resistance area.* The word *resistance* is used because at this point the index shows opposition to a further price rise. This term, along with *support,* is discussed at length in Chapter 15. When the demand/supply relationship comes into balance at *AA,* the market quickly turns in favor of the sellers because prices react. This temporary reversal may occur because buyers refuse to pay up for a security, or because the higher price attracts more sellers, or for both of these two reasons. The important fact is that the relationship between the two groups is temporarily reversed at this point.

Major Technical Principle   Transitions between a rising and falling trend are often signaled by price patterns.

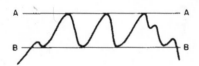

Figure 5-3 Trading range rectangle.

Following the unsuccessful assault on *AA*, prices turn down until line *BB*, known as a *support level*, is reached. Just as the price level at *AA* reversed the balance in favor of the sellers, so the support level *BB* alters the balance again. This time, the trend moves in an upward direction because at *BB* prices become relatively attractive for buyers who missed the boat on the way up, while sellers who feel that the price will again reach *AA* hold off. For a while, there is a standoff between buyers and sellers within the confines of the area bounded by lines *AA* and *BB*. Finally, the price falls below *BB*, and a major new (downward) trend is signaled.

To help explain this concept, the contest between buyers and sellers is like a battle fought by two armies engaged in trench warfare. In Fig. 5-4(*a*), armies *A* and *B* are facing off. Line *AA* represents army *A*'s defense, and *BB* is army *B*'s line of defense. The arrows indicate the forays between the two lines, as both armies fight their way to the opposing trench, but are unable to penetrate the line of defense. In Fig. 5-4(*b*), army B finally pushes through A's trench. Army *A* is then forced to retreat and make a stand at the second line of defense (line A_2A_2). In the stock market, line *AA* represents selling resistance, which, once overcome, signifies a change in the balance between buyers and sellers in favor of the buyers, so that prices will advance quickly until new resistance is met. The second line of defense, line A_2A_2, represents resistance to a further advance.

On the other hand, army *B* might quite easily break through A_2A_2, but the further it advances without time to consolidate its gains, the more likely it is to become overextended and the greater is the probability of its suffering a serious setback. At some point, therefore, it makes more sense for this successful force to wait and consolidate its gains.

If prices in financial markets extend too far without time to digest their gains, they too are more likely to face a sharp and seemingly unexpected reversal.

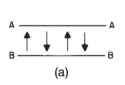

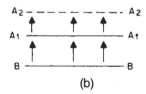

Figures 5-4 Trench warfare.

Introducing the Rectangle

The transitional or horizontal phase separating rising and falling price trends discussed previously is a pattern known as a *rectangle*. This formation corresponds to the line formation developed from the Dow theory. The rectangle in Fig. 5-3, marking the turning point between the bull and bear phases, is termed a *reversal* pattern. Reversal patterns at market tops are known as *distribution* areas or patterns (where the security is distributed from strong informed participants to weak uninformed ones), and those at market bottoms are called *accumulation* patterns (where the security passes from weak uninformed participants to strong informed ones) [see Fig. 5-5(*a*)]. If the rectangle were completed with a victory for the buyers as the price pushed through line *AA* [see Fig. 5-5(*b*)], no reversal of the rising trend would occur. The breakout above *AA* would therefore have reaffirmed the underlying trend. In this case, the corrective phase associated with the formation of the rectangle would temporarily interrupt the bull market and become a consolidation pattern. Such formations are also referred to as *consolidation* or *continuation* patterns.

During the period of formation, there is no way of knowing in advance which way the price will ultimately break; therefore, it should always be assumed that the prevailing trend is in existence until it is proved to have been reversed.

Size and Depth

The principles of price pattern construction and interpretation can be applied to any time frame, from 1-minute bars all the way through to monthly or even annual charts. However, the significance of a price formation or pattern is a direct function of its size and depth.

        (a)   (b)

Figures 5-5   (*a*) Reversal rectangle. (*b*) Consolidation rectangle.

> **Major Technical Principle** The longer a pattern takes to complete and the greater the price fluctuations within it, the more substantial the following move is likely to be.

Thus, a pattern that shows up on a monthly chart is likely to be far more significant than one on an intraday chart, and so forth. It is just as important to build a strong base from which prices can rise as it is to build a large, strong, deep foundation upon which to construct a skyscraper.

In the case of financial market prices, the foundation is an accumulation pattern that represents an area of indecisive combat between buyers and sellers. The term *accumulation* is used because market bottoms always occur when the news is bad. Such an environment stimulates sales by uninformed investors who were not expecting developments to improve. During an accumulation phase, more sophisticated investors and professionals would be positioning or accumulating the asset concerned in anticipation of improved conditions 6 to 9 months ahead. During this period, it is moving from weak, uninformed traders or investors to strong and knowledgeable hands. The longer the period of accumulation, the greater the amount of a security that moves from weak into strong hands and the larger is the base from which prices can rise.

At market tops, the process is reversed, as those who were accumulating at or near the bottom sell to less sophisticated market participants, who become more and more attracted as prices rise and the underlying fundamental conditions improve. Where a substantial amount of distribution develops, this is usually followed by a protracted period of price erosion or base building.

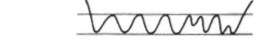

Figure 5-6 Long rectangle.

The time taken to complete a formation is important because of the amount of an asset changing hands, and also because a movement in price beyond the boundaries of a pattern means that the balance between buyers and sellers has altered. When the price action has been in a stalemate for a long time and investors have become used to buying at one price and selling at the other, a move beyond either limit represents a fundamental change, which has great psychological significance.

The depth of a formation also determines its significance. Consider the trench war analogy once more. If the opposing trenches are very close together, say, within 100 yards, this means that the victorious assault, when it comes, will be less significant than if they are separated by several miles; in such a case, the battles will have been much more intense and the victory that much greater. The same is true in the financial markets. The breeching of a wide trading range has far greater psychological significance than that of a narrow one.

Measuring Implications

Most of the results obtained with technical analysis procedures do not indicate the eventual duration of a trend. Price patterns are the exception, since their construction offers some limited forecasting possibilities. Before we examine this aspect, it is first necessary to draw the distinction between arithmetic and logarithmic or ratio scaling, because the choice determines the significance of the measuring implications.

Arithmetic Scale

Arithmetic charts consist of an arithmetic scale on the vertical or y axis, with time shown on the horizontal or x axis, as illustrated in Fig. 5-7. All units of measure are plotted using the same vertical distance, so that the difference in space between 2 and 4 is the same as that between 20 and 22. Arithmetic scaling is not a good choice for long-term price movements, since a rise from 2 to 4 represents a doubling of the price, whereas a rise from 20 to 22 represents only a 10 percent increase.

In the U.S. stock market, a price move in excess of 50 points for the Dow is normal. A 50 point move in 1932, though, when the average was traded well below 100, would have represented a huge move. For this reason, long-term movements should be plotted on a ratio or logarithmic scale. The choice of scale does not materially affect daily charts, in which price movements are relatively small in a proportionate sense. For periods over 1 year, in which fluctuations are much larger, I always prefer to use a ratio scale.

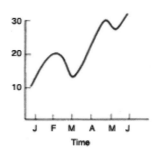

Figure 5-7 Arithmetic scaling (same vertical distance = same point move).

Chart 5-1 compares an arithmetic scale with a ratio scale for the Standard & Poor's Composite. The distortions on the arithmetic scale are self-evident.

Ratio Scale

Prices plotted on a ratio scale show identical distances for identical percentage moves. In Fig. 5-8, let's say that the vertical distance between 1 and 2 (a 2:1 ratio) is $^1/_2$ in. Similarly, the 2:1 distance between 4 and 2 is also represented on the chart as $^1/_2$ in. A specific vertical distance on the chart indicates the same percentage change in the price being measured, whatever the level. For example, if the scale in Fig. 5-8 was extended, $^1/_2$ in. would always represent a doubling, from 1 to 2, 16 to 32, 50 to 100, and so on, just as $^1/_2$ in. would indicate a rise of 50 percent and 1 in. would show a quadrupling of prices. Almost all computer software gives the user the option of choosing between arithmetic and logarithmic scales.

It is important to remember that market prices are a function of psychological attitudes toward fundamental events. Since these attitudes have a tendency to move proportionately, it makes sense to plot them on a scale that reflects proportionate moves equally.

Figure 5-9 shows a rectangle that has formed and completed a (distribution) top. The measuring implication of this formation is the vertical distance between its outer boundaries, that is, the distance between lines *AA* and *BB* projected downward from line *BB*. If *AA* represents 100 and *BB* 50, then the downside objective will be 50 percent, using a ratio scale. When projected downward from line *BB,* 50 percent gives a measuring implication of 25. Although this measuring formula offers a rough guide, it is usually a *minimum* expectation, and prices often go much further than their

Chart 5-1 S&P Composite arithmetic vs. ratio scale. This chart contains the S&P plotted on arithmetic and ratio scales. Note how the arithmetic scale totally obliterates any price fluctuations in the early part of the century and exaggerates the price movements in the last 20 years or so. The 1929–1932 period, the most severe on record, does not even appear as a blip on this scale. This is not true of the lower panel, which features a logarithmic or ratio scale. (*From Intermarket Review.*)

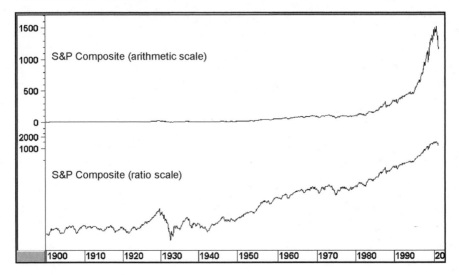

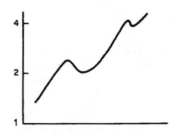

Figure 5-8 Ratio scaling (same vertical distance = same proportionate move).

implied objective. In a very high proportion of cases, the objective level derived from the measuring formula becomes an area of support or resistance when the price trend is temporarily halted.

The importance of using logarithmic scales whenever possible is shown in Fig. 5-10. In Fig. 5-10(*a*), the price has traced out and broken down from a rectangle. Projecting the vertical distance between 200 and 100 downward gives an objective of 0, clearly a very unlikely possibility. On the other hand,

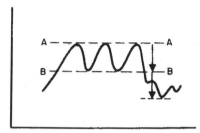

Figure 5-9 Measuring implication from a rectangle.

Fig. 5-10(b) uses the same projection based on a logarithmic scale. In this case, a more realistic objective of 50 is obtained.

If a rectangle appears as a bottom reversal pattern or as a consolidation pattern, the measuring rules remain consistent with the example given for the distribution formation. This is shown in Figs. 5-11(a)–(c).

If the minimal objective proves to be the ultimate extension of the new trend, a substantial amount of accumulation or distribution, whichever is appropriate, will usually occur before prices can move in their original direction. Thus, if a 2-year rectangle is completed and the downward price objective is reached, even though further price erosion does not take place, it is still usually, though certainly not always, necessary for a base (accumulation) to be formed of approximately the same size as the previous distribution (in this case 2 years) before a valid uptrend can take place.[1]

In many cases, the price will move beyond the objective. In really strong moves, it will move in multiples of it, where the various multiples or the objective itself becomes an important support and resistance area.

Confirmation of a Valid Breakout

Price

So far, it has been assumed that any move, however small, out of the price pattern constitutes a valid signal of a trend reversal (or resumption, if the pattern is one of consolidation). Quite often, misleading moves known as whipsaws occur, so it is helpful to establish certain criteria to minimize the

---

[1]Note: It is very important to remember that price objectives represent the *minimum ultimate* target and are not normally achieved in one move. Usually, a series of rallies and reactions in an upside breakout is required, or reaction or retracements in a downside breakout, before the objective is reached.

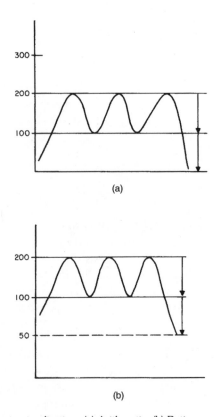

Figure 5-10 Measuring implication. (a) Arithmetic. (b) Ratio.

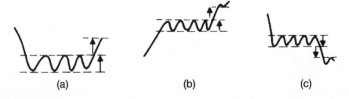

Figure 5-11 Measuring implications.

Major Technical Principle   A measuring objective is a minimum ultimate objective.

possibility of misinterpretation. Conventional wisdom holds that you should wait for a 3 percent penetration of the boundaries before concluding that the breakout is valid. This filters out a substantial number of misleading moves, even though the resulting signals are less timely.

This approach was developed in the first part of the twentieth century when holding periods for market participants were much longer. Today, with the popularity of intraday charts, 3 percent could represent the complete move and then some. I have no basic objection to the 3 percent rule for longer-term price movements in which the fluctuations are much greater. However, the best approach is a commonsense one based on experience and judgment in each particular case. It would be very convenient to be able to say that anything over a specific percentage amount represents a valid breakout, but unfortunately a lot depends on the time frame being considered and the volatility of the specific security.

For example, electric utilities are very stable in their price action compared to mining stocks where the volatility is far greater. Applying the same percentage breakout rule to both obviously doesn't make sense. What constitutes a decisive breakout, where the odds of a whipsaw are considerably reduced is then very much a matter of personal judgment based on experience, trial, and error. This judgment should take into consideration such factors as the type of trend being monitored, the volatility of the security, volume, and momentum characteristics.

Another factor that can help early on in deciding if a breakout is valid lies in the fact that a good breakout should hold for several periods. For example, you may observe a decisive upside breakout from a rectangle on a daily chart, but if it cannot hold for more than 1 day above the breakout level, the signal is highly suspect. Often the technical position is worse after such breakouts. This is because breakouts that cannot hold indicate exhaustion, and exhaustion moves are often followed by strong price trends in the opposite direction to that indicated by the (false) breakout. An example of a false breakout is featured in Chart 5-2 for June 2001 Gold.

On entering any trade or investment based on a price pattern breakout, it is important to decide ahead of time what type of price action would cause you to conclude that the breakout was a whipsaw. An example might be a break below a previous minor low, a decline below a predetermined level from the breakout point. A stop should then be placed *below* such a pivotal point. In this way, you will have calculated the loss you are willing to undertake and the point where the original premise for the trade; that is, the breakout is no longer operative. Failure to make such a decision ahead of time will mean that your decision to sell is more likely to be based on emotion and knee-jerk reactions to news events than on a logical preset plan. A

Chart 5-2 Gold futures and an exhaustion breakout. This chart of June (2001) Gold shows a nice decisive breakout from a reverse head-and-shoulders (H&S) pattern. Unfortunately, this proved to be an exhaustion move since the breakout was unable to hold above the neckline. In such situations, it is usually best to liquidate once it is realized that a false breakout has developed. There are three places to take action when the price slips decisively below the breakout point, it falls below the line joining the head with the right shoulder, or the price slips below the right shoulder itself. The violation of each of these benchmarks becomes progressively more reliable as a signal, but it encounters a greater potential loss. *(From Intermarket Review.)*

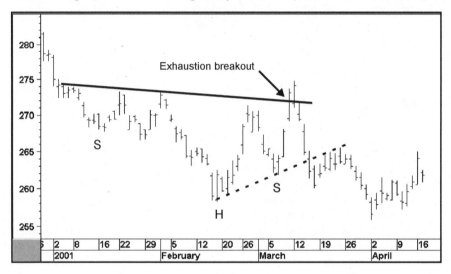

possible point of no return for the false breakout in Chart 5-2 would be at the point, where the dashed up trendline joining the lows was violated.

Volume

Volume usually goes with the trend; that is, volume advances with a rising trend of prices and falls with a declining one. This is a normal relationship, and anything that diverges from this characteristic should be considered a warning sign that the prevailing price trend may be in the process of reversing. Figure 5-12 shows a typical volume/price relationship.

Volume, the number of units of an asset (such as shares or contracts) that changes hands during a specific period, is shown by the vertical lines at the bottom of Fig. 5-12. Volume expands marginally as the price approaches its low at the beginning or rectangle AA, but as the accumulation pattern is formed, activity recedes noticeably.

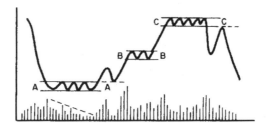

Figure 5-12 Volume considerations.

> **Major Technical Principle** Volume is always measured relative to its recent past.

As the pattern nears completion, disinterest prevails and volume almost dries up. As if by magic, activity picks up noticeably when the security moves above its level of resistance (bounded by the upper line in the rectangle). It is sometimes possible to draw a trend line joining the lower volume peaks, as shown in Fig. 5-12. It is this upward surge in trading activity that confirms the validity of the breakout. A similar move on low volume would be suspect and would result in a failure of volume to move with the trend.

Following the sharp price rise from the rectangle, enthusiasm dies down as prices correct in a sideways movement and volume contracts (rectangle BB). This is a perfectly normal relationship, since volume is correcting (declining) with price. Eventually, volume and price expand together, and the primary upward trend is once again confirmed. Finally, the buyers become exhausted, and the price forms yet another rectangle (rectangle CC) characterized, as before, by falling volume, but this time destined to become a reversal pattern.

It is worth noting that while the volume from the breakout in rectangle BB is high, it is relatively lower than that which accompanied the move from rectangle AA. In relation to the overall cycle, this is a bearish factor.

In this case, volume makes its peak just before entering rectangle BB, while the peak in prices is not reached until rectangle CC.

Volume contracts throughout the formation of rectangle *CC* and expands as prices break out on the downside. This expanded level of activity associated with the violation of support at the lower boundary of the rectangle emphasizes the bearish nature of the breakout, although expanding volume is not a prerequisite for a valid signal with downside breakouts, as it is for an upside move. Following the downside breakout, more often than not, prices will reverse and put on a small recovery or retracement rally. This advance is invariably accompanied by declining volume, which itself reinforces the bearish indications. It is halted at the lower end of the rectangle, which now becomes an area of resistance. Chart 5-3 shows an example of the Dow Jones Rail Average at the 1946 bull market high.

Major Technical Principle   Volume usually leads price.

It is now time to expand our discussion to some of the other price patterns, starting with one of the most notorious: the *head-and-shoulders* (H&S) formation.

H&S Patterns

H&S as Reversal Patterns

At Tops   The H&S is probably the most reliable of all chart patterns. It occurs at both market tops and market bottoms. Figure 5-13 shows a typical H&S distribution pattern. (See also Chart 5-4.)

This typical H&S distribution pattern consists of a final rally (the head) separating two smaller, although not necessarily identical, rallies (the shoulders). If the two shoulders were trends of intermediate duration, the first shoulder would be the penultimate advance in the bull market, and the second the first bear market rally. The head would, of course, represent the final intermediate rally in the bull market. Volume characteristics are of critical importance in assessing the validity of these patterns. Activity is normally heaviest during the formation of the left shoulder and also tends to be quite heavy as prices approach the peak. The real tip-off that an H&S pattern is developing comes with the formation of the right shoulder, which is invariably accompanied by distinctly lower volume. Quite often, the level of volume contracts as the peak of the right shoulder is reached. The line joining the bottoms of the two shoulders is called the *neckline*.

Chart 5-3 Dow Jones Rail Average, 1946. This chart shows a classic rectangle formation, as traced out by the Rail Average at the peak of the 1942–1946 bull market. Note the declining trend of volume, as indicated by the dashed line during the formation of the rectangle. Worth special mention is the saucer-like formation of the volume during the late July to early August rally. The expansion of activity accompanying the downside breakdown in late August signals the successful completion of this pattern. (*From Intermarket Review.*)

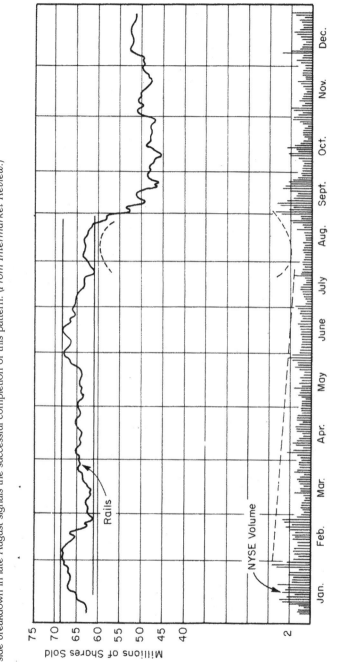

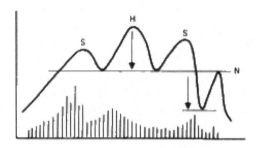

Figure 5-13 Classic H&S top.

If you look carefully at Fig. 5-13, you will appreciate that the violation of the neckline also represents a signal that the previous series of rising peaks and troughs has now given way to at least one declining peak and trough. The right shoulder represents the first lower peak and the bottom of the move following the breakdown represents a lower trough.

The measuring formula for this price formation is the distance between the head and the neckline projected downward from the neckline, as shown in Fig. 5-13. It follows that the deeper the pattern, the greater its bearish significance once it has been completed. Sometimes an H&S completion will be followed by a fairly extensive downtrend; at others, the negative effect of the pattern will be quickly cancelled by the completion of a base.

Often, traders will observe the formation of an H&S top and anticipate a breakdown. This is an incorrect tactic based on this evidence alone because it is not known until later whether the prevailing trend will continue or if a reversal signal will be given with a decisive break below the neckline. Over the years, I have seen many analysts, who should know better, forecast a bearish trend based on an incomplete H&S top. Remember, *in technical analysis, the prevailing trend is assumed to be in force until the weight of the evidence proves otherwise.* An incomplete H&S is not evidence, just a possible scenario.

H&S patterns can be formed in 10 to 15 minutes or take decades to develop. Generally speaking, the longer the period, the greater the amount of distribution that has taken place, and therefore the longer the ensuing bear trend is likely to be. The larger H&S formations are often very complex and comprise several smaller ones, as shown in Fig. 5-14.

The H&S patterns illustrated in Figs. 5-13 and 5-14 have a horizontal neckline, but there are many other varieties [see Fig. 5-15(a)–(c)], all of which possess the same bearish implications as the horizontal variety once they have been completed.

Chart 5-4 *The New York Times* average, 1928. This chart of *The New York Times* average of 50 railroad and industrial stocks shows the formation of an upward-sloping H&S during March, April, and May 1928. The minimum downside objective of about 182 was achieved fairly quickly, but a 3-month period of base building commensurate with the H&S pattern was still necessary before the effect of the distribution was canceled out and prices were able to resume their primary advance. Note the heavy volume on the left shoulder and head, and the relatively low volume on the right shoulder. Also, activity declined substantially during the formation of the triangle, but began to expand during the breakout in September.

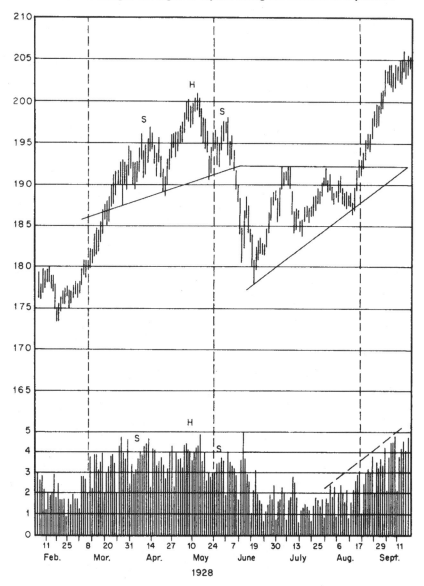

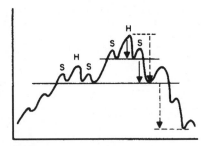

Figure 5-14   Complex H&S.

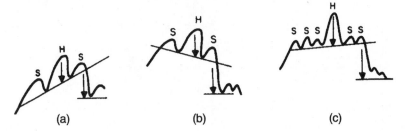

Figure 5-15   H&S variations.

At Bottoms   Figure 5-16 indicates how an H&S pattern would look at a market bottom; this is usually called an *inverse H&S,* a *reverse H&S,* or an *H&S bottom.*

Normally, volume is relatively high at the bottom of the left shoulder and during the formation of the head. The major factor to watch for is activity on the right shoulder, which should contract during the decline to the trough and expand substantially on the breakout (see Chart 5-5). Like the H&S distribution patterns, the inverse (accumulation) H&S can have a number of variations in trend line slope, number of shoulders, and so on. Usually, the more complex the formation, the greater its significance. This goes back to the idea that price formations represent battles between buyers and sellers: the more battles that go on, the greater the complexity and the more significant the new trend is once the battle has been resolved. Some of these reverse H&S variations are shown in Figs. 5-17(*a*)–(*c*).

H&S patterns are extremely reliable formations, and their successful completion usually gives an excellent indication of a trend reversal.

Chart 5-5 DJIA, 1898. This downward-sloping inverse H&S pattern developed in the spring of 1898. Note that the April rally developed on very low volume. The subsequent reaction successfully tested the March low and the ensuing breakout rally was accompanied by a bullish expansion of volume. By August, the Dow Jones Industrial Average (DJIA) had reached 60.97 and by April 1899 it rose to 77.28.

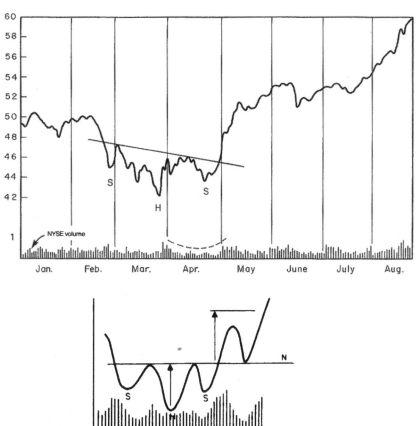

Figure 5-16 Classic reverse H&S.

H&S Formations as Continuation Patterns

H&S and reverse H&S formations occasionally show up on the charts as continuation patterns. Measuring implications and volume characteristics are the same as for the reversal type. The only difference is that these patterns develop *during* a trend rather than at the end. Chart 5-6 shows an example of an H&S consolidation during a decline.

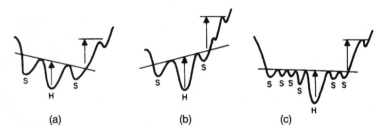

(a)   (b)   (c)

Figure 5-17   Reverse H&S variations.

H&S Failures

Sometimes the price action exhibits all the characteristics of an H&S distribution pattern, but it either refuses to penetrate the neckline or penetrates it temporarily and then starts to rally. This represents an H&S failure and is usually followed by an explosive rally. It is probably due to misplaced pessimism. Once the real fundamentals are perceived, not only do new buyers rush in, but also traders holding short positions are forced to cover. Since fear is a stronger motivator than greed, these bears bid up the price very aggressively.

Chart 5-7, which shows the daily close for the DJIA in 1975, illustrates this phenomenon very clearly, as the failure of an H&S pattern results in a fairly worthwhile rally. Nevertheless, an H&S that does not work indicates that while there is still some life left in the situation, the end may not be far off. In Chart 5-6, the rally ended rather abruptly in July.

Unfortunately, the pattern itself gives no indication that it is going to fail. Sometimes such evidence can be gleaned from other technical factors. For example, if a countertrend signal looks as if it may be taking place, this is just as likely to result in a failure. For instance, the H&S failure in Chart 5-7 was a sell signal in a bull market. Chart 5-8 shows another example of an H&S failure for Alberto Culver.

Failures used to be fairly rare, but now seem to be more common, which indicates the necessity of waiting for a decisive breakout on the downside. If any action is contemplated, it should be taken when the price breaks above the right shoulder on heavy volume (see Fig. 5-18). Usually, such signals offer substantial profits in a very short period of time and are well worth acting on. Inverse H&S patterns can also fail. Again, the failure is usually followed by an extremely sharp sell-off, as participants who bought in anticipation of an upward breakout are flushed out when the new bearish fundamentals become more widely known.

Chart 5-6 Citigroup consolidation H&S top. This chart shows a consolidation H&S top for Citigroup in 1998. Note how the volume is much heavier during the formation of the left shoulder and the head. Also notice how it expands as the price breaks below the neckline. *(From Intermarket Review.)*

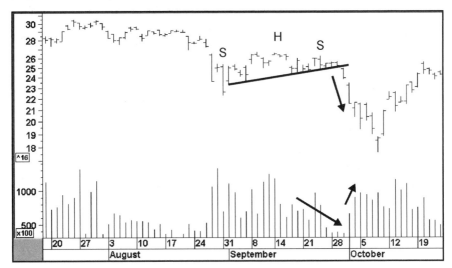

Major Technical Principle If a technical signal is going to fail, it is often because it is taking place in the *opposite* direction to the main trend.

Double Tops and Bottoms

A double top consists of two peaks separated by a reaction or valley in prices. Its main characteristic is that the second top is formed with distinctly less volume than the first (see Chart 5-9). It is normal for both peaks to form at the same price level, but it is also possible for the second peak to slightly exceed the first or to top out just a little below it. Remember, this is not an exact science, but a commonsense interpretation of a battle between buyers and sellers.

Minimum downside measuring implications for double tops, as shown in Fig. 5-19, are similar to H&S patterns.

Chart 5-7 DJIA 1974–1975 double bottom. Notice the lower volume established on the second low in December 1974. Also, in the spring of 1975, we see an example of a failed H&S top. (*From Intermarket Review.*)

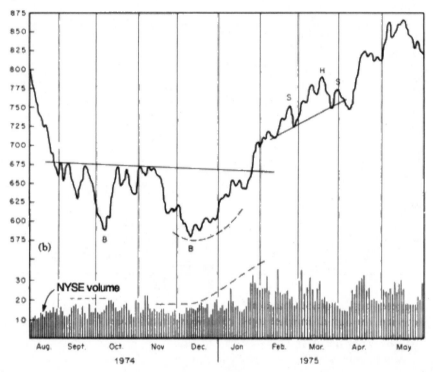

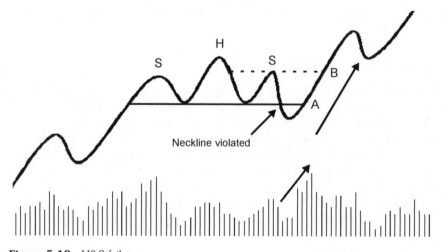

Figure 5-18 H&S failure.

Chart 5-8   Alberto Culver and a failed H&S top. This chart of Alberto Culver shows a classic H&S failure. The neckline was violated in mid-1993. A retracement followed, but the yellow flags began to come out when the early 1994 decline failed to make a new low. If the H&S was going to work, this should have happened. Later, the price rallied back above the neckline. At that point, the viability of the pattern was very much open to question. The real tipoff came when the price rallied above the down trendline joining the head and the right shoulder and finally when it rallied above the right shoulder at arrow *X*. (*From Intermarket Review.*)

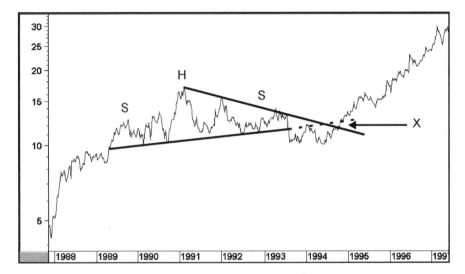

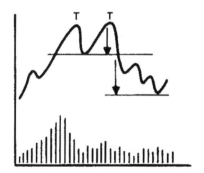

Figure 5-19   Double top.

A double bottom is shown in Fig. 5-20. This type of pattern is typically accompanied by high volume on the first bottom, very light volume on the second, and very heavy volume on the breakout. Usually, the second bottom is formed above the first, but these formations are equally valid whether or not the second reaction reaches (or even *slightly* exceeds) the level of its predecessor.

Chart 5-9 DJIA 1936–1937 double top. Following a substantial advance from 1932, the first post-Depression bull market ended in 1937. The chart shows a classic double top. Note that the volume during the July-to-August rally was substantially below that of the January-to-March peak. (*From Intermarket Review.*)

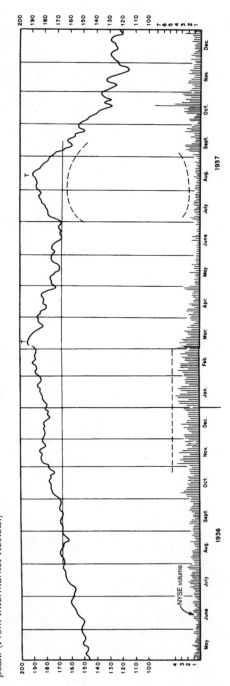

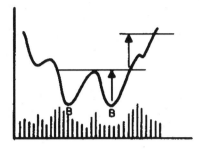

Figure 5-20 Double bottom.

Double patterns may extend to form triple tops or bottoms, or sometimes even quadruple or other complex formations. Some variations are shown in Figs. 5-21(a)–(c).

The measuring implications of all these patterns are derived by calculating the distance between the peak (trough) and lower (upper) end of the pattern and projecting this distance from the neckline. Chart 5-7, shown earlier, and Chart 5-10 show two classic double bottoms in the DJIA in 1974 and 1962, respectively.

Broadening Formations

Right Angled

Broadening formations occur when a series of three or more price fluctuations widen out in size so that peaks and troughs can be connected with two diverging trendlines. The easiest types of broadening formations to detect are those with a "flattened" bottom or top, as shown in Figs. 5-22(a) and (b).

The pattern in Fig. 5-22(a) is sometimes referred to as a *right-angled broadening formation*. Since the whole concept of widening price swings suggests highly emotional activity, volume patterns are difficult to characterize, although at market tops, volume is usually heavy during the rally phases. The patterns at both bottoms and tops are similar to the H&S variety, except that the head in the broadening formation is always the last to be formed. A bear signal comes with a decisive downside breakout. Volume can be heavy or light, but additional bearish emphasis arises if activity expands at this point.

Since a broadening formation with a flattened top is an accumulation pattern, volume expansion on the breakout is an important requirement, as shown in Fig. 5-22(b). Examples of broadening formations are shown in Charts 5-11 and 5-12. These two types of broadening formations can also

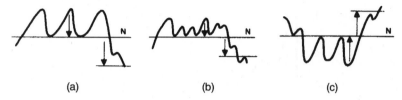

Figure 5-21 Triple tops and bottoms.

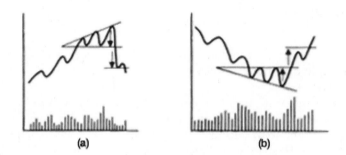

Figure 5-22 Broadening formations.

Chart 5-10 DJIA, 1962, double bottom. This chart depicts a classic double bottom in the DJIA, which formed during 1962. Note that the second one was accompanied by lower volume than the first. While volume expanded during the 1962 breakout, the increase in activity was not particularly spectacular. (*From Intermarket Review.*)

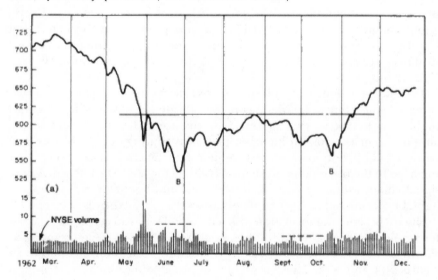

Chart 5-11 DJIA, 1938, right-angled triangle. This excellent example of a right-angled triangle occurred at the bottom of the 1937–1938 bear market. Note the substantial volume that accompanied the upside breakout. Following the breakout, the average traced out a right-angled broadening formation with a flat top. Usually, breakouts from these consolidation patterns are followed by a dramatic rise. In this case, however, the 158 level in November was destined to become the high for the 1938–1939 bull market. (*From Intermarket Review.*)

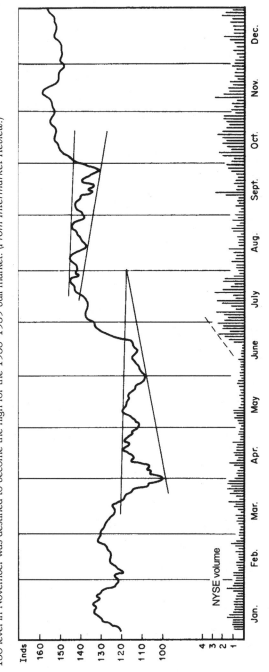

Chart 5-12 WW Grainger: a right-angled broadening formation. This chart of WW Grainger shows a right-angled broadening bottom. Note that it is not always possible to draw the outer boundaries of the pattern so that they connect all the peaks or troughs exactly. The most important thing is to make sure that the bottoms diverge and the tops form roughly at the same level. The concept is one of growing instability on the downside that is unexpectedly reversed to the upside. (*From Intermarket Review.*)

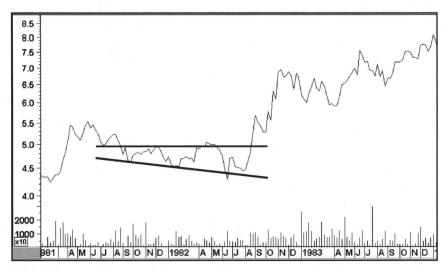

develop as consolidation patterns, as shown in Figs. 5-23(*a*) and (*b*). Charts 5-13 and 5-14 show several more examples of right-angled broadening formatting.

Broadening formations occasionally fail to work. Some possibilities are shown in Figs. 5-24(*a*) and (*b*). Unfortunately, there does not appear to be a reliable point beyond which it is safe to say that the pattern has failed to operate. The best defense in such cases is to extend the diverging trendlines, that is, the dashed lines in the figures, and await a decisive penetration by the price as confirmation.

When completed, right-angled broadening formations of both the reversal and the continuation type usually result in a particularly dynamic move. It is almost as if they are aborted H&S formations in which the move is so powerful that there is not time to complete the right shoulder.

Orthodox

The final type of broadening formation, known as an *orthodox broadening top,* is shown in Fig. 5-25. This pattern comprises three rallies, with each

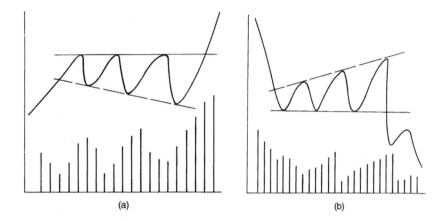

Figure 5-23   Consolidation broadening formations.

Chart 5-13   T-Bills, 90 days, various price patterns. (*From Intermarket Review.*)

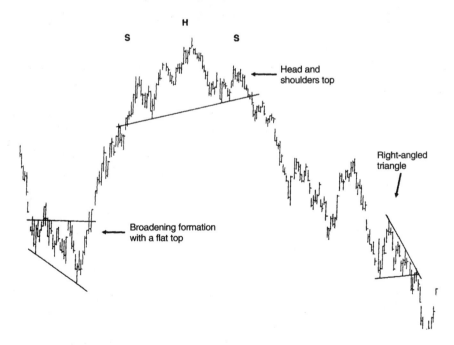

Chart 5-14 IBM—broadening formations. This chart of IBM shows a form of right-angled broadening top. There is no doubt that the chart reflects a bull market that is becoming more and more unstable. However, it is more likely that the price would experience a sharp sell-off immediately after the breakout. In the case of IBM, however, it hung around in a trading range for quite a while before moving significantly lower. Note also another broadening formation in 1991 to 1992. This one is not exactly "right-angled" because the lower line has a slight upward trajectory. Also, a classic pattern contains three complete price swings, and this one only has two. However, the rallies are progressively higher, thereby injecting the feeling of instability that is required for any broadening formation. (*From Intermarket Review.*)

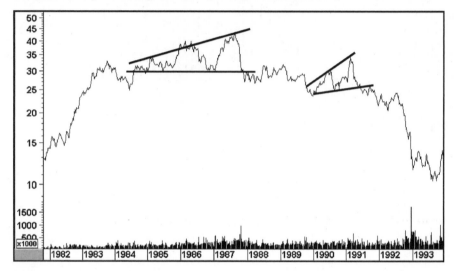

Figure 5-24 Broadening formation failures.

succeeding peak higher than its predecessor, and each peak separated by two bottoms, with the second bottom lower than the first. Orthodox broadening formations are associated with market peaks rather than market troughs.

These patterns are extremely difficult to detect until some time after the final top has been formed since there is no clearly definable level of support, the violation of which could serve as a benchmark. The violent and

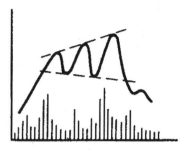

Figure 5-25 Orthodox broadening formation.

emotional nature of both price and volume swings further compounds the confusion and increases the complexity of defining these situations. Obviously, a breakout is difficult to pinpoint under such conditions, but if the formation is reasonably symmetrical, a decisive move below the descending trendline joining the two bottoms, or even a decisive move below the second bottom, usually serves as a timely warning that an even greater decline is in store.

Measuring implications are similarly difficult to determine, but normally the volatile character of a broadening top formation implies the completion of a substantial amount of distribution. Consequently, price declines of considerable proportions usually follow the successful completion of such patterns.

Triangles

Triangles, perhaps the most common of all the price patterns discussed in this chapter, are unfortunately the least reliable. Triangles may be consolidation or reversal formations, and they fall into two categories: symmetrical and right-angled.

Symmetrical Triangles

A symmetrical triangle is composed of a series of two or more rallies and reactions in which each succeeding peak is lower than its predecessor, and the bottom from each succeeding reaction is higher than its predecessor (see Fig. 5-26). A triangle is therefore the opposite of a broadening formation since the trendlines joining peaks and troughs *converge*, unlike the (orthodox) broadening formation in which they *diverge*.

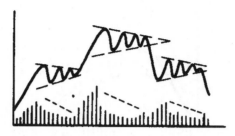

Figure 5-26 Symmetrical triangles.

These patterns are also known as *coils*, because the fluctuation in price and volume diminishes as the pattern is completed. Finally, both price and (usually) volume react sharply, as if a coil spring had been wound tighter and tighter and then snapped free as prices broke out of the triangle. Generally speaking, triangles seem to work best when the breakout occurs somewhere between one-half and three-fourths of the distance between the widest peak and rally and the apex (as in Fig. 5-27). The volume rules used for other patterns are also appropriate for triangles.

Right-Angled Triangles

Right-angled triangles are really a special form of the symmetrical type, in that one of the two boundaries is formed at an angle of 90 degrees, that is, horizontal to the vertical axis [see Figs. 5-28(*a*) and (*b*)]. (An example is illustrated in Chart 5-11.) The symmetrical triangle does not give an indication of the direction in which it is ultimately likely to break, but the right-angled triangle does, with its implied level of support or resistance and contracting price fluctuations. An example of a bearish right-angled triangle is shown in Chart 5-13.

One difficulty in interpreting these formations is that many rectangles begin as right-angled triangles. Consequently, a great deal of caution should be used when evaluating these elusive patterns. An example is shown in Fig. 5-29(*a*), where a potential downward-sloping right-angled triangle develops into a rectangle in Fig. 5-29(*b*).

Traditionally, measuring objectives for triangles are obtained by drawing a line parallel to the base of the triangle through the peak of the first rally. This line (*BB* in Fig. 5-30) represents the price objective that prices may be expected to reach or exceed.

Figure 5-30(*a*) and (*b*) show this concept for a right-angled and symetrical triangle at bottom.

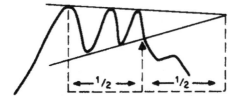

Figure 5-27   Classic symmetrical breakout.

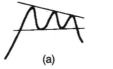

Figure 5-28   Right-angled triangles.

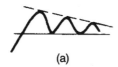
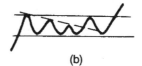

Figure 5-29   Triangle failure.

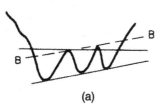
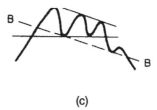

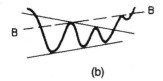
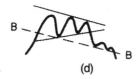

Figure 5-30   Triangle measuring implications.

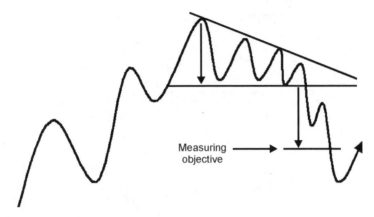

Figure 5-31   Alternative triangle measuring implications.

The reverse procedure at market tops is shown in Figs. 5-30(*c*) and (*d*). The same technique is used to project prices when triangles are of the consolidation variety. However, in my own experience, I have not found this method to be particularly useful. I prefer instead to treat the triangle as any other pattern by calculating its maximum depth and then projecting this distance at the breakout. An example of this alternative method is shown in Fig. 5-31.

Summary

- Prices in financial markets move in trends. A reversal is characterized by a temporary period in which the enthusiasm of buyers and sellers is roughly in balance. This transitional process can usually be identified by clearly definable price patterns that, when completed, offer good and reliable indications that a reversal in trend has taken place.
- Until a pattern has been formed and completed, the assumption should be that the prevailing trend is still operative, that is, that the pattern is one of consolidation or continuation. This principle is more important when the trend has been in existence for only a relatively short period, because the more mature it is, the greater the probability of an important reversal.

- Price patterns can be formed over any time period. The longer the time required to form a pattern and the greater the price fluctuations within it, the more substantial the ensuing price movement is likely to be.
- Measuring formulas can be derived for most types of patterns, but these are generally minimum objectives. Prices usually extend much further.
- Price objectives are not normally achieved in one move, but are often reached after a series of rallies and reactions have materialized.

6
Smaller Price Patterns

Most of the price patterns described in Chapter 5 can be observed in both reversal and continuation formations. The majority of those discussed in this chapter materialize during the course of a price trend and are therefore of the continuation variety. Since many of them are reflections of controlled profit taking during an advance and controlled digestion of losses during a decline, these patterns, for the most part, take a much smaller time to form than those described in the previous chapter. They most commonly appear in the daily charts.

Flags

A *flag*, as the name implies, looks like a flag on the chart. It represents a quiet pause accompanied by a trend of declining volume that interrupts a sharp, almost vertical rise or decline. As the flag is completed, prices break out in the same direction that they were moving in prior to its formation. Flags for both an up and a down market are shown in Figs. 6-1(*a*) and (*b*). Essentially, they take the form of a parallelogram in which the rally peaks and reaction lows can be connected by two parallel lines. The lines move in a countercyclical direction. In the case of a rising market, the flag is usually formed with a slight downtrend, but in a falling market, it has a slight upward bias. Flags may also be horizontal.

In a rising market, this type of pattern usually separates two halves of an almost vertical rise. Volume is normally extremely heavy just before the point at which the flag formation begins. As it develops, volume gradually dries to almost nothing, only to explode as the price works its way out of the com-

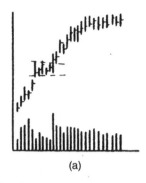 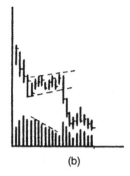

(a)   (b)

Figure 6-1 Flags.

pleted formation. Flags can form in a period as short as 5 days or as long as 3 to 5 weeks. Essentially, they represent a period of controlled profit taking in a rising market.

The formation of the flag in a downtrend is also accompanied by declining volume. This type of flag represents a formation with an upward bias in price, so the volume implication is bearish in nature, that is, rising price with declining volume. When the price breaks down from the flag, the sharp slide continues. Volume tends to pick up as the price breaks below the flag's lower boundary, but it need not be explosive. Only upside breakouts in bull markets require this characteristic.

It is important to make sure that the price and volume characteristics agree. For example, the price may consolidate following a sharp rise in what *appears* to be a flag formation, but volume may fail to contract appreciably. In such cases, great care should be taken before coming to a bullish conclusion since the price may well react on the downside. A flag that takes more than 4 weeks to develop should also be treated with caution, because these formations are, by definition, temporary interruptions of a sharp uptrend. A period in excess of 4 weeks represents an unduly long time for profit taking and therefore holds a lower probability of being a true flag.

Flag formations are usually reliable patterns from a forecasting point of view because not only is the direction of ultimate breakout indicated, but the ensuing move is usually well worthwhile from a trading point of view. Flags seem to form at the halfway point of a move. Once the breakout has taken place, a useful method for setting a price objective is to estimate the size of the price move in the period immediately before the flag formation began and then to project this move in the direction of the breakout. In technical jargon, flags in this sense are said to fly at half-mast, that is, halfway up the move. Since flags take a relatively short period to develop, they do not show up on weekly or monthly charts.

Pennants

A pennant develops under exactly the same circumstances as a flag and has similar characteristics. The difference is that this type of consolidation formation is constructed from two converging trendlines, as shown in Figs. 6-2(*a*) and (*b*). In a sense, the flag corresponds to a rectangle, and the pennant to a triangle, because a pennant is in effect a very *small* triangle. If anything, *volume* tends to contract even more during the formation of a pennant than during that of a flag. In every other way, however, pennants are identical to flags in terms of measuring implication, the time taken to develop, volume characteristics, and so on.

Chart 6-1 features a pennant for Alcoa in a down market. Note how the volume shrinks during the formation of the pattern. It then expands on the breakout.

Wedges

A wedge is very similar to a triangle in that two converging lines can be constructed from a series of peaks and troughs, as shown in Figs. 6-3(*a*) and (*b*). However, whereas a triangle consists of one rising and one falling line, or one horizontal line, the converging lines in a wedge both move in the *same* direction. A falling wedge represents a temporary interruption of a rising trend, and a rising wedge is a temporary interruption of a falling trend.

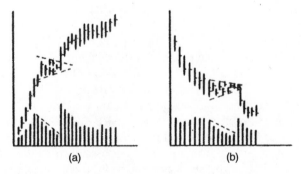

(a)   (b)

Figure 6-2 Pennants.

Chart 6-1 Alcoa pennant. (*From Intermarket Review.*)

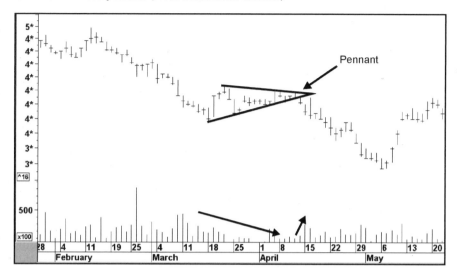

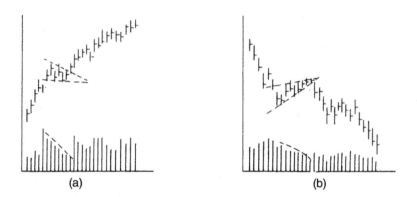

Figure 6-3 Wedges.

It is normal for volume to contract during the formation of both wedges. Since wedges can take anywhere from 2 to 8 weeks to complete, they sometimes occur on weekly charts but are too brief to appear on monthly charts.

Rising wedges are fairly common as bear market rallies. Following their completion, prices usually break very sharply, especially if volume picks up noticeably on the downside.

Saucers and Rounding Tops

Figures 6-4(*a*) and (*b*) show the formation of a saucer and a rounding top. A saucer pattern occurs at a market bottom, while a rounding top develops at a market peak. A saucer is constructed by drawing a circular line under the lows, which roughly approximates an elongated or saucer-shaped letter U. As the price drifts toward the low point of the saucer and investors lose interest, downward momentum dissipates. This lack of interest is also characterized by the volume level, which almost dries up at the time the price is reaching its low point. Gradually, both price and volume pick up until eventually each explodes into an almost exponential pattern.

The price action of the rounded top is exactly opposite to that of the saucer pattern, but the volume characteristics are the same. As a result, if volume is plotted below the price, it is almost possible to draw a complete circle, as shown in Fig. 6-4(*b*). The tip-off to the bearish implication of the rounded top is the fact that volume shrinks as prices reach their highest levels and then expands as they fall. Both these characteristics are bearish and are discussed in greater detail in Chapter 22.

Rounding tops and bottoms are fine examples of a gradual changeover in the demand/supply balance that slowly picks up momentum in the direction opposite to that of the previous trend. Quite clearly, it is difficult to obtain breakout points for these patterns since they develop slowly and do not offer any clear support or resistance levels on which to establish a potential benchmark. Even so, it is worth trying to identify them since they are usually followed by substantial moves. Rounding and saucer formations can also be observed as consolidation as well as reversal phenomena and can take as little as 3 weeks to as long as several years to complete.

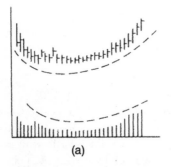 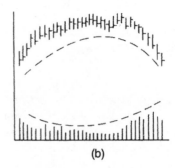

      (a)   (b)

Figure 6-4   A saucer and rounding top.

Gaps

A gap occurs when the lowest price of a specific trading period is above the highest level of the previous trading period [see Fig. 6-5(*a*)] or when the highest price for a specific trading period is below the lowest price of the previous trading period [see Fig. 6-5(*b*)]. On a daily bar chart, the trading period is regarded as a day, whereas on a weekly chart, it is a week, and so on.

By definition, gaps can occur only on bar charts on which intraday, weekly, or monthly prices are plotted. A gap is represented by an empty vertical space between one trading period and another. Gaps form in overnight trading as good or bad news is disseminated by the market. Daily gaps are far more common than weekly ones because a gap on a weekly chart can fall only between Friday's price range and Monday's price range; that is, it has a 1 in 5 chance relative to a daily chart. Monthly gaps are even more rare since such "holes" on the chart can develop only between monthly price ranges. The most common place to find gaps is on intraday charts at the open. I will have more to say on that point later.

A gap is closed or "filled" when the price comes back and retraces the whole range of the gap. For daily charts, this process sometimes takes a few days, and at other times it takes a few weeks or months. On even more rare occasions, the process is *never* completed.

It is certainly true that almost all gaps are eventually filled, but this is not *always* the case. Because it can take months or even years to fill a gap,

---

Major Technical Principle There is an old saying that the market abhors a vacuum, which means that most gaps are eventually filled.

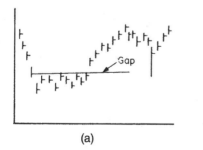

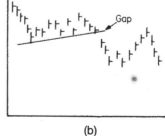

(a)   (b)

Figure 6-5 Gaps.

trading strategies should not be implemented solely on the assumption that the gap will be filled in the immediate future. *In almost all cases, some kind of attempt is made to fill the gap,* but quite often a partial filling on a subsequent test is sufficient before the price again reverts to the direction of the prevailing trend. The reason why most gaps are closed is that they are emotional affairs and reflect traders who have strong psychological motivations. We could say excess fear or greed, depending on the direction of the trend. Decisions to buy or sell *at any cost* are not objective ones, which means the odds of people having second thoughts when things have cooled down are pretty high. The second thoughts in this case are represented by the closing of the gap or at least a good attempt at closing it.

Gaps should be treated with respect, but their importance should not be overemphasized. Those that occur during the formation of a price pattern, known as *common gaps* or *area gaps,* are usually closed fairly quickly and do not have much technical significance. Another type of gap, which has little significance, is the one that results from a stock going ex-dividend. There are three other types of gaps that are worthy of consideration: breakaway, runaway, and exhaustion gaps.

Breakaway Gaps

A breakaway gap is created when a price breaks out of a price pattern (as in Figs. 6-5(*a*) and (*b*). Generally speaking, the presence of the gap emphasizes the bullishness or bearishness of the breakout, depending on which direction it takes. Even so, it is still important for an upside breakout to be accompanied by a relatively high level of volume. It should not be concluded that every gap breakout will be valid because the "sure thing" does not exist in technical analysis. However, a gap associated with a breakout is more likely to be valid than one that is not. Gap breakouts that occur on the downside are not required to be accompanied by heavy volume.

Continuation or Runaway Gaps

Runaway gaps occur during a straight-line advance or decline when price quotations are moving rapidly and emotions are running high. Either they are closed very quickly, such as within a day or so, or they tend to remain open for much longer periods and are not generally closed until the market makes a major or intermediate swing in the opposite direction to the price movement that was responsible for the gap. This type of gap often occurs halfway between a previous breakout and the ultimate duration of

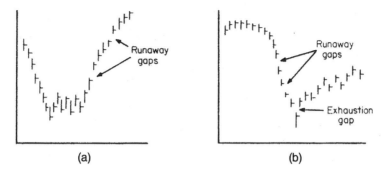

Figure 6-6 Runaway and exhaustion gaps.

the move. For this reason, continuation gaps are sometimes called *measuring gaps* [see Figs. 6-6(*a*) and (*b*)].

Exhaustion Gaps

A price move sometimes contains more than one runaway gap. This indicates that a very powerful trend is in motion, but the presence of a second or third gap should also alert the technician to the fact that the move is likely to run out of steam soon. Hence, there is a possibility that a second or third runaway gap will be the final one. An exhaustion gap is therefore associated with the terminal phase of a rapid advance or decline and is the last in a series of runaway gaps [see Fig. 6-6(*b*)].

One clue that an exhaustion gap may be forming is a level of volume that is unusually heavy in relation to the price change of that day. In such a case, volume usually works up to a crescendo well above previous levels. Sometimes the price will close near the vacuum (or gap) and well away from its extreme reading. If the next day's trading creates an "island" on which the gap day is completely isolated by a vacuum from the previous day's trading, this is usually an excellent sign that the gap day was in fact *the* turning point. This indicates only temporary exhaustion, but should be a red flag that signals to highly leveraged traders that they should liquidate or cover their positions.

If the gap is the first one during a move, it is likely to be a runaway rather than a breakaway type, especially if the price objective called for by a price pattern has not yet been achieved. An exhaustion gap should not be regarded as a sign of a major reversal, but merely as a signal that, at the very least, some form of consolidation should be expected.

The Importance of Gaps as Emotional Points

As we shall learn later, the places where gaps start or terminate are potential pivotal points on a chart because they represent high emotion. If you have an argument with a friend and one of you really shouts loudly at one point, you will both remember that particular moment because it represents an emotional extreme. The same principle can be applied to technical analysis since charts are really a reflection of psychological attitudes. This means that gaps have the potential to become important support-resistance levels that have the power to reverse short-term trends. We will have more to say on this matter in Chapter 15.

Gaps on Intraday Charts

There are really two types of *opening* gaps in intraday charts. The first develops as prices open beyond the trading parameters of the previous session, as in Chart 6-2. I'll call these *classic gaps* since these are the ones that also appear on the daily charts.

The second, more common gap develops *only* on intraday charts as the opening price of a new day gaps well away from the previous sessions' closing bar. I'll call these gaps *intrabar gaps* because they only fall between two bars calculated on an intraday time frame. For example, in Chart 6-3, the price opened up higher and created a gap. However, if you look back you

Chart 6-2   March 1997 bonds' 15-minute bar. (*From Martin Pring's Introduction to Daytrading.*)

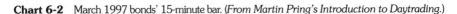
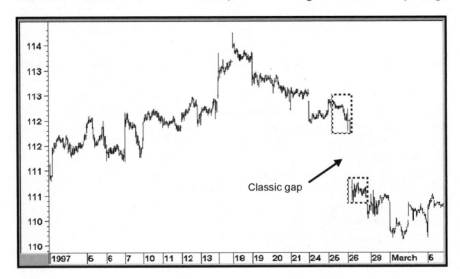

Classic gap

will see that the trading range of the previous day (contained within the box on the left) was not exceeded at the opening price; thus, on a daily chart, there would have been no gap.

If you are a trader with a 2- to 3-week time horizon using intraday charts, you should approach gaps in a different way than if you have a 1- or 2-day time horizon.

The first category should try to avoid initiating trades at the time the gap is created. This is because almost all gaps are eventually closed. Sometimes this happens within a couple of hours, and at others it can take 2 or 3 weeks. Consequently, if you buy on an opening gap on the upside, as in Chart 6-3, you run the risk that it will soon be closed. The problem is you do not know whether it will be in 2 days or 4 weeks.

Intraday traders are also advised to step aside when the market opens sharply higher or lower. In the case of stocks, this is caused by an order imbalance. That means that the market makers are forced to go short so that they can satisfy the unfilled demand. They naturally try to get the price a little higher at the opening so that it will come down a little, enabling them to cover all or part of the short position. The process will be reversed in the case of a lower opening. The key then is to watch what happens to the price *after* the opening range. Normally, if prices work their way higher after an upside gap and opening trading range, this sets the tone of the market for at least the next few hours, often longer.

Chart 6-3 March 1997 bonds' 15-minute bar. (*From Martin Pring's Introduction to Daytrading.*)

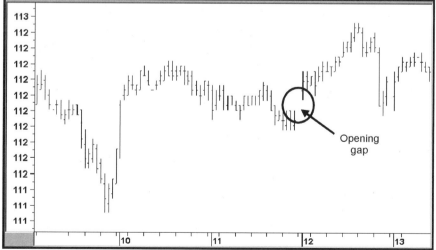

On the other hand, if the price starts to close the gap after a few bars, then the tone becomes a negative one. In Chart 6-4 featuring Merrill Lynch, there is an opening gap on Wednesday. After a bit of backing and filling, the price gradually works its way lower throughout the day. The signal that the opening could be an aberration develops after the price slips below the trendline. Note how the trendline proves to be resistance for the rest of the session. Thursday again sees an opening gap, but this time there is very little in the way of a trading range since the price continues to climb. Again, the rally away from the opening bar sets the tone for the rest of the day. On Friday another gap appears, but this time the opening trading range is resolved on the downside as the price breaks below the $86 level flagged by the line. Once again, this proves to be resistance for the rest of the day.

Island Reversals

An island reversal is a compact trading range created at the end of a sustained move and isolated from previous price behavior by an exhaustion gap and a breakaway gap. A typical island reversal is shown in Fig. 6-7 and in Chart 6-5.

Chart 6-4   Merrill Lynch's 7- to 5-minute bar. (*Telescan.*)

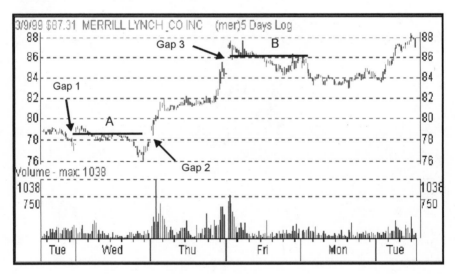

Chart 6-5 American Airlines (AMR) and an island reversal. (*From Intermarket Review.*)

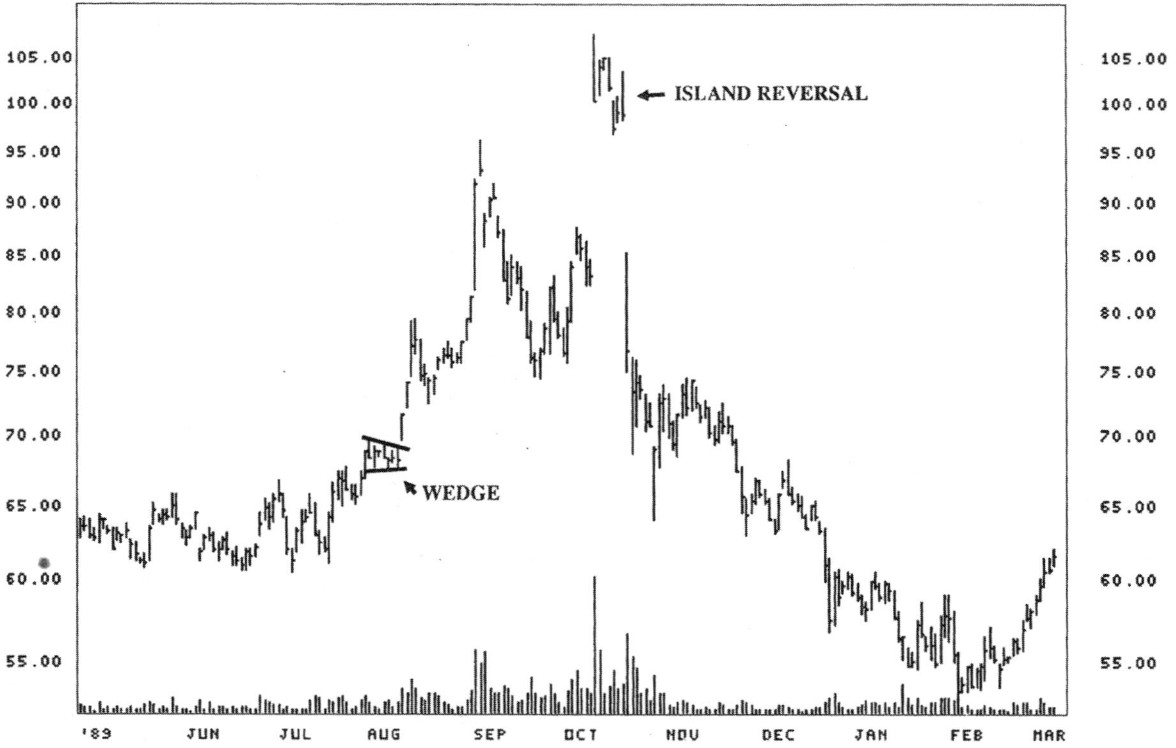

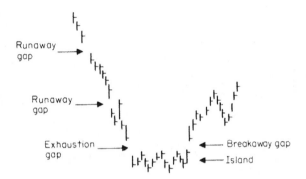

Figure 6-7   Island reversal.

The island itself is not usually a pattern denoting a major reversal. However, islands often appear at the end of an intermediate or even a major move and form part of an overall price pattern such as the top (or bottom) of a head-and-shoulders (H&S) pattern (or an inverse H&S pattern). Islands occasionally occur as 1-day phenomena.

Summary

- Flags, pennants, and wedges are short-term price patterns that usually develop halfway along a sharp price movement. Their development is normally complete within 3 weeks, and they represent periods of quiet price movement and contracting volume. They are almost always continuation patterns.
- Saucer formations and rounding tops are usually reversal patterns and are typically followed by substantial price movements. In both formations, volume contracts toward the center and is at its highest at either extremity.
- A gap is essentially a vacuum or hole in a bar chart. Ex-dividend and area gaps have little significance. Breakaway gaps develop at the beginning of a move, runaway gaps in the middle of a move, and exhaustion gaps at the end.
- Island reversals are small price patterns or congestion areas isolated from the main price trend by two gaps. They often signal the termination of an intermediate move.

7

One- and Two-Bar Price Patterns

Background

The price patterns we have considered so far take some time to complete, usually at least 15 bars. They all reflect changes in the relationship between buyers and sellers, which tells us that there has been a reversal in psychology.

Historically, the patterns described in this chapter were called 1- and 2-day patterns or 1- and 2-week patterns. With the advent of intraday charts, the title "inside days, outside days," and so on is no longer a generic term. Therefore, I have chosen to use the term "bar" with these patterns since it applies to all charts from 1-minute bars up to monthly ones.

> **Major Technical Principle** One- and two-bar patterns reflect changes in psychology that have a very short-term influence on prices.

We have already established that a key factor influencing the significance of a pattern is its size. Since these one- and two-bar patterns do not take very long to form, they are, by definition, only of short-term significance. For example, a 1-day pattern would only be expected under normal circumstances to affect the price over a 5- to 15-day period. A two-bar pattern created from 10-minute bars would influence the trend over the course of the next 50 minutes to an hour or so. Even so, the more I study these patterns, the more impressed I become with their capability to reliably signal short-term trend reversals.

> **Major Technical Principle**   One- and two-bar patterns should be interpreted as shades of gray rather than as black and white because some patterns offer stronger signs of exhaustion than others.

Not all one- and two-bar patterns are therefore created equal. What we are doing is hunting for clues as to the degree of exhaustion being signaled by a particular reversal phenomenon. I could *say* the word "help," for example, but if I *shout it* from the rooftop, you will get the message that I need help far more clearly. The same principle operates in the marketplace. For example, if an outside bar (discussed later) encompasses the trading range of three or four bars, it is likely, other things being equal, to be more significant than if it barely encompasses the trading range of one, and so forth.

There are a couple of ground rules to bear in mind when interpreting one- and two-bar patterns:

- They generally signal an exhaustion point. In the case of an uptrend, such formations develop when buyers have temporarily pushed prices up too far and need a rest. In the case of downtrends, there is little if any supply, because sellers have completed their liquidation. Such patterns are almost always associated with a reversal in the prevailing trend.
- In order for these formations to be effective, there must be something to reverse. This means that top reversals should be preceded by a meaningful rally, and bottom formations should be preceded by a sharp sell-off.
- It is important to interpret these patterns not so much as black and white, but as shades of gray, because not all patterns are created equal. Some show all of the characteristics I will be describing later in a very strong way. Others will reflect just a few characteristics in a mild way. What we might call a five-star pattern, with all the characteristics, is more likely to result in a strong reversal than, say, a two-star pattern that has mild characteristics. It is therefore necessary to apply a certain degree of common sense to their interpretation rather than jumping to an immediate conclusion that the presence of one of these patterns guarantees a quick, profitable price reversal.

Outside Bars

Outside bars are those in which the trading range totally encompasses that of the previous bar. They develop after both downtrends and uptrends, and represent a strong signal of exhaustion. An example of a top reversal is shown in Figs. 7-1 (*a*) and (*b*) and a bottom reversal in Figs. 7-2 (*a*) and (*b*).

For those not familiar with bar charts, the top of the bar represents the high, and the bottom, the low. The tick to the left indicates the opening price, and that to the right, the closing price.

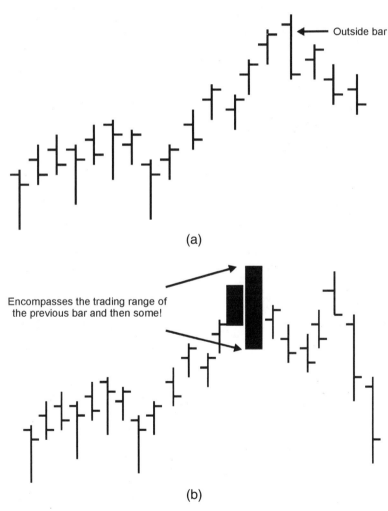

Figure 7-1 Outside bars at tops.

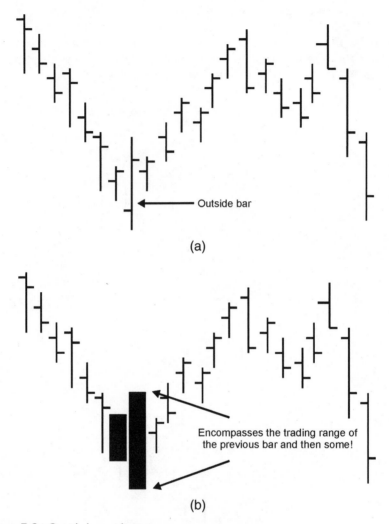

Figure 7-2   Outside bars at bottoms.

There are several guidelines for deciding on the potential significance of an outside bar. They are as follows:

- The wider the outside bar relative to the preceding ones, the stronger the signal.
- The sharper the rally (reaction) preceding the outside bar, the more significant the bar.

- The more bars encompassed, the better the signal.
- The greater the volume accompanying the outside bar relative to previous bars, the stronger the signal.
- The closer the price closes to the extreme point of the bar away from the direction of the previous trend, the better. For example, if the previous trend is down and the price closes very near to the high of the outside bar, this is more favorable than if it closes near the low and vice versa.

Some comparative examples of strong and weak outside bars are featured in Fig. 7-3.

When considering outside bars or any of the other 1- and 2-bar price patterns, it is important to ask yourself the question: What is the price action of this bar telling me about the underlying psychology? Wide bars, sharp preceding rallies or reactions, and high volume all suggest a change in the previous trend of sentiment.

Chart 7-1 features an example of an outside bar for Merrill Lynch. It represents what I would call a five-star signal since it has pretty well all of the characteristics of a strong reversal.

The price was in a persistent downtrend for the afternoon of the 21st. Then, a strong bar develops, totally encompassing the trading range of the previous bar. This is a pretty strong statement because the bar opens close to its low and closes almost at its high. Note also the very high volume that accompanies this outside bar.

Several outside bars are apparent in Chart 7-2. Example *A* is a good one because it is preceded by a relatively strong rally and is reasonably wide.

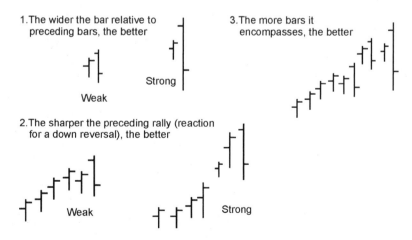

Figure 7-3 Assessing the significance of outside bars.

Chart 7-1   Merrill Lynch's 10-minute outside bar. (*From Pring Research.*)

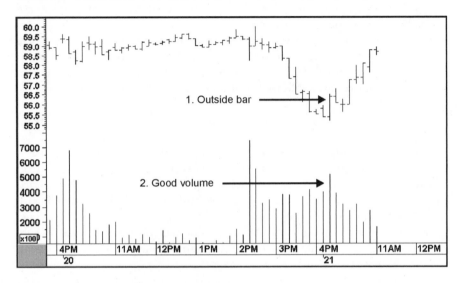

Chart 7-2   S&P Composite 5-minute outside bars. (*From Pring Research.*)

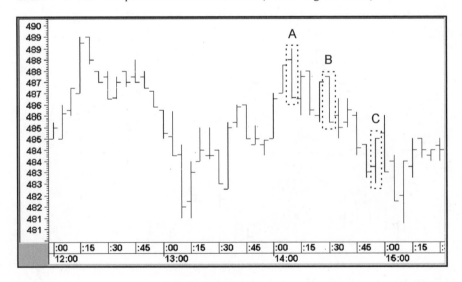

Example *B* completely fails. The reasons lie in the fact that the close is right on the low, the bar is not much larger than the previous one, and is not preceded by much of a decline. Thus, while in a strict technical sense it is an outside bar, it is not signaling much in the way of a change in sentiment.

Even though Example *C* is not really successful and it is preceded by a decline, it is a reasonable size larger than its predecessor, and closes at its high. I purposely put in this example to show that even when a substantial number of the requirements are present, this does not guarantee the success of a pattern.

Finally, Chart 7-3 shows two more examples of outside bars for the Dow Jones Industrial Average (DJIA) in March 2001. The first represents a reversal from a downtrend to an uptrend. The second marks the top of a very sharp rally. Note that it is very wide, encompasses the three previous bars,

Major Technical Principle   Not all one- and two-bar patterns are followed by a reversal in trend. Some, for example, may be followed by a change in trend, as prices consolidate after an up- or down-move.

Chart 7-3   DJIA 60-minute outside bars. (*From Pring Research.*)

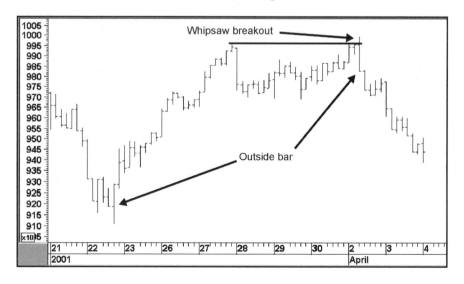

and also violates a good up trendline. Add to this the fact that it also experiences a whipsaw break to the upside and you have all the ingredients of a dramatic change in sentiment.

Inside Bars

Inside bars are the opposite of outside bars in that they form totally within the trading range of the preceding bar. An outside bar indicates a strong reversal in sentiment, but an inside one reflects a balance between buyers and sellers following a sharp up- or down-move, which is usually later resolved by a change in trend. During the period preceding the second bar of this formation, buyers or sellers have everything going their way depending on the direction of the trend. Then a more even balance sets in during the formation of the inside bar, which then gives way to a trend in the opposite direction. Examples of inside bars are shown in Figs. 7-4(*a*) and (*b*) and Figs. 7-5(*a*) and (*b*).

The guidelines for determining the significance of an inside bar are as follows:

- The sharper the trend preceding the pattern, the better.
- The wider the first bar and its immediate predecessors in relation to previous bars, the better. This brings the strong underlying momentum of the prevailing trend to a sort of climax.
- The smaller the inside bar relative to the outside bar, the more dramatic the change in the buyer/seller balance and therefore the stronger the signal.
- Volume on the inside bar should be noticeably smaller than that of the preceding bar since it indicates a more balanced situation.

Chart 7-4 shows two examples of inside bars. The first marks the end of the sharp September/November decline. Note the substantial width of the first bar and the paltry range of the actual inside bar. During the formation of the first bar, volume is very heavy and the price declines sharply. No doubt here that sentiment is strongly on the bearish side. Then, on the second day, volume dries up appreciably and the trading range is dramatically reduced, thereby indicating a fine balance between buyers and sellers. Although this marks the bottom of the move, the next short-term trend is essentially a sideways one. Quite often we find that with inside bars there is a change as opposed to a reversal in trend.

The second inside pattern develops just under halfway up the rally and is followed by a sideways trading range. The move is topped off by a two-bar reversal, which is discussed in the next section.

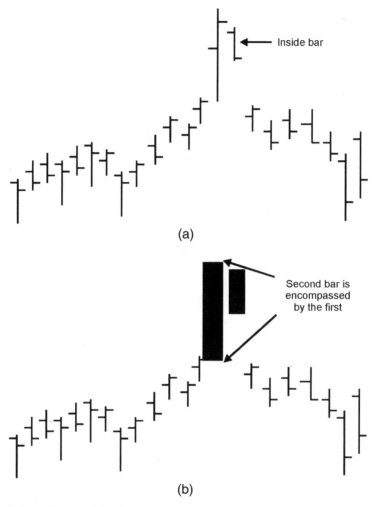

Figure 7-4 Inside bars at tops.

Chart 7-5 shows some more inside bars, this time on an intraday chart. Example *A* is followed by a pretty good rally, though the quality of the signal is not that great since there is not much of a contrast between the actual inside bar and its predecessor. Example *B* is an outright failure since the price continues to advance. This shows that when a strong trend is underway, price patterns can and do fail. Indeed, their very failure can often be a clue to the strength of that trend.

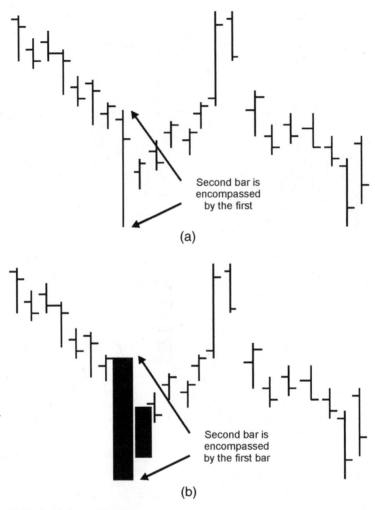

Figure 7-5 Inside bars at bottoms.

Finally, example *C* is a classic. The two final bars expand considerably in size. The actual inside bar is relatively small. Note also how the open and close develop at almost identical prices, thereby confirming the idea of a very fine balance between supply and demand.

Chart 7-4 Oxford Industries' 2000–2001 two-bar reversal and inside bars. (*From Pring Research.*)

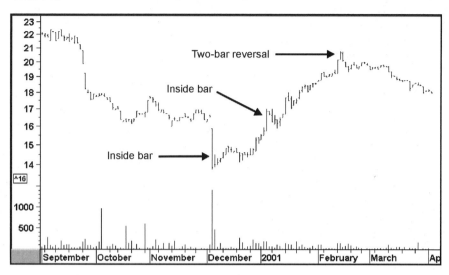

Chart 7-5 The S&P Composite's 5-minute inside bars. (*From Pring Research.*)

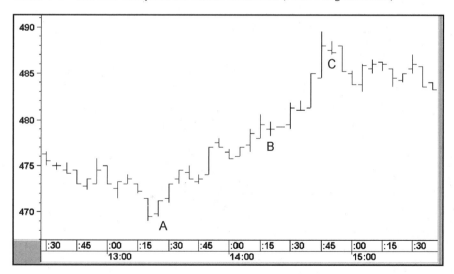

Two-Bar Reversal

A two-bar reversal is a classic way in which charts signal exhaustion. These patterns develop after a prolonged advance or decline. Examples are shown in Figs. 7-6 to 7-8.

The first bar of the formation develops strongly in the direction of the then prevailing trend. For a five-star signal in an uptrend, we need to see the close

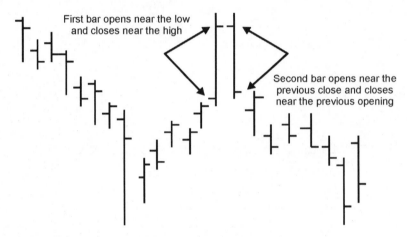

Figure 7-6   Two-bar reversals at tops.

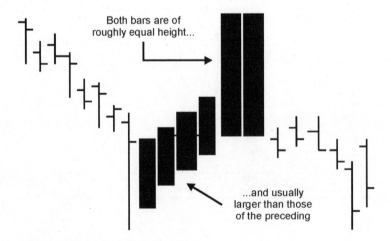

Figure 7-7   Two-bar reversals at the rally peak.

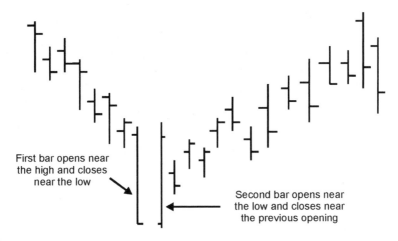

First bar opens near
the high and closes
near the low

Second bar opens near
the low and closes near
the previous opening

Figure 7-8 Two-bar reversals at bottoms.

of the bar at, or very close to, its high. At the opening of the next period, buyers come in expecting more of the same. This means the price should open very close to the high of the previous bar. However, the whole point of the two-bar reversal is that a change in psychology takes place as the bar closes slightly above or slightly below the low of the previous bar. Hence, the high expectations of participants at the opening of the bar are totally dashed at the end of the period, indicating a reversal in sentiment. To be effective, this has to be a climactic experience. This means that the two-bar reversal should contain as many of the following elements as possible:

- It needs to be preceded by a persistent trend—the sharper the better.
- Both bars should stand out as having exceptionally wide trading ranges relative to previous bars (see Fig. 7-7 for an uptrend).
- The openings and closings of both bars should be close to the extreme points of the bar.
- An expansion of volume on both bars enhances the concept of a change in sentiment.

Chart 7-6 shows a two-bar reversal for June gold in March of 2001. In many cases, such patterns will be followed by an immediate advance. In this case, the advance was delayed a day as an additional piece of evidence indicated a trend reversal. This came in the form of an inside bar that developed on the day after the two-bar reversal. I have noticed that such "double" patterns are often quite effective in signaling reversals. Note also that the second bar

Chart 7-6   June 2001 Gold Futures' two-bar reversal. (*From Pring Research.*)

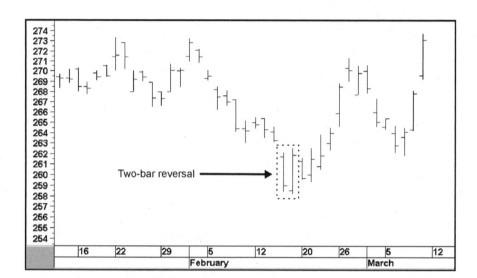

in the two-bar reversal encompasses the first bar. In effect, this is an outside bar. The two-bar reversal pattern rule does not require an outside bar, but its very presence reinforces the idea that sentiment has definitely reversed. If we are looking at the quality of a signal, I would certainly add points for this and the inside bar.

Chart 7-7 shows a two-bar reversal at the climax of a rally in US Bancorp in the fall of 2000. Note how the volume expands dramatically. Also, volume on the second day is slightly higher than that on the first, thereby providing an additional clue that the tide has turned in favor of the sellers.

These one- and two-bar price patterns generally have an effect for a very short period of time. They are not therefore suitable for long-term investors. However, for traders who are looking for clear-cut entry and exit points, they can be of immense value.

Key Reversal Bars

A key reversal bar is one that develops after a prolonged rally or reaction. Often the trend will be accelerating by the time the price experiences the key reversal bar. The classic pattern has the following characteristics:

Chart 7-7 US Bancorp 2000 two-bar reversal. (*From Pring Research.*)

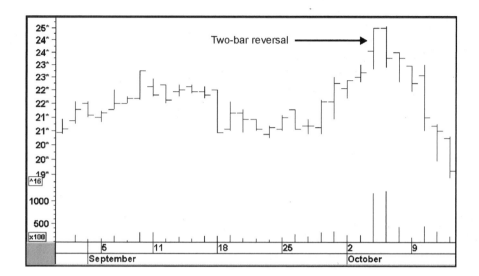

- The price opens strongly in the direction of the prevailing trend.
- The trading range is very wide relative to the preceding bars.
- The price closes near or below the previous close (or near or above the previous close in a downtrend reversal).
- Volume, if available, should be climactic on the key reversal bar.

An example of a key reversal bar is featured in Fig. 7-9. In many cases, a retracement move (see Fig. 7-10) follows a key reversal bar (see Fig. 7-11), especially if the initial reversal in trend is unduly sharp. Normally, the extreme point of the reversal bar is not exceeded. Figure 7-11 shows a key reversal bar at a bottom.

Chart 7-8 shows a classic example beginning in September 1999, as the short-term rally is climaxed by an explosion of volume and a wide key reversal bar. Quite often a key reversal is followed by a sharp change in trend and a subsequent retracement. That is exactly what happens in this case as the price rallies in the fourth and fifth sessions following the key reversal. Note that the termination of this brief collective advance is signaled by an outside day. Even though these one- and two-bar patterns only have short-term significance as a general rule, quite often they can prove to be the first domino in a major trend reversal. It all depends on the maturity of the trend in question together with the position of the longer-term indicators.

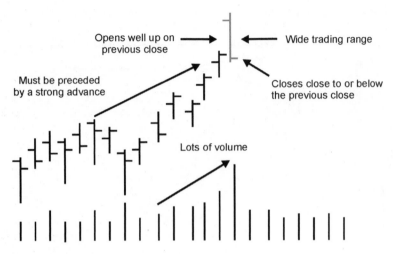

Figure 7-9   Key reversal bar at tops.

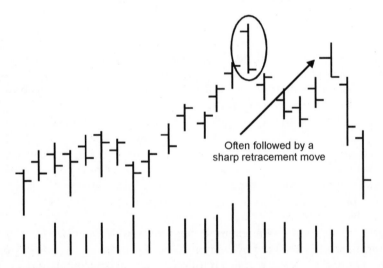

Figure 7-10   Key reversal bar and retracement moves.

The second example of a key reversal to the right is also a good one in that volume expands along with the trading range. However, it is not preceded by much of a rally and would not therefore earn as many stars as the first one.

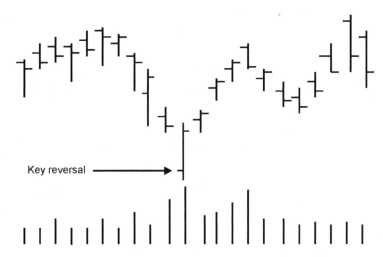

Figure 7-11 Key reversal bar at bottoms.

Chart 7-8 Barrick Gold, 1999–2000 two-bar reversals. (*From Pring Research.*)

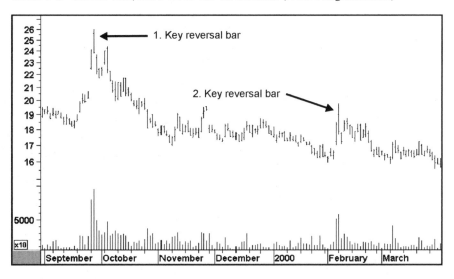

Chart 7-9 features the 1998 bottom for Merrill Lynch. Note that the actual day of the bottom experiences a classic key bar reversal. The volume also cooperates by expanding as the stock bottoms. It is also possible to construct a small down trendline, the violation of which confirms the signal being given by the reversal bar.

Chart 7-9   Merrill Lynch 1998 key reversal bar. (*From Pring Research.*)

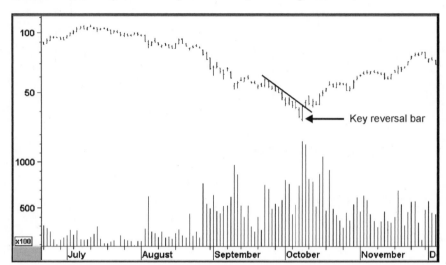

The intraday example in Chart 7-10 almost meets all of the qualifications, except that the opening is only slightly above the previous close. Even so, this bar does indicate exhaustion. One tip-off is the fact that the upper end of the bar sticks out like a sore thumb above the previous two sessions. In other words, the price broke out strongly to the upside, but was unable to hold its gains, and by the close it had given up ground over the previous period.

Exhaustion Bars

Exhaustion bars develop after a really sharp up- or down-move. They are a form of key reversal, but differ sufficiently enough to warrant their own category.

The requirements for an exhaustion bar are as follows:

- The price opens with a large gap in the direction of the then-prevailing trend.
- The bar is extremely wide relative to previous bars.
- The opening price develops in the lower half of the bar in a downtrend and in the upper half in an uptrend.

Chart 7-10 S&P Composite 5-minute pinocchio bar. (*From Pring Research.*)

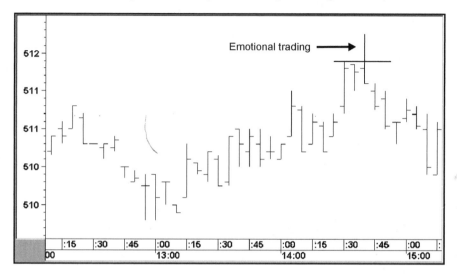

- The closing price should be both above the opening and in the top half of the bar in a downtrend and in the lower half and below the opening in an uptrend.
- The bar is completed with a gap to the left still in place.

Examples of exhaustion bars for both a bottom and top are featured in Figs. 7-12 and 7-13. They differ from the one-bar island reversal in that there is no gap between the exhaustion bar and its successor. Examples of one-bar island reversals are shown in Fig. 7-14.

What we are looking for here is for an extreme movement in the price that is preceded by an already strong move. The idea that the bar opens with a huge gap and closes in the opposite direction reflects the concept of a reversal in psychology. The large gap and wide trading range also point out the kind of frenzied activity associated with a turn.

Chart 7-11 shows an example of the daily price action of Kellwood. It was followed by a 10-day rally, a stark reminder that all these one- and two-pattern formations have short-term significance.

The exhaustion bar in Chart 7-12 does prove to be the actual bottom. Note how the termination of the test in mid-October was signaled by an inside day.

You will find that gaps almost always develop on the intraday charts at the open due to some overnight change in psychology. This means that

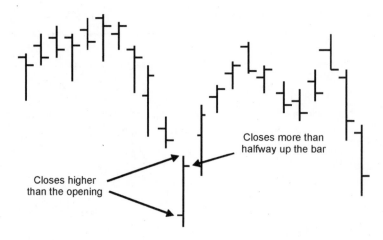

Figure 7-12 Emotional bar at bottoms.

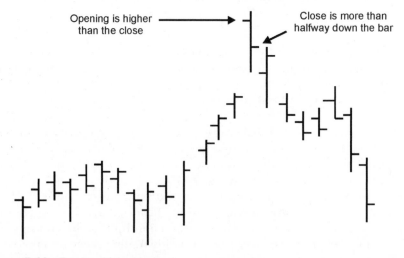

Figure 7-13 Emotional bar at tops.

exhaustion bars tend to be more prevalent in these very short term charts. Chart 7-13 shows an exhaustion bar for the NYSE Composite. It has all the characteristics: a large gap, a close higher than the opening, a wide range, and so on. It is also followed by an inside bar that adds a further piece of evidence that the trend had changed.

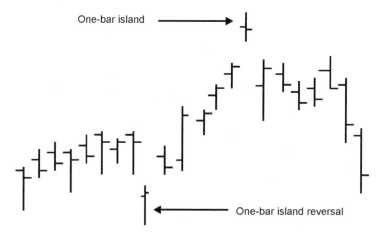

Figure 7-14   One-bar island reversals.

Chart 7-11   Kellwood 2001 exhaustion bar. (*From Pring Research.*)

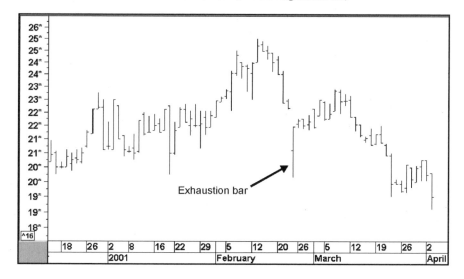

Pinocchio Bars

Exhaustion also shows itself in other forms that are different from the characteristics we have so far been looking at. I call these *Pinocchio bars* because

Chart 7-12   Warnaco exhaustion bar. (*From Pring Research.*)

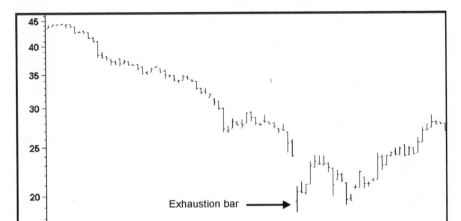

Chart 7-13   NYSE Composite 5-minute 1997 exhaustion bar. (*From Pring Research.*)

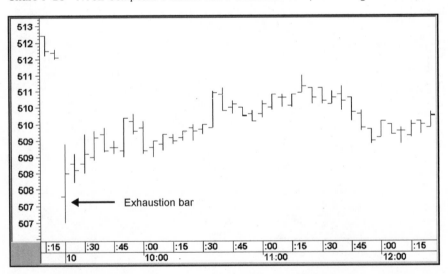

they temporarily give us a false sense of what is really going on. They are bars in which the bulk of the trading takes place outside the previous and subsequent trading ranges and that therefore give a false impression of a breakout. The character Pinocchio cannot hide that he is lying because his nose gets bigger. In the case of our Pinocchio bar, it is the isolated part of the bar above (below in a down trend) the open and close that is the big nose, which signals a probable false move by the end of the bar. Figures 7-15 and 7-16 offer two examples of false upside Pinocchio breaks. Figure 7-16 offers the idea that when a false break develops above a down trendline, this is indicative of exhaustion since the price cannot hold above the strong resistance reflected by the trendline.

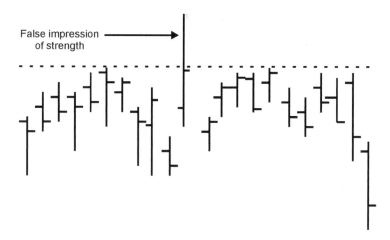

Figure 7-15 Pinocchio bars.

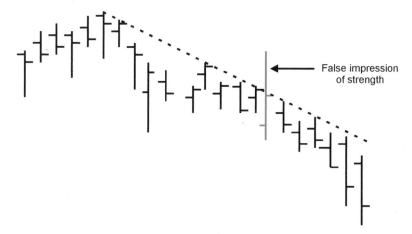

Figure 7-16 Pinocchio bars and down trendlines.

Marketplace examples of Pinocchio bars are featured in Charts 7-14 and 7-15. The first shows a break above the trading range, which was nullified by the time the bar closed. The second shows a false break to the downside.

Chart 7-14   S&P Composite 10-minute 1997 Pinocchio bar. (*From Pring Research.*)

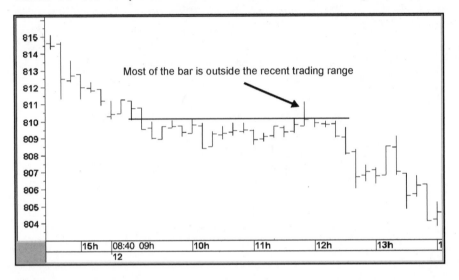

Chart 7-15   S&P Composite 10-minute 1997 Pinocchio bar. (*From Pring Research.*)

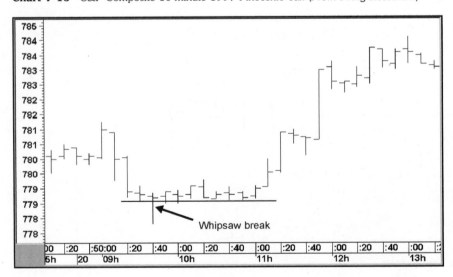

As so often happens following whipsaws, the price moves in the direction opposite to that indicated by the break.

One important fact about exhaustion is that the extremity of the move often proves to be an important support or resistance point. In this respect, it is often a good idea to place a stop loss a little bit beyond the extremity of the Pinocchio bar, provided, of course, that it still results in a reasonable risk reward.

Summary

- One- and two-bar reversals reflect exhaustion and signal a change, usually a reversal in trend.
- To be effective, they must be preceded by a worthwhile move.
- Their trend reversal significance is only of short-term duration. What constitutes as short-term will depend on the time span of the bar or bars in question. Daily or weekly reversal patterns will be far more significant than 10-minute bars.
- Reversal bars that contain more of the required characteristics normally provide stronger signals than those that only have a few.

8
Trendlines

A review of any chart will quickly reveal that prices usually move in trends. Quite often, a series of ascending bottoms in a rising market can be joined together by a straight line, and so can the tops of a descending series of rally peaks. These lines, known as *trendlines,* are a simple but invaluable addition to the technical arsenal [see Figs. 8-1(*a*) and (*b*)].

How to Draw Trendlines

A proper trendline has to connect two or more peaks or troughs; otherwise, it will be drawn in space and will have no significance. I often see people constructing lines that only touch one point, as in Fig. 8-2. See how the line misses the second trough. This is a fundamentally important point because whenever you draw or interpret a trendline, never ever forget that a true trendline is a graphic way of representing the underlying trend. Consequently, if it only touches one point, it is not a true *trendline.*

Ideally, an up trendline is constructed by connecting the final low with the first bottom in the rally, as line *A–D* in Fig. 8-3. In the case of a primary trend, this would be the bear market low and the first intermediate bottom,

(a)   (b)

Figure 8-1 Up and down trendlines.

> **Major Technical Principle**   A trendline is a dynamic area of support and resistance.

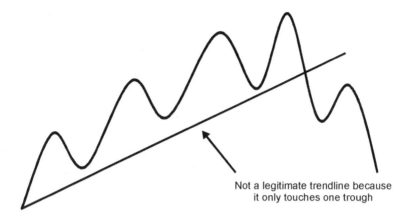

Figure 8-2   A nontrendline.

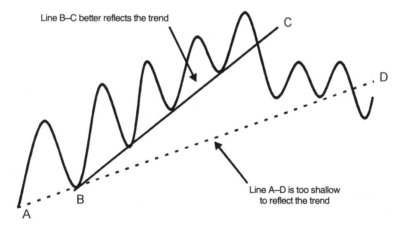

Figure 8-3   Commonsense trendlines.

and vice versa. For line *A–D* in Fig. 8-3, the first low develops fairly close to the final bottom, which results in a fairly shallow line. However, the price rallies sharply, which means that the violation of the line will develop well

> **Major Technical Principle**   Constructing trendlines is very much a matter of using common sense rather than applying hard and fast rules.

after the final peak. In such situations, it is better to reconstruct the trend-line as the price moves up. In Fig. 8-3, this is line *B-C*, which is obviously a better reflection of the underlying trend. Down trendlines are constructed using the same principles, but in reverse.

Bar Versus Line or Close-Only Charts

You probably already have noticed from previous chapters that some charts are plotted with bars and others as line charts. The question naturally arises as to which form of chart should be used for the purposes of trend and trendline analysis. In most cases, bar charts offer quicker signals, whether it is a peak-trough progression, price pattern completion, or trendline vio-lation. The problem in technical analysis is that speed comes with a price, and the price in this case is more whipsaws. It is important to remember that with traditional daily or weekly charts, the closing price is very impor-tant because it separates those who are willing to take home a position overnight or over a weekend from those who are not. *Closing prices have there-fore traditionally been considered to be more important chart points than highs or lows.*

Also, since there is much excitement during the day as unexpected news breaks, highs and lows often represent random points on the chart. For this reason, it is often a better idea to construct trendlines using closing data. I am not going to say that is always the case because some bar trendlines have greater significance than close-only ones based on the rules outlined for sig-nificance and described later in this chapter. Thus, *it is always crucial to apply common sense as much as strict technical rules.*

Trendline Breaks Can Signal Reversals or Consolidations

Some trends can be sideways, that is, a trading range, so it follows that trend-lines can also be drawn horizontally. The neckline of a head-and-shoulders (H&S) pattern or the upper or lower boundary of a rectangle is really a trendline. The penetration of these lines warns of a change in trend, as does the penetration of rising or falling trendlines. In effect, these lines represent points of support (rising trendline) and resistance (declining trendline).

The completion of a rectangle pattern can signify either (1) a reversal in the previous trend, in which case it becomes known as a *reversal pattern,* or (2) a resumption of the previous trend, when it is defined as a *consolidation* or *continuation pattern.* Similarly, the penetration of a trendline will result in either a reversal of that trend or its continuation. Figure 8-4 illustrates this point from the aspect of a rising price trend. In Fig. 8-4(*a*), the trendline joining the series of troughs is eventually penetrated on the downside. The fourth peak represents the highest point in the bull market, so the downward violation of the trendline signals that a bear market is underway.

The upward price trend and (solid) trendline penetration in Fig. 8-4(*b*) are identical to those in Fig. 8-4(*a*), but the action following this warning signal is entirely different because the trendline violation merely signals that the advance will continue, but at a greatly reduced pace. A new (dashed) trendline is subsequently constructed.

Unfortunately, there is no way of telling at the time of the violation which possibility will prove to be the outcome.

Also, valuable clues can be gleaned by applying other techniques described in subsequent chapters and by evaluating the state of health of the market's overall technical structure (examined in Parts II through IV).

Major Technical Principle   As a general rule, the violation of trendlines with a sharp angle of ascent or descent is more likely to result in a consolidation than a reversal.

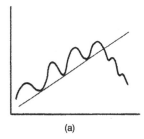
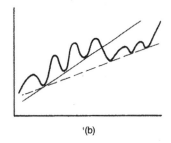

(a)   '(b)

Figure 8-4   A reversal and a continuation break.

Using the techniques discussed in Chapter 5 also help. For example, in a rising market, a trendline penetration may occur at the time of, or just before, the successful completion of a reversal pattern. Some possibilities are shown in Fig. 8-5 and Chart 8-1. In Fig. 8-5(*a*), the rising trendline joins a series of bottoms, but the last two troughs represent reactions from a right shoulder and head that are part of an ascending H&S pattern. Figures 8-5(*b*) and (*c*) represent a similar situation for a rectangle and a broadening top.

Figure 8-6 illustrates the same phenomenon from the aspect of a bear market reversal. If the violation occurs simultaneously with or just after the completion of a reversal pattern, the two breaks have the effect of reinforcing each other. Sometimes, however, as in Fig. 8-7, the trendline violation occurs before the completion of the pattern. In such cases, the break should be regarded as a sign of an interruption of the prevailing movement rather than as a sign of reversal, because a trend is assumed to continue until the weight of the evidence indicates otherwise.

During an advance, a setback below the previous trough should develop. This would confirm an actual reversal. The opposite will occur in the case of a declining market [see Fig. 8-7(*b*)]. Further clues as to the significance of a specific trendline violation can be gleaned from volume characteristics, as described in Chapters 5, 6, 7, and 22.

For example, if a series of ascending peaks and troughs is accompanied by progressively lower volume, it is a sign that the advance is running out of steam (since volume is no longer going with the trend). In this instance, a trendline violation is likely to be of greater significance than if volume had continued to expand with each successive rally. It is not necessary for a downside penetration to be accompanied by high volume, but a violation that occurs as activity expands emphasizes the bearish undertone because of the obvious switch in the demand/supply balance in favor of sellers.

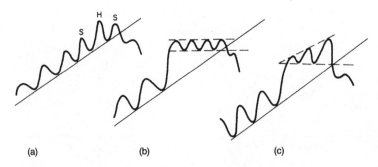

Figure 8-5 Simultaneous trendline and price pattern breaks at tops.

Chart 8-1 Invesco Energy Fund and simultaneous trendline price pattern violations. This chart shows two examples of a trendline break and pattern completion developing close together. At the end of 1990, the Invesco Energy Fund violates a nice up trendline and shortly after completes a right-angled broadening top. The end of the decline is signaled with another down trendline break and the completion of a reverse H&S pattern. (*From www.pring.com.*)

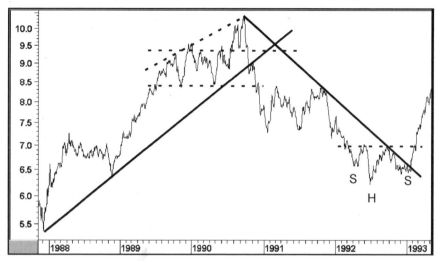

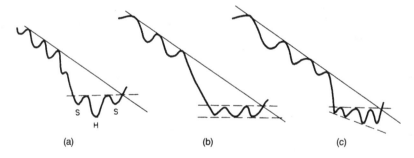

Figure 8-6 Simultaneous trendline and price pattern breaks at bottoms.

Extended Trendlines

Most people observe the violation of a trendline and then assume that the trend has changed and forget about the line. This is a mistake because an extended line can become just as important as the previous violated line.

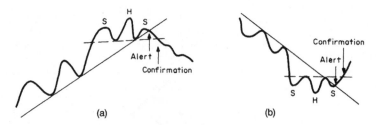

Figure 8-7   Delayed price pattern breaks at tops and bottoms.

> **Major Technical Principle**   An extended line reverses its support/resistance role.

Just as a return move often happens following a breakout from a price pattern, a similar move, known as a *throwback*, sometimes develops following a trendline penetration. Figure 8-8(*a*) shows a trendline reversing its previous role as support, while the throwback move turns it into an area of resistance. Figure 8-8(*b*) shows the same situation for a declining market.

Chart 8-2, for instance, shows an up trendline break for the Morgan Stanley Capital International (MSCI) Eastern European (Stock) Index. The penetration of this relatively steep line resulted in a consolidation break. As the price worked its way higher, it found resistance on two occasions.

Chart 8-3 shows the same idea but for a down trendline for the Euro. In this instance, the line continually reversed its role, starting out as resistance, then support, and finally resistance again.

Logarithmic (Ratio) Versus Arithmetic Scales

The importance of plotting charts on a logarithmic as opposed to an arithmetic scale was discussed in Chapter 5. The choice of scale is even more critical for a timely and accurate use of trendline analysis, because at the end of a major movement, prices tend to accelerate in the direction of the prevailing trend; that is, they rise faster at the end of a rising trend and decline more sharply at the termination of a bear market [see Figs. 8-9(*a*) and (*b*)].

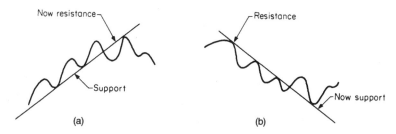

Figure 8-8 Extended trendlines at tops and bottoms.

Chart 8-2 MSCI Eastern Europe Index showing the importance of extended lines. (*From www.pring.com.*)

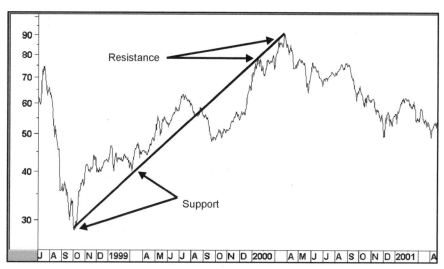

In a bull market, prices rise slowly after an initial burst, and then advance at a steeper and steeper angle as they approach the ultimate peak, looking rather like the left-hand cross section of a mountain.

Chart 8-4 shows that this exponential movement in late 1999 for the Athens General SE Index took the price well away from the trendline in the upper, arithmetically based chart. Consequently, the price had to fall that

Chart 8-3 Euro FX showing lines as support/resistance areas. (*From www.pring.com.*)

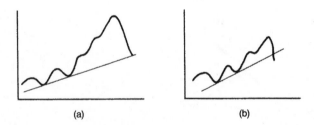

Figure 8-9 Arithmetic and ratio scale breaks at tops.

much farther before a penetration of the trendline could take place. As a result, up trendlines are violated more quickly on a logarithmic than on an arithmetic scale. This can be seen from the vertical arrow. Conversely, down trendlines are violated sooner on an arithmetic scale. Note that at the end of the chart, the up trendline on the arithmetic scale has been violated, whereas the logarithmically based one has not.

Generally speaking, penetration of a logarithmically based trendline is more accurate in reflecting trend reversals than the penetration of an arithmetically based trendline.

Chart 8-4   Athens General showing the differences between arithmetic and ratio scaling. (*From www.pring.com.*)

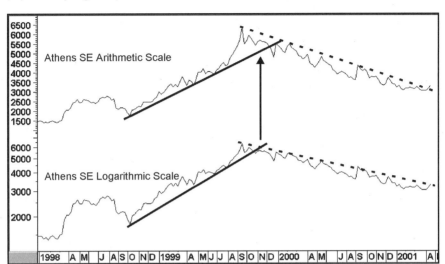

Significance of Trendlines

It has been established that a break in trend caused by the penetration of a trendline results in either an actual trend reversal or a slowing in the pace of the trend. Although it may not always be possible to assess which of these alternatives will develop, it is still important to understand the significance of a trendline penetration; the following guidelines should help in evaluation.

> **Major Technical Principle**   The significance of a trendline is a function of its length, the number of times it has been touched, and the angle of ascent or descent.

Length of the Line

The size or length of a trend is an important factor, as with price patterns. If a series of ascending bottoms occurs over a 3- to 4-week span, the resulting trendline is only of minor importance. If the trend extends over a period of 1 to 3 years, however, its violation marks a significant juncture point. Just remember, big trends result in big signals, small trends in small signals.

Number of Times the Trendline Has Been Touched or Approached

A trendline derives its authority from the number of times it has been touched or approached; that is, the larger the number, the greater the significance. This is true because a trendline represents a dynamic area of support or resistance. Each successive "test" of the line contributes to the importance of this support or resistance role, and thus the authority of the line is a true reflection of the underlying trend. Just remember that a close encounter with the line (an approach) is almost as important as an actual touching of the line because it still reflects the line's importance as a support or resistance area.

Also, if a line gains significance from the fact that it has been touched or approached, the extended line will become equally as important, but from a reverse point of view since extended lines reverse their support/resistance functions.

Angle of Ascent or Descent

A very sharp trend, as in Fig. 8-10, is difficult to maintain and is liable to be broken rather easily, even by a short sideways movement. All trends are eventually violated, but the steeper ones are likely to be ruptured more quickly. The violation of a particularly steep trend is not as significant as that of a more gradual one. The penetration of a steep line usually results in a short corrective movement, following which the trend resumes, but at a greatly reduced and more sustainable pace. Usually, the penetration of a steep trendline represents a continuation rather than a reversal break.

Measuring Implications

Trendlines have measuring implications when they are broken, just as price patterns do. The vertical distance between the peak in the price and the

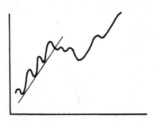

Figure 8-10   Sharp-angled trendlines.

trendline is measured during a rising trend (A_1 in Fig. 8-11). This distance is then projected down from the point at which the violation occurs (A_2).

The term *price objective* is perhaps misleading. Objectives are usually reached when a trendline violation turns out to be a reversal, but because they are more often exceeded (as with price patterns), the objective becomes more of a minimum expectation. When prices move significantly through the objective, as in Fig. 8-12, this area often becomes one of resistance to the next major rally or support for a subsequent reaction. Figure 8-13 shows the same possibilities for an upside breakout.

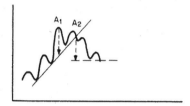

Figure 8-11   Measuring implications.

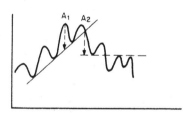

Figure 8-12   Downside measuring objectives.

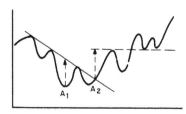

Figure 8-13   Upside measuring objectives.

Time and again, these price objective areas prove to be important support or resistance points. Unfortunately, there is no way to determine where the actual juncture point will be for any rally or reaction. This emphasizes a point made earlier that there is no known way of consistently determining the duration of a price movement. It is only possible to speculate on the *probability* that a specific area will prove to be an important turning point.

Corrective Fan Principle

At the beginning of a new primary bull market, the initial intermediate rally is often explosive, and so the rate of ascent is unsustainably steep. This happens because the advance is often a technical reaction to the previous overextended decline, as speculators who were caught short rush to cover their positions. As a result, the steep trendline constructed from the first minor reaction is quickly violated.

This is represented as line *AA* in Fig. 8-14. A new trendline is then constructed, using the bottom of this first intermediate decline (*AB*). The new line rises at a less rapid rate than the initial one. Finally, the process is repeated, resulting in construction of a third line, *AC*. These lines are known as *fan lines*. There is an established principle that once the third trendline has been violated, the end of the bull market is confirmed. In some respects these three rally points and trendlines can be compared to the three stages of a bull or bear market, as outlined in Chapter 3. The fan principle is just as valid for downtrends and can also be used for determining intermediate as well as primary trend movements.

Trend Channels

So far, only the possibilities of drawing trendlines joining bottoms in rising markets and tops in declining ones have been examined. It is also useful to

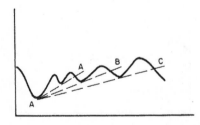

Figure 8-14   Corrective fan principle.

draw lines that are parallel to those basic trendlines, as shown in Figs. 8-15(*a*) and (*c*). In a rising market, the parallel line known as a *return trendline* joins the tops of rallies [*AA* in Fig. 8-15(*a*)], and during declines the return line joins the series of bottoms [*BB* in Fig. 8-15(*c*)]. The area between these trend extremities is known as a *trend channel*. Figure 8-15(*b*) is a rectangle, which is a horizontal form of a trend channel.

The return line is useful from two points of view. First, it represents an area of support or resistance, depending on the direction of the trend. Second, and perhaps more important, the penetration of the return trendline represents a signal that either the trend will accelerate or that a reversal of at least a temporary proportion in the basic trend is about to take place.

In Fig. 8-16(*a*), the violation of the return line signifies that the price advance has begun to accelerate. Figure 8-16(*b*) shows the same idea for a downside breakout. In effect, the channel in Fig. 8-16(*a*) represents a rising rectangle and the trendline violation represents a breakout.

On the other hand, if the angle of the trend channel is much steeper, as in Fig. 8-17(*a*), the violation of the return line represents an exhaustion move. The failure of the price to hold above (below) the return line then signals an important reversal in trend. This is often the case if the action is accompanied by high volume.

Consider a situation in which a man is sawing a thick piece of wood. At first, his sawing strokes are slow but deliberate; gradually, he realizes that his task is going to take some time, becomes frustrated, and slowly increases the speed of his strokes. Finally, he bursts into a frantic effort and is forced to give up his task for at least a temporary period because of complete exhaustion. Figure 8-17(*b*) shows an exhaustion move in a declining market. In this case, the expanding volume at the low represents a selling climax. As a general rule, the steeper the channel, the more likely it is that the breakout will turn out to be an exhaustion move.

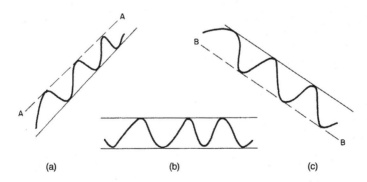

(a)   (b)   (c)

Figure 8-15   Trend channels.

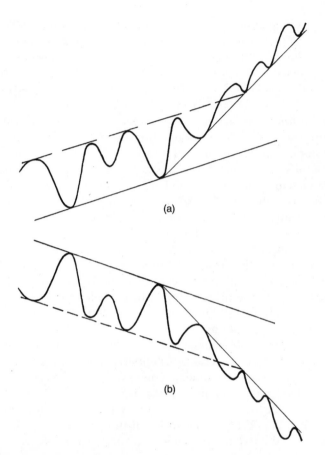

Figure 8-16   Successful channel breakouts.

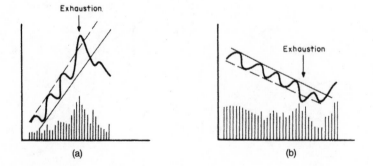

Figure 8-17   Exhaustion (whipsaw) breakouts.

Exhaustion

This temporary break often represents a signal that the prevailing trend has much further to run, in the same way as a whipsaw breakout from a price pattern. It also raises a dilemma in the way in which a trendline should be constructed. In Fig. 8-18, for instance, we see a false break above trendline *AB*. Should *AB* now be abandoned or should the peak of the exhaustion break be connected to the rally high to form a new trendline? Again, it is a matter of common sense. On the one hand, the whipsaw break is technically the correct place to draw the line, but common sense suggests that the original line is a better reflection of the underlying trend. After all, at the time of the whipsaw, it has been touched three times. If the line is then drawn to reflect the break, it will only have been touched twice, once at the outset and once at the whipsaw peak. In a sense, *the whipsaw is adding further credibility to the initial line because the price was unable to hold above it.* If we had come upon this situation after the whipsaw break and tried to construct a line, it would have been even more obvious that line *AB* was far superior to line *AC* because it has been touched or approached on far more occasions.

Major Technical Principle   Exhaustion develops when a price rallies temporarily above a down trendline (or below an up trendline) and then breaks back below (above) it.

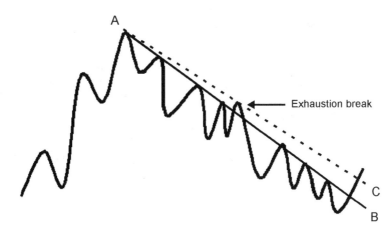

Figure 8-18   Exhaustion break in a downtrend.

Summary

- Trendlines are perhaps the easiest technical tool to understand, but considerable experimentation and practice are required before the art of interpreting them can be successfully mastered.
- Trendline violations signal either a temporary interruption or a reversal in the prevailing trend. It is necessary to refer to other pieces of technical evidence to determine which is being signaled (see Chart 8-5).
- The significance of trendlines is a function of their length, the number of times they have been touched or approached, and the steepness of the angle of ascent or descent.
- A good trendline reflects the underlying trend and represents an important support and resistance zone.
- Extended trendlines are an important concept and should not be overlooked (see Chart 8-6).
- Exhaustion breaks often possess good predictive power.

Chart 8-5 Value Line Composite Index, 1989–1990. This represents an example of a major trendline violation occurring in combination with a price pattern completion. In this case, the formation was a broadening one with a slightly rising trendline (the almost flat bottom). Some form of poetic license is often needed in interpreting charts since this particular one could not strictly be interpreted as a broadening formation with a flat bottom, but the effects were certainly the same. (*From www.pring.com.*)

Chart 8-6 S&P Composite 1966–1989 showing an exhaustion breakout. This chart shows that a resistance trendline joining the 1974 low and 1978 highs was temporarily violated. This proved to be an exhaustion move since the S&P Composite was unable to hold above the line. This failure was followed by the 1987 crash. Not all exhaustion moves result in such dynamic consequences, but they certainly warn of potential trouble and should never be ignored. (*From www.pring.com.*)

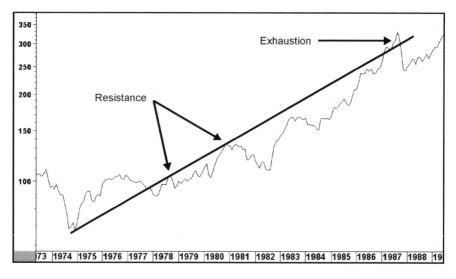

9
Moving Averages

It is evident that trends in stock prices can be very volatile, almost haphazard at times. One technique for dealing with this phenomenon is the moving average (MA). An MA attempts to tone down the fluctuations of any price series into a smoothed trend, so that distortions are reduced to a minimum. There are many variations of MAs used in technical analysis. The three most common are: simple, weighted, and exponential. The construction and use of these averages are different; therefore, each type will be dealt with in turn.

Simple MAs

A simple MA is by far the most widely used. It is constructed by totaling a set of data and dividing the sum by the number of observations. The resulting number is known as the *average,* or *mean average.* In order to get the average to "move," a new item of data is added and the first item on the list subtracted. The new total is then divided by the number of observations, and the process is repeated.

For example, the calculation of a 10-week MA would follow the method shown in Table 9-1. On March 12, the total of the 10 weeks ending on that date is 966, and 966 divided by 10 results in an average of 96.6. On March 19, the number 90 is added, and the observation of 101 on January 8 is deleted. The new total of 955 is then divided by 10. The calculation of a 13-week MA would require totaling 13 weeks of data and dividing by 13. This calculation is then repeated in order to get the average to move. A 13-week MA is shown in the upper panel of Chart 9-1 by the dashed line. Generally speaking, a rising MA indicates market strength and a declining one denotes weakness.

Table 9-1 Simple MA Calculation

Date		Index	10-week total	MA
Jan.	8	101		
	15	100		
	22	103		
	29	99		
Feb.	5	96		
	12	99		
	19	95		
	26	91		
Mar.	5	93		
	12	89	966	96.6
	19	90	955	95.5
	26	95	950	95.0
Apr.	2	103	950	95.0

Chart 9-1 Cash Wheat centered versus a noncentered average. (*From www.pring.com.*)

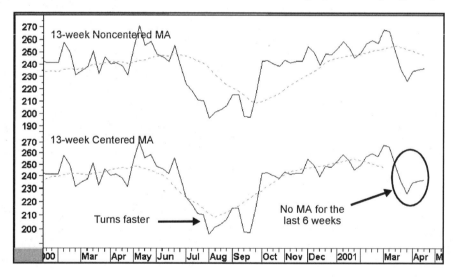

A comparison of the price index with its 13-week MA shows that the average changes direction well after the peak or trough in the price and is therefore "late" in changing direction. This is because the MA is plotted on the thirteenth week, whereas the average price of 13 weeks of observations actually occurs halfway through the 13-week time span, that is, in the seventh week.

> **Major Technical Principle**   Changes in the price trend are identi-
> fied by the price crossing its MA, not by a reversal in direction of
> the MA.

If it is to reflect the underlying trend correctly, the latest MA should be centered, or plotted, on the seventh week, as shown in the lower panel of Chart 9-1.

If the centering technique had been used in the example, it would have been necessary to wait 6 weeks before ascertaining whether the average had changed direction. That is why the blank area on Chart 9-1 exists between the last plot for the average and the last plot for the data point.

A time delay, though it is an irritant, is not particularly critical when analyzing other time series such as economic data. However, given the relatively rapid movement of prices in the financial markets and the consequent loss of profit potential, a delay of this nature is totally unacceptable. Technicians have found that, for the purpose of identifying trend reversals, the best results are achieved by plotting the MA on the final period.

A change from a rising to a declining market is signaled when the price moves below its MA. A bullish signal is triggered when the price rallies above the average. Since the use of MAs gives clear-cut buy and sell signals, they help to eliminate some of the subjectivity associated with the construction and interpretation of trendlines.

More often than not, it pays to take action based on MA crossovers, provided the particular time span in question has proved reliable in the past. The degree of accuracy depends substantially on the choice of MA, as discussed later, as well as the volatility of the security in question. The length of the moving average will also have an influence on its accuracy. Generally speaking, the longer the time span, the more reliable the average. In effect, a moving average for any given time span on an intraday chart is likely to be much less reliable than one constructed from month-end data on a monthly chart. Now though, we need to examine some of the characteristics of MAs in greater detail.

Characteristics of Simple MAs

Although the examples in this and the following sections feature simple MAs, the principles outlined can be applied to weighted and exponential

MAs, which are discussed later. The major technical principles of interpreting MAs are as follows:

- *An MA is a smoothed version of a trend, and the average itself is an area of support and resistance.* In a rising market, price reactions are often reversed as they find support in the area of the MA. Similarly, a rally in a declining market often meets resistance at an MA and turns down. The more times an MA has been touched, that is, when it acts as a support or resistance area, the greater the significance when it is violated.
- *A carefully chosen MA should reflect the underlying trend; its violation therefore warns that a change in trend may already have taken place.* If the MA is flat or has already changed direction, its violation is fairly conclusive proof that the previous trend has reversed.
- *If the violation occurs while the MA is still proceeding sharply in the direction of the prevailing trend, this should be treated as a preliminary warning that a trend reversal has taken place.* Confirmation should await a flattening in the angle of ascent or descent, a change in direction in the MA itself, or alternative technical sources. The crossover of a moving average with a sharp angle of ascent or descent is akin to the violation of a trendline with a sharp angle.
- *Generally speaking, the longer the time span covered by an MA, the greater the significance of a crossover signal.* For instance, the violation of an 18-month MA is substantially more important than the crossover of a 30-day MA.
- *Reversals in the direction of an MA are usually more reliable than an MA crossover.* In instances in which a change in direction occurs close to a market turning point, a very powerful and reliable signal is given. However, in most instances, an average reverses well after a new trend has begun and so is only useful as a confirmation.

In short, think of an average as a type of moving trendline that obtains its significance from its length (time span), the number of times it has been touched or approached, and its angle of ascent or descent.

What Constitutes a Valid Crossover

A *crossover* is any penetration of an MA. However, close observation of any chart featuring an MA will usually reveal a number of whipsaw, or false, signals. How can we tell which ones are going to be valid? Unfortunately, there is no way of knowing for certain. Indeed, many whipsaws cannot be avoided and should be regarded as a fact of life. However, it is possible to avoid some of these close calls by using filtering techniques. The type of filter to be used depends on the time span in question and is very much a matter of individual experimentation.

For example, we may decide to take action on MA crossovers for which a 3 percent penetration takes place and to ignore all others. Violations of a 40-week MA might result in an average price move of 15 to 20 percent. In this instance, a 3 percent penetration would be a reasonable filter. An example is shown in Chart 9-2. On the other hand, since 3 percent would probably encompass the whole move signaled by a 10-day MA crossover, this kind of filter would be of no use whatsoever.

Some analysts, recognizing that one-period whipsaws are quite common, require an MA crossover to hold for at least one period. In the case of daily

> **Major Technical Principle**   If an MA crossover takes place at the same time a trendline is violated or a price pattern completed, these signals strongly reinforce each other and therefore need less in the form of a filter requirement.

Chart 9-2   Eurotop 40-week MA and 3-percent bands. This chart features the Eurotop Index of European blue chips together with a 40-week MA (the dashed line). The solid lines have been plotted at ±3 percent. Buy signals are generated when the price crosses above the upper line, and sell signals when it crosses below the lower one. (*From www.pring.com.*)

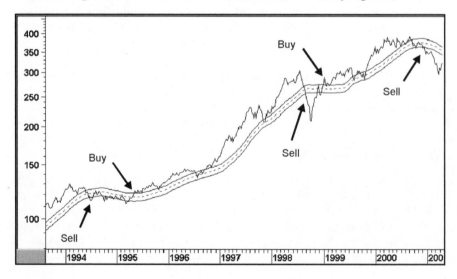

data, this approach would mean waiting for the second or third day before concluding that the average had been violated. A more sensible method is to use a combination of the period *and* percentage penetration for deciding whether a crossover is valid.

An example is shown in Chart 9-3, where a joint trendline and MA violation develop for the Philadelphia Gold and Silver Share Index in August 1994. Later, we see an MA violation and a head-and-shoulders (H&S) top completion, both of which developed around the same time. Chart 9-4 shows a similar situation with Alberto Culver and a 50-day MA.

MAs are usually constructed from closing data. Closing prices are more reliable than highs, lows, or openings because they reflect positions that investors are willing to carry overnight or, in the case of weekly charts, over the weekend. Intraday trading can be subject to manipulation or distorted by an unwarranted emotional attitude to news events. For this reason, it is best to wait for the closing price to penetrate the average before concluding that a crossover has taken place. If intraperiod activity is used for MA violations, it is usually best to calculate an MA based on daily lows or highs.

One exception would occur when a bar chart touches an MA on numerous occasions. In many instances, the MA is clearly a significant support/resistance point and its violation should be treated with respect.

Chart 9-3   Philadelphia Gold and Silver Share Index 1994. (*From Martin Pring's Introduction to Technical Analysis.*)

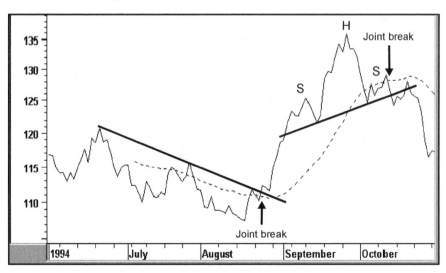

Chart 9-4 Alberto Culver and a simultaneous MA trendline break. This chart features Alberto Culver together with a 50-day MA. Note how it was possible to construct a trendline that intersected with the MA. Since both represent resistance, their joint violation represents two pieces of evidence that prices were headed higher. A third came in the form of an expansion in volume. (*From www.pring.com.*)

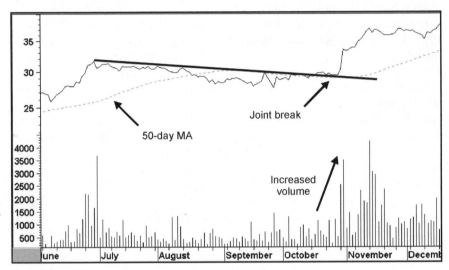

In Chart 9-5, the dotted line shows a 25-day MA calculated from intraday lows. The solid line represents the same average based on closing-only data. If intraday crossovers of the former had been used as stop-loss signals on the downside, considerably fewer whipsaws would have been generated than if the MA had been based on closing data.

Choice of Time Span

MAs can be constructed for any time period, whether a few days, several weeks, many months, or even years. The choice of length is very important. For example, if it is assumed that a complete bull and bear cycle lasts for 4 years, an MA constructed over a time span longer than 48 months will not reflect the cycle at all. This is because it smoothes out all the fluctuations that take place during the period and will appear more or less as a straight line crossing through the middle of the data. On the other hand, a 5-day MA will catch every minor move in the stock cycle and will be useless for the purpose of identifying the actual top and bottom of the overall cycle.

Chart 9-5 Canadian dollar and two MAs. (*From www.pring.com.*)

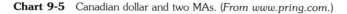

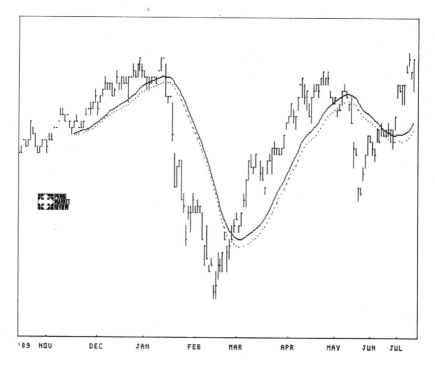

Even if the 48-month average were shortened to 24 months and the 5-day average expanded to 4 weeks, for example, using the crossover signals would still cause the 24-month average to give an agonizingly slow confirmation of a change in trend. The 4-week average would be so sensitive that it would continually give misleading or whipsaw signals [see Fig. 9-1(*a*)]. Only an MA that can catch the movement of the actual cycle will provide the optimum trade-off between lateness and oversensitivity, such as the 10-month MA in Fig. 9-1(*b*).

The choice of MA depends on the type of market trend that is to be identified: short, intermediate, or primary. Because different markets have different characteristics and the same markets go through different cyclic phenomena, there is no such thing as a perfect MA. In recent years, extensive computer research has been done on the optimum MA time span. The conclusion from all sources is that there is no one perfect time span.

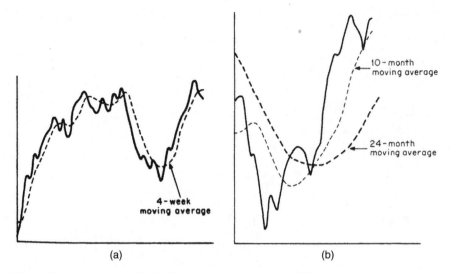

Figure 9-1 (a) 4-week MA. (b) 10-month versus 24-month MA.

What may work extremely well in one market over one specific period of time is unlikely to be duplicated in the future. When we talk about choice of time span, we are really trying to identify an MA that will work most of the time with a specific time frame, that is, short, intermediate, or long. Generally speaking, long-term time spans are less influenced by manipulation and knee-jerk random reactions to unexpected news than are short-term ones. This is why long time spans usually give the best test results. Examples of a 40-week span are featured in Chart 9-6. Research also shows that simple averages generally outperform weighted and exponential ones. Recognizing these limitations, the time spans in Table 9-2 are suggested.

The important thing to remember is that an MA is *one* technical tool in the technical arsenal that is used with other techniques as part of the *art* of identifying trend reversals.

Advancing Simple Moving Averages

A technique that has a lot of potential, but is not widely used, is to advance an MA. In the case of a 25-day MA, for example, the actual plot would not

Chart 9-6 Standard & Poor's (S&P) Composite, yen, MSCI World Stock Index, and 40-week MAs. This chart shows a 40-week MA at work in three different markets. Crossovers of each index are subject to whipsaws from time to time, but on balance this average is still fairly reliable. Note that the 40-week average is continually being used as a support or resistance level. (*From www.pring.com.*)

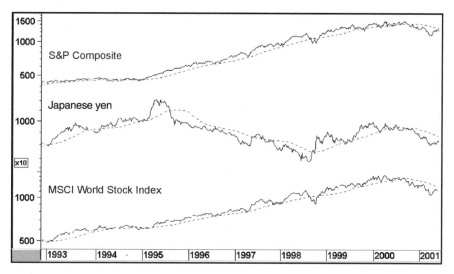

Table 9-2 Suggested Time Frames

Short-term	Intermediate-term	Long-term
10-day	30-day	200-day/40-week/9-month*
15-day	10-week (50-day)	45-week†
20-day	13-week (65-day)	
25-day	20-week	12-month‡
30-day	26-week	18-month
	200-day	24-month

*Recommeneded by Willaim Gordon, *The Stock Market Indicators,* Investors Press, Palisades Park, N.J., 1968.

†Reported by Robert W. Colby and Thomas A. Meyers in *The Encyclopedia of Technical Market Indicators,* Dow Jones-Irwin, Homewood, Ill., 1988, to be the best average for the U.S. stock market using weekly data.

‡Ibid.; reported to be the best average for the U.S. stock market using monthly data.

be made on the 25th day, but advanced to the 28th or 30th, and so forth. The advantage of this approach is that it delays the crossover and filters out occasional whipsaws or false signals. In *Profits in the Stock Market,* H. M. Gartley[1] calculated that during the period of 1919 to 1933, which covered almost all kinds of market situations, the use of a simple 25-day MA crossover netted 446 Dow points (slightly better than 433 points for the 30-day MA and far better than the 316 and 216 for 40- and 15-day MAs, respectively). However, when the 25-day average was plotted on the 28th day, crossovers resulted in an increase of 231 points to 677. The 30-day MA, when advanced 3 days, also produced superior results, with an additional gain of 204 points for a total of 637. Chart 9-7 represents three MAs, as calculated by Gartley. Although these MAs are plotted normally, the whipsaw signals would be avoided by moving the MA forward 3 days, as shown on the chart.

Although the 25-day MA that advanced 3 days may not ultimately prove to be the best combination, the technique of advancing an MA is clearly one that could be usefully incorporated into the technical approach. It is always difficult to know how much to advance an MA. Experimentation is the answer. One possibility is to advance the average by the square root of the time span. For example, a 36-day MA would be advanced by 6 days (the square root of 36 = 6).[2] See Chart 9-8 featuring the Madrid General Index.

Convergence of Simple MAs

A sharp price move is often preceded by a gradually narrowing trading range. In effect, decreasing price fluctuations reflect a very fine balance between buyers and sellers. When the balance is tipped one way or the other, the price is then free to embark upon a major move.

This kind of situation can often be identified by plotting several MAs and observing them when they are all at approximately the same point. Chart 9-9 shows the Spot Euroyen between 2000 and 2001 together with three MAs

[1]DJ Industrials and three MAs. (H.M. Gartley's *Profits in the Stock Market,* Lambert Gann Publishing, Pomeroy, WA, 1981.)
[2]Arthur Skarew, *Techniques of a Professional Commodity Chart Analyst,* Commodity Research Bureau, New York, 1980.

Chart 9-7 The DJIA and three MAs (H.M. Gartley, *Profits in the Stock Market*, Lambert Gann Publishing, Pomeroy, Washington, 1935.)

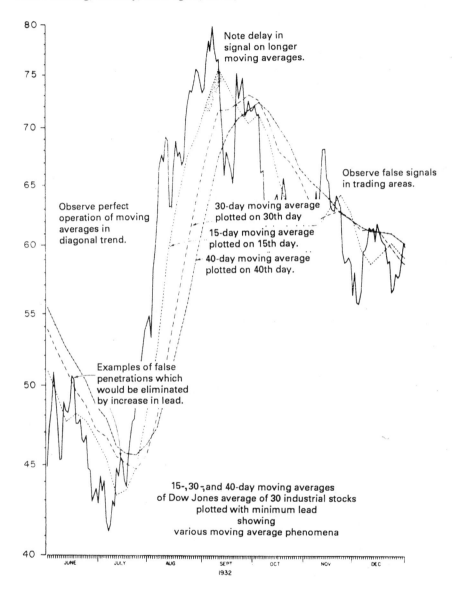

Chart 9-8   Madrid General and an advanced MA. Here we see a 50-day MA together with a 50-day average advanced by seven periods. Note how the advanced average filtered out several whipsaw signals. This is by no means a perfect approach, but it definitely comes into its own after a sharp rally or decline. (*From www.pring.com.*)

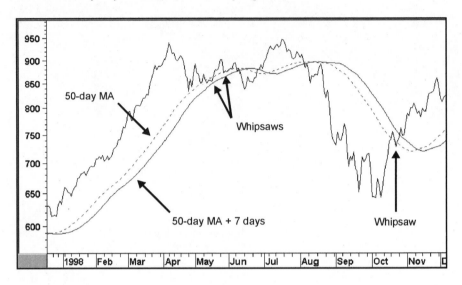

Chart 9-9   Spot Euroyen and three MAs. (*From www.pring.com.*)

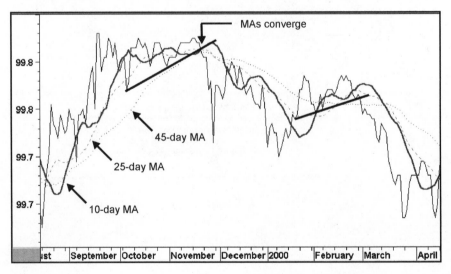

of differing time spans. Note how the three MAs almost completely converge just before the price embarks on a sharp decline in November 2000. The convergence of the averages tells us that the balance between buyers and sellers is very evenly matched and warns that a major move is likely. The actual signal comes from the violation of the up trendline. A similar combination develops in February 2001, only this time the 25-day average does not participate in the convergence.

Multiple Simple MAs

Some techniques of trend determination involve more than one MA at a time. Signals are given by a shorter-term MA crossing above or below a longer one. This procedure has the advantage of smoothing the data twice, which reduces the possibility of a whipsaw, yet it warns of trend changes fairly quickly after they have taken place (see Chart 9-10). Two averages that have

Chart 9-10 MSCI World Stock Index and two MAs. In this chart of the Morgan Stanley Capital International (MSCI) World Stock Index, the 10-week MA crosses below the 30-week MA in early 1998 and late 1999. However, the 30-day series is still advancing, so no sell signal is given. The late 1998 decline shows the weakness of this system because the sharp intermediate correction resulted in a sell signal almost at the bottom. Because the bottom was V-shaped, the counterveiling buy signal was not triggered until the price had experienced a good rally. After that, the 10/30 system would have maintained a long position until just after the final peak. (*From www.pring.com.*)

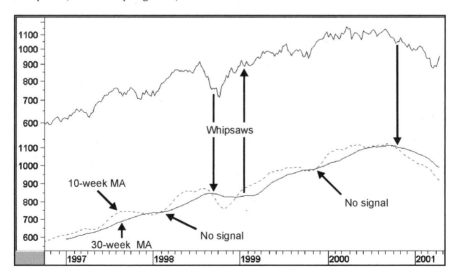

been found reliable in determining primary market moves are the 10- and 30-week MAs, when used together. For the purpose of simplifying the calculation, the weekly closing price is used, rather than a 5-day average.

Signals are given when the 10-week average moves below the 30-week average and when the 30-week average itself is declining. This development warns that the major trend is down. It is not assumed to have reversed until both averages are rising simultaneously, with the 10-week higher than the 30-week MA. A valid signal is not given if the 10-week average rises above the 30-week average while the longer average is still declining (and vice versa for bull markets). By definition, these warning signals always occur after the ultimate peak or trough of stock prices and serve as *confirmation* of a change in trend rather than as actual juncture points in themselves.

MAs should *always* be used in conjunction with other indicators. This is because prices occasionally fluctuate in a broad sideways pattern for an extended period of time, resulting in a series of misleading signals. Chart 9-11, featuring the U.S. Dollar Index in 1995, shows an example of a period in which many misleading crossovers were experienced. Usually, such frustrating trading-range action is followed by an extremely strong trend in which the losses incurred from the trendless period of whipsaw signals are more than made up for.

Whenever it is obvious that an MA has entered a trading range, and this might take two or three whipsaws, it is best to ignore it and concentrate on trendlines joining peaks and troughs of the range shown in Charts 9-11 and 9-12, using their breakouts as a basis for buying or selling.

Weighted MAs

An MA can correctly represent a trend from a statistical point of view only if it is centered, but centering an average delays the signal, for the reasons discussed previously. One technique that attempts to overcome this problem is to weight the data in favor of the most recent observations. An MA constructed in this manner can *turn* or reverse direction much more quickly than a simple MA, which is calculated by treating all the data equally.

There are countless ways in which data can be weighted, but the most widely used method is a technique whereby the first period of data is multiplied by 1, the second by 2, the third by 3, and so on until the latest one

Chart 9-11 U.S. Dollar Index 1995. (*From Martin Pring's Introduction to Technical Analysis.*)

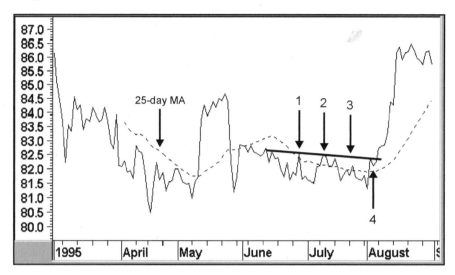

Chart 9-12 The Eurotop Index 1993–1995.

is multiplied. The calculations for each period are then totaled. The divisor for a simple MA is the number of periods, but for this form of weighted average, the divisor is the sum of the weights; that is, $1 + 2 + 3 + 4 + 5 + 6 = 21$. For a 10-week weighted MA, the sum of the weights would be $1 + 2 + 3 + 4 + 5 + 6 + 7 + 8 + 9 + 10 = 55$. Table 9-3 illustrates how the calculations are made.Another method is to calculate a simple MA, but, in doing so, to use the most recent observation twice, which doubles its weight.

The interpretation of a weighted average is different from that of a simple average because the weighted average is more sensitive. Warning of a trend reversal is given by a change in the direction of the average rather than by a crossover.

Exponential MAs

Weighted MAs are helpful for the purpose of identifying trend reversals. However, the time-consuming calculations required to construct and maintain such averages prior to the widespread use of computers greatly detracted from their usefulness. An exponential moving average (EMA) is a shortcut to obtaining a form of weighted MA. In order to construct a 20-week EMA, it is necessary to calculate a simple 20-week MA first, that is, the total of 20 weeks of observations divided by 20. In

The 20-week average becomes the starting point for the EMA. It is transferred to column 2 for the following week. Next, the entry for the 21st week (January 8 in the previous example) is compared with the EMA, and the difference is added or subtracted and posted in column 3; $100 - 99 = 1.00$. This difference is then multiplied by the exponent, which for a 20-week EMA is 0.1. This exponentially treated difference, 1.00×0.1, is then added to the previous week's EMA, and the calculation is repeated each succeeding week. In the example, the exponentially treated difference for January 8 is 0.1, which is added to the previous week's average, 99.00, to obtain an EMA for January 8 of 99.10. This figure in column 6 is then plotted.

If the difference between the new weekly observation and the previous week's EMA is negative, as in the reading 99.00 versus 99.64 for January 29, the exponentially treated difference is subtracted from the previous week's EMA.

The exponent used varies with the time span of the MA. The correct exponents for various time spans are shown in Table 9-5, where the time periods have been described as weekly. In effect, however, the exponent 0.1 can be used for any measure of 20—hours, days, weeks, months, years, or an even longer period.

Exponents for time periods other than those shown in Table 9-5 can easily be calculated by dividing 2 by the time span. For example, a 5-week average will need to be twice as sensitive as a 10-week average; thus, 2 divided by 5 gives an exponent of 0.4. On the other hand, since a 20-week average should be *half* as sensitive as for a 10-week period (0.2), its exponent is *halved* to 0.1.

If an EMA proves to be too sensitive for the trend being monitored, one solution is to extend its time period. Another is to smooth the EMA by another EMA. This method uses an EMA, as calculated previously, and repeats the process using a further exponent. There is no reason why a third or fourth smoothing could not be tried, but the resulting EMA, while smoother, would be far less sensitive. Remember, all forms of MAs represent a compromise between timeliness and sensitivity.

By definition, EMA crossovers and reversals occur simultaneously. Buy and sell signals are therefore triggered in the same way as simple MA crossovers.

In their book *The Encyclopedia of Technical Market Indicators,*[3] Colby and Meyers tested all the time spans between 1- and 75-week EMAs for the U.S. stock market between 1968 and 1987. They discovered that the 42-week EMA gave the best performance, offering an equity gain of 97+ points, but lagged behind the 45-week simple MA, which experienced a gain of 111+ points. Chart 9-13 features a 65-week EMA for Albertson's.

[3]Robert W. Colby and Thomas A. Meyers, *The Encyclopedia of Technical Market Indicators,* Dow Jones-Irwin, Homewood, Ill., 1988.

Table 9-3 Weighted MA Calculation

Date	Index (1)	6 x col. 1 (2)	5 x col. 1 1 week ago (3)	4 x col. 1 2 weeks ago (4)	3 x col. 1 3 weeks ago (5)	2 x col. 1 4 weeks ago (6)	1 x col. 1 5 weeks ago (7)	Total cols. 2-7	Col. 8 ÷ 21 (9)
Jan. 8	101								
15	100								
22	103								
29	99								
Feb. 5	96								
12	99	594	480	396	309	200	101	2080	99.1
19	95	570	495	384	297	206	100	2052	97.7
26	91	546	475	396	288	198	103	2006	95.5
Mar. 5	93	558	455	380	297	192	99	1981	94.3
12	89	534	465	364	285	198	96	1924	92.5

Table 9-4 EMA Calculation

Date	Price (1)	EMA for previous week (2)	Difference (col. 1 − col. 2) (3)	Exponent (4)	Col. 3 × col. 4 ±/− (5)	Col. 2 + col. 5 EMA (6)
Jan. 1	. . .	. . .	. . .	. . .	. . .	99.00
8	100.00	99.00	1.00	0.1	+0.10	99.10
15	103.00	99.10	3.90	0.1	+0.39	99.49
22	102.00	99.49	2.51	0.1	+0.25	99.74
29	99.00	99.64	(0.64)	0.1	−0.06	99.68

Table 9-5 Expontential Factors for Various Time Frames

Number of weeks	Exponent
5	0.4
10	0.2
15	0.13
20	0.1
40	0.05
80	0.25

Chart 9-13 Albertson's simultaneous price pattern completion and MA crossover. One of my favorite averages is the 65-week EMA. As featured in this chart, we see an H&S top for Albertson's at the end of 1999. Note how the EMA and neckline both intersect in approximately the same area. This type of action emphasizes the significance of the break. (*From www.pring.com.*)

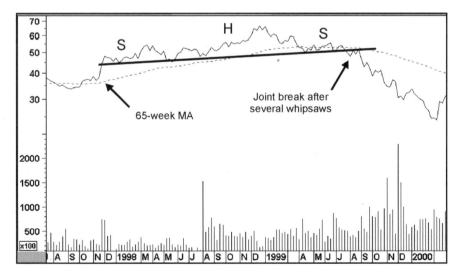

Envelopes

It has already been established that MAs can act as important juncture points in their roles as support and resistance areas. In this respect, the longer the time span, the greater the significance of the average. This support and resistance principle can be taken one step further by constructing symmetrical lines parallel to an MA called *envelopes* (refer to Fig. 9-2). This technique is based on the principle that stock prices fluctuate around a given trend in cyclical movements of reasonably similar proportion. In other words, just as the MA serves as an important juncture point, so do certain lines drawn parallel to that MA. Looked at in this way, the MA is really the center of the trend, and the envelope consists of the points of maximum and minimum divergence from it.

There is no hard and fast rule about the exact position at which the envelope should be drawn, since that can be discovered only on a trial-and-error basis with regard to the volatility of the price being monitored and the time span of the MA. This process can be expanded, as in Fig. 9-3, to include four or more envelopes (that is, two above and two below the MA), each drawn at an identical proportional distance from its predecessor. In this example, the envelopes have been plotted at 10 percent intervals. If the MA is at 100, for example, the envelopes should be plotted at 90, 110, and so on. An example featuring Masco appears in Chart 9-14.

Bollinger Bands

A useful addition to envelope analysis is a new approach devised by John Bollinger.[4] Rather than being plotted as fixed percentages above and below

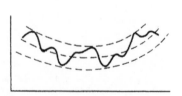

Figure 9-2 Single envelopes.

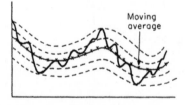

Figure 9-3 Multiple envelopes.

[4]John Bollinger, Bollinger Capital Management, P.O. Box 3358, Manhattan Beach, CA 90266 (*www.Bollingerbands.com*).

Chart 9-14   Masco 1998–2001 using a ±15% band of a 10-day simple MA.

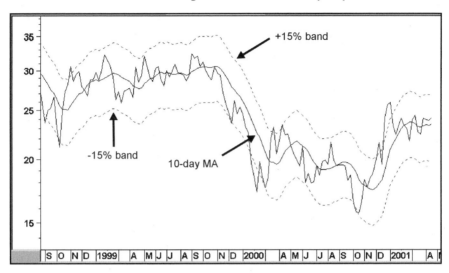

an MA, Bollinger bands are calculated as standard deviations above and below an average based on closing prices. They are designed with the concept that the bands widen and narrow as the price trend becomes more or less volatile.

Rules for Interpretation

The deviation setting for the Bollinger bands determines the distance between the outer bands and the center one. Chart 9-15 shows an average set to 20 and a deviation to 6; all the other charts in this section have been plotted with a 20 × 2 parameter. It is fairly evident that this wider setting has no significance because its bands are never touched. Similarly, if they are set at too narrow a basis, there will be far too many whipsaws.

There are several rules for interpreting the bands:

• When the bands narrow, there is a tendency for sharp price changes to follow. This, of course, is another way of saying that when prices trade in a narrow range and lose volatility, demand and supply are in a fine state of balance. In this context, a narrowing of the band is always relative to the recent past, and that's where Bollinger bands can help in visually

Chart 9-15   Northern States and the Bollinger band (20 × 6). (*From www.pring.com.*)

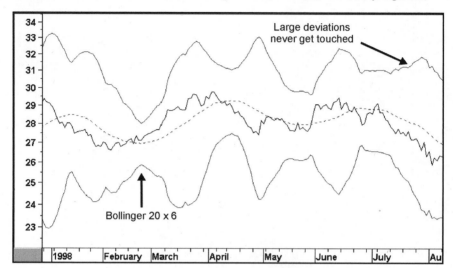

showing the narrowing process. They also give us some indication of when a breakout might materialize because they start to diverge once the price begins to take off. Two examples are shown in Chart 9-16, where it is also possible to construct some trendlines marking the breakout point.

- If the price exceeds a band, the trend is expected to continue. This is really another way of saying that if the price moves above the band, upside momentum is strong enough to support higher ultimate prices and vice versa. After both breakouts in Chart 9-16, we see the price immediately move outside the band. The crossover of the Bollinger band usually indicates short-term exhaustion and it quickly pulls back again. However, this is just a process of pausing for breath until the trend is then able to extend again. By now, you will have noticed that the price often crosses the bands several times before the trend reverses. The obvious question at this point is: How do you know when the band has been crossed for the last time? In other words, how do you know how to spot the bottom and top of a move? The answer lies in the following rule.

- When the price traces out a reversal formation after it has crossed outside a band, expect a trend reversal. Some examples are shown in Chart 9-17, first in April and then in June. In both situations, the price tried and failed to cross the band successfully before completing a price pattern.

Chart 9-16 Oneok and narrowing Bollinger bands. (*From www.pring.com.*)

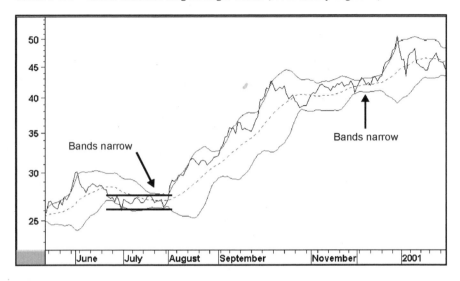

Chart 9-17 Northern States and Bollinger bands (20 × 2) (*From www.pring.com.*)

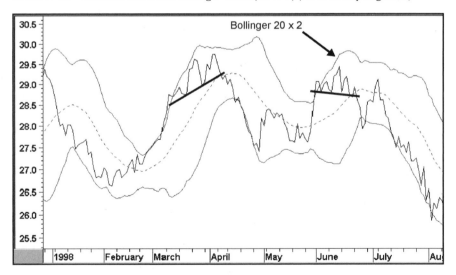

Summary

- One of the basic assumptions of technical analysis is that stocks move in trends. Since major trends comprise many minor fluctuations in prices, an MA is constructed to help smooth out the data so that the underlying trend will be more clearly visible.
- Ideally, a simple MA should be plotted at the halfway point of the time period being monitored (a process known as *centering*), but since this would involve a time lag during which prices could change rapidly and lose much of the potential profit of a move, the MA is plotted at the end of the period in question.
- This drawback has been largely overcome by the use of MA crossovers, which provide warnings of a reversal in trend and by the use of weighted EMAs, which are especially sensitive to changes in the prevailing trend since they weight data in favor of the most recent periods.
- There is no such thing as a perfect average. The choice of time span always represents a trade-off between timeliness (catching the trend at an early stage) and sensitivity (catching the trend turn too early and causing an undue amount of whipsaws). For short-term trends, 10-, 25-, 30-, and 50-day spans are suggested, but for longer-term time spans, 40-week simple and 65-week EMA averages are recommended. Helpful time spans using monthly data are 6, 9, 12, 18, and 24 months.

10
Momentum Principles

The methods of trend determination considered so far have been concerned with analysis of the movement of the price itself through trendlines, price patterns, and moving averages (MAs). These techniques are extremely useful, but they identify a change in trend *after it has taken place.*

This chapter will examine the general principles of momentum interpretation that apply in some degree or other to *all* momentum indicators. The *rate of change* (ROC) will be used as a case study. The next two chapters will discuss other specific momentum indicators.

Introduction

The concept of upside momentum is illustrated in the following example. When a ball is thrown into the air, it begins its trajectory at a very fast pace; that is, it possesses strong momentum. The speed at which the ball rises gradually diminishes until it finally comes to a temporary standstill. The force of gravity then causes it to reverse course. This slowing-down process, known as a *loss of upward momentum,* is a phenomenon that is also

---

Major Technical Principle The use of momentum indicators can warn of latent strength or weakness in the indicator or price being monitored, often well ahead of the final turning point.

---

experienced in financial markets. The flight of a ball can be equated to a market price. The price's rate of advance begins to slow down noticeably before the ultimate peak in prices is reached.

On the other hand, if a ball is thrown inside a room and hits the ceiling while its momentum is still rising, the ball and the momentum will reverse at the same time. Unfortunately, momentum indicators in the marketplace are not dissimilar. This is because there are occasions for which momentum and price peak simultaneously, either because a ceiling of selling resistance is met or because buying power is temporarily exhausted. Under such conditions, the *level* of momentum is often as helpful as its *direction* in assessing the quality of a price trend.

The idea of downward momentum may be better understood by comparing it to a car that is pushed over the top of a hill. The car begins to roll downhill and, due to the gradient of the hill, the car starts to accelerate until it reaches maximum velocity at the bottom. Although its speed then begins to decrease, the car continues to travel, but finally it comes to a halt. Market prices act in a similar fashion: The rate of decline (or loss of momentum) often slows ahead of the final low. This is not always the case, however, since momentum and price sometimes (as at peaks) turn together, as prices meet a major level of support. Nevertheless, momentum leads price often enough to warn of a potential trend reversal in the indicator or market average that is being monitored.

Momentum is a generic term. Just as fruit describes apples, oranges, grapes, and so on, so momentum embraces many different indicators. Examples include ROC, the relative strength indicator (RSI), the moving average convergence divergence (MACD), the know sure thing (KST), breadth oscillators, and diffusion indexes.

There are two broad ways of looking at momentum. The first uses price data for an individual series, such as a currency, commodity, stock, or market average. It is then manipulated in a statistical form that is plotted as an oscillator. We will call this *price momentum* (although volume can be manipulated in the same way). The second is also plotted as an oscillator, but is based on statistical manipulation of a number of market components, such as the percentage of New York Stock Exchange (NYSE) stocks above a 30-week MA. This measure is referred to as *breadth momentum* and is discussed

---

Major Technical Principle The principles or characteristics of momentum interpretation are the same for all indicators, but some are specially constructed to bring out a particular characteristic.

in Chapter 24. Price momentum can be constructed for any price series, but breadth momentum can only be calculated for a series that can be broken down into various components.

This chapter outlines a number of these basic principles using the ROC as an example. Remember that it is only *one* type of price momentum indicator. Chapters 11, 12, 23, and 24 will discuss other oscillators for price and breadth momentum.

It should be noted that the type of trend reversal signaled by a momentum indicator depends upon the time span over which it has been calculated. It is accepted practice to use daily data for identifying short-term trends, weekly data for intermediate trends, and monthly data for primary trends.

It is very important to note that the use of momentum indicators assumes that the price of the security is experiencing a normal cyclic rhythm, which is expressed in price action by rallies and reactions. However, in some instances, countercyclical reactions are almost nonexistent. Price movement is then reflected as a linear uptrend or downtrend. This is an unusual phenomenon, and when it develops momentum, oscillators fail to work. This is why the following principle is so very important.

> **Major Technical Principle** It is of paramount importance to use momentum analysis in conjunction with some kind of trend-reversal signal in the price series itself.

The ROC Indicator

The simplest way of measuring momentum is to calculate the rate at which a security price changes over a given period of time, which is known as an ROC indicator. If it is desired, for example, to construct an ROC using a 10-week time span, the current price is divided by the price 10 weeks ago. If the latest price is 965 and that 10 weeks ago was 985, the ROC or momentum indicator will read 98.0, that is, 965 divided by 985. The subsequent reading in the indicator will be calculated by dividing next week's price by the price 9 weeks ago (see Table 10-1). The result is a series that oscillates around a central reference point. This horizontal equilibrium line represents the level at which the price is unchanged from its reading 10 weeks ago (see Fig. 10-1). If an ROC calculation were made for a price that remained unchanged, the oscillator would be represented by a horizontal straight line.

Table 10-1   Ten-Week ROC Calculation

Date	DJIA (1)	DJIA 10 weeks ago (2)	10-week rate of change (col. 1 divided col. 2) (3)
Jan. 1	985		
8	980		
15	972		
22	975		
29	965		
Feb. 5	967		
12	972		
19	965		
26	974		
Mar. 5	980		
12	965	985	98.0
19	960	980	98.0
26	950	972	97.7
Apr. 2	960	975	98.5
9	965	965	100.0
16	970	967	100.3
23	974	972	100.2
30	980	965	101.6
May 7	985	974	101.1

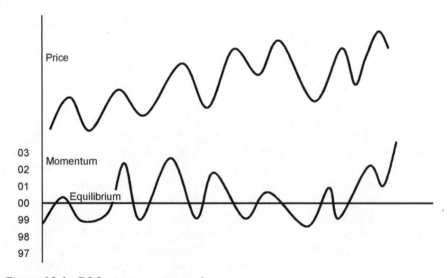

Figure 10-1   ROC using percentage scaling.

When an ROC is above the reference line, the market price that it is measuring is higher than its level 10 weeks ago. If the ROC is also rising, the difference between the current reading of the price and its level 10 weeks ago is growing. If it is above the central line but declining, the price is still above its level 10 weeks ago, but the difference between the two readings is shrinking. When the ROC is below its central line and falling, the price is below its level 10 weeks ago, and the difference between the two is growing. If the indicator is below its central line but rising, the price is still lower than its level 10 weeks ago, but its rate of decline is slowing.

In short, a rising ROC implies expanding velocity, and a falling one a loss of momentum. Rising momentum should be interpreted as a bullish factor, and declining momentum as a bearish one.

The ROC may also be calculated by the subtraction method; that is, the current price is subtracted rather than divided by a price N periods ago. This indicator is called the momentum indicator on several charting packages, but it is really a rate of change. My own preference is strongly for the division calculation since it expresses proportionate moves in a similar manner to the ratio scale. This means that the indicator will not be distorted in longer-term charts, as will an ROC calculated with the subtraction method.

There are two methods of scaling an ROC chart. Since the choice does not affect the trend or level of the indicator, the method used is not important, but a brief explanation is in order because the two alternatives can be confusing. The first method is the one described previously and shown in Fig. 10-1, where 100 becomes the central reference point. In the example, 100 (this week's observation) divided by 99 (the observation 10 weeks ago) is plotted approximately as 101, 100 divided by 98 as 102, 100 divided by 102 as 98, and so on.

The alternative is to take the difference between the indicator and the 100 level and plot the result as a positive or negative number using a reference line of 0. In this case, 101 is plotted as $+1$, 102 as $+2$, 98 as -2, and so on (see Fig. 10-2).

Selection of Time Span

Choice of the correct time span is important. For longer-term trends, a 12-month or 52-week time span is generally the most reliable, although a 24- or 18-month period can also prove useful. For intermediate trends, a 9-month, 26-week (6-month), or 13-week (3-month) span works well. Price movements of even shorter duration are often reflected by a 10-, 20-, 25-, or 30-day span. Reliable short/intermediate movements are often reflected with a 45-day (9-week) and 65-day (13-week) span.

> **Major Technical Principle**   The analysis of any technical situation
> will be enhanced by the calculation of several momentum indicators,
> each based on a different time span.

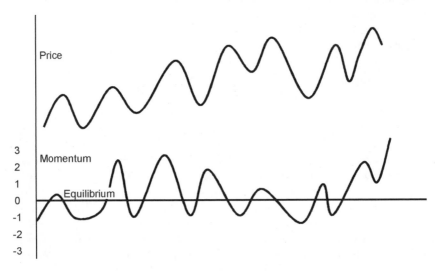

Figure 10-2   ROC using plus and minus scaling.

In this way, trendlines, price patterns, and divergences, which may not be
obvious in one period, are more apparent in another. The discovery of signs
of a trend reversal in several indicators constructed from different time
spans adds further fuel to the weight of the evidence. An example of this is
featured in Chart 10-1.

Principles and Applications of Momentum Indicators

The following description of the principles and use of momentum indicators applies to all forms of oscillators, whether constructed from an individual price series or from an indicator that measures internal market
momentum, such as those described in Chapter 24.

These principles can be roughly divided into two broad categories:

Chart 10-1   Long's Drugs, 1996–1997, and three ROCs. (*From www.pring.com.*)

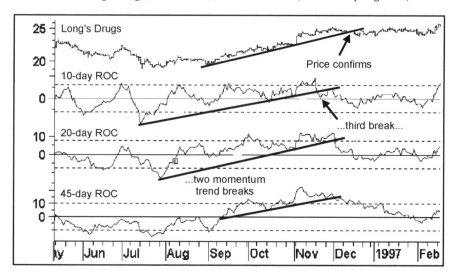

- **Those that deal with overbought and oversold conditions, divergences, and the like**   I will call these *momentum characteristics.* If you study momentum indicators or oscillators, you will find that they have certain characteristics that are associated with subsurface strengths or weaknesses in the underlying price trend. It is rather like looking under the hood of an engine. Most of the time you can identify mechanical trouble before it becomes self-evident. Momentum and sentiment are closely allied, and the relationship between them is discussed in Chapter 26, dealing with market sentiment.
- **The identification of trend reversals in the momentum indicator itself (momentum trend-reversal techniques)**   In this case, we are making the assumption that when a trend in momentum is reversed, prices will sooner or later follow.

Trend-determining techniques, such as trendline violations, MA crossovers, and so on, when applied to momentum are just as valid as when utilized with price. The difference, and it is an important one, is that a trend reversal in momentum is just that, a reversal in momentum. Momentum typically reverses along with price, often with a small lag, *but just because oscillators change direction doesn't always mean that prices will too.* Normally, a reversal in the momentum trend acts as confirming evidence of a price trend reversal signal. In effect, this momentum signal performs the act of supplementary "witness" in our weight of the evidence approach. I will have more to say on this one a little later, but for now take special note of the fact that *actual buy and sell signals can only come from a reversal in trend of the actual price, not the momentum series.*

Interpreting Momentum Characteristics

Overbought and Oversold Levels

Perhaps the most widely used method of momentum interpretation is the evaluation of overbought and oversold levels. This concept can be compared to a person taking an unruly dog for a walk. The leash is continually being pulled from one side of the person to the other as the dog struggles to get free. Despite all its activity, however, the dog can move no farther away than the length of the leash.

The same principle holds true for momentum indicators in the marketplace, except that the market's "leash" should be thought of as made of rubber, so that it is possible for particularly strong or weak price trends to extend beyond the normal limits known as *overbought* and *oversold* levels. These areas are drawn on a chart at some distance above and below the equilibrium level, as in Fig. 10-3. The actual boundaries will depend on the volatility of the price being monitored and the time period over which the momentum indicator has been constructed.

For example, an ROC indicator has a tendency to move to wider extremes over a longer period than over a shorter one. It is highly unlikely that a price

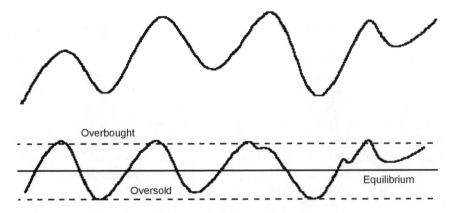

Figure 10-3 Overbought and oversold zones.

will move 10 percent over a 10-day period; yet over the course of a primary bull market extending over a 12-month period, a 25-percent increase would not be uncommon. Some indicators, such as RSI and stochastics, have been specially constructed to move within definite predetermined boundaries.

When a price reaches an overbought or oversold extreme, the probabilities favor but by no means guarantee a reversal. An overbought reading is a time to be thinking about selling, and an oversold one warns that the current technical position may warrant a purchase. In many cases when a price reaches an overbought extreme, the news is good, participants are optimistic, and human nature tells us to buy. Unfortunately, the opposite is more likely to be the case. On the other hand, an oversold reading is usually associated with a negative news background. The last thing we want to do is raise our shaking hand, pick up the phone, call our friendly broker, and tell him or her to buy, but that is often a reasonable time to do it, provided the overall technical position is favorable.

In view of the variability of indicators such as the ROC, there is no hard and fast rule about where the overbought and oversold lines should be drawn. This can be determined only by studying the history and characteristics of the security being monitored. The lines should be drawn such that they will act as pivotal points that, when touched or slightly exceeded, are followed by a reversal in the oscillator. When a particularly sharp price movement takes place, these boundaries will become totally ineffective. Unfortunately, this is a fact of life, but by and large it is usually possible to construct overbought and oversold benchmarks that are price-sensitive. Again, the market leash is made of rubber and can remain in overbought or oversold territory for long periods. Consequently, it is essential to get confirmation from a reversal in the trend of the price itself before taking any drastic action.

Oscillator Characteristics in Primary Bull and Bear Markets

I mentioned much earlier that the character of an oscillator alters according to the price environment. In a bull market, oscillators tend to move into an overbought condition very quickly and stay there a long time. In a bear market, they can and do remain in an oversold condition for considerable periods.

In effect, an oscillator is not unlike a migrating bird in the Northern Hemisphere. I have divided the price action in Fig. 10-4 into a bear market, followed by a bull, and finally another bear market. As we enter the bear phase, the true range of the oscillator shifts to the south, in a similar way to a bird in the Northern Hemisphere migrating south to escape the cold northerly winter. Then, when the bull market starts, the oscillator's trading pattern migrates north again, just like the bird, finally shifting south again

> **Major Technical Principle**   Oscillators behave in different ways, depending on the direction of the primary trend.

as a new bear market begins. This is useful information in itself because if it is possible to draw parallel horizontal lines like these against an oscillator, it provides a valuable clue as to whether the prevailing primary trend is bullish or bearish.

The second point is that if you have an idea of the direction of the primary trend, you can anticipate what might come from a specific overbought or oversold reading. In a bull market, the price is extremely sensitive to an oversold condition. That means that when you are lucky enough to see one, look around for some confirming signals that the price is about to rally. An example might be the violation of a down trendline and so on. The reason for this sensitivity lies in the fact that the oversold reading very likely reflects an extreme in short-term sentiment. Market participants are focusing on the latest bad news and are using that as an excuse to sell. Because this is a bull market, they would be better served by remembering the positive long-term fundamentals that will soon emerge and by using this weakness as an opportunity to buy.

The same thing happens in reverse during a bear market. Traders are focused on bad news that sends the price down. Then some unexpectedly good news hits the wires and the price rallies. However, when it is fully

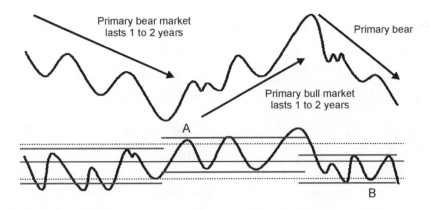

Figure 10-4   Changes in momentum characteristics in bull and bear markets.

digested, most people realize that things really have not changed at all, and the price declines again. Thus, the overbought reading more often than not will correspond with the top of a bear market rally.

Looking at it from another perspective, during a bull market the price will be far less sensitive to an overbought condition. Often it will be followed by a small decline or even a trading range, as at point *A* in Fig. 10-4. The rule then is do not count on a short-term overbought condition to trigger a big decline in a bull market because the odds do not favor it.

Finally, people often point to an oversold condition and use that as their rationale for a rally. Your favorite financial columnist might say, "Analysts point out that the market is deeply oversold and a snap back rally is expected." Once again, it very much depends on the environment. In a bull market, yes, that is true, but the columnist is more likely to say that "despite a short-term oversold condition, analysts are expecting lower prices because . . ." and then the columnist will go on to list a load of bearish factors justifying his or her position. Remember, as a general rule, the media reflect the crowd, which is usually wrong at turning points, and do not make accurate forecasts, especially when quoting "experts."

In a bear market, on the other hand, a market or stock is far less sensitive to an oversold reading, often failing to signal a rally or possibly being followed by a trading range, as at point *B* in Fig. 10-4.

The maturity of the trend, whether primary or intermediate, often has an effect on the limits that an oscillator might reach. For example, when a bull market has just begun, there is a far greater tendency for an oscillator to move quickly into overbought territory and to remain at very high readings for a considerable period of time. In such cases, the overbought readings tend to give premature warnings of declines. During the early phases of the bull cycle, when the market possesses strong momentum, reactions to the oversold level are much more responsive to price reversals, and such readings therefore offer more reliable signals. It is only when a bull trend is maturing, or during bear phases, that overbought levels can be relied upon to signal that a rally is shortly to be aborted. The very fact that an indicator is unable to remain at, or even to achieve, an overbought reading for a long period is itself a signal that the advance is losing momentum. The opposite is true for a bear trend.

Overbought and Oversold Crossovers

In most cases, excellent buy and sell alerts are generated when the momentum indicator exceeds its extended overbought or oversold boundary and then crosses back through the boundary on its way to zero. Figure 10-5 demonstrates this possibility. This approach filters out many premature buy

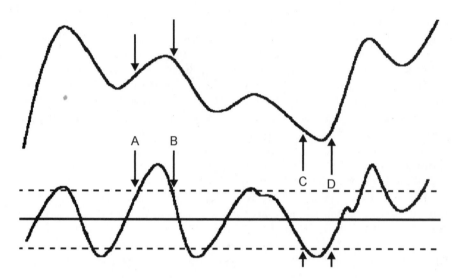

Figure 10-5   Overbought and oversold recrossovers.

and sell signals generated as the indicator just reaches its overextended boundary, but one should still wait for a trend reversal in the price itself before taking action.

Mega-Overboughts and Oversolds

As discussed in Chapter 26, there is a close connection between market sentiment indicators and the characteristics of oscillators. Since market sentiment differs widely during bull and bear markets, it follows that such mood swings are occasionally reflected in changing characteristics of momentum indicators. Observing these changing characteristics through short-term oscillators is one of the few techniques that enables us to identify primary trend reversals at an early stage.

As discussed in previous chapters, I have termed some of these phenomena *mega-overboughts* and *mega-oversolds*. A mega-overbought is the initial thrust in a bull market following the final bear market low. It is a reading in the momentum indicator well beyond the normal overbought condition witnessed in either the previous bull or bear market and should represent a multiyear high. Such conditions are usually a sign of a very young and vibrant bull market. The very fact that an oscillator is able to rally to such a high level can be used, along with other trend-reversal evidence, to signal that a new bull market has begun. It represents a sign that the balance between buyers and sellers has unequivocally shifted in favor of buyers. Think of a situation where a person uses all his or her strength to crash through a locked door. It takes a tremendous amount of energy to achieve, but once the door is finally shoved open, there is nothing to hold that person back any longer. In the same way, a mega-overbought removes the price from its bear market constraints, leaving it free to experience a new bull market. An example is shown in Fig. 10-6.

A mega-overbought is about the only instance when opening a long position from an overbought condition can be justified. Even so, it can only be rationalized by someone with a longer-term time horizon. This is due to the fact that whenever an oscillator experiences a mega-overbought, higher prices almost always follow after a short-term setback or consolidation has taken place. A highly leveraged trader may not be able to withstand the financial pressure or the countertrend move, whereas the long-term investor can. In most instances, you will probably find that the immediate correction following the mega-overbought is sideways, rather than downward, but there are just enough exceptions to trip up the overleveraged trader.

Since a mega-overbought condition is associated with the first rally in a bull market, it is a good idea to check and see if volume is also expanding. If it takes the form of record volume for that particular security, the signal is far louder, because record volume coming after a major decline is usually a reliable signal of a new bull market. Expanding volume is a more or less necessary condition since it is consistent with the idea that buyers now have the upper hand and that the psychology has totally reversed.

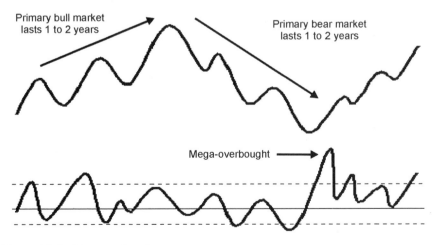

Figure 10-6 Mega-overbought.

Having said that, there are occasions when a mega-overbought condition is followed not by a reversal, but by a change in trend. In other words, the previous bear market emerges into a multiyear trading range rather than a full-fledged bull market. The point here is that the low preceding the mega-overbought is not normally decisively violated for many years.

The same concept also appears in reverse for oversold extremes. Consequently, when a price decline following a bull market high pushes a momentum indicator to a multiyear extreme low, well beyond anything witnessed either during the previous bull or bear market, the implication is that sellers now have the upper hand. The fact that it is possible for the momentum indicator to fall so sharply and so deeply is in itself a sign that the character of the market has changed. When you see this type of action, you should, at the very least, question the bull market scenario. Look for telltale signs that a new bear market may be underway. What are the volume configurations on the subsequent rally? Does volume now trend lower as the price rises compared to previous rallies that were associated with trends of rising volume?

The same possibilities of a change, as opposed to a reversal in trend, also apply in the sense that a mega-oversold is typically the first decline in a bear market, but occasionally it can also signal a change in trend from a primary bull market to a multiyear trading range. An example of a mega-oversold is shown in Fig. 10-7. Both mega-conditions are usually best observed in short-term oscillators ranging from 10 to as many as 30 days in a time span. They never develop from indicators whose construction constrains their fluctuations between 0 and 100, such as the RSI and stochastic indicators. Examples of a mega-overbought and a mega-oversold are shown in Chart 10-2.

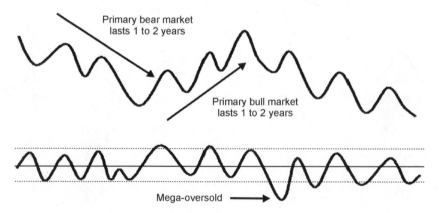

Figure 10-7   Mega-oversold.

Chart 10-2 Beckon Dickenson, 1981–1985, and a mega-overbought and oversold. (*From www.pring.com.*)

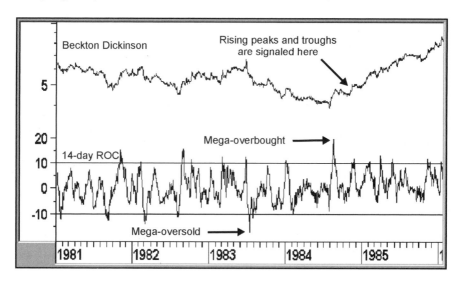

Extreme Swings

The extreme swing is another phenomenon that signals a dramatic shift in psychology. It reflects the idea that some primary trend reversals are signaled by a swing from unbelievable exuberance, as the bull market reaches its peak, to one of complete despondency and depression, as the first bear market setback gets under way. The opposite is true of a transition from a primary bear to a primary bull market. In order for an extreme swing to develop, it is necessary for the market to experience a prolonged up- or downtrend. The extreme swing then appears in a momentum indicator by an extremely strong move in the direction of the then-prevailing trend, as shown in Fig. 10-8. This is followed by an extreme reading in the opposite direction.

In Fig. 10-8, we see a exhaustion blowoff to the bull move as the oscillator reaches a very overbought reading. This is subsequently followed by a price decline that pushes it to the other extreme. Such action indicates a dramatic shift in sentiment as market participants change from a mood of euphoria to one of despondency as the security eventually reacts in the direction opposite to that originally expected.

In order to qualify for an extreme swing, the first swing must represent the strongest move in several years, certainly the strongest since the initial

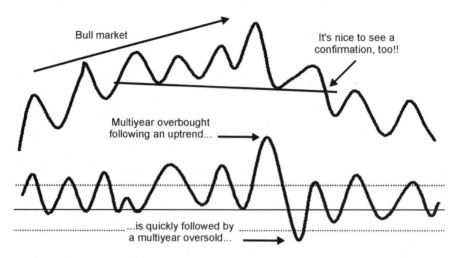

Figure 10-8   Bearish extreme swing.

thrust from the previous bear market bottom. It is really a climax move for the bull market. The second swing to the downside should really be a mega-oversold, though in some cases an extreme oversold will suffice.

This phenomenon is undoubtedly formed because the first swing encourages the participants who have been right about the prevailing trend and discourages those who have been wrong. In the case of a bull market, the final rally also squeezes out all of the remaining shorts, so when the trend reverses, there is virtually no buying activity from speculators covering short positions. The preceding sharp advance also encourages buyers who could see that there was only one way prices could go, and that was up. As a result, decisions on the buy side are made carelessly and without thought for the fact that prices may move the other way. When they do, such individuals are flushed out of the market with no quarter given. Since there are few short sellers able to pick up the pieces, the price drops ferociously.

Extreme swings also develop between a bear and bull primary trend, as featured in Fig. 10-9. In this case though, the mood swing is from total despondency and depression as the bear market squeezes out the last of the bulls from the sharp and persistent downtrend. Even the strongest bulls are forced to capitulate and eventually there is no one left to sell. Then during the rally phase, the shorts are forced to cover and new buying comes in because of the perceived improvement in the fundamentals. Since there is virtually no one left to sell, prices shoot up, and a mega- or extreme over-bought is registered.

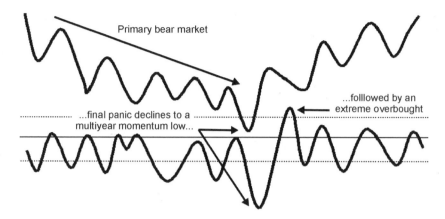

Figure 10-9 Bullish extreme swing.

Needless to say, extreme swings are quite unusual, but when you can spot them, it really pays to follow their lead since a new trend invariably results. An example of a bullish extreme swing is shown in Chart 10-3 featuring VF Corp.

Divergences

The ball example used at the beginning of the chapter showed that maximum velocity was obtained fairly close to the point at which the ball leaves the hand. Similarly, prices in financial markets usually reach their maximum level of momentum ahead of the final peak in prices. In Fig. 10-10, this is shown at point *A*. If the price makes a new high, which is confirmed by the momentum index, no indication of technical weakness arises. On the other hand, if momentum fails to confirm (point *B*), a *negative* divergence is set up between the two series, and a warning of a weakening technical structure is given. Such discrepancies normally indicate that the price will undergo a corrective process. It can take the form of either a sideways or a horizontal trading range, or (more likely) a downward one. However, the price will sometimes continue upward to a third top and be accompanied by even greater weakness in the momentum index (point *C*). Occasionally, the third peak in the momentum index may be higher than the second, but lower than the first. Either circumstance requires some degree of caution, since this characteristic is a distinct warning of a sharp reversal in price or a long corrective period.

Chart 10-3   VF Corp., 1989–1993, and a positive extreme swing. (*From www.pring.com.*)

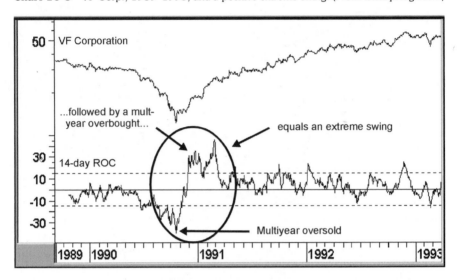

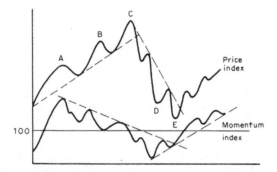

Figure 10-10   Momentum and divergences.

Major Technical Principle   It is extremely important to note that divergences only warn of a weakening or strengthening technical condition and do not represent actual buy and sell signals.

Figure 10-10 also shows a *positive divergence*. In this instance, the price makes its low at point *E*, but this is preceded by the oscillator that bottomed at *D*.

Whenever any divergence between momentum and price occurs, it is essential to wait for a confirmation from the price itself that its trend has also been reversed. This confirmation can be achieved by (1) the violation of a simple trendline, as shown in Fig. 10-10, (2) the crossover of an MA, or (3) the completion of a price pattern or (4) a reversal in peak/trough progression. This form of insurance is well worth taking, since it is not unknown for a security to continually lose and regain momentum without suffering a break in trend during a long cyclical advance. Examples of this phenomenon occurred during the 1990's bull market in U.S. stocks and in Japanese stocks between 1982 and 1990.

A good example can be seen in Chart 10-4, which shows the Nikkei Dow violating an important $3^1/_2$-year secondary trendline after the 13-week ROC indicator had negatively diverged several times with the index. As a result, the final rally was accompanied by very little upside momentum. It would have been a mistake to sell on any of the prior divergences, but a very timely sell signal was generated by waiting for a confirmation in the form of a trend break in the index itself.

At point *C* in Fig. 10-11, the price moves to a significant new high, but the momentum indicator is barely able to remain above the equilibrium line. Such a situation demands the utmost caution *when accompanied by a trend break,* because it is usually a sign of extreme technical weakness and is often, though certainly not always, followed by an above average decline. The opposite type of situation (see Fig. 10-12) in a bear market should be viewed as a very positive characteristic, especially if the upward trend break in price is accompanied by high volume. The more explosive the volume, the more reliable the signal.

In a sense, it is possible to equate momentum divergences and price trend breaks with dark clouds and rain. If you look up at the sky and observe dark clouds, common sense tells you that it will probably rain, but you do not know for sure until you can hold out your hand and actually feel rain falling. In other words, the clouds (like the divergences) warn of the deteriorating

---

Major Technical Principle   As a general rule, the greater the number of negative divergences, the weaker the underlying structure and vice versa.

Chart 10-4 Nikkei, 1985–1990, and negative divergences. At the 1990 peak, the Nikkei experienced numerous divergences with its 13-week ROC. They were confirmed when the price eventually violated its 1986–90 up trendline and later on crossed below its 65-week exponential moving average (EMA). These negative divergences took place over a 3-year period so it was not surprising that the Nikkei experienced a major bear market following this event. (*From www.pring.com.*)

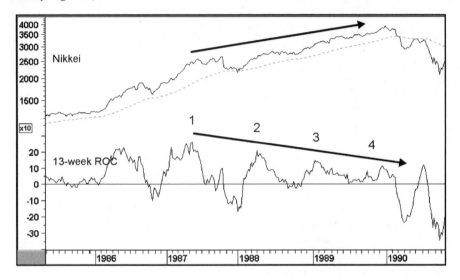

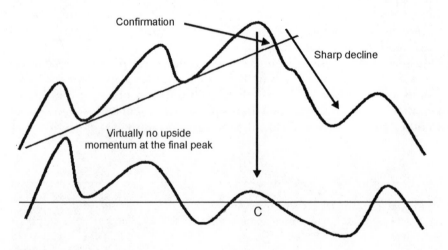

Figure 10-11 Extreme bearish divergence.

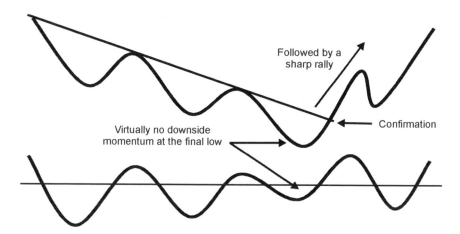

Figure 10-12   Extreme bullish divergence.

Major Technical Principle   A divergence that develops close to the equilibrium line is often followed by a sharp price move.

---

weather (technical condition), but the change in weather is signaled only by the first raindrop (reversal in the price). It is possible to take the analogy a step further by concluding that the darker the clouds (the greater the number of divergences), the heavier the rainstorm (the sharper the price decline).

Price Discrepancy Divergences

A further indication of subtle strength or weakness is given when the momentum series moves strongly in one direction, but the accompanying move in the price index is a much smaller one. Such a development suggests that the security is tired of moving in the direction of the prevailing trend, because despite a strong push of energy from the oscillator, prices are unable to respond. This unusual but powerful phenomenon is illustrated for both tops and bottoms in Figs. 10-13 and 10-14.

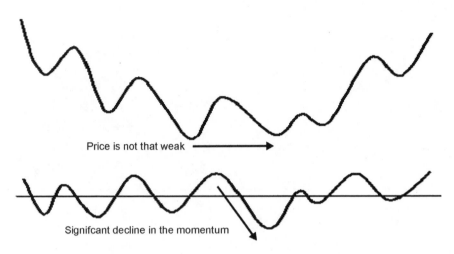

Price is not that weak ⟶

Signifcant decline in the momentum

Figure 10-13   Bullish price discrepancy divergence.

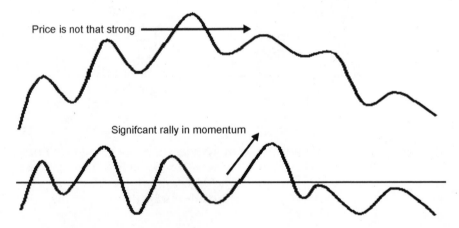

Price is not that strong ⟶

Signifcant rally in momentum

Figure 10-14   Bearish price discrepancy divergence.

Complex Divergences

It is widely recognized that price movements are simultaneously influenced by several cyclic phenomena. Because a single momentum indicator can monitor only one of these cycles, it is always a good idea to compare several different momentum indicators based on differing time spans.

One approach is to plot two momentum indicators of differing time spans on the same chart, as shown in Fig. 10-15. Since this method tries to monitor two separate cycles, it is just as well to choose two widely different time spans. For example, not much could be gained from the comparison of 12- and 13-week ROCs since they would move very closely together. On the other hand, comparing 13- and 26-week spans would clearly reflect different cycles.

Most of the time, the two indicators are moving in gear, so this study does not give us much information. On the other hand, when the longer-term indicator reaches a new peak and the shorter one is at or close to the equilibrium line, they are clearly in disagreement or out of gear (see point A_2 in Fig. 10-15). This normally, but not necessarily, indicates that a reversal in trend will take place, and it is usually a significant one. Even so, it is very important to make sure that any such divergence is confirmed by a reversal in the price trend itself. In Fig. 10-15, a trend break does occur, but in Fig. 10-16, no reversal takes place and the price continues upward.

Complex divergences also occur in a positive combination, as indicated at point B_1 in Fig. 10-15, but again, it is mandatory to wait for that trend-reversal signal in the price itself.

An example in Chart 10-5 features Lowe's using 20- and 45-day ROCs. The 45-day series makes its bottom in January of 1995, but by that time the 20-day series is already around zero. Soon after, the price confirms this divergence by rallying above a small resistance trendline.

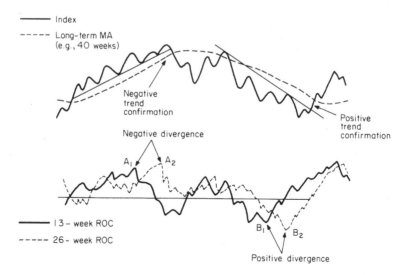

Figure 10-15 Complex divergence.

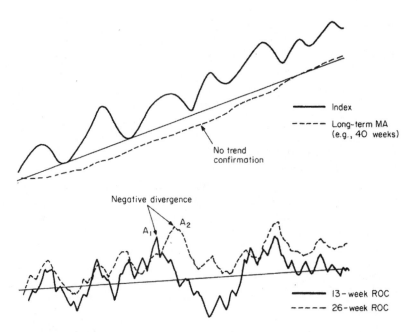

Figure 10-16   Complex divergence with nonconfirmation.

Chart 10-5   Lowe's, 1994–1995, and a complex divergence. (*From www.pring.com.*)

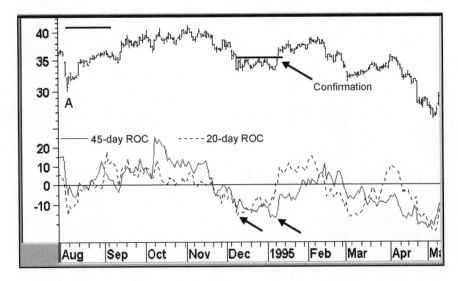

Momentum Trend-Reversal Techniques

Trendline Violations

Occasionally, it is possible to construct a trendline on the momentum indicator by connecting a series of peaks or troughs. An example of an uptrend reversal is shown in Fig. 10-17. When the line is violated, a trend-reversal signal for the oscillator is generated.

The construction and significance of the break should be based on the principles outlined in Chapter 8. This type of momentum weakness must be regarded as an alert, and action should be taken only when confirmed by a break in the price trend itself (indicated at point *AA* in Fig. 10-17). In effect, the momentum trend break is reinforcing the price trend break and offers an additional piece of evidence that the trend has reversed.

An example signaling a new uptrend is featured in Fig. 10-18. It is possible for the momentum trend break to precede that of the price by some time, yet it does not generally lose its potency because of this.

Major Technical Principle When the trendlines for the oscillator and price are violated simultaneously, the signal is usually stronger.

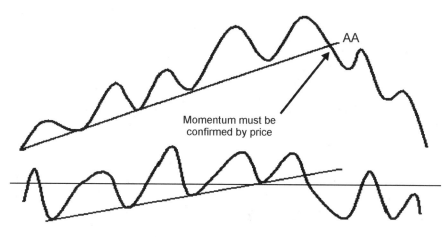

Figure 10-17 Bearish momentum trend break.

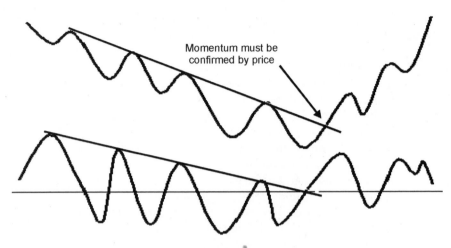

Figure 10-18 Bullish momentum trend break.

It should also be noted that momentum trendline breaks can be confirmed by any legitimate trend-reversal technique in the price, be it an MA crossover, a price pattern or peak-trough progression reversal, and so on. Of all the methods of momentum interpretation, the joint trendline violation technique is one of the simplest and without doubt one of the most effective.

Momentum Price Patterns

Momentum indicators are also capable of tracing out price patterns. Because of the shorter lead times normally associated with reversals of falling momentum, a breakout from an accumulation pattern, when accompanied by a reversal in the downward trend of the price itself, is usually a highly reliable indication that a worthwhile move has just begun. An example is shown in Fig. 10-19 and Chart 10-6.

It is important to use a little common sense in interpreting momentum price patterns. Figure 10-20, for example, shows a breakout from a reverse *head-and-shoulders* (H&S) pattern that takes place as a result of an overbought condition. This is not to say that such signals will never be valid, but it stands to reason that a breakout from an extreme level is very unlikely to result in a sustainable price move. Remember, *technical analysis deals with probabilities*, and the odds of a favorable outcome in this case are low.

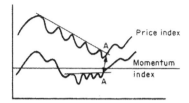

Figure 10-19   Momentum price pattern completion.

Chart 10-6   Alcoa, 1999–2000, and momentum price patterns. This chart features Alcoa with a 10-day ROC. Note how a reverse H&S in the 10-day ROC was completed just before the price broke a nice trendline to the upside. Adding to the significance of the signal was the fact that the price crossed above its MA more or less simultaneously with the trendline violation. Since both the line and the MA represent resistance, the breakout offered two pieces of evidence that the trend had reversed. As soon as the ROC had broken out, it began to form an H&S top. The break from this momentum distribution pattern was then confirmed by the price violating a small up trendline. (*From www.pring.com.*)

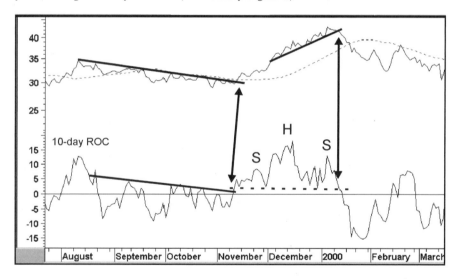

Equilibrium Crossovers

Some technicians have devised indicators that offer buy and sell signals when the momentum indicator crosses above and below its equilibrium or zero line. Many markets do not lend themselves to this approach, so its implementation depends very much on a trial and error basis through

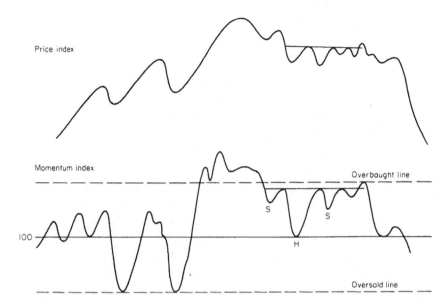

Figure 10-20   Overbought momentum pattern completion.

experimentation. In any event, it is always a good idea to use this method in conjunction with a reversal in the price itself. Chart 10-7 shows how zero 12-month ROC crossovers, used in conjunction with 12-month MA crossovers, have consistently given reliable buy signals for the Economist All Items Commodity Index. The two sets of ellipses point out few whipsaw signals.

Momentum and MAs

By now, it is apparent that all the trend-determining techniques used for price are also applicable to momentum. The interpretation of oscillators, as described previously, depends to a considerable extent on judgment. One method of reducing this subjectivity is to smooth the ROC index by using an MA. Warnings of a probable trend reversal in the price being monitored are offered by momentum MA crossovers, as indicated in Fig. 10-21.

One of the problems associated with this approach is that the momentum indicator is often much more jagged than the price index that it is trying to measure, causing an unacceptable number of whipsaw signals. It is possible to filter out some of these whipsaws by using a combination of two MAs, as shown in Fig. 10-22. Buy and sell alerts are given when the shorter-term MA crosses above or below its longer-term counterpart.

Chart 10-7 The Economist Commodity Index, 1968–2001, and zero crossovers. (*From www.pring.com.*)

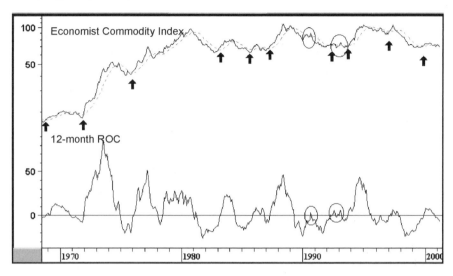

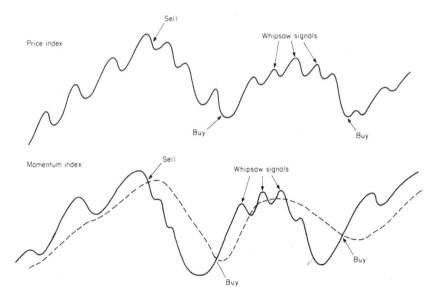

Figure 10-21 MA crossovers.

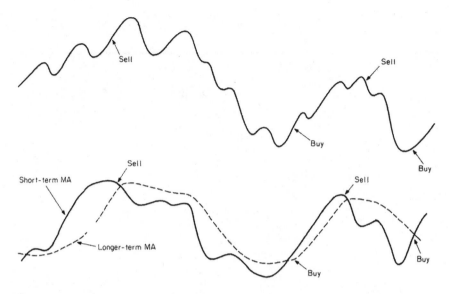

Figure 10-22   MA crossovers smoothed.

This concept of momentum is explained in greater detail in the next chapter, since smoothed momentum forms the basis of the trend deviation and MACD indicators.

Smoothed Momentum Indicators

Another way of incorporating MAs into momentum studies is to smooth the momentum indicator by a long-term MA. The meaning of long-term in this case will depend on the type of trend being monitored. For example, a 20- to 30-day time span would be suitable for a short-term price movement, but a 6-, 9-, or 12-month smoothing, or one even longer, is more appropriate for a primary trend. Warnings of a probable trend reversal in the price would be offered by a reversal in the smoothed momentum index itself, as shown in Fig. 10-23(a), or by a penetration of the MA through a designated over-bought or oversold level, as in Fig. 10-23(b). The level of the dashed over-bought and oversold barrier would be determined on a trial and error basis, with reference to a historical study of the relationship between the price and the momentum curve.

If the momentum curve is found to be unduly volatile, it is always possi-ble to smooth out fluctuations by calculating an even longer-term MA or by

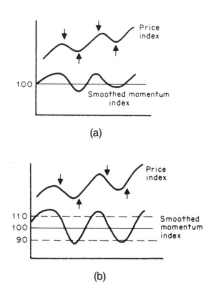

Figure 10-23 (a) Directional changes of smoothed momentum MAs. (b) Overbought/over-sold recrossovers of smoothed momentum MAs.

smoothing the MA itself with an additional calculation. Another possibility is to construct an oscillator by combining the MAs of three or four ROCs and weighting them according to their time span. This possibility is discussed at length in Chapter 12.

Chart 10-8 shows the effectiveness of combining two smoothed ROC indicators. In this case, the smoothing is a 10-month weighted average of 11- and 14-month ROCs of the S&P Composite monthly closing prices. Since this indicator has been found useful for market bottoms rather than tops, the momentum curve is significant only when it falls below the zero reference line and then rises. The arrows show that bull market signals between 1960 and 2000 were particularly timely. The ellipse represents a signal where the indicator was timely, although in this case it did not drop below zero. I have traced this indicator back to 1900 and found that very few whipsaws were triggered. These could have been eliminated by waiting for a 12-month MA crossover as confirmation. Clearly, this is an excellent track record (derived from an approach discovered by E.S.C. Coppock).

A further variation on the construction of a smoothed momentum index is to take the ROC of an MA of a price index itself. This method reverses the process described previously, because instead of constructing an ROC

Chart 10-8 S&P Composite and the Coppock Indicator, 1960–2001. (*From www.pring.com.*)

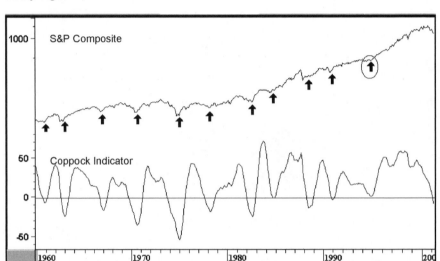

and then smoothing the resulting momentum index, the price index itself is first smoothed with an MA, and an ROC is taken of that smoothing.

Summary

- *Momentum* is a generic term embracing many different types of oscillators.
- Momentum measures the rate at which prices rise or fall and gives useful indications of latent strength or weakness in a price trend. This is because prices usually rise at their fastest pace well ahead of their peak and normally decline at their greatest speed before their ultimate low.
- Since markets generally spend more time in a rising than a falling phase, the lead characteristic of momentum indicators is normally greater during rallies than during reactions.
- Oscillators reflect market sentiment and have different charactersistics in primary bull and bear markets.
- There are two basic methods of interpreting momentum: momentum characteristics and momentum trend reversal.
- Momentum signals should *always* be used in conjunction with a trend-reversal signal by the actual price.

11

Individual Momentum Indicators I

In this and the next chapter, several specific momentum indicators will be examined. It is recommended that you study them all and then choose three or four in which you have confidence and with which you feel intuitively comfortable. Following too many indicators usually leads to confusion.

Relative Strength Indicator

The Formula

The relative strength indicator (RSI) was developed by Welles Wilder.[1] It is a momentum indicator, or oscillator, that measures the relative internal strength of a security against *itself*. This should not be confused with comparative relative strength, which compares the performance of one security to another. The formula for the RSI is as follows:

$$RSI = 100 - \frac{100}{1 + RS}$$

$$RSI = \frac{\text{average of } x \text{ days' up closes}}{\text{average of } x \text{ days' down closes}}$$

[1]Wells Wilder, *New Concepts in Technical Trading Systems*, Trend Research, Greensboro, NC, 1978.

211

where RS = the average of *x* days' up closes divided by the average of *x* days' down closes. The formula aims to overcome two problems involved in the construction of a momentum indicator: (1) erratic movements and (2) the need for a constant trading band for comparison purposes. Erratic movements are caused by sharp alterations in the values, which are dropped off in the calculation. For example, in a 20-day rate of change (ROC) indicator, a sharp decline or advance 20 days in the past can cause sudden shifts in the momentum line even if the current price is little changed. The RSI attempts to smooth out such distortions.

The RSI formula not only provides this smoothing characteristic, but also results in an indicator that fluctuates in a constant range between 0 and 100. The default time span recommended by Wilder is 14 days, which he justified on the basis that it was half of the 28-day lunar cycle.

The RSI Enables Comparisons Between Securities

The nature of the RSI calculation enables the accurate comparison of different securities on the same chart. In Chart 11-1, there are two series, the Dow Jones Utilities Index and the Philadelphia Gold and Silver Share Index. The upper panel plots a 45-day ROC and the lower one a 45-day RSI. With the ROC, it is not easily possible to compare the two because the Utilities Index is far less volatile. On the other hand, you can see that the divergence in volatility is far less. Because of this, it is much easier to establish universal standards for the overbought and oversold benchmarks. Using the 14-day default, these levels are traditionally set at 30 for oversold and 70 for overbought.

Constructing Overbought/Oversold Lines

The default time span for the calculation of an RSI is 14 periods. The overbought and oversold lines are typically drawn at 70 and 30, respectively. In an article entitled "How The RSI Behaves,"[2] Peter W. Aan argued that the average value of an RSI top and bottom occurred close to the 72 and 32 levels, respectively. This research would indicate that the 70 and 30 levels recommended by Wilder should be moved farther apart to better reflect the average overbought and oversold values.

It is important to note that the magnitude of the oscillations of the RSI is inverse to that of most other momentum series. For example, the ROC indicator is subject to wider fluctuations the longer the time span. It works

[2] *Futures,* January 1985.

Chart 11-1   RSI versus the ROC. (*From www.pring.com.*)

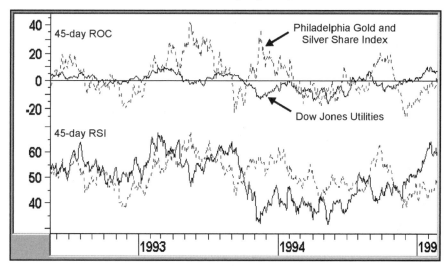

in an opposite way for the RSI. For the RSI, equilibrium is the halfway point, which in this case is the 50 level. It is therefore traditional to place the overbought and oversold lines equidistant from this point.

We should remember that longer time spans in the RSI calculation result in shallower swings and vice versa. Consequently, the 70/30 combination is inappropriate when the time span differs appreciably in either direction from the standard 14-day period. Chart 11-2, for example, features a 14-day RSI for the Eurodollar for which an 80/20 combination gives a much better feel for the overbought/oversold extreme than the 70/30 default value. This is due to the fact that shorter time spans result in wider RSI oscillations. The lower panel features a 65-day RSI in which the narrower swings result in a more appropriate 65/35 combination. In this instance, neither of the default 70/30 values is reached at any time.

The terms *long* and *short time spans* refer to the type of data under consideration in a relative sense. For example, a 60-day RSI would represent a long span for daily data, but for monthly numbers, a 60-day (2-month) span

Major Technical Principle   The longer the time span, the narrower the RSI overbought and oversold lines should be constructed and vice versa.

Chart 11-2   Eurodollar, 1994–1997, RSI overbought/oversold lines. (*From www.pring.com.*)

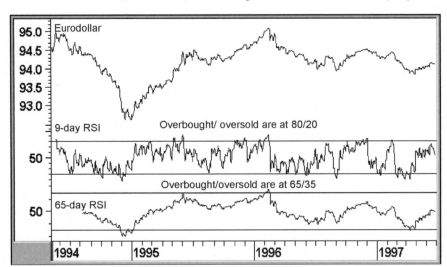

would be very short. Some consideration should therefore be given to this factor when the choice of a specific RSI time span is being made. Chart 11-3 plots two RSIs for identical time periods (60 days or 3 months). However, the overbought and oversold lines are drawn at different levels because one calculation is based on daily and the other on monthly data.

Because RSIs based on shorter-term time spans experience greater volatility, they are more suitable for pointing out overbought and oversold conditions. On the other hand, longer-term spans are more stable in their trajectories and therefore lend themselves better to the purpose of constructing trendlines and price patterns.

Time Spans

The RSI can be plotted for any time span. In his book *New Commodity Trading Systems,* Perry Kaufman questions the exclusivity of the 14-day time span selection (the default for most charting packages). He points out that maximum divergence occurs when the *moving average* (MA) is exactly half the time span of the dominant cycle. In other words, if you make the assumption that the primary trend of the stock market revolves around the 4-year business cycle, an MA of 24 months will give you the greatest divergence between the high and low points of the cycle. In the case of the 28-day cycle, 14 days is the correct choice, but it is important to understand that there

Chart 11-3 RSI comparing time frames. (*From www.pring.com.*)

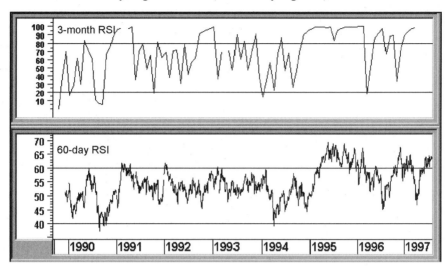

are many other cycles apart from the lunar cycle. Working on this assumption, for example, would mean that a 14-hour RSI would be inappropriate if the dominant cycle was something other than 28 hours. The same would be true for weekly and monthly data.

In practice, a 14-day time span works quite well, but only for shorter periods. I also use 9-, 25-, 30-, and 45-day spans. For weekly data, the calendar quarters operate effectively, so 13-, 26-, 39-, and 52-week spans are adopted. As for monthly charts, the same recommended spans for the ROC are also suitable for the RSI, that is, 9, 12, 18, and 24 months.

For longer-term charts, covering perhaps 2 years of weekly data, a time span of about 8 weeks offers enough information to identify intermediate-term turning points. A 26-week RSI results in a momentum series that oscillates in a narrower range, but nevertheless usually lends itself to trendline construction. Very long term charts, going back 10 to 20 years, seem to respond well to a 12-month time span. Crossovers of the 30 percent oversold and 70 percent overbought barriers provide a very good indication of major long-term buying and selling points. When the RSI pushes through these extremes and then crosses back toward the 50 level, it often warns of a reversal in the primary trend.

To isolate major buy candidates, it is important to remember that the best opportunities lie where long-term momentum, such as a 12-month RSI, is oversold. If you can also identify an intermediate- and a short-term oversold condition, all three trends, primary, intermediate-term, and short-term, are then in a classic conjunction to give a high-probability buy signal.

RSI Interpretation

Extreme Readings and Failure Swings   Any time an RSI moves above its overbought zone or below its oversold zone, it indicates that the security in question is ripe for a turn. The significance depends upon the time frame under consideration. For example, an overbought reading in a 14-day RSI, as shown in Chart 11-4, is nowhere near as significant as an RSI constructed with a 12-month time span, as in Chart 11-5. An overbought or oversold reading merely indicates that, in terms of probabilities, a counterreaction is overdone or overdue. It presents an *opportunity* to consider liquidation or acquisition, but not an *actual* buy or sell signal. This can come *only* when the price series itself gives a trend-reversal signal.

For instance, in Chart 11-6 featuring Centura Banks, the overbought reading in June 2000 was confirmed by a nice trend break in the price, as was the oversold reading that had previously been registered in February. Compare this to the December 1999 oversold reading that was not confirmed by a price break and did not generate any meaningful rally.

More often than not, the RSI traces out a divergence, as indicated in Fig. 11-1. In this case, the second crossover of the extreme level at points *A* and

Chart 11-4   German Bunds, 1995–1996, RSI and trendlines. (*From www.pring.com.*)

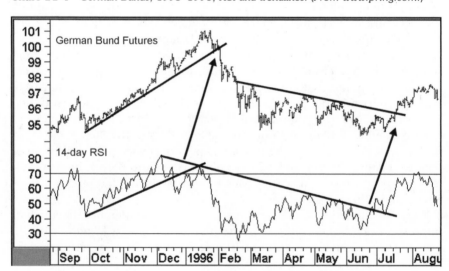

Chart 11-5   Spot Nickel, 1981–2001, RSI, trendlines, failure swings, and extreme crossovers. (*From www.pring.com.*)

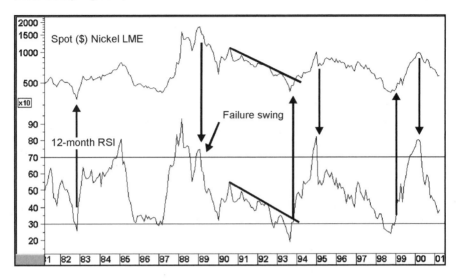

Chart 11-6   Centura Banks, 1999–2000 RSI, trendlines, and price patterns. (*From www.pring.com.*)

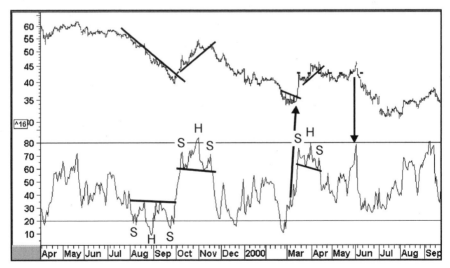

B usually offers good buy and sell alerts. These divergences are often called *failure swings*. Chart 11-7 shows an example of a bullish failure swing for J.P. Morgan in October 2000. Chart 11-5 shows a longer-term failure swing for Spot Nickel.

Trendline Violations and Pattern Completions   The RSI can also be used in conjunction with trendline violations. Generally speaking, the longer the time span for any particular period (daily, weekly, or monthly), the better the opportunity for trendline construction. Important buy and sell signals are generated when trendlines for both price *and* the RSI are violated within a relatively short period (refer to Chart 11-4). An example of the RSI's capability to form price patterns is shown in Chart 11-6, where we see three situations in which it traced out a *head-and-shoulders* (H&S) formation. Each one was confirmed by a trend break in the price. Note how the inverse pattern, formed in the summer of 1999, involved several false oversold crossover buy signals. However, it was not until the pattern was completed that the price confirmed any of this by rallying above its 3-month down trendline.

Smoothing the RSI   It is a perfectly legitimate technique to smooth the RSI. One of my favorite approaches is to smooth a 9-day RSI with an 8-day MA. Because the fluctuations are not as great as the raw data, the overbought and oversold lines are drawn at 70 and 30, not at my usual default of 80/20 for a 9-day span.

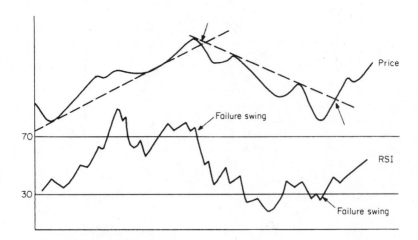

Figure 11-1   RSI failure swings.

Chart 11-7 J.P. Morgan, 2000–2001, RSI, trendlines, and failure swings. This chart shows a 14-day RSI for J.P. Morgan. Note the two trendline violations that signaled declines in September 2000 and February 2001. Also, there was a bullish failure swing at the October low. It's true that the price confirmed with a trendline violation, but the trendline was not that impressive since it was quite steep and was only touched by one rally. Little wonder that the stock needed to test the low again before taking off to the upside. (*From www.pring.com.*)

Chart 11-8 features such an indicator plotted inversely with the 30-year yield to correspond with movements in bond prices. This smoothing technique is very useful from the point of view of flagging reversals when the indicator moves beyond its normal overbought and oversold extremes. The dashed arrows point to changes in trends signaled by the RSI moving to an extreme, but where no reasonable price confirmation was given. The solid arrows show the three instances where the overbought and oversold extremes were confirmed with price trend breaks. This form of interpretation works pretty well except in periods experiencing strong linear up- or downtrends.

Application to Peak-and-Trough Progression

The RSI often traces out a series of rising or falling peaks and troughs, which, when reversed, offer important buy or sell alerts. Chart 11-9 shows that the 14-day RSI for SunTrust Banks experienced two peak-and-trough reversals, each of which was confirmed by a price trend break. These are flagged by the arrows.

Chart 11-8 30-year Government Yield, 1998–2001, RSI and overbought and oversold crossovers. (*From www.pring.com.*)

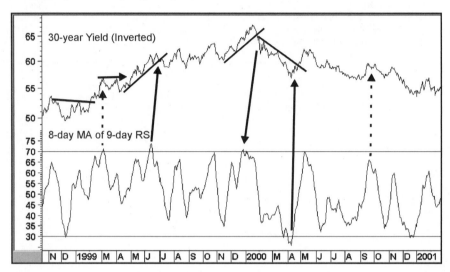

Chart 11-9 SunTrust Banks' 1997 RSI and peak-and-trough analysis. (*From www.pring.com.*)

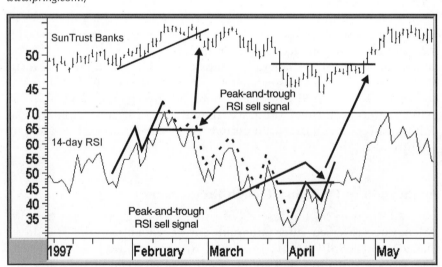

Two Variations on the RSI

Chaunde Momentum Oscillator

The Chande momentum oscillator (CMO), named after its inventor, Dr. Tushar Chande, is a variation on the RSI, yet is uniquely different. It has three characteristics:

- The calculations are based on data that have not been smoothed. This means that extreme short-term movements are not hidden, so the indicator reaches overbought and oversold extremes more often, but not enough to result in too many signals.
- The scale is confined within the −100 to +100 range. This means that the zero level becomes the equilibrium point. With the RSI, the 50 level is the equilibrium point and is not always readily identifiable. With zero as the pivotal point, it is easier to see those periods when momentum is positive, and those when it is negative. The zero equilibrium therefore makes comparisons between different securities that much easier.
- The formula uses both up and down days in the calculation.

Interpretation

Chart 11-10 compares a 14-day RSI with a 14-day CMO. The first thing to notice is that the CMO reaches an overbought and oversold extreme more times than the RSI, such as in February and June 2000 and in January 2001. Sometimes it is possible to construct more timely and better trendlines for the CMO, though occasionally it works the other way. The March 2000 break, for instance, came off as a better trendline for the CMO than the RSI; so too did the breaks from trendlines AB and CD. The two trendlines in the summer of 2000 were slightly better for the RSI. Note also that both series experienced positive divergences at the October 2000 low, but the one for the CMO was a much stronger signal since the September bottom was well above that of mid-October. It does not always work in favor of the CMO, but I prefer this indicator because of the more numerous overbought and oversold readings, and the plus and minus scaling, which makes it easier to spot positive and negative readings.

One approach that I have found helpful is to plot a 20-day CMO and smooth it with a 10-day MA, such as that plotted in Chart 11-11. I then take a smoothing of this indicator, in this case a 10-day simple MA, the dashed line that hugs the CMO. MA crossovers are then used to generate buy and sell alerts. However, since there are numerous crossovers, it is important to make an attempt at filtering out those that are not likely to work out by only

Chart 11-10 FTSE, 2000–2001, comparing the RSI with the CMO. (*From www.pring.com.*)

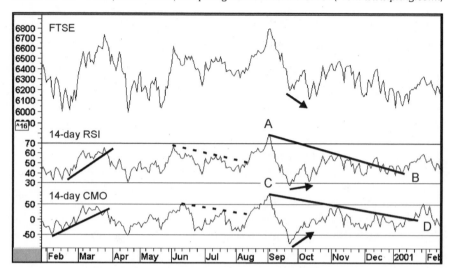

using those that develop at an extreme level in view of the fact that they tend to be more accurate. This should then be confirmed by a trend break in the price itself. Some examples are shown in Chart 11-11.

Relative Momentum Index

The relative momentum index, or RMI as it is known, is another variation on the RSI. In the calculation of the RMI, the standard RSI formula is modified to allow for a momentum factor. This indicator first came to my attention as an article in the February 1993 *Stocks and Commodities* magazine by Roger Altman.

This modification has two effects. First, it smooths the indicator and, second, it accentuates the degree of the fluctuation. The result is a less jagged oscillator that experiences more overbought and oversold readings. The RMI requires two parameters: the time frame and the momentum factor.

If the RMI has a momentum factor of 1, the indicator is identical to the RSI. It is only when the momentum factor is greater than 1 that the two series diverge.

Chart 11-12 shows two variations on the RMI. The middle panel features a 14-day span with an 8-day momentum factor, and the lower one a 45-day

Chart 11-11 Hang Seng's 1998–2000 smoothed CMO.

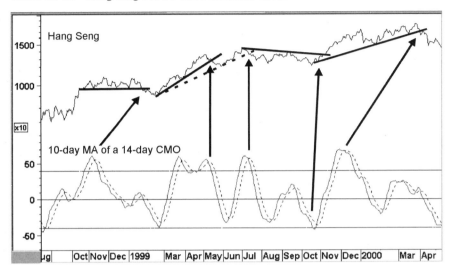

span with a 10-day momentum factor. Since it is an RSI-based indicator, longer-term spans involve less volatility. Note that the fluctuations in the 45-day series are much less pronounced than the 14-day RMI.

Generally speaking, the longer-term span offers slower and more deliberate movements that lend themselves more easily to trendline construction. Several examples are shown in Chart 11-12. I particularly like the late 1998 signal since it is confirmed by a simultaneous breakout above the trendline and the 200-day MA. Whenever a price crosses above a trendline and a reliable MA at the same time, it emphasizes the strength of the signal since they reinforce each other as dynamic resistance areas.

RSI Conclusion

Most of the time, the RSI and its two variations, like all oscillators, do not tell us very much. The RSI can be really useful when it triggers divergences, completes price patterns, or violates trendlines. When such an occurrence is *also* confirmed by a trend-reversal signal in the price itself, it is usually a wise policy to pay attention, because the RSI has a good record of reliability.

Chart 11-12   AT&T, 1996–2001, two RMI variations. (*From www.pring.com.*)

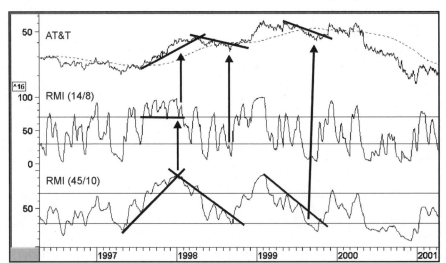

Trend Deviation (Price Oscillator)

A trend-deviation indicator is obtained by dividing or subtracting a security's price by a measure of trend, which is usually a form of MA. It is also possible to base a trend deviation using linear regression techniques. However, we will concentrate on the MA method here. This approach is also called a *price oscillator* in some charting packages. There are two methods of calculation: subtraction and division. Division is preferred, since it is more reflective of proportionate moves. For a discussion of this topic, you are referred to Chapter 5 and Chapter 8, which compare logarithmic and arithmetic scales.

Since the average represents the trend being monitored, this oscillator indicates how fast the price is advancing or declining in relation to that trend. An oscillator based on a trend-deviation calculation is, in fact, a horizontal representation of the envelope analysis discussed in Chapter 9, but in this graphic format, it also shows subtle changes of underlying technical strength and weakness.

Figures 11-2(*a*) and (*b*) show these two approaches for the same indicator. The upper and lower envelopes are both drawn at a level that is 10 percent from the actual MA, which means that when the price touches the 100 line, it is really at the same level as the MA. When the momentum index is at 110, the price index is 10 percent above its MA, and so on. Chart 11-13 for the S&P Composite Index also indicates how a trend-deviation indicator using the closing price and a 25-day MA is calculated.

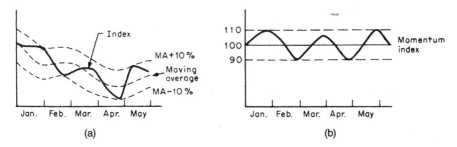

Figure 11-2 Envelopes and momentum.

Chart 11-13 S&P Composite, 1996–1997, calculation of a trend-deviation indicator. (*From www.pring.com.*)

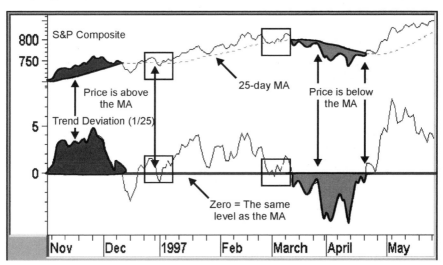

The interpretation of a trend-deviation indicator is based on the same principles described in Chapter 10. This method can be used to identify divergences as well as overbought and oversold zones, but it appears to come into its own when used in conjunction with trendline construction and MA crossovers.

Trendline Construction

Chart 11-14 shows the Morgan Stanley Capital International (MSCI) Hungary Index together with a trend deviation calculated from a close divided by a 45-day MA. This is a fairly jagged indicator and lends itself to overbought/oversold, trendline, and price pattern analysis. In March 2000, we see the completion of an H&S top in the indicator, which was later confirmed by a trendline violation in the price. Later, the oscillator traces out a double bottom formation and the price violates a 3-month down trendline and crosses above its 25-day MA. This should have warranted a good rally, but instead the price initially advanced and then traded in a sideways range, later to be followed by a new low.

In theory, this breakout should have worked. In retrospect, it was because the price had begun a bear market, but this example is a good reminder anyway that even the best laid technical principles can and do fail from time to time: *all the more reason to plan an exit strategy prior to making a trade or investment in case things do not go according to plan.*

Trend Deviation and MAs

An alternative approach with trend-deviation indicators is to smooth out unwanted volatility with the aid of two MAs, as shown in Chart 11-15. The actual trend-deviation series is calculated by taking a 26-week MA of the clos-

Chart 11-14 MSCI Hungary Index and a trend-deviation indicator, 1999–2000. (*From www.pring.com.*)

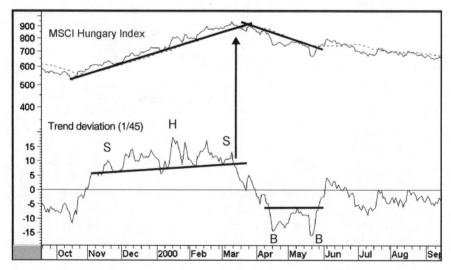

ing price divided by a 52-week MA. The second series is simply a 10-week MA of the first. Buy and sell alerts are then triggered as the smoothed trend-deviation indicator crosses above or below its 10-week MA. Then look for a confirmation from the price itself. Two examples are shown in Chart 11-15, one for a top and the other for a bottom.

This is very much a guerilla approach because the buy alert indicated by the dashed arrow was signaled almost at the top of the rally. This example demonstrates the importance of picking and choosing between signals, only selecting those that develop close to a turning point. If this filtering approach is not taken, then there is considerable risk that action will be taken close to the end of the trend.

A useful method that greatly reduces such whipsaw activity, but still offers timely signals, is to advance the 52-week MA by 10 weeks when the trend-deviation calculation is being made. This means that each weekly close is divided by the 52-week MA as it appeared 10 weeks before. This new calculation has been plotted in the center panel of Chart 11-16.

In this example, the whipsaw in late 2000 was filtered out since the trend-deviation indicator fails to cross decisively below its MA. I am not suggesting this as the only legitimate combination for weekly charts, but it is one that appears to operate quite well. There is always a trade-off when you try to make signals less sensitive and in this case we find that there is occasionally a small delay compared to the nonadvanced 52-week MA. The most obvious

Chart 11-15 S&P Airlines, 1995–2001, and a smoothed trend-deviation indicator. (*From www.pring.com.*)

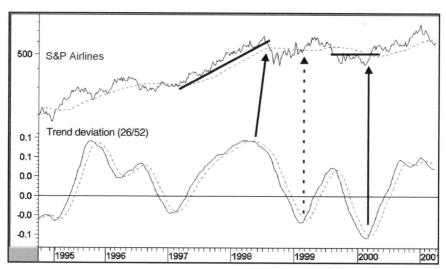

Chart 11-16   S&P Airlines, 1995–2001, and two smoothed trend-deviation indicators. (*From www.pring.com.*)

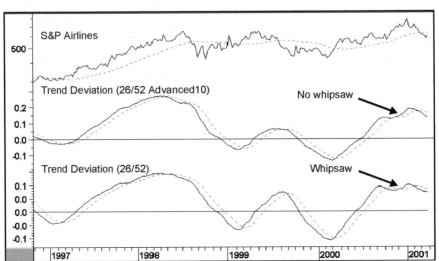

one on this chart developed at the beginning of 1997, where the lagged series in the center panel crossed its MA at a slightly higher price. In most instances though, this is a small price to pay if a costly whipsaw can be avoided.

Moving Average Convergence Divergence

The moving average convergence divergence (MACD) trading method is a form of a trend-deviation indicator using two MAs, the shorter being subtracted from the longer. The two MAs are usually calculated on an exponential basis, in which more recent periods are more heavily weighted than in the case of a simple MA. It is normal for the MACD to then be smoothed by a third exponential moving average (EMA), which is plotted separately on the chart. This average is known as the *signal line*, the crossovers of which generate buy and sell signals. This indicator obtains its name from the fact that the two EMAs are continually converging and then diverging from each other. The MACD has gained great popularity over the years, but in effect, it is really just another variation on a trend-deviation indicator that employs two EMAs as its method of deviation. A visual of its construction is therefore very similar to Chart 11-13.

MACDs can be used with many different time periods. Gerald Appel of Signalert,[3] who has done a considerable amount of research on the subject, recommends that buy signals on a daily chart be constructed from a combination of 8, 17, and 9 exponential MAs, but he feels that sell signals are more reliable when triggered on the basis of a 12, 25, and 9 combination. On the other hand, the popular MetaStock program plots the default values as 12 and 17 with the signal line at 9.

Chart 11-17 shows an example from General Electric with an MACD indicator. As mentioned before, one of the principal ways in which the MACD is interpreted is to use the signal-line crossovers as buy and sell alerts. The problem I have with this approach is that it results in far too many whipsaws. In Chart 11-17, we see numerous examples. A more reliable technique is to construct overbought and oversold lines, trendlines, and price patterns and to look for divergences. In the chart, both series complete H&S patterns at the end of the year 2000. The MACD also experiences a negative divergence. Note how the divergence, flagged by the right shoulder, is barely able to rally above zero. The result is an above-average decline. Note also that the indicator was unable to rally above zero and touched its oversold level several times during the balance of the period covered by the chart. This type of action reflects bear market activity. The MACD is often plotted in a histogram format along with the signal line as in Chart 11-18.

Chart 11-17 General Electric, 1999–2000, and MACD. (*From www.pring.com.*)

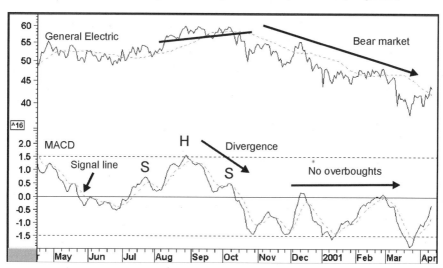

[3]Signalert, 150 Great Neck Road, Great Neck, NY 11021.

Alternatively, the MACD can be plotted as a smoother series using two relatively long-term MAs. This more deliberate series then lends itself better to signal-line crossovers. For example, on hourly charts, a 65/90 combination with a 12-period signal line appears to work quite well. The same principle can be applied to daily, weekly, or monthly charts. Ironically the default time span used for daily charts (26/12 with a 9-day signal line) appears to work better on monthly ones because it manages to retain the primary trend swings yet the signal line whipsaw crossovers are kept to a minimum.

Stochastic Indicators

Introduction and Formula

The stochastic indicator originally gained a great deal of popularity among futures traders, with the result that the standard formula uses very short term time spans. The theory behind the indicator, which was invented by George Lane,[4] is that prices tend to close near the upper end of a trading range during an uptrend. As the trend matures, the tendency for prices to close away from the higher end of the trading range becomes pronounced. In a downward-moving market, the reverse conditions hold true.

Chart 11-18   Homestake Mining and an MACD in histogram format. This chart shows a classic H&S pattern. Note that the MACD histogram gradually became weaker as the pattern progressed. This was only a short-term sell signal, but the price eventually fell below the signal level. (*From Telescan.*)

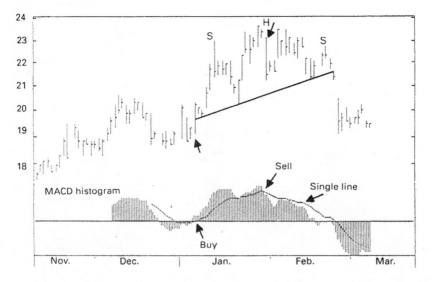

[4]Investment Educators Incorporated, Des Plaines, IL 60018.

The stochastic therefore attempts to measure the points in a rising trend at which the closing prices tend to cluster around the lows for the period in question, and vice versa, since these are the conditions that signal trend reversals. It is plotted as two lines, the $\%K$ line and the $\%D$ line. The $\%D$ provides the major signals and is therefore more important.

The formula for calculation of $\%K$ is

$$\%K = 100[(C - L_5)/(H_5 - L_5)]$$

where C is the most recent close, L_5 is the lowest low for the last five trading periods, and H_5 is the highest high for the same five trading periods. Remember that the calculation of stochastic indicators differs from that of most other momentum indicators in that it requires high, low, and closing data for the period in question.

The stochastic formula is similar to the RSI in that the plots can never exceed 0 or 100, but in this case, it measures the closing price in relation to the total price range for a selected number of periods. A very high reading, in excess of 80, would put the closing price for the period near the top of the range, while a low reading, under 20, would place it near the bottom of the range.

The second line, $\%D$, is a smoothed version of the $\%K$ line. The normal value is three periods. The $\%D$ formula is as follows:

$$\%D = 100 \times (H_3/L_3)$$

where H_3 is the three-period sum of $(C - L_5)$ and L_3 is the three-period sum of $(H_5 - L_5)$.

The momentum indicator that results from these calculations is two lines that fluctuate between 0 and 100. The $\%K$ line is usually plotted as a solid line, while the slower $\%D$ line is usually plotted as a dashed line. A good way to differentiate between them is to think of the fast $\%K$ as "kwick" and the slow $\%D$ as "dawdle."

The popularity of the stochastic can no doubt be explained by the smooth manner in which it moves from an overbought to an oversold condition, lulling a trader into a feeling that price trends are much more orderly than would appear from an observation of an RSI or an ROC indicator.

Longer-term time frames, used on monthly and weekly charts, appear to work much better than the shorter-term stochastic indicators used on daily futures charts. Colby and Meyers in *The Encyclopedia of Technical Market Indicators*[5] noted that the stochastic tested very poorly relative to MA crossovers and other momentum indicators.

[5]Robert W. Colby and Thomas A. Meyers, *The Encyclopedia of Technical Market Indicators,* Dow Jones-Irwin, Homewood, IL, 1988.

Overbought and oversold bands are usually plotted in the 75 to 85 percent area on the upside and in the 15 to 25 percent area on the downside, depending on the time span in question. An overbought indication is given when the %D line crosses the extreme band, but an actual sell alert is not indicated until the %K line crosses below it. When the two lines cross, they behave very similarly to a dual MA system. If you wait for the penetration, you can avoid getting trapped into shorting a strongly bullish move or buying into an extremely negative one.

Interpretation

Crossovers Normally, the faster %K line changes direction sooner than the %D line. This means that the crossover will occur before the %D line has reversed direction, as in Fig. 11-3(a). When the %D line reverses direction first, a slow, stable change of direction is indicated, and %D is regarded as a more reliable signal [see Fig. 11-3(b)].

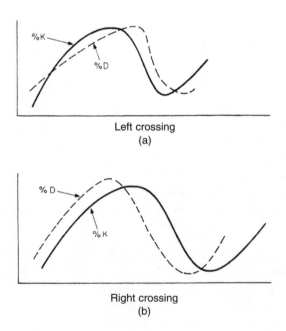

Left crossing
(a)

Right crossing
(b)

Figure 11-3 Stochastic crossovers.

Divergence Failure   An important indication of a possible change in trend arises when the %K line crosses the %D line, moves back to test its extreme level, and fails to cross the %D line, as in Fig. 11-4.

Reverse Divergence   Occasionally, during an uptrend, the %D line will make a lower low, which is associated with a higher low in the price, as in Fig. 11-5. This is a bearish omen, and conventional wisdom suggests looking for a selling opportunity on the next rally. This condition is sometimes referred to as a *bear setup*. A bull setup develops at the end of a downtrend.

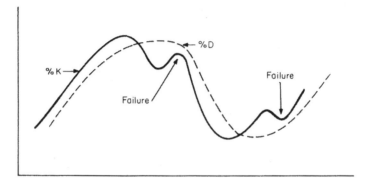

Figure 11-4   Stochastic failures.

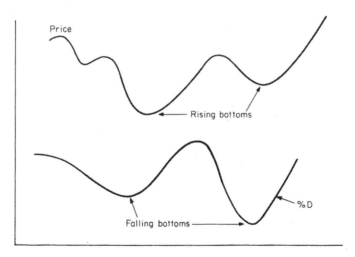

Figure 11-5   Stochastic reverse divergences.

Extremes   Occasionally, the %K value reaches the extreme of 100 or 0. This indicates that a very powerful move is underway, since the price is consistently closing near its high or low. If a successful test of this extreme occurs following a pullback, it is usually regarded as an excellent entry point.

Hinges   When either the %K line or the %D line experiences a slowdown in velocity, indicated by a flattening line, the indication is usually that a reversal will take place in the next period (see Fig. 11-6).

Divergences   The stochastic indicator often sets up positive and negative divergences in a similar manner to other oscillators. Some possibilities are indicated in Fig. 11-7. Buy and sell alerts are triggered when the %K line crosses %D after a divergence has taken place.

Slowed Stochastic Indicator   It is also possible to extend the calculation in order to invoke a slowed version of stochastic indicators. In this instance, the %K line is replaced with the %D line, and another MA is calculated for the %D. Many technicians argue that this modified stochastic version gives more accurate signals. Chart 11-19 shows the Amex Brokers Index together with a 10-day %K slowed by a factor of 5. The %D line has a slowing factor of 5 as well, hence the 10/5/5 label.

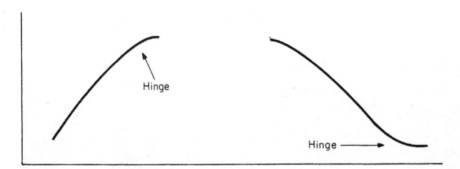

Figure 11-6   Stochastic hinges.

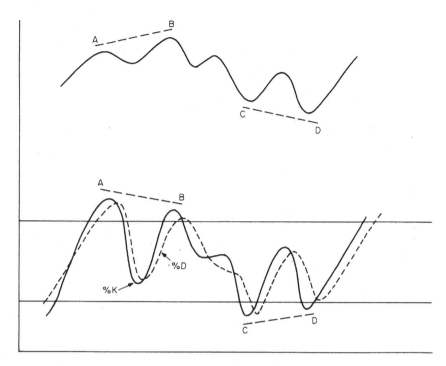

Figure 11-7 Stochastic divergences.

Chart 11-19 Amex Brokers Index, 2000–2001, stochastic and several interpretive techniques. (*From www.pring.com.*)

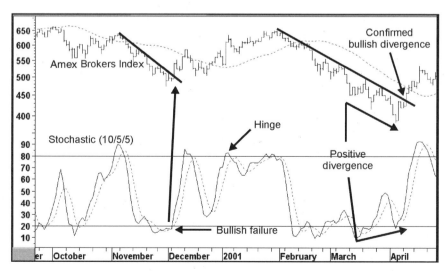

Summary

- The RSI is bounded by 0 and 100. Overbought and oversold lines should be wider the shorter the time span.
- The RSI lends itself more easily to comparing the momentum of different securities than does the ROC.
- The RSI can be used in conjunction with overbought and oversold lines, divergences, price patterns, trendlines, and smoothings.
- Trend-deviation indicators are calculated by dividing the close or a short-term MA by a longer-term one.
- Trend-deviation indicators can be used with trendlines, price patterns, and MAs. They also lend themselves to overbought-oversold and divergence analysis.
- The MACD is a form of trend-deviation indicator.
- The stochastic indicator assumes that prices close near the low at the end of a rally and near their highs at the end of a downtrend.
- The stochastic indicator is confined between 0 and 100 and consist of two lines, the %K and the %D.
- The stochastic indicators lend themselves to crossovers, divergences, hinges, extremes, and reverse divergences and are usually plotted in their slowed version.

12

Individual Momentum Indicators II

The Know Sure Thing (KST)

The Long-Term KST

Chapter 10 explained that the rate of change (ROC) measures the speed of an advance or decline over a specific time span and is calculated by dividing the price in the current period by the price N periods ago. The longer the time span under consideration, the greater the significance of the trend being measured. Movements in a 10-day ROC are far less meaningful than those calculated over a 12- or 24-month time span.

The use of an ROC indicator helps to explain some of the cyclical movements in markets, often giving advanced warning of a reversal in the prevailing trend, but a specific time frame used in an ROC calculation reflects only one cycle. If that particular cycle is not operating, is dominated by another one, or is dominated by a combination of cycles, it will be of little value.

> **Major Technical Principle** Price at any one time is determined by the interaction of many different time cycles. An indicator that takes this into consideration is likely to be more timely without losing too much in the way of sensitivity.

This point is illustrated in Chart 12-1, which shows three ROC indicators of different time spans: 6 months, 12 months, and 24 months. The 6-month ROC tends to reflect all of the intermediate moves, and the 24-month series sets the scene for the major swings. The arrows flag the major turning points. They show that for the most part all three ROCs are moving in the same direction once the new trend gets under way. A major exception occurred at the 1984 bottom. Here we see the price rise, but immediately after, the 24-month ROC declines while the others continue on up. During the period covered by arrow *A*, the speed of the advance is curtailed because of the conflict between the three cycles. Later, though, all three ROCs get back in gear on the upside and the rally approximated by arrow *B* is much steeper. In effect, major turning points tend to occur when several cycles are in agreement and speedy advances and declines develop when more cycles are operating in the same direction. This is a fairly limited view because there are far more than three cycles operating at any one point in time.

Clearly, one ROC time span taken on its own does not give us a complete picture. This was one of the factors that I considered when designing the KST. Another was that I wanted an indicator that fairly closely reflected the major price swings over the time period under consideration, primary trends for monthly charts, short-term trends for daily charts, and so forth.

Chart 12-1   S&P Composite, 1978–1988, and three ROCs. (*From www.pring.com.*)

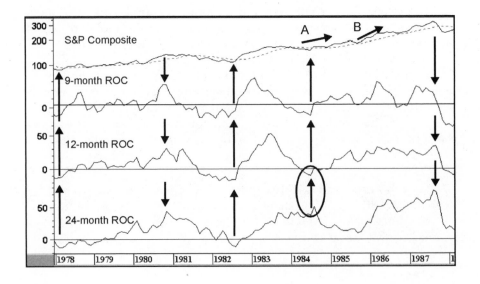

Chart 12-2 shows the Standard & Poor's Composite during the 1974–90 period. The oscillator is a 24-month ROC smoothed with a 9-month MA. This series certainly reflects all of the primary trend swings during this period. However, if we use the indicator's changes in direction as signals, close examination shows that there is a lot to be desired. For example, the 1984 low is signaled with a peak in the oscillator. Similarly, the 1989 signal develops almost at the rally peak. What was required was an indicator that reflected the major trend yet was sensitive enough to reverse fairly close to the turning points in the price. A good way of achieving this is to construct an indicator that includes several ROCs of differing time spans. The function of longer time frames is to reflect the primary swings, while the inclusion of the shorter ones helps to speed up the turning points. The formula for the KST is shown in Table 12-1.

Table 12-1   Formulas for Time Frames

Time Frame	Smoothing		Weight
9-month	6-MA	×	1
12-month	6-MA	×	2
18-month	6-MA	×	3
24-month	9-MA	×	4

Chart 12-2   S&P Composite, 1973–1991, and a smoothed ROC. (*From www.pring.com.*)

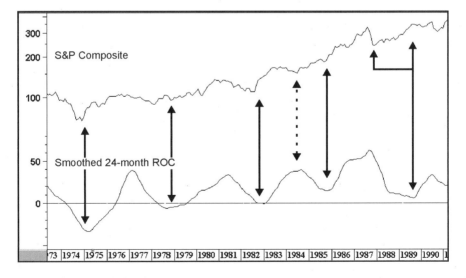

Since the most important thing is for the indicator to reflect the primary swings, the formula is weighted so that the longer, more dominant time spans have a larger influence.

Chart 12-3 compares the performance of the smoothed 24-month ROC to the long-term KST. It is fairly self-evident that the KST reflects all of the major swings being experienced by the smoothed 24-month ROC. However, the KST turning points develop sooner than those of the ROC. The vertical arrows slice through the ROC as it bottoms out. In every instance, the KST turns ahead of the arrow, the lead time varying with each particular cycle. Note how in 1988 the KST turns well after the 1987 bottom, but just at the time when the market begins to take off on the upside. The ROC reverses direction much later. There is one period when the KST underperformed, and that is contained within the 1986–1987 ellipse where the KST gave a false signal of weakness, unlike the ROC that continued to rise.

The dominant time frame in the KST's construction is a 24-month period, which is half of the 4-year business cycle. This means that the KST will work best when the security in question is experiencing a primary up- and downtrend based on the business cycle. For example, Chart 12-4 shows the KST during the 1960s and 1970s where the S&P was in a clearly defined business cycle–typetrading range. Periods of accumulation and distribution occur between the times when the KST and its MA change direction.

There are really three levels of signaling. The first occurs when the indicator itself changes direction, the second when it crosses its MA, and the

Chart 12-3 S&P Composite, 1973–1991, and a smoothed ROC versus the KST. (*From www.pring.com.*)

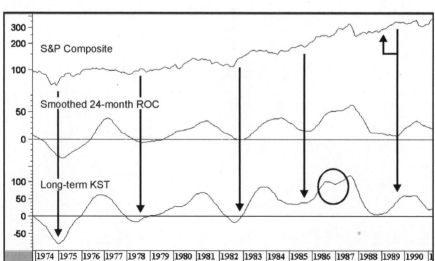

Chart 12-4 S&P Composite, 1963–1979, and a long-term KST. (*From www.pring.com.*)

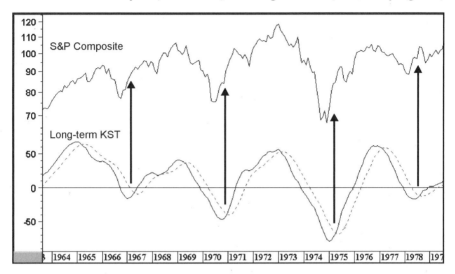

third when the MA also reverses direction. In most cases, the MA crossover offers the best combination of timely signals with a minimum of whipsaws. Changes in the direction of the 9-month MA offer the most reliable signals, but these usually develop well after the turning point. The most timely and reliable signals thereby develop in those situations where the MA reverses close to a turning point.

For the most part, the indicator has been very reliable, but like any other technical approach, it is by no means a perfect technique. For instance, the same calculation is shown in Chart 12-5, but this time for the Nikkei. During periods of a secular or linear uptrend (as occurred for Japanese equities in the 1970s and 1980s), this type of approach is counterproductive since many false bear signals are triggered. However, the vast majority of markets are sensitive to the business cycle, and so the summed ROC concept works extremely well. It is for this reason that I call this indicator the KST, which stands for *know sure thing*. Most of the time the indicator is reliable, but you *know* that it's not a *sure thing*.

Short- and Intermediate-Term KSTs

The KST concept was originally derived for long-term trends, but the idea of four smoothed summed ROCs can just as easily be applied to short, intermediate, and even intraday trends. Formulas for various time frames are shown in Table 12-2. The formulas presented here are by no means the last word and

Chart 12-5   The Nikkei, 1975–1992, and a long-term KST. (*From www.pring.com.*)

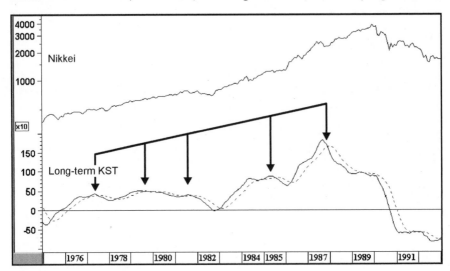

Table 12-2   Suggested KST Formulas*

	ROC	MA	Weight	ROC	MA	Weight	ROC	MA	Weight	ROC	MA	Weight
Short-term[†]	10	10	1	15	10	2	20	10	3	30	15	4
Short-term[‡]	3	3[¶]	1	4	4[¶]	2	6	6[¶]	3	10	8[¶]	4
Intermediate-term[‡]	10	10	1	13	13	2	15	15	3	20	20	4
Intermediate-term[‡]	10	10[¶]	1	13	13[¶]	2	15	15[¶]	3	20	20[¶]	4
Long-term[§]	9	6	1	12	6	2	18	6	3	24	9	4
Long-term[§]	39	26[¶]	1	52	26[¶]	2	78	26[¶]	3	104	39[¶]	4

*It is possible to program all KST formulas into MetaStock and the Computrac Snap Module (see Resources, at the end of the book).
[†]Based on daily data.
[‡]Based on weekly data.
[§]Based on monthly data.
[¶]EMA

are suggested merely as good starting points for further analysis. Readers may experiment with different formulas for any of the time frames and may well come up with superior results. When experimenting, strive for consistency, never perfection, for there is no such thing in technical analysis.

Chart 12-6 shows an intermediate KST for the London copper price. One of the things I like about the indicator, especially in its short-term and intermediate varieties, is its flexibility of interpretation. Pretty much all of the interpretive techniques discussed in Chapter 10 can be applied. In Chart 12-6, we see an overbought crossover at the tail end of 1994. It did not amount to anything because it was not possible to come up with any trend-reversal signals in the price. Later, though, in early 1995 we see a negative divergence,

Chart 12-6   Cash copper, 1993–2001, and an intermediate KST. (*From www.pring.com.*)

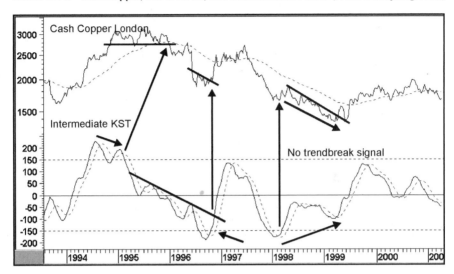

an overbought crossover, a 65-week exponential moving average (EMA) crossover, and a head-and-shoulders (H&S) top in the price—classic stuff. There were a couple of false buy signals on the way down, but the rally peaks in the KST lent themselves to a nice trendline construction. The violation of the line, the oversold crossover, and the completion of the base in the price combined to offer a nice buy signal in late 1996. The next time the KST crossed its oversold level in 1998 there was no good place to observe a trend-reversal signal in the price. That was not true in early 1999, where a positive divergence, an EMA crossover by the KST, and a trendline break in the price offered a good timely entry point. Note that after the price broke above the down trendline, it subsequently found support at the extended line.

Charts 12-7 and 12-8 feature a short-term KST suitable for use with daily data. First, the KST for the Bombay SE Index experienced nice fluctuations between 2000 and the first quarter of 2001. The arrows on the chart indicate the approximate periods when the KST reverses and crosses above or below its 10-day MA. These MA crossovers are a classic way in which the KST is used. Unfortunately, not all situations are as usable as this.

Chart 12-8, for instance, shows the KST with the Amex Brokers Index. After two false KST MA crossovers, the index finally succumbed to a trend break and a negative KST divergence in the spring of 1999. Occasionally, the KST will move in a very quiet and subdued manner, as indicated by the two converging trendlines in the fall of 1999. Once the indicator breaks out and this is confirmed by the price, a strong and reliable signal is usually given.

Chart 12-7   Bombay SE Index and a short-term KST. (*From www.pring.com.*)

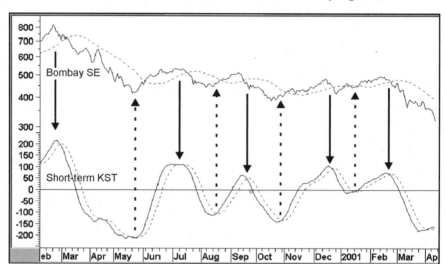

Chart 12-8   Amex Brokers Index, 1998–2000, and a short-term KST. (*From www.pring.com.*)

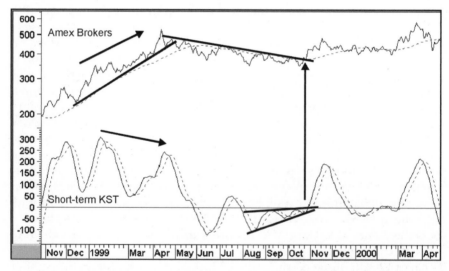

Chart 12-9 shows a 15-minute bar of Apple Computer with a short and intermediate KST suitable for intraday trading. Several oversold crossover signals are featured. Generally speaking, the monthly KST is far more reliable than its daily and weekly counterparts. The degree of success for any

Chart 12-9   Apple Computer and two intraday KSTs. (*From www.pring.com.*)

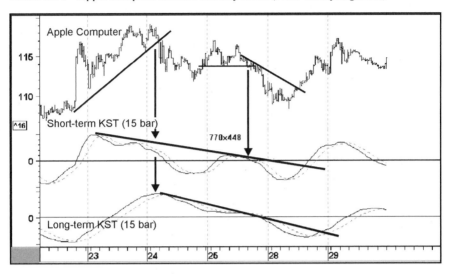

of these time frames will depend on the character of the market being monitored and the nature of the trend. By its very construction, the formula
assumes that markets are influenced by the usual 4-year business cycle.
Whenever that time frame is unduly shortened or lengthened, the monthly
KST suffers in its performance.

Using the KST with the Market Cycle Model

Three Main Trends   Chapter 1 explained that there are several trends
operating in the market at any particular time. They range from intraday,
hourly trends right through to very long term or secular trends that evolve
over a 20- or 30-year period. For investment purposes, the most widely
recognized trends are short term, intermediate term, and long term. Short-
term trends are usually monitored with daily prices, intermediate-term
trends with weekly prices, and long-term trends with monthly prices. A
hypothetical bell-shaped curve incorporating all three trends is shown in
Fig. 1-1 in Chapter 1.

From an investment point of view, it is important to understand the direction of the main, or primary, trend. This makes it possible to gain some perspective on the current position of the overall cycle. The construction of a
long-term KST is a useful starting point from which to identify major market cycle junctures. The introduction of short and intermediate series as well
now enables us to replicate the Market Cycle Model.

The best investments are made when the primary trend is in a rising mode and the intermediate- and short-term market movements are bottoming out. During a primary bear market, the best selling opportunities occur when intermediate- and short-term trends are peaking.

In a sense, any investments made during the early and middle stages of a bull market are bailed out by the fact that the primary trend is rising, whereas investors have to be much more agile during a bear market in order to capitalize on the rising intermediate-term swings.

Combining the Three Trends   Ideally, it would be very helpful to track the KST for monthly, weekly, and daily data on the same chart, but plotting constraints do not easily permit this. It is possible, however, to simulate these three trends by using different time spans based on weekly data, shown for the Chicago lumber price in Chart 12-10. This arrangement facilitates identification of both the direction and the maturity of the primary trend (shown at the bottom) as well as the interrelationship between the short and the intermediate trends. The lines above the price reflect primary bullish and bearish environments as reflected in the long-term KST crossing above and below its 26-week EMA. Note how the short-term KST rarely moves to the oversold zone during the bullish environments and rarely to overbought when the main trend is down.

Chart 12-10   Lumber, 1994–2001, and three KSTs. (*From www.pring.com.*)

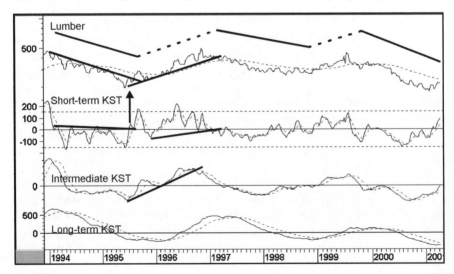

The best buying opportunities seem to occur either when the long-term index is in the terminal phase of a decline or when it is in an uptrend, but has not yet reached an overextended position. These indicators differ from the previous charts in that they are smoothed by EMAs rather than by simple MAs. Trial and error suggests this substitution as more suitable for this type of arrangement. The long-term indicator is constructed from the same time spans as the monthly series; thus, 12 months becomes 52 weeks, and so on.

Only an actual EMA crossover should be interpreted as a buy or sell alert for a momentum series based on exponential smoothing, not on a reversal in direction. Quite often, the long-term series stabilizes but does not reverse direction, thereby leaving the observer in doubt as to its true intention. Vital clues can often be gleaned from the action of the short-term and intermediate series in conjunction with the price action itself.

For example, in early 1997 the long-term KST stabilized, but preceding this event the intermediate series had crossed below its EMA and violated a trendline. The short-term series also completed a top and crossed below zero, while the price itself violated a nice up trendline. All these signals suggested that the price was at best likely to move sideways. Even under that scenario, the long-term KST could be projected to decline since there would be a tremendous dissipation of upside momentum resulting from these signals.

The KST can also be adapted to relative strength lines. This is especially useful for the long term when applied to industry groups or individual stocks. This is because the group rotation around the business cycle means that linear up- and downtrends are far less likely to develop than with absolute price data. For a fuller discussion on these matters, readers are referred to Chapter 16, on relative strength, Chapter 19, on group rotation, and Chapter 31, on individual stock selection. For those who do not have access to a charting package capable of plotting the KST, a useful substitute is the MACD, suitably smoothed with longer-term MAs.

The Directional Movement System

The objective of the Directional Movement System designed by Welles Wilder is to determine whether a market is likely to experience a trending or trading range environment. The distinction is important because a trending market will be better signaled by the adoption of trend-following indicators such as moving averages (MAs), whereas a trading range environment is more suitable for oscillators. In practice, I am not impressed with the capability of the Directional Movement System to accomplish this objective, other than to identify a change in trend. On the other hand, there are several other ways in which this indicator can be usefully applied.

The Concept

The calculation of the Directional Movement System is quite involved and time does not permit a full discussion here. For that, readers are referred to Wilder's *New Concepts in Technical Trading*.

To simplify matters, the directional movement indicator is plotted by calculating the maximum range that the price has moved, either during the period under consideration (a day, week, 10-minute bar, and so on) or from the previous period's close to the extreme point reached during the period. In effect, the system tries to measure directional movement. Since there are two directions in which prices can move, there are two directional movement indicators, called +DI and −DI. Since the raw data derived from the calculation are unduly volatile, they are each calculated as an average over a specific time period and the result is plotted on a chart. Normally, the DIs are overlaid in the same chart panel. The standard, or default, time span is 14 periods. Chart 12-11 shows the two DIs using a 14-day span. Crossovers of the DIs are then used as buy and sell signals.

There is one other important indicator incorporated in this system and that is the Average Directional Index (ADX). The ADX is simply an average of the +DIs and −DIs over a specific period. In effect, it subtracts the

Chart 12-11   IBM, 2000–2001, and two DIs. (*From www.pring.com.*)

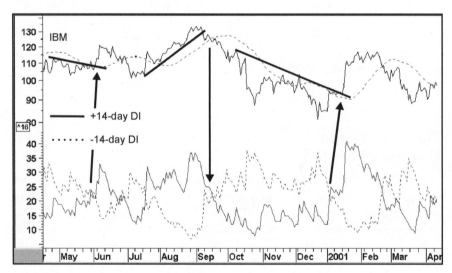

days of negative directional movement from the positive ones. However, when the −DI is greater than the +DI, the negative sign is ignored. This means that the ADX only tells us whether the security in question is experiencing directional movement or not. Again, the normal default time span is 14 days.

The ADX is calculated in such a way that the plot is always contained within the scale of 0 to 100. High readings indicate that the security is in a trending mode (it has a lot of directional movement), and low readings indicate a lack of directional movement and are more indicative of trading range markets. Unlike other oscillators, the ADX tells us nothing about the direction in which a price is moving, only its trending or nontrending characteristics. Use other oscillators for this task.

The Two DIs

Chart 12-11 features the price of IBM together with ± DIs using a 14-day time span. Buy alerts are signaled when the +DI crosses above the −DI and vice versa. In this example, there are several occasions when it is possible to confirm such crossovers with a trendline violation in the price. MA crossovers or price patterns could just as easily be substituted. In this example, the crossovers are pretty good and not subject to any whipsaws. Unfortunately, things do not always work out as well as this. That's one reason why it is important to make sure that such crossovers are confirmed by the price.

Chart 12-12 Alcoa, 1999–2000, two smoothed DIs, and an ADX. (*From www.pring.com.*)

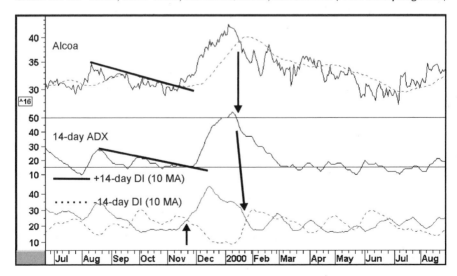

Another way around this is to smooth the two DIs, as I have done in Chart 12-12. This certainly reduces the whipsaws, but there is a trade-off in that the signals are occasionally delayed because this approach is less sensitive.

The ADX

A high ADX reading does not tell us that the market is overbought and about to do down. Please note that a *change* in trend is different from a *reversal* in trend since a change in trend can be from up to down, up to sideways, or down to up. Similarly, a downtrend could change to a trading range or to an uptrend.

In Chart 12-13, a 14-day ADX has been plotted against Alcoa. I have also placed an oversold (little directional movement) at 15 and an overbought (lots of directional movement) at 50. Since the volatility of each security is different, such lines should be drawn on a trial-and-error basis using the price history (as much as possible) as a guide. There are three periods when

Major Technical Principle When the ADX is at a high reading and starts to reverse, the prevailing trend is likely to change.

Chart 12-13 Alcoa, 1999–2001, and an ADX. (*From www.pring.com.*)

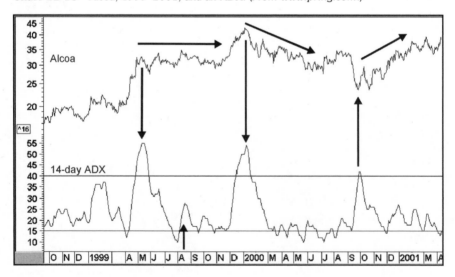

the ADX, having indicated a strong directional movement, then falls back below its 40 level. The reversal warns us that the trend or strong directional movement has now reversed, and we should be on the lookout for a change of trend. In the first instance, it was from up to sideways, in the second from up to down, and on the far right of the chart from down to up.

There is rarely an optimum time span for any indicator. However, for the ADX, the 14-period span and those very close to it appear to offer the best results. Chart 12-14 shows two extremes: a 6-day and a 30-day span. They demonstrate that shorter-term time frames return an ADX that is too volatile, while longer-term ones result in a step-like pattern.

The arrow against the 6-day series also goes to show that a reversal in direction does not always result in a change in trend. In this case, a reduction in directional movement was accurately predicted by the reversal. Unfortunately, the reduction was not sufficient to result in a change of trend, merely a slowing down in the existing (downward) one. Fortunately, this kind of action is the exception rather than the rule.

Chart 12-12 zeros in on one of these periods, but it also includes a 10-day MA of the 14-day up and down DIs. These are displayed in order to offer some idea as to the implication of the reversal in the ADX. In this case, the crossing of the 50 level (note that this overbought reading is not the same as that in Chart 12-13) is followed by a negative crossover of the smoothed DI above its +DI counterpart. This indicates that the reversal in the ADX is likely to be followed by a decline.

Chart 12-14   AT&T, 1998–2001, and two ADXs. (*From www.pring.com.*)

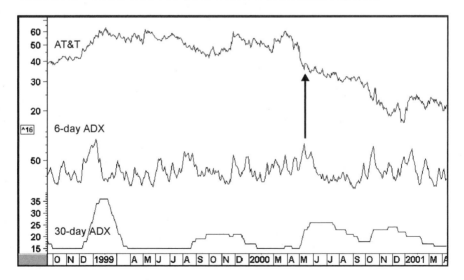

Low readings in the ADX indicate a lack of directional movement, and these can be helpful as well when it is fairly clear that a rising trend of directional movement is underway. Consider the situation in November 1999. The ADX had been in a narrow trading range at a very low level. Then it broke to the upside. This indicated that the price was now likely to trend, but in which direction? The answer lay in monitoring the two smoothed DIs and the price. In this instance, the +DI crossed above the minus series and the price was confirmed with a nice breakout. Remember that the rising ADX did not signal rising prices, only rising directional movement. If the −DI had crossed below the +DI and the price had broken to the downside, the rising ADX would then have been associated with a declining trend in the price.

The Parabolic Indicator

The Concept

The Parabolic System, devised by Welles Wilder, is not a momentum indicator, and so strictly speaking, it does not fall within the scope of this chapter. However, it is being mentioned briefly since it has become a very popular trading mechanism and can be used to generate timely stop-loss signals.

One of the most valid criticisms of trend-following systems is that the implied lags between the turning points and the trend-reversal signals obliterate a significant amount of the potential profitability of a trade. The Parabolic System is designed to address this problem by increasing the speed of the trend, so far as stops are concerned, whenever prices reach new profitable levels. The concept draws on the idea that time is an enemy, and unless a trade or investment can continue to generate more profits over time, it should be liquidated. Since it is a stop-loss system, it can be used with any momentum series, once that indicator has been used to filter out a good entry point for a trade. It is also a trailing stop-loss system, which means that the stop is continually being moved in the direction of the position, that is, up for a long position and down for a short one.

When the position is first initiated, it is given a relatively long leash, so to speak. Then, as time passes, and the price increases, the stop is gradually tightened. The expression *parabolic* arises from the shape of the curve of the stops as it appears on the chart. In a rising market, the stop is continually being raised, never lowered. In a declining market, the opposite will hold true.

How Does It Work?

The parabolic shows up on the chart as a parabolic-shaped curve that is plotted above and below the price, as in Chart 12-15. This curve is often referred to as the SAR, which stands for *stop and reversal system*. This is because the parabolic, when triggered, is often used not only to stop a position, but to actually reverse it. Thus, a parabolic would simultaneously trigger the liquidation of a long position and the entering of a short one.

Personally, I prefer to select an entry point and use the Parabolic System for the purposes of setting the stop, rather than continually reversing positions. Remember, *most losing trades develop when you go against the direction of the main trend.* Strict use of the parabolic with the stop and reversal approach totally ignores this discipline. That's why I prefer to use the Parabolic System as a stop system only, and not a stop and reverse system.

Strict use of the parabolic would involve buying when the price crosses above it, placing the stop well underneath the purchase price. This is the downside because there is considerable risk at this point. Gradually, the parabolic picks up steam and the risk is dramatically reduced as upside momentum increases. In Chart 12-15, the sell signal comes pretty close to the top of the rally. The short signal in November also results in a nice profit.

Like most other indicators, the parabolic does not do as well in a trading range. This is because it is unable to gather sufficient momentum to quickly

Chart 12-15 GM and a parabolic, 2000–2001. (*From www.pring.com.*)

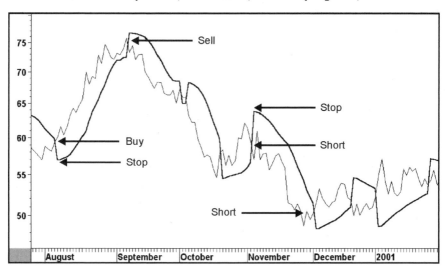

Chart 12-16   Hewlett-Packard and a parabolic. (*From www.pring.com.*)

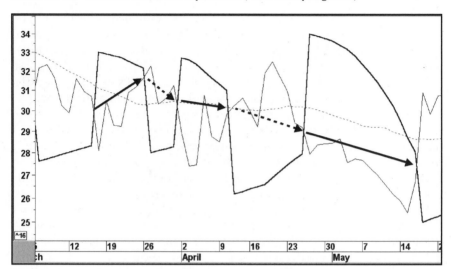

reduce the risk. In Chart 12-16, we see five trades, three long (the solid arrows) and two short (the dashed arrows). None make much money, but the winners slightly outnumber the losers three to two.

Setting the Parameters

Most charting packages enable the user to set two parameters. These are the acceleration factor and the maximum acceleration factor. The acceleration factor is the amount the parabolic is increased every time the price makes a new high in an uptrend (a new low in a downtrend). The maximum factor is a limit above which the acceleration factor cannot go. For example, if the acceleration factor is .2 and the maximum is .8, after the price has made four new highs since the parabolic began (that is, .2 times 4), the acceleration factor remains at .8 until the price crosses the parabolic and a new (SAR) trade is begun. The level of the acceleration factor is the most important.

With MAs, there is always a trade-off between timeliness and sensitivity. A short-term MA gives very timely signals, but is so sensitive that it also generates numerous whipsaws. On the other hand, a long-term average has fewer whipsaws, but crossovers are less timely. The Parabolic System works in exactly same way, but in this case the lower the acceleration factor, the less timely the signal, and the higher the acceleration factor, the more sensitive and timely are the signals. However, they result in more whipsaws.

In Chart 12-17, the upper panel features an acceleration factor of .01 with a maximum of .2, whereas the lower chart shows a more aggressive .2 acceleration with a .2 maximum. The difference is very clear. The smaller acceleration factor featured in the top panel results in far fewer whipsaws than that in the lower panel, but at the same time is less timely. Setting levels for the accelerating factor is a trial-and-error process just like the process of determining the optimum span for an MA. In my experience, the default value provided with many software programs and Wilder's recommendation of .02 and .2 are quite satisfactory in most situations.

A Practical Use

There are many ways in which the parabolic can be applied. One of my favorites is to enter a trade on an MA crossover and exit the trade on a reverse crossover. However, if the parabolic crosses the MA, then it should be used to exit the trade. An example is shown in Chart 12-18 with General Motors. For a more in-depth explanation, please refer to my own Momentum Explained book and CD-ROM tutorial.

Chart 12-17 Hewlett-Packard and two parabolics. (*From www.pring.com.*)

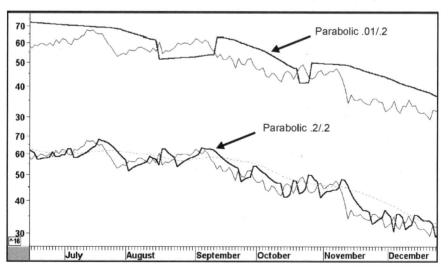

Chart 12-18 GM, a parabolic versus an MA crossover. (*From www.pring.com.*)

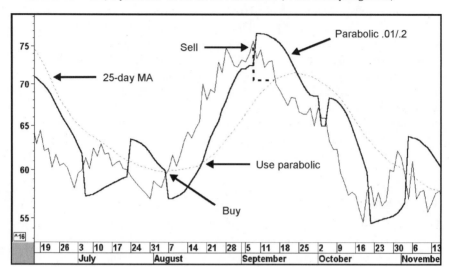

Summary

- The KST can be constructed for any time frame, from intraday to primary.
- The KST is calculated from the smoothed ROC of four time spans, each of which is weighted according to the length of time.
- Long-term, short-term, and intermediate KSTs can be combined on one chart to reflect the Market Cycle Model.
- The KST lends itself to numerous momentum-interpretive techniques and can successfully be applied to relative strength analysis.
- The +DIs and −DIs measure positive and negative short-term direction.
- When the raw or smoothed DIs cross, they trigger buy and sell momentum signals.
- The ADX measures the directional movement of a trend.
- A rising ADX indicates an increase in directional movement and vice versa.
- When the ADX reverses direction from a high reading, the prevailing trend is likely to change.
- The parabolic is a stop-loss system.
- The parabolic was originally designed as a stop and reversal method. However, it is better used as an exit mechanism due to the large risk often associated with the initiation of a position based on an initial parabolic stop.

13
Candle Charts

Candle Construction

Candle charts originated in Japan several centuries ago, but have recently gained a following in other countries. This system of plotting price data is an alternative to the familiar bar chart. Candles can be used to identify price patterns, and they also lend themselves to trendline construction. They are constructed from opening, high, low, and closing data for a specific period such as an hour, day, or week.

Bar charts are expressed as vertical lines, with the left and right handles representing the opening and closing levels. Candle charts, on the other hand, are plotted as vertical rectangular boxes that connect the opening and closing prices, and with vertical lines that extend from the rectangles to encompass the extreme high and low. Bar charts treat all data more or less equally. It is also important to differentiate between which is higher, the open or the close.

Candle charts can be plotted only for markets in which opening prices as well as closes, highs, and lows are known. Proponents of this system believe that it provides all the information contained in bar charts as well as additional ideas contained only in candle charts. Candle charts are not the Holy Grail, but they are certainly a useful adjunct to the technical

---

Major Technical Principle In candlestick charting, the greatest emphasis is given to the opening and closing prices and the trading range between them.

---

arsenal. In this description, we will refer to days since they are the most common timeframe, but bear in mind that candle charts can be constructed for any time period.

A typical candle consists of two parts: the real body, that is, the rectangular part, and the shadow or wick, that is, the two vertical extensions. The top and bottom of the rectangle are determined by the opening and closing prices for the day. If the closing price ends up *above* the opening (the real body), it is plotted in white. When it closes *below* the opening, it is plotted in black [see Figs. 13-1(*a*) and (*b*)]. The top of the real body represents the opening price, the bottom the close. This is reversed in the case of a white rectangle where the close is plotted at the top and the open at the bottom.

The thin, vertical shadow lines that protrude from the real body reflect the high and low for the day. Since the closing and opening prices can be identical, or identical with the high or low, there are a number of possible combinations that need to be represented. Some of them are shown in Fig. 13-1.

Candlesticks provide essentially the same information as bar charts, but their more pronounced visual representation of the material enables technicians to identify characteristics that are less obvious on bar charts. Certain phenomena illustrated in bar charts have been given their own names, such as *key reversal days* or *island reversal days*, likewise, with candle charts. Because of the large number of potential variations for both individual days and price formations encompassing several days, it has been common practice to give exotic names to the various possibilities. The characteristics of the more common candles are also shown in Fig. 13-1.

Figure 13-1(*a*) shows the *long white line*, a wide trading range where the opening is close to the low and the high is near the close. This candle has

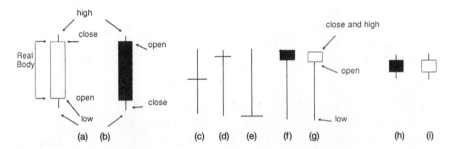

Figure 13-1   Selected one-bar candles.

a bullish tendency. Figure 13-1(*b*) is the *long black line*, a wide trading range where the opening is close to the high and the close near the day's low. This candle has a bearish tendency. Figures 13-1(*c*) to (*e*) show *doji lines*, where opening and closing prices are identical. Interpretation depends upon the context in which they appear, but they essentially indicate a balance between buyers and sellers. Figures 13-1(*f*) and (*g*) illustrate *umbrella lines*, where the real body is narrow and develops at the high end of the day's trading range. Umbrella lines are bullish at bottoms and bearish at tops. Figures 13-1(*h*) and (*i*) show *spinning tops*, representing days when the trading range is very small. They do not have any significance in trading ranges, but are important in some of the price formations discussed later.

Candle charts offer indications of both reversal and continuation phenomena, just as bar charts do. Some examples in this chapter demonstrate candlestick formations (see Charts 13-1 to 13-4). Candlesticks really come into their own in the identification of shorter-term reversals and continuation situations.

Chart 13-1 *Financial Times* Stock Exchange 100 cash, 1990. (*From www.pring.com.*)

Reversal Phenomena

Hammers and Hanging Men (Takuri and Kubitsuri)

These formations [see Figs. 13-1 (*f*) and (*g*)] have probably gained more notoriety than all the others because of their imposing titles. A *hanging man* is an umbrella line that develops after a rally. It looks rather like the body of a man with dangling legs and, as its name implies, is a bearish pattern. If a hanging man appears after a prolonged upmove, it should be treated with respect, especially if it occurs after a gap. A hanging man can be identified by the fact that the shadow, or wick, is at least twice the height of the real body. The color of the body is not important.

A *hammer* is identical to a hanging man, but occurs after a market decline when it is a bullish sign. It gets its name from the idea that the price is "hammering out" a bottom. In effect, it represents the kind of trading day when the price temporarily slips quite sharply, because there is a run on the selling stops. Nevertheless, the technical position is sufficiently constructive to cause buyers to come into the market and push the price back up toward or above the opening level.

Chart 13-2 New York light crude three-month perpetual, 1989–1990. (*From www.pring.com.*)

Chart 13-3 Microsoft, 2000–2001, candle volume. (*From www.pring.com.*)

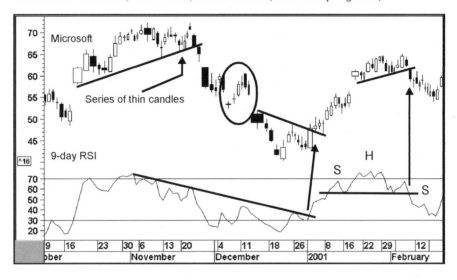

Chart 13-4 Treasury bonds, 1990. (*From www.pring.com.*)

Dark Cloud Cover (Kabuse)

In real life, dark clouds (see Fig. 13-2) hint at the possibility of rain, so a *dark cloud* candlestick formation implies lower prices. Its bearish connotations are most pronounced during an uptrend or in the upper part of a congestion zone. It is a form of key reversal, since the price closes down on the day after a gap's higher opening. It consists of 2 days. The first is a strong, white real body, and the second is a black body, in which the close occurs in the lower half of the previous white real body.

Piercing Line (Kirikorni)

This pattern (see Fig. 13-3) would be more aptly named "sunny sky" because it is the exact opposite of the dark cloud and is therefore bullish. It is important to note whether the second day's white body closes more than halfway above the previous body. If it does not, conventional wisdom indicates that additional weakness is likely.

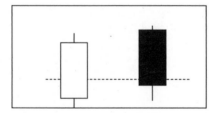

Figure 13-2   Dark cloud cover.

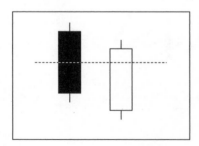

Figure 13-3   Piercing line.

Engulfing Pattern (Tsutsumi)

This formation (see Fig. 13-4) develops significance after a prolonged price move. It is characterized by two consecutive more or less shadowless real bodies, in which the second day "engulfs" the first. It is bullish in a downtrend, when the second day is a white body, and bearish in an uptrend, when it appears as a black one.

Stars (Hoshi)

Stars (see Fig. 13-5) are common phenomena in candle charts and come in four different reversal varieties. Stars are combinations of wide real bodies and spinning tops. The *morning star* heralds a new day (upmove) and is bullish. It consists of two long real bodies separated by a spinning top. The star is represented by the spinning top, which is made on a gap. The third body should be white and should result in a closing price more than halfway up the body of the first the dotted horizontal line in Fig. 13-5. The *evening star* is a precursor of night. It has the opposite characteristics and implications of a morning star.

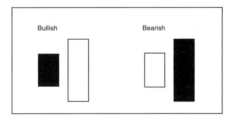

Figure 13-4 Engulfing patterns.

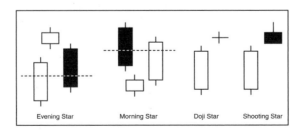

Figure 13-5 Stars.

A *doji star is* a bearish sign and occurs after a lengthy rally. It consists of a gap and a doji line. *A shooting star* is like a short-term top where the daily price action experiences a small gap and the black real body appears at the end of a long wick or upper shadow.

Upside Gap Two Crows (Narabi Kuro)

This bearish formation (see Fig. 13-6) consists of a long white line followed by two black lines. The first black line gaps to the upside. The third day often closes the gap, but because it is a black line where the close is below the open, its implication is bearish.

Three Black Crows (Sanba Garasu)

The *three black crows* pattern in Fig. 13-7 consists of three declining black candlesticks that form after an advance. They indicate lower prices. Each black candle should open within the real body of its black predecessor and close

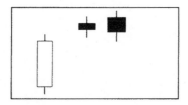

Figure 13-6   Upside gap two crows.

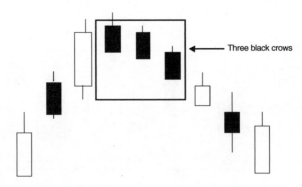

Figure 13-7   Three black crows.

at or close to its session low (see Fig. 13-8). You can see that none of the candles have a lower wick (see Fig. 13-9) and each of the three real bodies opens within the range of the previous session's real body.

Tweezer Tops and Bottoms (Kenuki)

If you hold a tweezer upside down, you will see that the two points are at identical levels (see Fig. 13-10). The same is true of a *tweezer top,* which consists of two candles that the high of the day is identical to. Actually, it's possible for a tweezer to consist of more than 2 days with an identical top. Make no mistake about it, we are talking about the high, which can be a shadow or real body close or open. This pattern is short-term bearish because the first day's high acts as resistance; when the second day is unable to punch

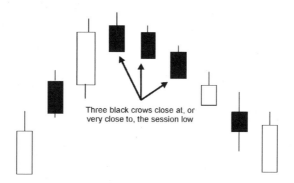

Figure 13-8 Three black crows.

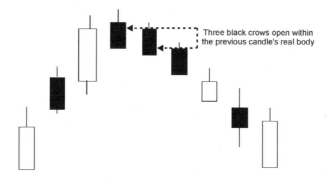

Figure 13-9 Three black crows.

through the horizontal line that marks the area of the top, it indicates a loss of upside momentum. In this example, the second day is also an engulfing pattern, which is an important point since a tweezer often contains a price pattern as part of its formation.

A *tweezer bottom* occurs when, after a decline, two or more candles make an identical low. This again indicates a loss of downside momentum since the price finds support in the area of the low. In Fig. 13-10, we see a tweezer literally hammered out because the second low to touch the horizontal line is a part of a hammer candle.

One factor that will increase the significance of a tweezer is the nature of the pattern being formed. For example, if the second day of a tweezer top is a hanging man, as in Fig. 13-11, we have two pieces of evidence that the trend may be about to reverse: the tweezer and the hanging man. Alternatively, the second day might be a doji, so the tweezer is really a harami cross (see Fig. 13-20). It could also be a shooting star. Finally, a tweezer bottom may also be a morning star, harami, hammer, and so forth.

Belt-Hold Lines (Yorikiri)

A bullish *belt hold* (see Fig. 13-12) is a one-candle pattern consisting of a long candle in which the price opens on the session low and then works its way higher throughout the session. The price does not have to close at the high, but the longer the real body, the more positive the candle. Also, if a belt hold has not appeared on the chart for quite a while, it is therefore an

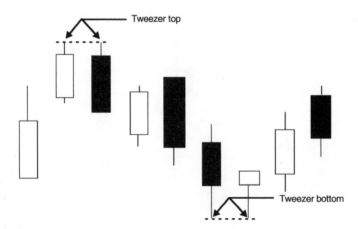

Figure 13-10 Tweezer tops and bottoms.

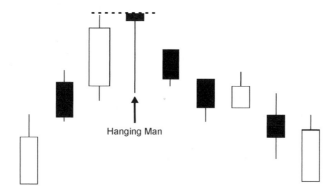

Figure 13-11 Tweezer top and a hanging man.

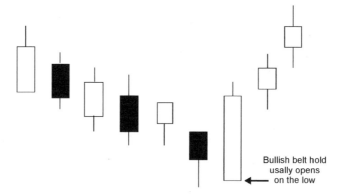

Figure 13-12 Bullish belt hold.

unusual phenomenon. As a result, it gains in importance. This is because traders are making a very strong statement about their feelings towards the market with a belt hold compared to the smaller candles that were previously the norm. Just think of a crowd murmuring, and then a loud voice comes from within the crowd. It is obviously a person who wants to be heard. Well, the belt hold following a long period of smaller candles amounts to the same thing. It's a 1-day pattern that says loudly, "Listen to me because I am telling you the short-term trend has changed."

A bearish belt hold (see Fig. 13-13) is the opposite. It is a long black candle in which the price opens at the high and then works its way lower as the session progresses. Belt holds are often important pivotal days since the high

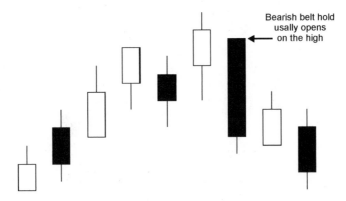

Bearish belt hold
usally opens
on the high

Figure 13-13   Bearish belt hold.

and low occasionally act as support and resistance areas in subsequent price action. The halfway point of the real body of a belt hold should also be monitored for a possible price reversal during later price swings.

Counterattack or Meeting Lines (Deai Sen/Gyakushu Sen)

A bullish *counterattack line* (see Fig. 13-14) develops when, after a decline, a black candle is followed by a white candle and both close or "meet" at the same level. This is why this 2-day pattern is sometimes referred to as a *meeting line.* The first day is usually a long black candle. The second day opens sharply lower, leading most traders to believe prices will continue to give way. However, by the end of the day, the price has regained everything lost (a counterattack by the buyers) and closes unchanged. The meeting line therefore indicates that the downside momentum has probably dissipated and a reversal in trend is likely.

A bearish counterattack or meeting line (see Fig. 13-15) is formed when, after an advance, a white candle is followed by a black candle and both close at the same level. The psychology behind this one is fairly evident. The sharply higher opening on the second day has the bulls in a euphoric mood since these new gains come on top of an already sharp rally. However, euphoria turns to disappointment as the price unexpectedly returns to the unchanged level.

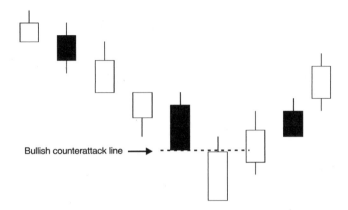

Figure 13-14 Bullish counterattack line.

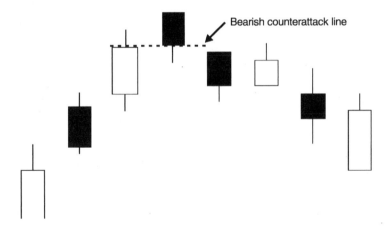

Figure 13-15 Bearish counterattack line.

More specific rules for identifying these patterns are as follows:

- The first day is colored in the direction of the prevailing trend and the second day forms in the opposite color (white/black for tops and black/white for bottoms).
- Both real bodies extend the prevailing trend and are long.
- The closes are identical.

Continuation Formations

Upside Gap (Tasuki)

A tasuki gap (see Fig. 13-16) occurs after an advance. The requirement is an upside, white line gap followed by a black line that does not close the gap. This type of pattern is usually followed by higher prices. However, if the gap is filled, the formation deteriorates into an upside gap with one crow and therefore loses its bullish portent.

Rising and Falling Three Methods (Uwa and Shita Banare Sanpoo Ohdatekomi)

These formations [see Figs. 13-17(*a*) and (*b*)] are very similar in concept to a flag in bar charting, except that they take only a few days, not weeks, to develop. The rising method is a bullish pattern and consists of a powerful white line followed by a series of three or four declining small black lines. These lines should be accompanied by a noticeable contraction in volume that indicates that a very fine balance is developing between buyers and sellers. The final part of the pattern is a very strong white line that takes the price to a new closing high. If volume data are available, this final day should record a significant increase in activity. The bearish falling three method is exactly the opposite except that volume characteristics are of no significance on the last day. An example is featured in Fig. 13-17(*b*).

Windows (Ku)

Japanese chartists refer to gaps as *windows* (see Fig. 13-18). Whereas gaps are said to be "filled" in traditional bar charts, windows are "closed" in candle charts. Windows therefore have the same technical implications as gaps. (Refer to Chapter 7.)

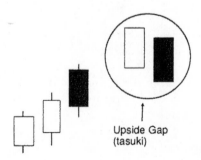

Upside Gap
(tasuki)

Figure 13-16 Upside gap.

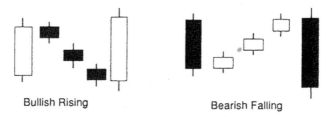

Bullish Rising   Bearish Falling

Figure 13-17 Rising and falling three methods.

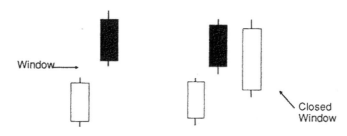

Figure 13-18 Windows.

Harami Lines (Yose)

In Chapter 8, it was mentioned that trendline violations are followed either by a reversal or a temporary consolidation. The *harami* formation, shown in Fig. 13-19, is similar to the consolidation trendline break in that it indicates a loss of momentum. The main difference is that harami lines are of much shorter duration and consist of 2 days' price action. The second one, the harami, forms a real body that is sufficiently small to be engulfed by the prior day's long real body. If the harami is also a doji, as in Fig. 13-20, it is called a *harami cross*. After a sharp rally or reaction, these patterns indicate a balance between buyers and sellers after one or the other has predominated. This means that haramis often warn of an impending trend change. In some instances, this will be from up or down to sideways and in others an actual reversal.

Harami

Figure 13-19   Harami.

Harami Cross

Figure 13-20   Harami cross.

Candle Charts and Western Techniques

There is a tendency among many technicians to look at candlesticks in isolation. My preference, remembering the weight of the evidence approach discussed earlier, is to combine selected Western charting techniques with candlesticks. This involves, amongst other things, the inclusion of price patterns, trendlines, and oscillators into the analysis.

Chart 13-5, for instance, shows a head-and-shoulders (H&S) top for Microsoft that was completed in November 2000. Note the sell off during the right shoulder was an identical three crow pattern. Later, we see a double bottom. The rally from the second low consisted of a bullish belt hold, which in itself indicated that prices were headed higher. This bottom was also associated with a reverse H&S in the RSI. Finally, the H&S top in the RSI was confirmed with a harami.

One important question is where to draw the trendlines. Should they touch the wicks, real bodies, or a combination of both? The answer lies in applying common sense. Since the opening and closing prices are generally more important than the high and low, lines that exclusively touch real bodies will generally be more significant than those only touching the wicks. However, a longer line that has been touched on more occasions and only touches the wicks will probably be more significant than one that is relatively short and only touches two real bodies.

Chart 13-5 Microsoft, 2000–2001, candles and an RSI. (*From www.pring.com.*)

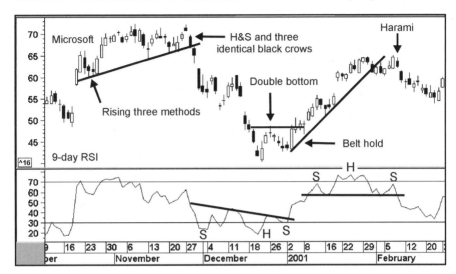

Candle Volume Charts

Candle volume charts are the same as regular candle charts with one important difference. The width of the real bodies varies with the level of volume during that particular session. The greater the volume, the wider the real body and vice versa. This is a very useful way of presenting the data because the signals from the regular candlesticks are preserved, yet the width of the real bodies offers a quick and simple overview of the volume pattern. We will have a lot to say on volume in Chapters 22 and 23, including the concept of equivolume on which the candle volume technique is based.

Chart 13-6 shows a candle volume chart for Wal-Mart. Notice how the early November window following the bullish engulfing pattern was closed soon after. However, the very thin candles that were involved in the retracement move indicated a lack of volume, which is precisely the type of thing that is required in a pullback of this nature. Heavy volume in such a situation would indicate selling pressure as opposed to the situation here where prices were clearly falling because of a lack of buying interest.

The previous rally experienced a series of very thin candles, which indicated that prices were rising on lower volume. This is opposite to the norm, where rising prices and volume are healthy. The very thin candles therefore warned that the days of the rally were numbered.

Chart 13-6 Wal-Mart, 2000–2001, and candle volume. (*From www.pring.com.*)

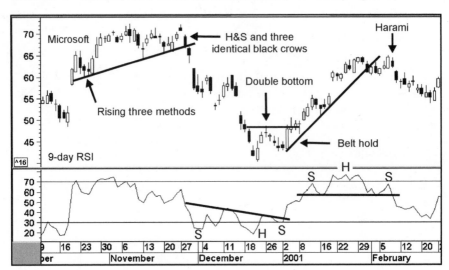

The late November/early December rally was associated with wider candles, which was a good sign. However, as we reach the week of the fourth, the candles move sideways, but are very thin. This indicates that the balance between buyers and sellers was more evenly matched. The doji on the day of the high also reflects the even balance. This characteristic is often followed by a trend reversal, especially if volume picks up on the downside. That's precisely what happened here, as the up trendline is violated and the candles thicken up.

The long white line that developed at the very end of December looked good at the time, since this candle was a pretty wide one, indicating heavy volume. However, there was no followthrough on the upside, which indicated that the long white line was a buying climax. This was confirmed first with the establishment of a harami on the subsequent day and by a long black candle that retraced all of the ground gained by the long white line.

Chart 13-7 shows the same period for Microsoft, as shown in Chart 13-5, but this time with candle volume. Note that from November 30 the bulk of the candles are thin, indicating low volume. The only thick candles are black ones, which indicate potential selling pressure. Finally, the right-shoulder rally consists of thin candles, indicating low (bearish) volume. The early December bear rally is also associated with thin candles. Rising prices on weak volume is bearish because it indicates that prices are rallying on a lack

Chart 13-7   Microsoft, 2000–2001, and candle volume. (*From www.pring.com.*)

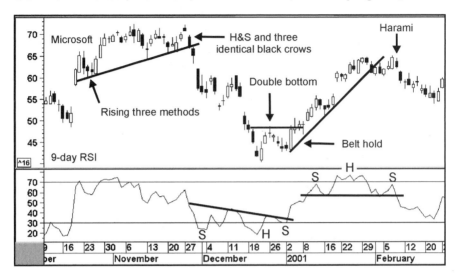

Chart 13-8   Boeing, 2000–2001, and candle volume. (*From www.pring.com.*)

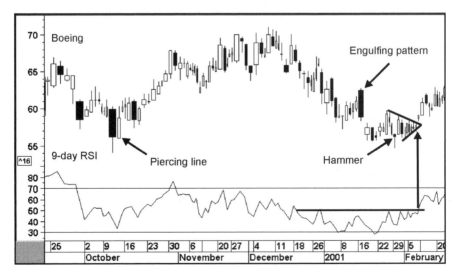

of selling rather than enthusiastic buying. Then, on the day of the rally high, the relatively thick black candle indicates that the days of the bulls are numbered because selling pressure has started to pick up.

You can see that the February down trendline break is associated with a thick belt hold and a trendline break in the RSI. Also, it's important to note that the nature of the RSI changes with candle volume, because the wider candles involve a slower, but more deliberate price action by the oscillator. Thin lines work in the opposite way, of course.

Chart 13-8, featuring Boeing, shows a piercing line in October. Note that the white candle is fairly thin. Normally, we would like to see a thick one because that would mean expanding volume. The engulfing day in January is a thick candle and the high volume that this reflects adds to the bearishness of the pattern. Finally, note how the candles break out from the symmetrical triangle at the same time the RSI completes a base.

Summary

- Candle charts can be constructed only from data that include opening prices, and therefore the technique is not one that can be applied to all markets.
- Candle charts provide a unique visual effect that emphasizes certain market characteristics not easily identifiable from bar or closing charts.
- Candle patterns can be reversal or continuation in nature.
- Western charting techniques can be used in conjunction with candles for superior results.
- Candle volume charts add an additional dimension to the analysis.

14
Point and Figure Charting

Point and Figure Charts versus Bar Charts

Point and figure charts differ from bar charts in two important ways. First, bar charts are plotted at specific time intervals regardless of whether there is any change in price. A new plot on a point and figure chart, on the other hand, is made only when the price changes by a given amount. Point and figure charts are only concerned with measuring price, whereas bar charts measure both price (on the vertical axis) and time (on the horizontal axis).

The second major difference is that bar charts record every change in price for the period they are measuring, but point and figure charts ignore all price movements that are smaller than a specified amount. For example, if a box is set at price movements of 5 points for the *Dow Jones Industrial Average* (DJIA), only price changes in excess of 5 points will be recorded, and smaller fluctuations will not appear.

Construction of Point and Figure Charts

Point and figure charts are constructed using combinations of X's and O's, known as boxes. The X shows that prices are moving up, the O that they are moving down. Once the amount of historical data to be plotted has been established, there are two important decisions to be made before a chart can be constructed.

First, the size of each box must be determined. For individual stocks, it is common practice to use a l-point unit or box for issues trading above $20 and a ½-point unit for lower-priced stocks. However, for very long term charts or for averages consisting of much higher numbers, it is more convenient to use 5-, 10-, or even 20-point boxes. As the box size is decreased, the detail of price movement graphically displayed is increased, and vice versa. In following the price action of a stock or market over many years, it is more convenient to use a relatively large box since small boxes will make the chart unduly large and unmanageable. Often, it is a good idea to maintain two or three different versions, just as daily, weekly, and monthly bar charts may be plotted.

The second decision is whether to use a regular point and figure formula or to use a reversal chart (which should not be confused with a reversal pattern). The straight point and figure chart is plotted just as the data are recorded. If the price moves from 64 to 65, five X's will be plotted on a 20¢-point chart, as in Fig. 14-1(*a*). If the price reverses from 67 to 66, five O's will be posted. Reversal charts, on the other hand, follow a predetermined rule: A new series of X's or 0's cannot begin until prices have moved by a specified amount in the opposite direction to the prevailing trend. The use of the reversal technique therefore helps to reduce misleading or whipsaw signals and to greatly compress the size of the chart so that more data can be plotted. Figure 14-1(*b*) shows the same data plotted as a line chart.

The construction of ½-point, 5-point, or 10-point charts, or charts by any other measure, is identical to the previous method except that a new box can be posted only when the price has moved by the degree specified, that is, by ½ point, 5 points, or 10 points, respectively. Since only price is recorded, it could take several days or even weeks before a new box is plotted. Hence, a common practice is to record dates either at the foot of the chart or in the boxes at the appropriate points. A combination of both date locations is used for longer-term charts. For example, the year is recorded at the bottom of the chart against the column that the first posting of that year was made for, and the beginning of each month is recorded in a box using the number of the month, 1 for January, 2 for February, and so on.

The decision about unit size (and thus the degree of price change required to trigger a new column of O's or X's) is essentially based on personal judgment. It is determined by the price range and degree of volatility of the indicator, stock, or market under consideration. Reducing the size of the units (figures) increases the detail of the price movement portrayed. Making the unit larger expands the base of data, that can be included, but this limits the number of fluctuations that can be illustrated (see Chart 14-1). Following a market with bar or line charts on a daily, weekly, or monthly

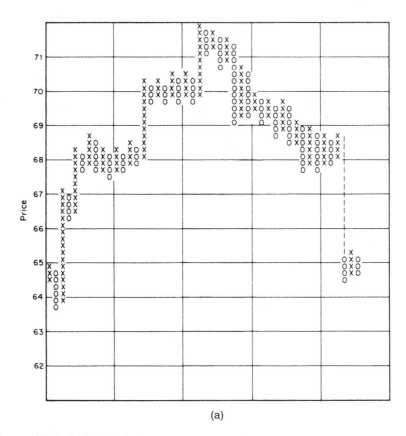

(a)

Figure 14-1 20¢ point chart.

basis corresponds to keeping several point and figure charts using various unit sizes.

Point and figure charts are plotted on an arithmetic scale. If drawn on paper, they would have traditionally been constructed with 8, 10, or 12 squares to the inch. Occasionally, point and figure charts are plotted on a semilogarithmic or ratio scale, though this is not the norm, because price objectives are calculated in a different way than those on regular charts with a time scale.

Data published in the financial press covering the high, low, and close for specific stocks are not suitable for accurate point and figure charts. For example, if a $15 stock has an intraday price range of $1½, it is impossible

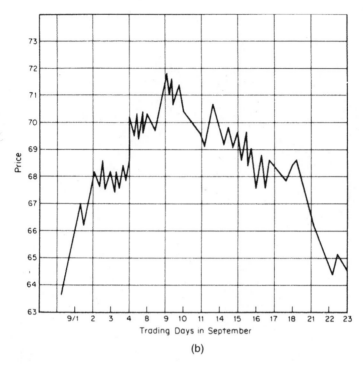

Figure 14-1 Closing prices (line chart).

to know for point and figure purposes the actual course of the stock from 14½ to 16. It could have risen from 14½ to 16 in one move, which for a ½-point chart would have been represented by three rising X's. Alternatively, it might have moved from 14½ to 15½, back to 14½, and then to 16, which would have resulted in two X's, two O's, and then a column of three X's. The character of the rally has a very important bearing on the appearance of a point and figure chart.

When dealing with data published in this form, it is better to use larger units so that intraday fluctuations do not distort the chart unduly. If more detail is required, the data should be purchased from a source that publishes intraday price movements. Charting packages featuring intraday data that have point and figure options are not affected by this problem.

Accepted rules for plotting point and figure data where the actual prices on the tape are not known are as follows:

- If the opening price is closer to the high than the low, assume that the course of prices is open, high, low, and close.

Chart 14-1 Gold price $5 and $2 reversals. These two charts show the gold price plotted on $5 and $2 reversals. The trendlines are self-explanatory. Note that the $5 chart captures 10 years of history very concisely. On the other hand, the 2-point reversal chart, which covers March to November 1982, offers far better detail. (*From Chart Analysis London.*)

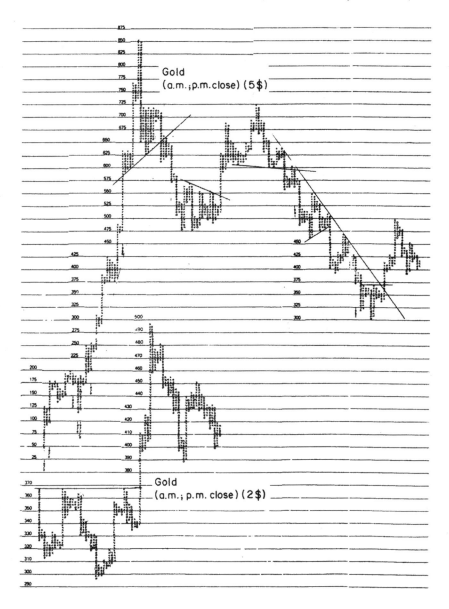

- If the opening price is closer to the low, assume open, low, high, and close.
- If the opening price is also the high, assume open, high, low, and close.
- If the opening price is also the low, assume open, low, high, and close.
- If the opening price is the low and the closing price is the high, assume open, low, close, and high.
- If the opening price is the high for the day and the close is the lowest price, assume open, high, close, and low.

Interpreting Point and Figure Charts

General

Since point and figure charts do not include volume, moving averages (MAs), or time, price action is the only element to be examined. In this respect, the basic principles of bar chart analysis are applied. There are certain disadvantages to using point and figure charts; for example, key reversal days, islands, gaps, and other such formations do not show up. On the other hand, if properly constructed, these charts represent all important price swings, even on an intraday basis. They effectively emphasize important support and resistance areas. For example, on a weekly bar chart, a single bar representing a weekly price action can take up only one line. However, if there was considerable volatility during the week in which support and resistance were each tested three or four times, this would most likely show up on a point and figure chart as a congestion area. As a result, the importance of these levels would be drawn to the attention of the technician, who would then be in a good position to interpret the significance of any breakout that might develop.

Point and figure patterns are similar in nature to those of price patterns and may be of the continuation or reversal type. The most common ones are shown in Fig. 14-2. Head-and-shoulders (H&S) and inverse H&S patterns, double tops and bottoms, and rounding tops and bottoms can easily be recognized as the point and figure equivalent of regular bar or close-only price formations, discussed previously. Most of the price patterns shown in Fig. 14-2 are explained in Chapter 5.

The Count Method

Chapter 5 pointed out that the minimum downside projection from an H&S top is derived by projecting the vertical distance from the top of the head

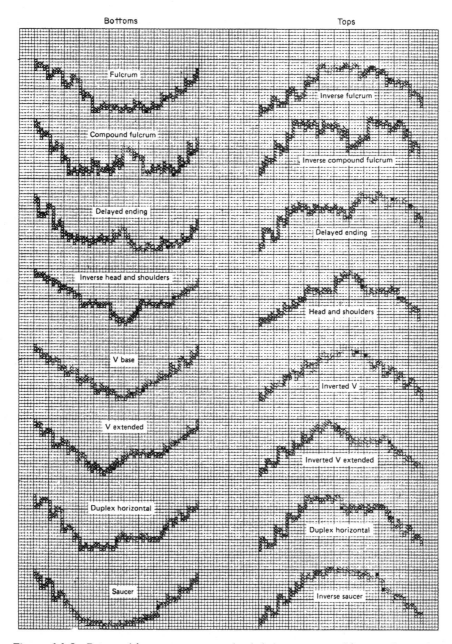

Figure 14-2 Point and figure price patterns (study helps in point and figure techniques).

to the neckline downward at the point of breakout. In point and figure charting, the *width* of the pattern is used to determine the measuring objective, which is again projected from the breakout point. No one to my knowledge has thus far satisfactorily explained why this principle appears to work. It seems to be based on the idea that lateral and vertical movements are proportional to each other on a point and figure chart. In other words, the more times a price has undergone price swings within two given levels (as dictated by the price pattern), the greater the *ultimate* move is likely to be once the breakout has taken place. On a point and figure chart, the dimensions of the consolidation or reversal pattern can be easily discerned by adding up the number of boxes and projecting the number downward or upward, depending on which way prices break out.

The problem with the count method is that formations with irregular outlines can generate confusion about where the count should begin. The best approach is to select an important horizontal line in the formation, measure across it, and add (or subtract) the number of boxes in the line to (or from) the level of the line.

Price projections for point and figure formations are by no means 100 percent accurate in all situations. In general, upside projections are likely to be exceeded in bull markets, and downside projections surpassed in bear markets. Projections that are made counter to the prevailing trend have a tendency not to be achieved, such as a downside projection in a bull market. Chart 14-2 shows a couple of examples of the count method in action.

Trendlines on Point and Figure Charts

It is possible to construct trendlines on point and figure charts by joining a series of declining peaks. Up trendlines are drawn by connecting a series of rising lows, and horizontal trendlines are created by joining identical sup-

Major Technical Principle The fundamental difference between price projections based on point and figure charts and those based on bar or close-only charts is that the measuring formula of point and figure charts is derived from a horizontal rather than a vertical count.

Chart 14-2 Honeywell (.50 × 1). This chart features a number of price formations for Honeywell using a .50 × 1 combination. Note that the measuring objective from the base on the left was reached almost to the dollar. The H&S top that followed offered a nice sell signal as the neckline was penetrated. The objective in this case called for the price to fall back to its previous low. As it turned out, this was exceeded. Note how the subsequent rally found resistance in approximately the same area as the objective. Finally, we see a nice trendline break in the right-hand side of the chart. (*From www.pring.com.*)

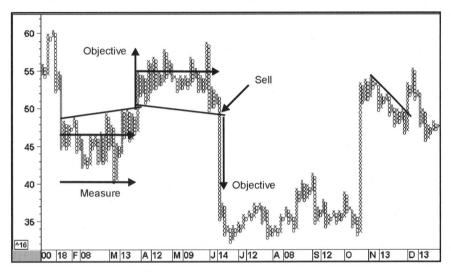

port or resistance levels. The same principles of interpretation discussed in Chapter 8 apply to trendlines drawn on point and figure charts. The trendline takes its significance from a combination of length, the angle of descent or ascent, and the number of times it has been touched. Misleading or whipsaw signals occur occasionally. However, if a carefully chosen reversal amount is used as a filter in the construction of the chart, such whipsaws can be kept to a minimum. Another possibility would be to draw a parallel line one box above (or below) the actual trendline as a filter and use this as the signal to buy (or sell). Although some timeliness is clearly lost with this type of approach, it does offer some protection from misleading price moves.

It is also possible to construct oscillators and plot them underneath point and figure charts. Since time is ignored in the point and figure charts, oscillators will appear differently than on regular charts where the time scale is plotted for each unit (hour, day, week, and so on). An example using a 14-period relative strength indicator (RSI) is shown in Chart 14-3.

Chart 14-3 Boeing (1 × 1) and an RSI. This chart of Boeing shows that it is possible to combine an oscillator with a point and figure chart. The joint breakout by the price and RSI offered a timely buy signal on June 16. *(From www.pring.com.)*

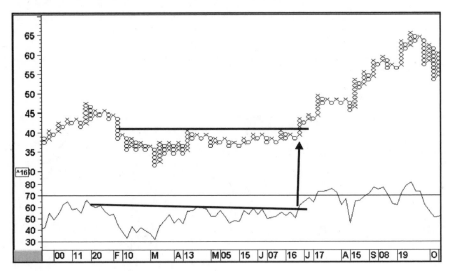

Summary

- Point and figure charts measure only one dimension: price.
- Point and figure charts are constructed from columns of X's and O's, known as figures, which represent a specified, predetermined price movement.
- Point and figure charts often point up support/resistance zones better than bar charts because they emphasize the number of price swings that take place within a given congestion area.
- Point and figure charts are interpreted similarly to bar charts, the main exception being the measuring formula, which is achieved by the principle of the count.

15

Miscellaneous Techniques for Determining Trends

Introduction

The two techniques discussed in this chapter, *support and resistance* and *proportion,* are concerned with estimating the potential extent or duration of a trend. This contrasts with most of the indicators previously examined that attempt to confirm a change in trend after it has already occurred. These techniques should be used only as an indication of the *probable* extent of the move, not as the basis of an actual forecast.

Support and Resistance Defined

Support and resistance are terms that we hear bandied about quite a lot, but to many of us their meaning is quite vague. Quite often seasoned pros

> **Major Technical Principle** There is no known method of predicting the exact magnitude or duration of a price trend.

say resistance when they actually mean support, and support when they really mean resistance. It's no wonder there is a lot of confusion. Support and resistance are points on a chart where the probabilities favor a halt or even a reversal in the prevailing trend.

Support is where a declining trend can be expected to halt temporarily due to a concentration of demand. Resistance is where an advancing trend can be expected to halt temporarily due to a concentration of supply.

Obviously, demand and supply are always equal, so the concentration of demand means that buyers are more enthusiastic than sellers and are therefore more willing to bid up prices and vice versa.

At the beginning of Fig. 15-1, the price is in a downtrend. The price rallies from point *B*. Since *previous bottoms and tops represent potential pivotal points on the charts*, it would be reasonable to expect the price to bottom at level *B* the next time its falls. However, this is not the case and it quickly falls to *A*. At this point, the bear market is interrupted by a consolidation pattern (rectangle) from which prices ultimately break down as the price is unable to hold at *A*. In technical jargon, we say that the support level was violated. If you jump up and down on the tenth floor of an old and decrepit multi-story building, eventually the floor gives way. The floor was your support area, which has now been violated. Thinking of personal safety, you must now look out for the next area of support, which is the floor of the ninth story. The same is true in markets; when a particular support level is violated, you need to look for the next one down.

The price reaches its low and then, after a brief period of consolidation, mounts a rally. This advance is halted at the dashed line, which is at the same level as the lower end of the rectangle. People who bought during the period when the rectangle was being formed have all lost money up to this point, and many of them are keen to liquidate their positions and break even.

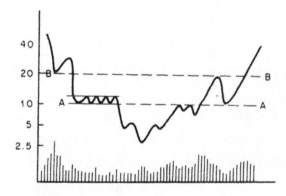

Figure 15-1 Support and resistance.

Consequently, there is a concentration of supply at this level, transforming what was formerly a zone of support to one of resistance. Such levels are often formed at round numbers such as 10, 50, or 100 since they represent easy psychological points upon which investors often base their decisions. Prices then fall off slightly and mount another assault on the resistance level at *A*, but still more of the asset is put up for sale. This is important, because it is a rule of technical analysis that *what becomes support on the way down turns out to be resistance on the way up.* Just remember our analogy of falling through the tenth floor and finding support at the ninth. If you want to get back to the tenth, you are going have to jump through the ceiling of the ninth floor because that now becomes resistance. It's the same in the markets.

Eventually, the resistance level is violated and prices advance to the next level of resistance at *B*. Once again, the previous level of support on the way down is reversed to one of resistance on the way up. The rationale for this lies in the fact that quite a few people bought at *B*, and when the price broke below it, they ended up with a paper loss. Now that the price has returned to *B* again, they have the chance to pretty well break even, so a lot of them take advantage of the opportunity and sell. You will also find that once a resistance level has been violated on the upside, subsequent declines will find support there. Consequently, the final decline on the chart halts at *A*. Thus, resistance levels once violated reverse their role to support.

Estimating Future Support/Resistance Levels

There are certain guidelines for identifying potential areas of support or resistance:

- Round numbers often become pivotal points on a chart. How often do we hear people say, "I'm going to sell when it reaches so and so." Well, if they are picking a number out of the air, chances are it's going to be a round number like 25, 50, 100, and so forth. The same thing works on the downside where you might say, "I'll buy some if it comes down to 10, 5, or a certain value." Round numbers, then, have a tendency to become support and resistance zones. I say zones as opposed to levels because prices will often move a little bit beyond or just fail to reach the actual round numbers, so zone is a more accurate description.
- Previous peaks and troughs have a strong tendency to become support or resistance zones. Again, you might hear someone say, "I'll sell it if it gets back to its old high of so and so," or "I'll buy it if it ever falls to so and so again." For example, if a stock rallies to $20, falls back, and then moves up to, say, $24, an intelligent place to anticipate a correction to

terminate would be the $20 area. This is because the previous high could well reverse its role from resistance to support on the way back.
- Trendlines and moving averages (MAs) are dynamic levels of support and resistance. We saw in previous chapters that a good trendline and a reliable MA are themselves support and resistance levels. Thus, it makes sense during an uptrend to buy a security when the price falls back to the area of the trendline. If the other indicators agree, this is a low-risk trade or investment because you can place a stop directly under the line. If it is hit, you then know that the support level reflected by the trendline has been violated.
- Emotional points on charts often represent significant potential support or resistance points. Possibilities include the opening and closing of gaps, key reversal highs and lows, Pinocchio highs or lows, and so forth.
- Retracement points and Fibonacci and Gann fans, as described later in this chapter, are a final possibility for anticipating potential support points.

Chart 15-1 shows some interesting support and resistance characteristics. First, the zone around the round number 50 halted two declines at the end of 2000, became resistance for a series of daily rallies in early 2001, and served as an opening for a gap a little bit afterward. The lower part of the downside gap in October 2000 became very important resistance for the next few months. Even after the price managed to rally above this level for a few sessions, the rally found resistance there before the price fell sharply. Finally, the opening of the gap in April 2001 became support for the sharp 1-day decline.

How to Determine the Significance of Support and Resistance Areas

There are several rules for determining the significance of any support or resistance area, but the four most important are as follows:

- The more times a zone has been able to halt or reverse a price trend, the greater its significance. This is perhaps the most important rule. Just think of it this way. If the price keeps bouncing off a support level, people get used to the idea. Then, when it is finally breached, those who have become accustomed to buying there and selling at a profit are forced to sell at a loss. Others would have placed stop losses below the support level. The longer it is established, the more obvious it becomes that this is the

Chart 15-1 Applied Micro, 2000–2001, and support and resistance zones. (*From www.pring.com.*)

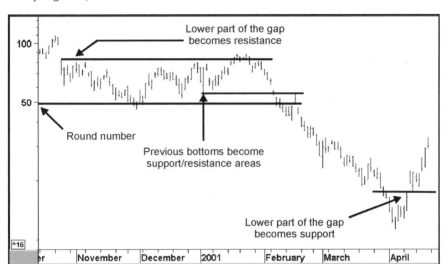

level at which to place stops. As the support gives way, confidence is lost until a new level at a lower price is established. The same principle in reverse works for a resistance zone.

- The steeper the price move preceding a given support or resistance zone, the greater its significance. Just think of trying to lift a heavy weight. If you make the attempt after running a fast race, you are less likely to succeed than someone who has not had to make such a dash. Markets are the same way. A modest support or resistance barrier is likely to be much more significant if prices have been racing ahead or declining sharply than if the price has been experiencing a slow, steady advance or decline.
- The greater the quantity of security that changes hands at a given support or resistance level, the greater its importance. People tend to remember their own experiences. This means that the larger the number of people who have bought or sold at a particular level, the greater the significance that level will have as a potential support or resistance zone. If a lot of participants bought at $8 and the price declines to $6, there will be a rush of sell orders at $8 when the price rallies because people have a problem taking losses, but are far more comfortable about breaking even.

- The fourth rule for establishing the potency of a support or resistance zone is to examine the amount of time that has elapsed between the formation of the original congestion and the nature of general market developments in the meantime. A supply that is 6 months old has greater potency than one established 10 or 20 years previously. Even so, it is almost uncanny how support and resistance levels repeat their effectiveness time and time again even when separated by many years.

Proportion

The law of motion states that for every action there is a reaction. Prices established in financial markets, as reflected in various trends, are really the measurement of crowd psychology in motion and are also subject to this law. The measuring implications of price patterns, trendlines, MAs, and envelopes are examples of this concept of proportion in practice.

Support and resistance levels can help to give an idea of just where a trend in prices may be temporarily halted or reversed. The principles of proportion can also help, but these principles go much further. For example, when a security is exploring new, all-time high ground, there is no indication of where a resistance level may occur, because no transactions have taken place. In such cases, the concept of proportion offers a clue to potential juncture points.

Perhaps the best-known principle of proportion is the *50 percent rule*. For instance, many bear markets, as measured by the Dow Jones Industrial Average (DJIA), have cut prices by half. For instance, the 1901–1903, 1907, 1919–1921, and 1937–1938 bear markets recorded declines of 46, 49, 47, and 50 percent, respectively. The first leg of the 1929–1932 bear market ended in October 1929 at 195, just over half the September high. Sometimes the halfway mark in an advance represents the point of balance, often giving a clue to the ultimate extent of the move in question or, alternatively, indicating an important juncture point for the return move. Thus, between 1970 and 1973, the market advanced from 628 to 1067. The halfway point in that rise was 848, or approximately the same level at which the first stage of the 1973–1974 bear market ended.

> **Major Technical Principle**   Support and resistance levels represent intelligent places for anticipating a trend to be reversed and therefore represent one more tool in the technical arsenal.

By the same token, rising markets often find resistance after doubling from a low; the first rally from 40 to 81 in the 1932–1937 bull market was a double.

In effect, the 50 percent mark falls halfway between the one-third to two-thirds retracement described in Chapter 3. These one-third and two-thirds proportions can be widely observed in the stock market and also serve as support or resistance zones. Ratio scale charts are helpful in determining such points since moves of identical proportion can easily be projected up and down.

The principle of proportion can also be applied to individual stocks. Chart 15-2 shows GM's habit of rising in proportions of about 50 percent. In down moves, this results in a 33 percent decline from high to low. The 55 and 35 percent proportions and multiples thereof tend to act as pivotal points for support and resistance areas. Thus, the 1974 low of about 32, when multiplied by 150 percent, results in an objective of just over 65. The 65 area proved to be one of strong support in 1976 and 1977, and it was one of resistance in 1978 and 1979.

Chart 15-2 GM's 1972–1983 50-Percent swing xones. (*From Securities Research, Boston, MA.*)

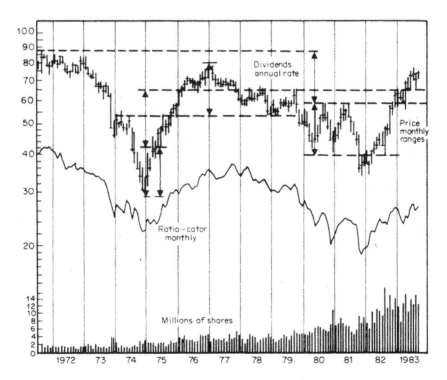

It is not possible to project which proportion will result from a specific move. However, these swings occur with sufficient consistency to offer possible reversal points at both peaks and troughs. If general market conditions and additional technical analysis of the price are consistent, there is a good chance that the projections based on this approach may prove accurate.

Remember, technical analysis deals with probabilities, which means that forecasts using only this method should not be undertaken. If you are making a projection based on the rules of proportion, it is always a good idea to see whether the projection corresponds to a previous support or resistance point. If so, the odds will be much higher that this zone will represent a reversal point or at least a temporary barrier. When a market is reaching new, all-time high ground, another possibility is to try to extend up trendlines. The point at which the line intersects with the projection using the rules of proportion may well represent the time and place of an important reversal. Experimentation will show that each market, stock, or commodity has a character of its own, some lending themselves more readily to this approach, and others not at all.

Chart 15-3, featuring SDL, shows another example of how proportionate retracements may be applied. The 0 percent represents the top of the move and therefore no retracement. The 100 percent signifies a retracement of the whole move.

Speed Resistance Lines

This concept incorporates the one-third and two-thirds proportions, but instead of using them as a base for a probable price objective, the speed of an advance or a decline is substituted. During a downward reaction, a price may be expected to find support when it reaches a line that is advancing at either two-thirds or one-third of the rate of advance from the previous trough to the previous peak. This is illustrated in Figs. 15-2(a) and (b). In the figures, A marks the peak and B the trough. The advance from A to B is 100 points and takes 100 days, so the speed of the advance is 1 point per day. A one-third-speed resistance line will advance at one-third of that rate (that is, one-third a point per day), and a two-thirds line will move at two-thirds a point per day.

A rally or decline is measured from the extreme intraday high or low and not the closing price. In order to construct a one-third-speed resistance line from Fig. 15-2(a), it is necessary to add 33 points (one-third of the 100-point advance) to the price at A and plot this point directly under B. In this case,

Chart 15-3 SDL, 1998–2001, and proportionate retracements. This chart shows several lines representing retracement percentages from the 1998 low to the bull market high set in the summer of 2000. Notice that the 33 percent retracement level marked the approximate lower end of a trading range. The 50 percent level acted as resistance for two rallies that flagged the top of two shoulders of a *potential head-and-shoulders* (H&S) pattern. Note that the word potential has been emphasized because the pattern had not yet been completed. Finally, the 66 percent level was the pivotal point at which the two declines in early and late 2000 were reversed. (*From www.pring.com.*)

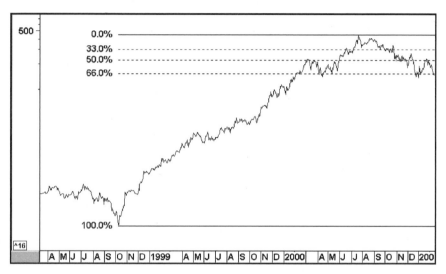

A is 100 points, so a plot is made at 133 under *B*. This point is then joined to *A* and the line extended to the right-hand portion of the graph. Similarly, the two-thirds line joins *A* and the 166 level on the same date as *B*.

If the chart were plotted on a ratio scale, the task would be much easier. All that would be required would be a line joining *A* and *B* [this is shown in Fig. 15-2(*b*)]. The angle of ascent, in this case 30 degrees, would then be recorded. Two lines at one-third (10 degrees) and two-thirds (20 degrees) of this angle are then drawn. Figure 15-3 illustrates the same process for a declining market. Once constructed, the speed resistance lines act as important support and resistance areas.

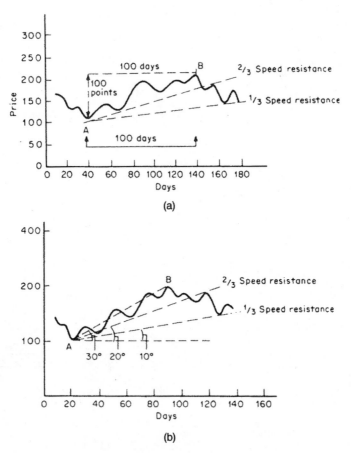

Figure 15-2 Speed resistance line (bull retracements).

Rules for Interpretation

More specifically, the application of these lines is based on the following rules:

- A reaction following a rally will find support at the two-thirds-speed resistance line. If this line is violated, the support should be found at the one-third-speed resistance line. If the index falls below its one-third line, the probabilities indicate that the rising move has been completed and that the index will decline to a new low, possibly below that upon which the speed resistance lines were based.

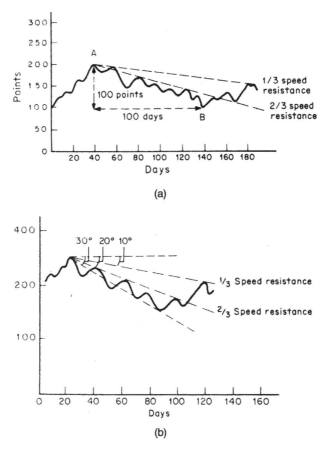

Figure 15-3 Speed resistance lines (bear retracements).

- If the index holds at the one-third line, a resistance to a further price advance may be expected at the two-thirds line. If the index moves above the two-thirds line, a new high is likely to be recorded.
- If the index violates its one-third line and then rallies again, it will find resistance to that rally at the one-third line.
- The previous rules apply in reverse for a declining market.

Chart 15-4 shows the application of these rules in the marketplace.

Chart 15-4 DJIA, 1975–1978, and speed resistance lines. (*From www.pring.com.*)

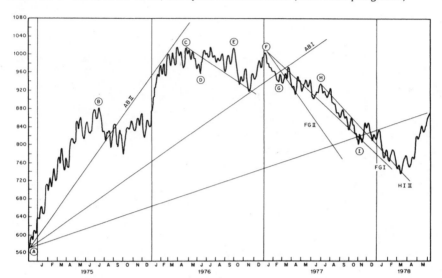

Fibonacci Retracements

The term *Fibonacci numbers* refers to a sequence of numbers discovered by the thirteenth-century mathematician Leonardo Fibonacci. The sequence is derived by taking the number 2 and adding it to the previous number in the series. Thus, $2 + 1 = 3$, $3 + 2 = 5$, $5 + 3 = 8$, and so forth. The sequence starts 1, 2, 3, 5, 8, 13, 21, 34, 55, 89, 144, 233, and so on.

It has a number of properties. For example, the ratio of one number to its next highest is 61.8 to 100. The ratio of any number to its next lower one is 161.8 to 100. The ratio 1.68 multiplied by the ratio .618 equals 1.

Fibonacci numbers, both for time and price, are widely used by technicians in projecting future pivotal points. One of the most practical uses of the sequence is for Fibonacci retracements. The first step is to measure the distance between a major low and high. In the case of Chart 15-5, this is indicated by the thick black arrow. Then Fibonacci numbers are used as possible retracement targets. These are represented in the chart by the other horizontal lines. The initial decline falls by 61.8 percent (to *A*), and the subsequent rally retraces 100 percent of the move because it forms the second top in a double top formation (*B*). When a subsequent decline takes the price to a new low, the next rally finds resistance at the 50 percent mark (*C*). The next thing to note is that the series of peaks between June and April finds resistance at the 100 percent retracement, that is, the starting point. Finally, the series of three lows, set between September and December 2000, all develop in the 161.8 percent vicinity.

Clearly, not every turning point has a Fibonacci flavor to it. However, it certainly makes sense to examine the technical picture for other evidence as the price approaches a known Fibonacci retracement level.

Fibonacci Fans

Another technique is to measure the vertical distance between a low and a high (or vice versa in a declining market). The next step is to measure certain Fibonacci points along the line. In Chart 15-6, I have labeled 38.2, 50, 61.8, and 100 percent. The 100 percent represents the whole distance of the vertical line. The 61.8 represents 61.8 percent of the total distance of the line from its peak and so on. The next step is to construct a line by joining the points on the vertical line to the original low and extending it to the right. These are the "fans" that are then used as possible turning points for prices. Chart 15-6 shows that the 38.2 and 61.8 lines held back a couple of serious declines for Sanmina.

Chart 15-5 Staples, 1999–2001, and Fibonnacci retracements. (*From www.pring.com.*)

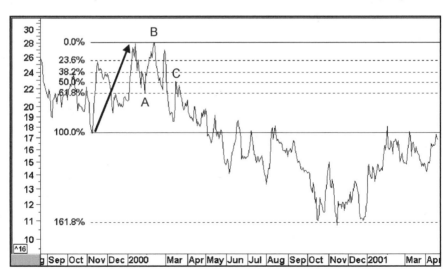

Chart 15-6   Sanmina, 1998–2001, and Fibonacci fan lines. (*From www.pring.com.*)

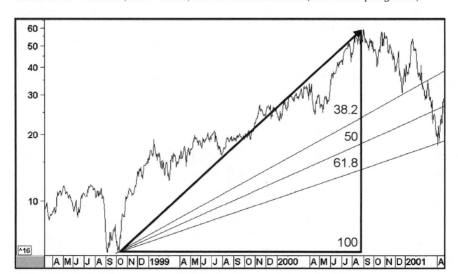

Having shown two good examples of Fibonacci retracements and fan lines in action, it is very important to emphasize that things do not always work out that well. This emphasizes the point already made that one should always use these techniques along with other indicators. As with any other techniques in the technical arsenal, they should never be used in isolation because all indicators can and will fail.

Gann Fans

Gann lines are named for the early twentieth-century commodity trader W. D. Gann. They come in three forms: Gann lines, fans, and grids. The most practical appears to be the fan approach. The concept and application are very similar to the speed resistance lines discussed previously. Gann's idea was that specific geometric patterns and angles had unique characteristics for the prediction of price turning points. Essential to this approach was a balance between time and price. Thus, to him, a 45-degree angle offered a perfect balance between price and time. That could only be achieved if the

Chart 15-7 Advanced Micro Circuit 2000 and Gann fan lines. (*From www.pring.com.*)

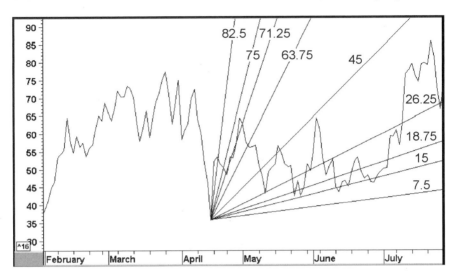

distance on the chart is the same for price and time, thus mandating an arithmetic scaling on the price axis. An example is shown in Chart 15-7, where the nine Gann-recommended angles are plotted.

Chart 15-8 shows an example of some Gann fans. This time the central line connects the high with the December low. The rise and run proportions are also the same; the centerline reflects a 1×1, the upper line 8×1, and so forth. However, because the time and price distances are different, the lines are at different angles. The principles of interpretation are the same, in that it is assumed that when one line is penetrated, the price will find resistance at the next one or support at the line it has just penetrated on the way down. Thus, the lines are continually reversing their support and resistance functions. See how the initial rally finds resistance at the 2×1 line. This line is subsequently penetrated on the way up, but acts as support for the next two reactions. Once again, there are far more exceptions than those reversal points that make up the rules. This means, of course, that Gann fans should be used as a place for anticipating a reversal, depending on what the other indicators are saying.

Chart 15-8 Advanced Micro Circuit, 2000–2001, and Gann fan lines. (*From www.pring.com.*)

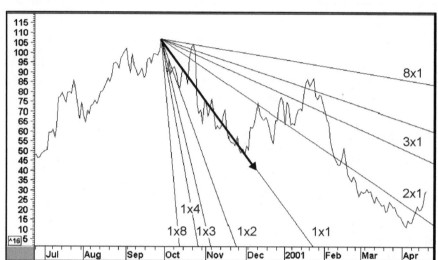

Summary

- A support area is a concentration of demand, which is sufficient to halt a decline at least temporarily.
- A resistance area is a concentration of supply, which is sufficient to turn back an advance at least temporarily.
- Once violated, a support zone reverses its role to resistance on the way back up, and resistance reverses its role to support on the way down.
- Once penetrated, a resistance zone reverses its role to one of support on the way down.
- Support and resistance zones gain significance from the number of times they have successfully turned back a trend, the amount of volume that has been transacted at that level, and the greater the speed of the preceding price movement.
- Places to look for potential support and resistance zones are previous highs and lows, retracement percentages, trendlines, MAs, and emotional points.

- Support and resistance zones are just one more tool in the technical arsenal that should be used in conjunction with others. They never guarantee a reversal; they just provide an intelligent place for anticipating one.
- Price often moves in proportion, and the most common proportions are one-half, one-third, and two-thirds.
- The Fibonacci sequence of numbers can be used for projecting future turning points. The techniques include retracements, fans, actual numbers, and time points that fall into the Fibonacci sequence.
- Gann believed that specific geometric patterns and angles have unique characteristics for the prediction of price turning points.

16
The Concept of Relative Strength

The Concept

Relative strength (RS) is a technical concept that measures the relationship between two securities. It's important to note that relative strength as we will be using it here should in no way be confused with Welles Wilder's relative strength indicator (RSI), which is outlined in Chapter 11.

RS as discussed here is comparative RS where one security is divided by another and the result is plotted as a continuous line. There are several ways in which RS can be used:

- RS can be used to compare one asset to another in order to decide which one to buy or to better understand an intermarket relationship. In this case we might compare gold to bonds to see whether the gold price is in a rising trend relative to bonds. If so, this could mean that an inflationary trend is unfolding. Another possibility might arise when a review of the technical position indicates that both the U.S. and the Japanese stock markets are in a bullish trend. Analyzing the trend of the RS between the two would show which market was likely to outperform the other.
- In commodity trading, a spread is a form of RS. A spread involves the relationship between one commodity and another, such as corn to hogs. Alternatively, a spread captures the relationship between a distant contract and a nearby one. In this instance traders are attempting to discover relationships that have diverged from the norm and riding on the spread until the two contracts come back into line.

- A currency is really a relative relationship. For example, there is no such thing as the "U.S. dollar" in an external sense because each currency is really a relationship between itself and other currencies—the dollar/euro cross, the euro/yen cross, and so forth.
- The most common and important use of RS is to compare a stock to a market average. For example, we might compare the performance of Microsoft to the S&P Composite. When RS is used in this way, it becomes a powerful concept for individual stock selection. It is this concept of comparing an individual security to a market average that we will be concentrating on in this chapter. Please note that unless otherwise stated, all RS comparisons in this chapter are against the S&P Composite.

Construction of an RS Line

An RS line is obtained by dividing the price of one item by another. The numerator is usually a stock and the denominator is a measurement of the market—for example, the NASDAQ or the S&P 500. The concept can also be expanded to the commodity area by comparing the price of an individual commodity, such as corn, to a commodity index, such as the Commodity Research Board (CRB) Composite. Figure 16-1 shows the closing price of the stock in the upper panel and its RS in the lower one. When the line is rising, it means that the stock is outperforming the market. In this case the denominator is the S&P Composite, so a rising line means that the stock is outperforming the S&P. Later, the stock continues to rally, but the RS line peaks out. This means that it is now underperforming the market. Another possibility might involve the comparison of an individual country's stock or index to a global indicator, such as the Morgan Stanley World Stock Index. As long as the appropriate currency adjustments are made, the principles are the same.

The interpretation of relative trends is subject to exactly the same principles as that of the price itself. It is important to note that an RS indicator is just what its name implies—*relative.* A rising line does not mean that an item, such as a stock, is advancing in price, but merely that it is outperforming the

---

Major Technical Principle RS moves in trends, just like the absolute price. This means that RS lends itself to trend-reversal techniques such as price patterns, trendlines, and moving average (MA) crossovers.

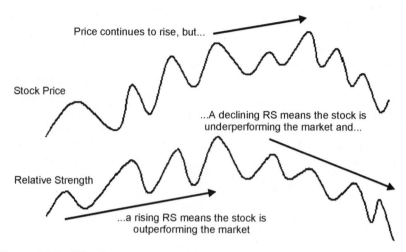

Figure 16-1   RS and price.

market or rising *relative* to the market index. For example, the market, as measured by the S&P Composite, may have fallen by 20 percent and the stock may have fallen by 10 percent. Both have lost value, but the RS line would be rising because the stock retreated less than the market.

RS Interpretation

Relative trends can be interpreted in similar ways to trends in absolute prices. However, the introduction of relative analysis into the equation offers an additional dynamic. This arises from a comparison of the two series that often throws up subtle differences in much the same way as a comparison between the price and an oscillator.

Since RS trends tend to experience more random noise than absolute price trends, we generally find that charts based on weekly and monthly data tend to be more reliable than those constructed from daily RS data. This same principle is true for the absolute price, but more so for relative action.

Positive and Negative RS Divergences

When both the price and the RS are rising, they are said to be "in gear." Important trends usually begin with both series acting in concert, but eventually the RS line fails to confirm new highs being set by the price itself. This type of situation indicates that the odds favor the stock beginning a period of underperformance against the market. However, weakness in RS is not an absolute sell signal—that is, one indicating that the price will go down; it is merely a relative signal—that is, one implying a switch from an issue that has started to become out of favor to one that is coming into favor.

Quite often, though, a divergence or series of divergences between the price and RS following an advance represents an early warning sign of trouble, which is later confirmed by a trend-reversal signal in the price itself. In Fig. 16-2 the two are in gear at the start, but later on the RS line diverges negatively with the price on three occasions. Finally, the price completes a top and declines.

The opposite set of circumstances holds true in a declining market in which an improvement in RS ahead of price is regarded as a positive sign. An example is shown in Fig. 16-3. This time the confirmation comes from a trendline break in the price.

Trend-Reversal Techniques

MA Crossovers Sometimes it's a good idea to run an MA through the price using the crossovers as legitimate signals of a change in trend. It's also possible to do the same thing for an RS line, but because the RS line tends to be much more volatile, this technique often proves unprofitable because

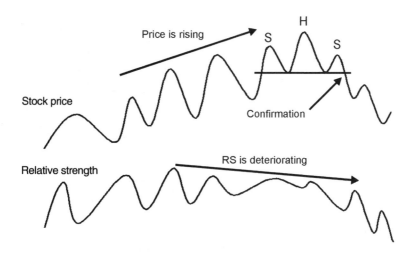

Figure 16-2 RS and a negative divergence.

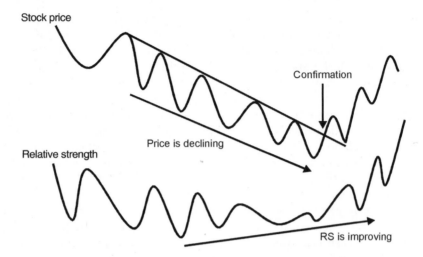

Figure 16-3   RS and a positive divergence.

of the numerous whipsaws that are generated. This is especially true for short-term trends, but even long-term MAs, such as a 40-week simple or 65-week exponential, often result in more whipsaw signals than we might like. Figure 16-4 offers an alternative. It involves plotting two MAs, a short-term and a longer-term average, using the crossovers for signaling trend reversals. This approach definitely eliminates whipsaws, but the trade-off is that several signals are less timely.

An example is shown in Chart 16-1 for General Motors. Note the numerous whipsaws for the 65-week EMA being flagged by the ellipse. Chart 16-2 shows an alternative, where the 65-week exponential moving average (EMA) is used with its 10-week EMA as a method of signaling trend changes. Note that pretty much all of the 1996–1998 whipsaws have been eliminated. We are still left with a couple, but the 1996–1998 pounding is totally avoided, as the 65-week dashed line remains below the solid blue line during the whole period.

Trendline Violations   I feel that a better alternative to the MA approach is to construct trendlines against the RS line. The concept is to construct a trendline for the RS line and when that is violated to look around for a legitimate trend-reversal signal in the price itself to act as confirmation. Figure 16-5 shows an example of a reversal from an uptrend to a downtrend.

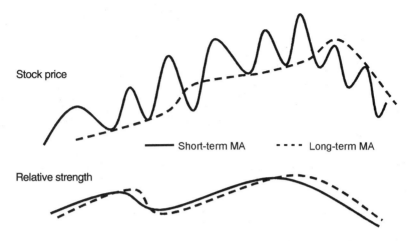

Figure 16-4 RS and MAs.

Chart 16-1 General Motors, 1993–2001, and RS MA crossovers. (*From www.pring.com.*)

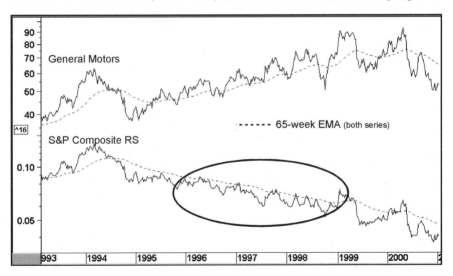

Figure 16-6 shows that this is also a useful way to identify "buy" candidates. The first thing to do is wait for a violation of the RS line. Then, when the price also confirms with a trend-reversal signal, you can take some action. These joint violations do not occur that often, but when they do, it's usually

Chart 16-2 General Motors, 1995–2000, and RS MA crossovers. (*From www.pring.com.*)

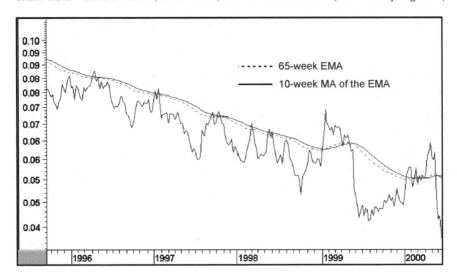

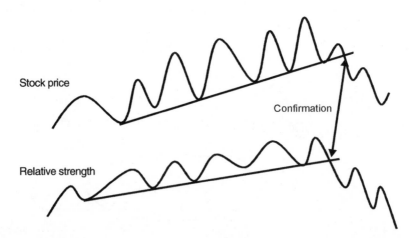

Figure 16-5 RS and uptrendlines.

a signal of an important reversal. In this case the strength of the signal has been enhanced because it was preceded by a positive divergence. The divergence did not represent a signal to buy, but it did set the scene for some positive action later by indicating that the technical position is improving.

Incidentally, the confirmation by the absolute price does not have to be a trendline break; it could be a price pattern completion, a reliable—and I emphasize the word *reliable*—MA crossover, or even a reversal to a series of rising peaks and troughs. Remember at all times that the size of the new trend depends principally on the time frame being charted and the length of the lines. Intraday breaks, for example, reflect small trends and have nowhere near the significance of trendline violations on the monthly charts.

Price Patterns Price patterns can also be employed to analyze trends in RS. In Fig. 16-7 the RS line completed a head-and-shoulders (H&S) top. This certainly indicates that the RS trend has reversed and provides enough evidence to justify a switch from this stock in favor of one where the RS trend was emerging in a positive way. However, it does not signal that the price itself is going to decline, though in many instances that will prove to be the case. In this particular example the absolute trend reversal is signaled when the short-term low flagged by the small horizontal trendline is violated because this confirms that the series of rising bottoms and tops has now been reversed. Note that even though the price subsequently rallies back through the line, this does nothing to reverse the peak trough progression to the upside, so the trend is still regarded as negative.

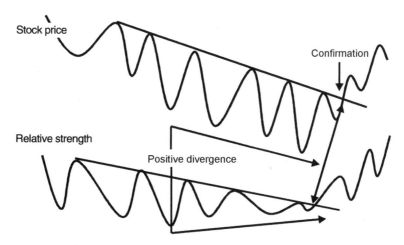

Figure 16-6 RS and downtrendlines.

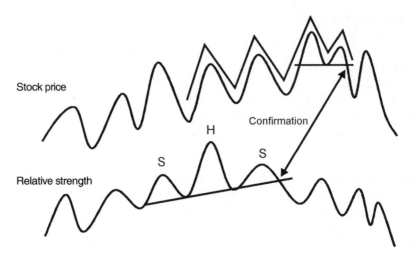

Figure 16-7 RS and price patterns.

Figure 16-8 features a reversal from a downtrend to an uptrend. First the RS line diverges positively with the price. This is our initial indication that both trends may be about to reverse. Then the RS line traces out a rectangle and breaks to the upside, later to be followed by the price completing a broadening formation with a flat top.

Long-Term RS

Chart 16-3 features a quarterly close of the S&P Domestic Oil RS line—relative, that is, to the S&P Composite. This is a very long term chart that encompasses much of the twentieth century. It is useful in that it demonstrates that the RS line lends itself to price pattern and trendline construction. These formations are not completed often, but they are usually followed by a relative price move that lasts for many years. It's important to bear this in mind because most of the patterns look small on the chart but extend over considerable periods of time. Their completion therefore signals a change in the environment that typically lasts for many years, even decades. For example, it traces out a 15-year H&S top in the late 1950s. A break of this magnitude signals a change in sentiment for a long time. Indeed, it was not until the late 1960s that the RS line returned to the level of the breakdown point.

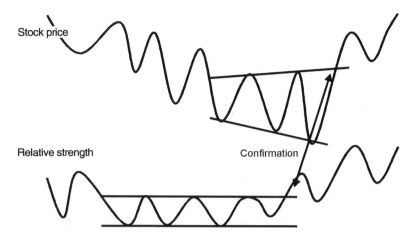

Figure 16-8 RS and price patterns.

Next we see a breakout from a double bottom formation that forms the right shoulder of an approximate 25-year reverse H&S pattern. The neckline is flagged with the dashed line, but the SHS labeling has been omitted so that the chart is not too busy. A huge pattern warrants a huge move, and that was definitely the case in this instance. A consolidation symmetrical triangle forms approximately halfway up the move.

Finally, note the fact that the Oil Index experienced a substantial rally between 1980 and the end of the century. Does this mean that oils would have been a good place to invest in this 20-year period? Hardly, because the persistent decline in the RS line indicated that the oils were consistent underperformers.

Obviously, we would not make a practice of studying these long-term charts every week or so, but say once a quarter it does make sense to review the long-term picture of the RS technical structure to see whether any major trends might be emerging. On a more regular basis, we would look at monthly charts covering a far shorter period of time, later moving down to the weekly and daily ones.

Individual Stocks and RS Analysis

Chart 16-4 compares General Motors to its RS line in the 1984–1987 period. The two large arrows point up a negative divergence between the two series. This indicated technical vulnerability but was not an outright sell signal for

Chart 16-3   S&P Domestic Oil, 1940–2001, and RS price patterns. (*From www.pring.com.*)

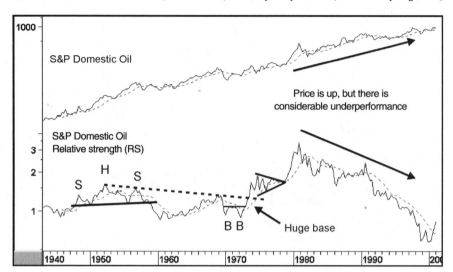

the stock. Later, the RS line completes a H&S top, which indicated that how-ever much GM might rally, it would be far less than the market. This was a definite sign of forthcoming weakness. As the RS line tries to rally back to the extended neckline, we see another small divergence as flagged by the two small dashed arrows. Finally, the price was confirmed by violating a sec-ondary 1984–1987 up trendline.

RS and Momentum

Long-Term Trends   Since classic trend-determining techniques can be applied to RS lines, it is a small step to expand the analysis to embrace momentum indicators derived from RS lines. While it is certainly practical to apply oscillators to short-term momentum of RS lines, by far the best use of momentum in relative work, I believe, is to use oscillators based on long-term spans that have been carefully smoothed to iron out unwanted fluc-tuations.

Chart 16-5 features the RS line of ConAgra Inc., together with a long-term know sure thing (KST) of RS. The waves against the RS line reflect the waves in the KST. Peaks in the KST roughly correspond with peaks in the waves and vice versa. As we shall learn in Chapter 19, RS lines are far more cycli-cal in their patterns than absolute prices. This makes the use of smoothed

Chart 16-4   General Motors, 1984–1987, and RS trendline breaks. (*From www.pring.com.*)

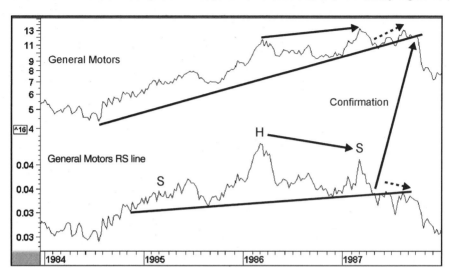

long-term oscillators such as the KST (see Chapter 12) far more accurate in their reflection of the primary trend. Remember, absolute prices can be subject to strong linear trends, which means that even the best-designed smoothed long-term momentum indicator will offer premature buy and sell signals. We cannot say this will never happen with a KST constructed from relative action, but it is certainly a lot less likely.

The principal objective is to identify a stock when its long-term KST is below zero and is starting to poke above its 26-week EMA. Incidentally, the average plotted against the RS line is a 65-week EMA. Note, even with a substantial time span such as this, there were still numerous whipsaws between 1987 and 1989 and 1994 and 1997. This is one of the reasons why I prefer to use trendline violations of the RS line in conjunction with long-term RS KST reversals. They are certainly not perfect, but they tend to be relatively more reliable. In this example I used a KST, but it is possible to substitute any smoothed long-term momentum indicator. The KST just happens to be my preference. Alternatives could be a stochastic, a moving average convergence divergence (MACD), or another trend deviation indicator. The basic idea is to use an indicator that closely resembles the primary up and down waves yet turns reasonably close to the turning points. When experimenting, always try for consistency over a number of stocks in different time periods; never go for perfection because it just isn't there.

Chart 16-5 ConAgra, 1985–2001, and a smoothed RS long-term momentum. (*From www.pring.com.*)

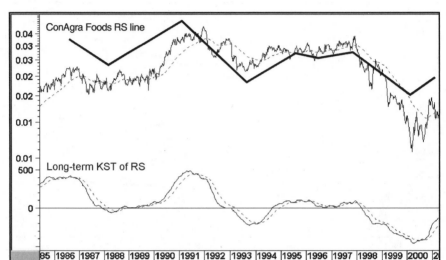

Once the direction and maturity of the long-term trend of RS has been established, it is then time to move to the shorter-term charts.

Short-Term Trends   Chart 16-6 features the relative action of Abbott Labs in the top panel, followed by a 14-day RSI of the RS line and in the lower panel an MACD of the RS line. It is fairly evident by looking at the chart that there are two main environments—a bear market between the end of 1999 and the start of the year 2000, followed by a bull move. Now take a closer look at the MACD. During the bear market, the MACD fails to reach an overbought condition yet oversold readings fail to signal rallies. The opposite is true during the bull phase. This is typical of oscillators since they change their characteristics in primary bull markets. Just like birds in the Northern Hemisphere, they migrate to the south during the winter or bear market and to the north in the summer or bull market. Whenever you can spot a situation where an oversold oscillator fails to trigger much in the way of a rally, this represents a tip that the prevailing trend may be bearish. It does not happen every time, of course, but in most cases this rule will work out. In this case, the failure of the January 1999 MACD oversold condition to generate a rally and its failure to register an overbought reading a little bit later pointed to a bear market environment.

Chart 16-6 Abbott Labs, RS 1998–2001, and short-term RS momentum. (*From www.pring.com.*)

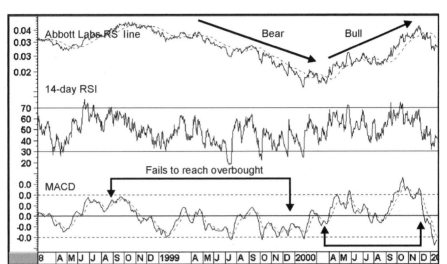

A sign that a bull market was starting did not come when the MACD reached an overbought reading, which, after all, is still possible in a bear market. Instead, it came when the May decline in the oscillator did not fall back to an oversold reading but was held just above zero. Such action indicated that the underlying character of the MACD had probably changed for the better.

Chart 16-7 shows an analysis of the relative action in greater detail starting with the October 1998 top. Signs of weakness started to appear as both the RSI and the MACD of RS violated up trendlines. This was then confirmed by the RS line itself violating an up trendline. This joint action was not important enough to signal a bear market, but it definitely indicated that the uptrend would be stalled for several months. In effect Abbott Labs was unlikely to outperform the market during that period. If you look carefully, you can see that the RSI trendline was, in fact, the neckline of a H&S top.

As we move on the price, action becomes progressively disappointing. The January oversold condition merely triggers a sideways trading range after which the relative downtrend is resumed. Also, look at the three dashed down trendline breaks. They should have been followed by a good rally, but they were not—the type of action that is often indicative of a bear market.

Chart 16-7 Abbott Labs, RS 1998–2001, and short-term RS momentum. (*From www.pring.com.*)

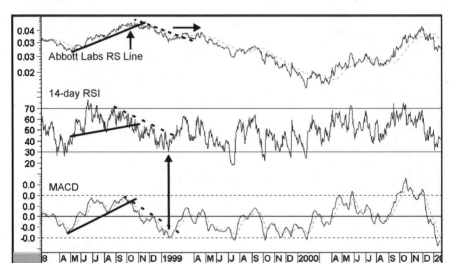

Chart 16-8 shows the same period but also includes the actual price. The dashed up trendline marks the approximate point where we got our relative sell signal, but note that the absolute price continued to extend its rally. It then diverged negatively with the RS line, indicating underlying technical weakness. However, it remained above its solid up trendline until January 1999. If the sell signals in the RS line that had developed previously were not sufficient evidence to justify liquidation, the violation of this trendline in the absolute price certainly was.

Chart 16-9 shows a closeup of the bullish period featured in Chart 16-6. Remember, coming into this period the RS line had been in a strong bear market where the momentum indicators had been triggering false signals. However, in March 2000 some positive action by both momentum series starts to develop since they barely fell below the equilibrium level at the time the RS line was reaching its second low in the top panel. Also, the MACD moved above its previous high, indicating a probable change in character more suitable for a bull than a bear market.

Finally, the RS line confirmed by breaking above the horizontal line marking the top of a double bottom formation. At the same time, it confirmed that a series of rising peaks and troughs was now under way. Throughout the bear market each rally high was lower than its predecessor; this was also the case with the bottoms.

Chart 16-8 Abbott Labs, 1998–1999, and short-term RS momentum. (*From www.pring.com.*)

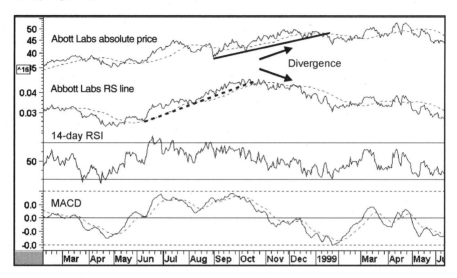

Chart 16-9 Abbott Labs, RS 1999–2000, and short-term RS momentum. (*From www.pring.com.*)

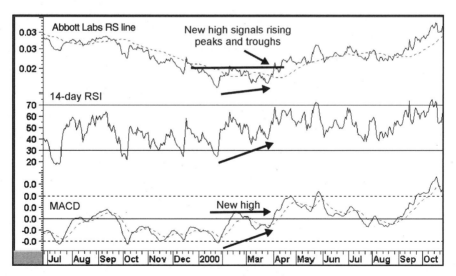

Spreads

RS is widely used in the futures markets under the heading "spread trading" in which market participants try to take advantage of market distortions. These discrepancies arise because of unusual fundamental developments that temporarily affect normal relationships. Spreads are often calculated by subtracting the numerator from the denominator rather than dividing. I prefer the division method because it presents the idea of proportionality. However, if a spread is calculated over a relatively short period (for example, less than 6 months), it is not important whether subtraction or division is used.

Spread relationships arise because of six principal factors:

- *Product relationships* such as soybeans versus soybean oil or meal, or crude oil versus gasoline or heating oil
- *Usage* such as hogs, cattle, or broilers to corn
- *Substitutes* such as wheat versus corn, or cattle versus hogs
- *Geographic factors* such as copper in London versus copper in New York, or sugar in Canada versus sugar in New York
- *Carrying cost* such as when a specific delivery month is out of line with the rest
- *Quality spreads* such as T-bills versus eurodollars, or S&P versus Value Line

Some of these relative relationships, such as London versus New York copper, *really* represent arbitrage activity and are not suitable for the individual investor or trader.

On the other hand, the so-called TED Spread, which measures the relationship between (high-quality) T-bills and (low-quality) eurodollars, is a popular trading vehicle.

In some cases, spreads move to what was previously an extreme and then proceed to an even greater distortion. For this reason it is always important to wait for some kind of trend-reversal signal before taking a position. While the risk associated with such transactions is by no means eliminated, it will certainly be reduced.

Other relationships between various asset categories are further analyzed in subsequent chapters. These relationships may be used for different purposes, but all are subject to trends, reversals of which can be identified by the techniques already described.

Summary

- Comparative RS compares one security with another. The result is plotted as a continuous line called the RS line.
- The most common application is to compare a stock with a market average. When the line is rising, it means that the stock is outperforming the market and vice versa.
- Divergences between the absolute price and RS warn of latent strength and weakness.
- RS moves in trends. Any legitimate trend-determining technique can be applied to a relative strength line.
- One of the most useful techniques for analyzing the primary trend of relative action is the use of smoothed long-term oscillators, especially the KST.

17
Putting the Indicators Together: The DJ Transports 1990–2001

It is now time to combine the indicators that we have covered so far into an analysis of the long-term picture. For this purpose I've chosen the Dow Jones transportation average between 1990 and 2001. Chart 17-1 shows the average together with its 9-month MA. This was one of the best testing averages derived by optimizing from 1931 through to the year 2000.

The upward and downward pointing arrows indicate the principal turning points in this period. The 1990 bottom was not an easy one to recognize because the average virtually reversed on a dime. Chart 17-2 shows that the 18-month rate of change (ROC) violated a sharp down trendline just before the price.

The relative strength (RS) line, in the center panel of Chart 17-3 actually broke its bear market trendline ahead of the absolute price. This indicated that the DJ Transports were likely to outperform the market during the early stages of the new bull market.

The vertical line in Chart 17-4 shows that this was one of the few occasions in which all three oscillators were simultaneously oversold. This chart also offered the strongest buy signal because the down trendline for the price was violated at approximately the same time as the 65-week exponential

Chart 17-1 Dow Jones Transports, 1989–2001, and turning points. (*From www.pring.com.*)

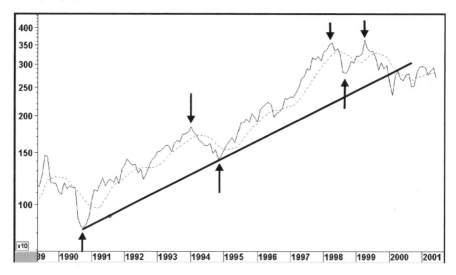

Chart 17-2 Dow Jones Transports, 1989–2001, and long-term Momentum. (*From www.pring.com.*)

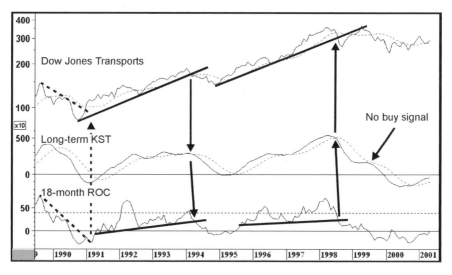

Chart 17-3 Dow Jones Transports, 1989–2001, and relative strength. (*From www.pring.com.*)

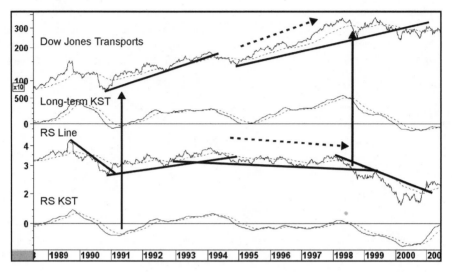

Chart 17-4 Dow Jones Transports, 1989–2001, and three weekly CMOs. (*From www.pring.com.*)

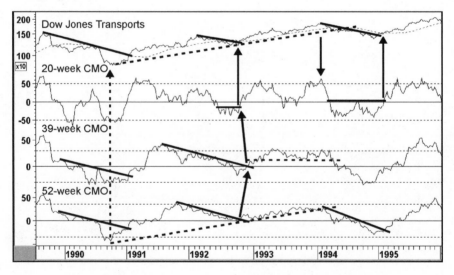

moving average (EMA). Also, the 39-week CMO completed a base. By February 1991, several positive signs had therefore developed, all of which indicated that downside momentum had probably dissipated sufficiently to allow the long-term know sure things (KSTs) to reverse to the upside.

The next major event was the intermediate peak in 1992. The average briefly crossed below its 12-month (Chart 17-2) and 65-week EMAs (Chart 17-3), and the long-term KST also triggered a negative whipsaw signal. These events could certainly have justified the conclusion that the Transports had begun a bear market. However, once the average and the long-term KST (Chart 17-2) had crossed back above their respective moving averages (MAs), there was little reason to maintain a bearish stance.

Unfortunately, this whipsaw type activity occasionally develops from an intermediate correction. Under such circumstances it is important to keep an open mind on the indicators. In this case, Chart 17-4 shows that the 20-week Chande momentum oscillator (CMO) broke out from a base and several down trendlines were broken, so there was plenty of evidence that the tide had turned.

The top of the bull market developed 2 years later in early 1994. Signs of a major top were quite widespread. In Chart 17-2 the Transports simultaneously violated a 4-year up trendline and the 12-month MA. The KST gave a decisive sell signal, and the 18-month ROC completed a head-and-shoulders (H&S) top. In the whole 11 years covered by the chart, there were only two completed chart patterns for this indicator, so the early 1994 breakdown was very significant.

Chart 17-4 was equally significant in its bearish entrails. The 39- and 52-week CMOs diverged negatively with the price, and both series completed a top or experienced a major trendline violation. At the peak itself, the 20-week CMO was actually overbought. The chart shows that, except for the strongest of up- or downtrends, the overbought and oversold conditions were often associated with intermediate-type reversals. Later in the year something more ominous started to happen, and this was a trendline break in the RS line. For the first time since the bull market in RS began the long-term RS, KST (shown in Chart 17-3) triggered a decisive sell signal. Although it was not apparent at this point, the transports had begun a long period of underperformance.

Because the ensuing bear market was relatively mild, the bottom in early 1995 was only signaled on the weekly charts. Once again, Chart 17-4 holds the key, as the down trendline in the 52-week CMO was violated and a base in the 20-week series completed. The Transports themselves more or less simultaneously broke above their bear market down trendline and 65-week EMA. The long-term KST in Chart 17-3 also turned positive around the same time.

The average remained above its 65-week EMA for the next 4 years and the series of rising peaks and troughs continued. Then, some extremely serious trend breaks developed. First, the average itself crossed below its 12-month MA and violated its bull market trendline (Chart 17-2). The KST also triggered a sell signal and the 18-month ROC completed a top.

Chart 17-5 shows that the Transports also completed and broke down from an upward-sloping H&S top and crossed below its 65-week EMA more or less at the same time. Notice how the 39- and 52-week CMOs were actually below zero at the time the average was forming the right shoulder. This distinct lack of upside momentum was a very bearish sign. Not surprisingly, the Transports experienced a pretty sharp decline into the fall of 1998.

The most serious technical damage of all came from Chart 17-3 in the form of a major breakdown in the RS line below a 6-year support trendline. This happened as the absolute price was crossing below its 65-week EMA. Trouble on the RS front had been signaled long before this, because it had utterly and completely failed to confirm the bull market in the absolute price. By the time of the 1998 peak in the Transports themselves, the RS line had experienced a major negative divergence. When the RS line moved

Chart 17-5 Dow Jones Transports, 1995–2001, and three weekly CMOs. (*From www.pring.com.*)

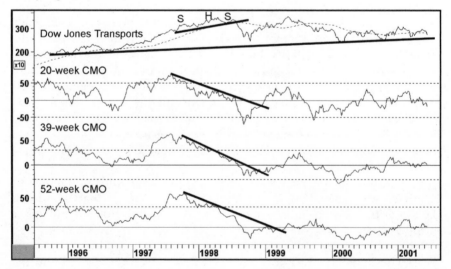

to a new post-1993 low at the end of 1996, this should have been warning enough that there were far better places for exposure than transportation stocks.

The 1998 bottom, like that of 1990, was an elusive affair, but more so because the turn was so sharp. All three CMOs in Chart 17-5 violated down trendlines, but the average itself did not cross above its average until it had rallied a long way from the bottom. No down trendlines could be drawn against the price, so it was not really possible to build a timely and convincing bullish case. In cases where the evidence of a trend reversal is incomplete, it is always better to avoid the security in question. In any event, the overriding factor should have been the early 1998 breakdown in the RS line, as this set the scene for the next several years of trading action.

Indeed, as it turned out, the 1998–1999 advance was really an above-average reflex rally since all the price was able to do was to rally back to resistance in the form of its 1998 high and the extended bull market trendline. During this whole period the KST failed to give a buy signal and the RS line in Chart 17-3 never crossed back above its 65-week EMA.

Finally, the average violated its 1990–2000 up trendline at the start of the new century. This was not a great trendline, for, although it was quite long, it had only been touched on two occasions and was not therefore a great reflection of the underlying trend. However, it did result in a sideways trading range over the ensuing 2 years. The critical point after this would be the trendline joining a series of lows between 1996 and 2001. A break below it, notwithstanding other evidence, would be a serious technical blow.

Summary

This has been a brief account of the technical position of the Transports between 1990 and 2000. Although it was not possible to include too many indicators, it has enabled us to describe how trend indicators for price, momentum, and RS can be combined to help identify major turning points.

PART II
Market Structure

18

Price: The Major Averages

Price is the most logical starting point for any attempt to analyze the strength of the overall market structure.

No index represents the ideal movement of "the market." Although the majority of stocks move together in the same direction most of the time, there is rarely a period when specific stocks or several groups of stocks are not moving contrary to the general direction of the trend. There are basically two methods for measuring the general level of stock prices. The first, known as an *unweighted index,* takes a mean average of the prices of a wide base of stocks; the second also takes an average of the prices of a number of stocks, but in this case the prices are weighted by the outstanding capitalization (that is, the number and market value of shares) of each company. The first method monitors the movement of the vast majority of listed stocks, but since the second gives a greater weight to larger companies, movements in a market average constructed in this way more fairly represent changes in the value of the nation's portfolios. For this reason, weighted averages are usually used as the best proxy for the market. These averages are compiled from stocks representing public participation, market leadership, and industry importance.

Several price indexes have been developed that measure various segments of the market. Their interrelationship offers useful clues about its overall technical condition. Chapter 3 discussed in detail the relationship between the Dow Jones Industrial Average (DJIA) and the *Dow Jones Transportation Average,* but there are many other useful indexes, such as, the *Dow Jones Utility Average,* unweighted indexes, and a few bellwether stock groups. These indexes are examined in this chapter in the context of their contribution to the U.S. market's overall technical structure.

Composite Market Indexes

The DJIA is the most widely followed stock market index in the world. It is constructed by totaling the prices of 30 stocks and dividing the total by a divisor. The divisor, which is published regularly in *The Wall Street Journal* and *Barron's,* is changed from time to time because of stock splits, stock dividends, and changes in the composition of the average. Strictly speaking, it is not a composite index, since it does not include such industries as transportation and utilities. Yet, the capitalization of the DJIA stocks is equivalent to a substantial percentage of the outstanding capitalization on the New York Stock Exchange (NYSE), and it has normally proved to be a reliable indicator of general market movements.

The original reason for including a relatively small number of stocks in an average was convenience. Years ago the averages had to be laboriously calculated by hand. With the advent of the computer, the inclusion of a much more comprehensive sample became much easier.

One of the drawbacks of the method used in the construction of the DJIA is that if a stock increases in price and is not split, its influence on the average will become substantially greater, especially if many of the other Dow stocks are growing and splitting at the same time. In spite of this and other drawbacks, the Dow has, over the years, acted fairly consistently with many of the more widely capitalized market averages.

The Standard and Poor's (S&P) *Composite,* which comprises 500 stocks representing well over 90 percent of the NYSE market value, is another widely followed bellwether average. It is calculated by multiplying the price of each share by the number of shares outstanding, totaling the value of each company, and reducing the answer to an index number.

Over the years, the S&P 500 has become the benchmark against which the professional money manager is judged. It is also the most widely traded equity futures contract.

Most of the time, the DJIA and S&P 500 move in the same direction, but there are times when a new high or low is achieved in one index but not the other. Generally speaking, the greater the divergence, the more substantial the subsequent move in the opposite direction. Chart 18-1 shows that in late 1968, the S&P 500 reached a new all-time high, unlike the DJIA, which was not able to surpass its 1966 peak. This development helped to signal a bear market that wiped nearly 40 percent off the value of both averages. On the other hand, the 1973–1974 bear market was completed with a double bottom. In the case of the DJIA, the second bottom in December 1974 was lower than the October one, yet the S&P 500 failed to confirm the new low in the DJIA. In the space of the next 2 years, the DJIA rose by some 80 percent. This is also shown in Chart 18-1.

Chart 18-1 Key market averages, 1965–1978. (*From Securities Research.*)

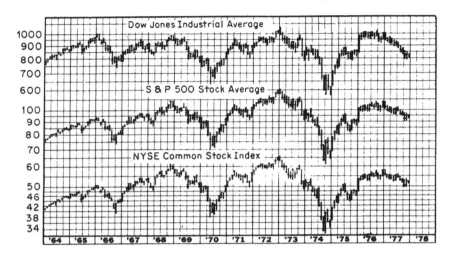

Chart 18-2 compares the DJIA to the S&P Composite for the turn of the century. For most of the 1990s, both series were in gear. However, the DJIA made its peak in January 2000, and the S&P topped out in March and September of that year. This indicated that both averages were out of gear with each other. The confirmation of a bear trend came later in the year when each one violated important up trendlines.

The *NASDAQ Composite* is a capitalization-weighted index consisting of 5000 stocks. Since it contains most of the technology heavyweights, such as Microsoft, Cisco, and Intel, it is very much a technology-driven index, and is discussed in greater detail later in this chapter.

The NYSE compiles an all-encompassing index called the *NYSE Composite*. In a sense, it represents the ideal average, since its value is based on the capitalization of all shares on the exchange. Its movements are similar to those of the DJIA and the S&P 500. Nevertheless, divergences between the trends of these three averages offer additional confirmation of changes in the overall technical structure.

The most comprehensive indicator of all is the *Wilshire 5000 Equity Index*, a composite that represents the value-weighted total in billions of dollars of most of the actively traded common stocks in the United States. Originally, it included 5000 securities, hence the name, but at the turn of the century this had grown to include over 6500 issues. Conceptually, this is the indicator that should be used for monitoring trends of the overall market, but because of the lethargy of the investment community and the obvious vested

Chart 18-2   The DJIA versus the S&P Composite, 1998–2001, and divergences. (*From www.pring.com.*)

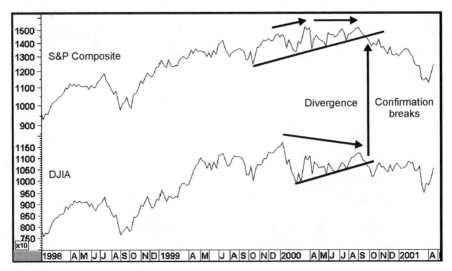

interest of the sponsors of the other popular averages, it has not received the widespread recognition that it justly deserves.

The Wilshire 5000 is compared to the DJIA in Chart 18-3. The relationship, just like that between the DJIA and the S&P Composite, is in gear for the vast majority of the time. It is when they disagree that a warning of a potential reversal in trend is given. We saw one develop in 1997. However, this was not followed by a trend change. In such situations it is often best to await some kind of trend-reversal signal to act as confirmation. In this instance neither series violated its 40-week MA, although the DJIA came pretty close. Later we saw a positive divergence at the 1998 bottom. Both series subsequently confirmed by crossing above their respective averages. Finally, the 2000 top experienced a divergence as the DJIA topped out in January and the Wilshire in March. The MA crossovers were not reliable in this instance, but there was little doubt once the Wilshire had violated its 2-year secondary up trendline. In actual fact this was the neckline of an upward-sloping head-and-shoulders pattern.

The Market Averages Using MAs

When experimenting with an MA from the point of view of trend determination, it is necessary to first assess the type of cycle to be considered. The

Chart 18-3 DJIA versus the Wilshire 5000, 1995–2001, and divergences. (*From www.pring.com.*)

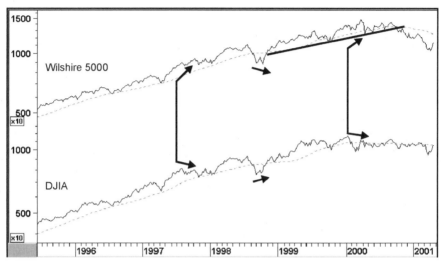

4-year stock market cycle has corresponded to the U.S. business cycle for many decades. Since the stock market is greatly influenced by business cycle developments, this 4-year (or to place it more exactly, 41-month) cycle is of great significance in trend determination. Consequently, the choice of an MA to detect such swings is limited to anything less than the full period, that is, 41 months, since an MA covering this whole time span would smooth out the complete cycle and theoretically become a straight line. In practice, the MA does fluctuate, since the cycle is rarely limited exactly to its average 41 months and varies in magnitude of price change. Through computer research[1] it has been found that a 12-month MA for the S&P Composite was the most reliable between 1910 and the early 1990s. This was not true for every decade but for the period as a whole.

In his book *The Stock Market Indicators,* William Gordon calculated that a 40-week crossover gave 29 buy and sell signals for the DJIA between 1897 and 1967. The average gain for all bull signals (that is, between the buy and sell signals) was 27 percent, and the average change from sell signals was 4 percent. For investors using the buy signals to purchase stocks, nine of the

[1]Robert W. Colby and Thomas A. Meyers, *The Encyclopedia of Technical Market Indicators,* Dow Jones-Irwin, 1988. Investors Press, Palisades, N.J., 1968. The actual rule used for buy signals was as follows: "If the 200-day (40-week) average line flattens out following a previous decline, or is advancing and the price of the stock penetrates that average line on the upside, this comprises a major buying signal."

signals resulted in losses, although none greater than 7 percent, while gains were significantly higher. This approach has worked reasonably well since 1967, though it is important to note that 40-week MA crossovers of the S&P Composite resulted in many whipsaws in the late 1970s. As so often happens after a number of whipsaws, the 1982 buy signal was superb. It captured most of the initial advance of the 1982–1987 bull market. The February 1984 sell signal was reasonably timely as was the August 1984 buy signal, which would have kept investors in the market until the Friday before the 1987 crash.

Chart 18-4 shows the DJIA and its 40-week MA between 1990 and 2001 in the lower panel. The upper panel is the equity line based on a 40-week crossover. Only long positions were taken, and a 4 percent interest rate was earned when the index was below its MA. No margin was involved, and an allowance for a 1 percent commission for a round trip was made. The approach worked reasonably well except for the trading ranges of 1994 and 1999–2001. This demonstrates why it is often a good idea to use a trend-following approach, such as moving averages with oscillators, which come into their own during trading ranges.

For intermediate swings, crossovers of 13- and 10-week (50-day) averages have proven to be useful benchmarks, but naturally an MA covering such a brief time span can result in many misleading whipsaws and is, therefore, less reliable than the 40-week average. For even shorter swings, a 30-day (6-week) MA works well, although some technicians prefer a 25-day average.

Chart 18-4   DJIA, 1990–2001. (*From www.pring.com.*)

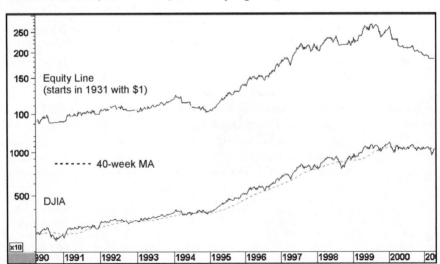

The Major Averages and ROCs

There are many ways in which the techniques described in Chapter 10 can be adapted to the major averages. In Charts 18-5 and 18-6, for instance, the S&P Composite is featured with a 9-month ROC. It seems that an excellent signal of an intermediate to primary trend bottom develops when the ROC either recrosses above its oversold line at −20 percent or touches the −20 percent level and then reverses. Alternatively, a recrossing of the +20 percent level offers a reasonably reliable intermediate peak or bear market signal. Obviously, this is not a perfect indicator, but for the most part it works with a high degree of statistical reliability. Some of the most glaring errors are flagged by the ellipses. The first in 1929–1930 was obviously premature, and the second in the late 1990s experienced several whipsaw signals that completely failed. In really strong or weak markets, premature signals are triggered so it's a good idea to wait for confirmation from a 9- or 12-month MA crossover.

Another technique is to construct an up trendline joining the bear market low with the first intermediate bottom. This is then combined with a 12-month ROC where a similar trendline is constructed or a price pattern, if available, flagged. That is the idea behind the trendlines drawn in Charts 18-7 and 18-8. Sometimes it is not possible to construct such lines unless they are extremely steep. Consequently, we are left with the alternative of a secondary trendline such as the situation in the early 1990s. When both lines are violated, this is usually a good sign that the bull move is over. Most of

Chart 18-5 S&P Composite, 1900–1950, and a 9-Month ROC. (*From www.pring.com.*)

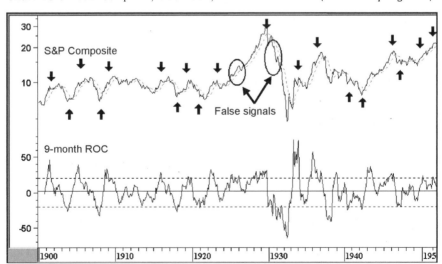

Chart 18-6   S&P Composite, 1950–2001, and a 9-Month ROC. (*From www.pring.com.*)

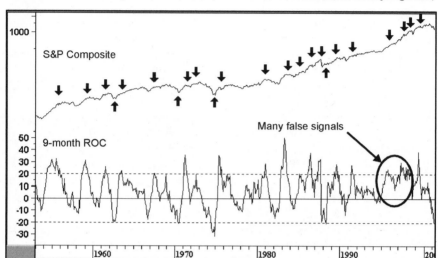

> **Major Technical Principle**   In cases where it is obvious that trend-
> lines are going to be violated well after the turning point, it is usually
> best to disregard them and rely on other evidence.

---

the time the signals come fairly close to the bull market peak. However, in
the 1982 and 1987 instances, the breaks obviously came too late to be of
any practical use.

Even though this approach worked pretty well in the twentieth century,
there were some failures. One example developed in 1998, where a good
joint trendline break in the price and momentum turned out to be whipsaws. Chart 18-9 shows the same type of approach, but this time using weekly
data and a 52-week ROC.

This technique, substituting a 13-week ROC, can also be used for identifying intermediate trend reversals. An example is shown in Chart 18-10. It
involves the drawing of trendlines for both the weekly closing price of the
DJIA and its 13-week momentum. When a break in one series is confirmed
by the other, a reversal in the prevailing trend usually takes place. Such signals are illustrated in the chart by the arrows. This type of analysis should
be supported where appropriate with price pattern analysis for the S&P and
with other techniques using the principles described in Chapter 10. The

Chart 18-7   S&P Composite, 1966–1983, and trendlines. (*From www.pring.com.*)

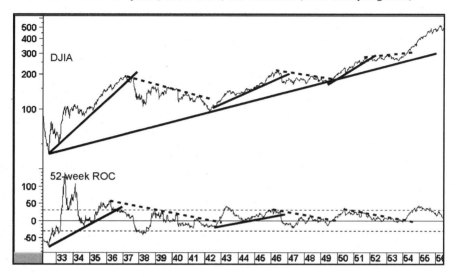

Chart 18-8   S&P Composite, 1984–2001, and trendlines. (*From www.pring.com.*)

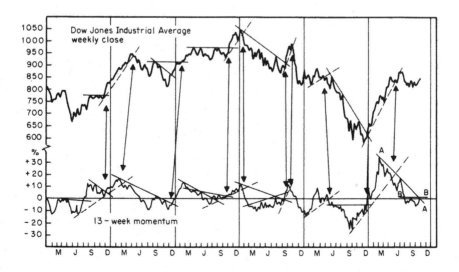

Chart 18-9   DJIA, 1931–1956, and a 52-Week ROC. (*From www.pring.com.*)

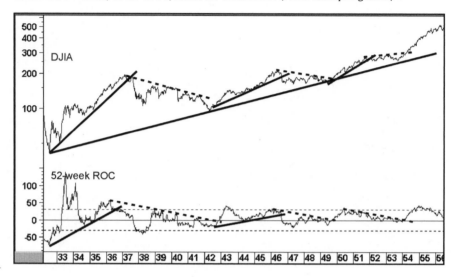

Chart 18-10   DJIA, 1970–1975, and a 13-Week ROC. (*From www.pring.com.*)

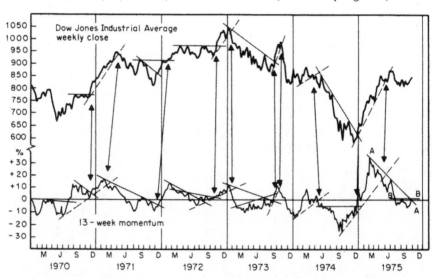

trendline technique does not always give a signal, but whenever there are clearly definable violations of trendlines that have been touched three or more times, the conclusions drawn are usually extremely reliable.

An alternative possibility is to use overbought and/or oversold crossovers in conjunction with price trend breaks or pattern completions in the average. The vertical solid lines in Chart 18-11 indicate where this could have been done for intermediate peaks. The dashed lines are drawn where the overbought crossover was not confirmed by any type of confirmation from the average itself.

The Dow Jones Transportation Average

In the last part of the nineteenth century and the early part of the twentieth century, rail was the dominant form of transportation and, therefore, an average composed solely of rails represented a good proxy for transportation stocks. In 1970, the Rail Average was expanded to embrace other transportation segments, and the index was renamed the Transportation Average.

The Transportation Average is basically affected by two factors: volume of business and changes in interest rates. First, when a business recovery gets under way, inventories are low, and raw materials are needed to initiate production. Transportation volume picks up, and investors, anticipating such a trend, bid up the price of transportation shares. At business cycle peaks, companies typically overbuild their stocks; the result is that when sales start

Chart 18-11 DJIA, 1990–2000, and a 13-Week ROC. (*From www.pring.com.*)

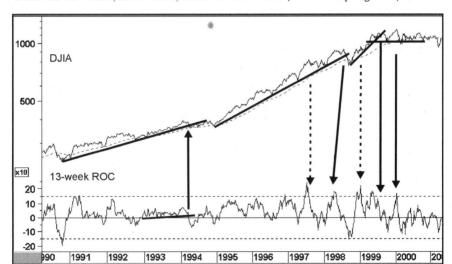

to fall, their requirements for raw materials are reduced. Transportation volume then falls sharply, and the stocks react accordingly. Second, transport companies tend to be more heavily financed with debt than industrials. Because of the leverage of this heavy debt structure, their earnings are also more sensitive to changes in interest rates and business conditions than those of most industrial companies. As a result, the Transportation Average quite often leads the Industrial Average at important juncture points.

The significance of the Dow Theory rule requiring confirmation of both the Industrials and Transport should now be more obvious since a move by the producer stocks (the Industrials) really has to be associated with an increased volume of transportation, which should be reflected by a similar move in the transportation stocks. In a similar vein, increased business for the transportation stocks is likely to be of temporary significance if the industrial companies fail to follow through with a rise in sales and production levels. The longer-term cycles of the Transportation Average and the Industrial Average are more or less the same as a result of their close association with business conditions. The techniques and choice of time spans for MAs, ROCs, and so forth are, therefore, similar to those described previously for the Industrials.

One principle that is not normally used for the Industrials but can be applied to the Transport is that of relative strength (RS). This technique is particularly useful during periods of nonconfirmation between the two averages, when RS can offer a useful clue as to how the discrepancy will be resolved. One such example occurred in the summer of 1998, when the DJIA made a marginal new high. Chart 18-12 shows that the Transports remained above their 40-week MA, but the average had already violated a secondary up trendline, thereby indicating potential weakness. As it turned out, when the Industrials reached their new high, the Transports rallied back to the extended trendline that they had previously violated. However, the real tip-off that the Transports were unlikely to confirm the Industrials came from the fact that the RS line had crossed below its MA and secondary up trendline in April 1998. The 26-week ROC of relative strength also violated an up trendline. Thus, at the time when the Industrials were making a new high in July, the Transport RS line was declining and well below its MA. Finally, the ROC was unable to rally above zero, which represented an additional sign of vulnerability.

The Dow Jones Utility Average

The Dow Jones Utility Average comprises 15 utility stocks drawn from electric utilities, gas pipelines, telephone companies, and so forth. This average has historically proved to be one of the most reliable barometers of the

Chart 18-12   Transports, 1996-1999, and three indicators. (*From www.pring.com.*)

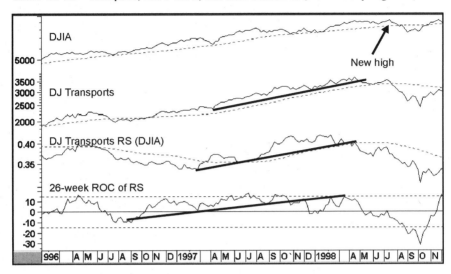

Industrials. This is because utility stocks are extremely sensitive to changes in interest rates and interest rates generally lead the overall stock market.

Interest rate changes are important to utility stocks for two reasons. First, utility companies require substantial amounts of capital because they are usually highly financed with debt relative to equity. As interest rates rise, the cost of renewing existing debt and raising additional money puts pressure on profits. When interest rates fall, these conditions are reversed and profits rise. Second, utility companies generally pay out their earnings in the form of dividends, so that these equities are normally bought just as much for their yield as for their potential capital gain. When interest rates rise, bonds, which are also bought for their yield, fall in price and thus become relatively more attractive than utilities. As a result, investors are tempted to sell utility stocks and buy bonds. When interest rates fall, the money returns once again to utility stocks, which then rise in price.

Generally speaking, when the Utility Average flattens out after an advance or moves down while the Industrials continue to advance, it is usually a sign of an imminent change in trend for the Industrials. Thus, the Utilities led the Industrials at the 1937, 1946, 1953, 1966, 1968, 1973, 1987, and 1994 bull market peaks. Conversely, at the 1942, 1949, 1953, 1962, 1966, 1974, 1982, and 1998 bottoms, the Utilities made their bear market lows ahead of the Industrials. At most major juncture points, the Utilities coincided with the Industrials, and occasionally, as at the 1970 bottom and the 1976 top, the Utilities lagged.

> **Major Technical Principle**   Since changes in the trend of interest rates usually occur ahead of reversals in the stock market, the interest-sensitive Utility Average more often than not leads the DJIA at both market tops and market bottoms.

The relationship between the Utilities and the Industrials is often over-looked because they usually give their loudest message when other market activity is at its most exciting. At market tops, the Utility Average quietly declines while investors, analysts, and the media are excited about huge price advances yet to be seen. Chart 18-13 shows a classic example in 1987. In August, the Industrials were at an all-time high, but the Utility Average was already in a well-established bear market. At market bottoms, fear, depression, and sometimes panic reign while the Utility Average is quietly in the process of turning up.

The Unweighted Indexes

An unweighted index is calculated by adding the prices of a universe of stocks and dividing the total by that number. The resulting average is then weighted by price rather than capitalization. The most widely followed is the *Value Line Arithmetic.*

Unweighted indexes are useful because they closely represent the price of the average stock often found in individual portfolios, as opposed to the blue chips toward which institutional investment is more oriented. Unweighted indexes are also helpful in gaining an understanding of the market's technical structure, since they have a tendency to lead the market (that is, the DJIA) at market tops. When a persistent divergence of this nature between the DJIA and the Value Line develops, it almost always results in the Dow being dragged down as well. Once a divergence starts, a cautious approach should be maintained until both the DJIA and the Value Line break out from price patterns, declining trendlines, and so forth.

A show of good relative strength by the unweighted indexes at a time of sustained weakness in the major averages often signifies that an important rally will follow when the decline is over. This occurred in 1978, when the Value Line Arithmetic Index made its low in late 1977, several months ahead of the DJIA. Chart 18-14 shows the Value Line Arithmetic against the S&P Composite between 1985 and 1990. In late 1985, the Value Line made a

Chart 18-13   DJIA versus DJ Utilities, 1985–1987. (*From www.pring.com.*)

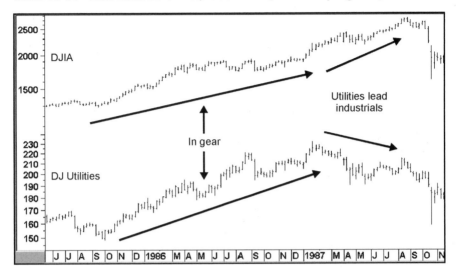

lower low than it did at the beginning of the year, but the S&P made a higher low. This out-of-gear situation was a negative sign but was never confirmed by the S&P violating its 40-week MA. We see a similar type of situation in 1986, but again, this potentially negative discrepancy was not confirmed by a negative S&P MA crossover. The situation in 1990 was different because the S&P not only penetrated its MA but violated a major up trendline as well.

This reaffirms an important principle—that of confirmation. There are countless situations where we can compare two indicators or averages and observe disagreements. However, just as divergences in oscillators should be confirmed by price, so these disagreements between averages, whether they are positive or negative in nature, must be confirmed before we can come to a conclusion that the trend has reversed.

The NASDAQ

The technology boom of the 1990s brought the NASDAQ Composite into the kind of prominence that it had never experienced before. This capitalization-weighted Index is dominated by large technology companies and has become a proxy for the technology sector. The NASDAQ has no leading characteristics, such as the Utilities, but it can be used with relative strength analysis.

Chart 18-14   Value Line Arithmetic versus the S&P Composite. (*From www.pring.com.*)

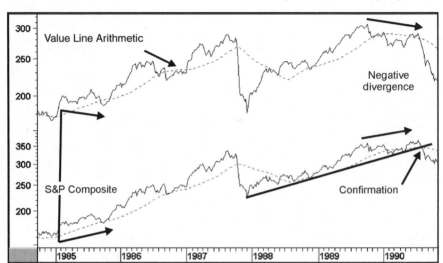

Chart 18-15 features the NASDAQ together with its RS line against the S&P Composite. Note how a joint trendline break in 1991 signaled a major rally. Later, another down trendline break in the RS line was confirmed. This time it was confirmed by a solid break above a resistance trendline in the index itself. This was then followed by an acceleration in the speed of the bull market as the NASDAQ raced toward its ultimate peak.

General Motors

It has been claimed that "what is good for General Motors is good for America," and the record for the last 50 years or so certainly bears out this statement as far as the stock market is concerned, for General Motors (GM) is a bellwether stock par excellence.

GM has hundreds of thousands of employees and more than 1 million shareholders, and its business is extremely sensitive to credit conditions. It is still the largest auto manufacturer in the country, and a significant number of American jobs are either directly or indirectly dependent on the auto industry.

As a result, most of the time GM tends to rise and fall in concert with the trend of the DJIA or the S&P 500. At market tops, GM usually leads the market, so that a new high in the DJIA or S&P Composite that is unconfirmed by GM is a warning signal of a reversal in trend. On the other hand, GM is

Chart 18-15 NASDAQ Composite, 1982–2001, and relative strength. (*From www.pring.com.*)

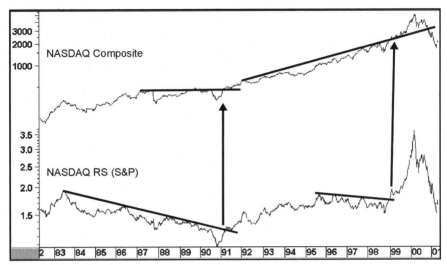

not as helpful at market bottoms because it usually lags. The long-term chart of GM in Chart 18-16 shows this quite clearly. It is also worth noting the huge *head and shoulders* (H&S) formed between 1928 and 1929, as well as the right-angled broadening top between 1964 and 1966. The completion of both these long-term distribution patterns led to substantial declines in the stock.

Chart 18-17 compares GM to the S&P for the closing years of the twentieth century. The dashed vertical line points up the fact that GM often lags at bottoms. In this case, the stock tested its low but did not exceed it, whereas the S&P made a higher bottom following that at the vertical line. This time we are considering GM's leading characteristics for intermediate as well as bull market peaks. The 1997 and 1998 declines were both signaled with a negative GM divergence. There was also a negative divergence where GM led the S&P in the Spring of 2000. However, there was an even greater discrepancy in that the 1999 and 2000 peaks in GM developed at the same level, yet the S&P peak was much higher in 2000 than it was in 1999. This major disagreement was then followed by a commensurately significant decline in both series.

Proponents of GM have developed a useful principle. Known as the *4-month rule* (although some analysts prefer a 19- to 21-week rule), it states that if in a bull market GM fails to make a new high within 4 calendar months (for example, February 27 to June 27, or March 31 to July 31) of its previous peak, the bullish trend of the market has reversed or is just about

Chart 18-16 Market profile of General Motors, 1924–1935 and 1948–1973. (*From M.C. Horsey.*)

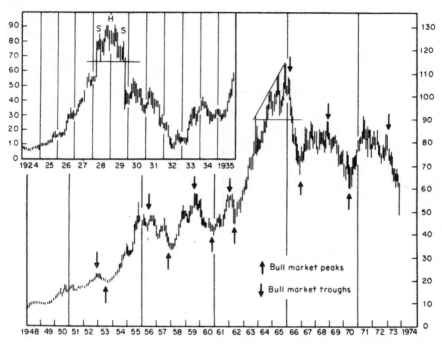

Chart 18-17 General Motors versus the S&P Composite, 1996–2001. (*From www.pring.com.*)

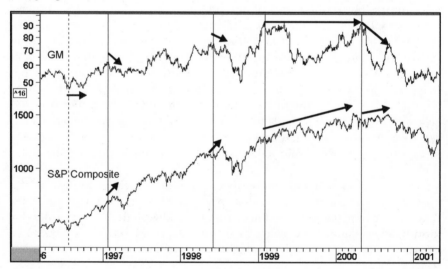

to do so. Similarly, during a market decline, if GM fails to make a new low within 4 months of its previous trough, a reversal in the downward trend of the market has already taken place or is just about to occur. The GM rule is not infallible, but its record is extremely good.

In effect, the relationship between GM and the DJIA or S&P Composite is another technical tool. As such, it should not be used in isolation but in combination with other indicators and relationships.

The Russell Indexes

The Frank Russell organization, among other things, publishes three important indexes: the Russell 3000, 2000, and 1000. The Russell 1000 is a composite capitalization-based series containing the 1000 largest stocks in the country. The Russell 2000 represents the next 2000 issues based on capitalization. Finally, the Russell 3000 is a composite index of the others and in 2001 represented approximately 98 percent of the investable U.S. equity market. The three are plotted in Chart 18-18.

Normally, they are all in gear, either on the up- or downside, but when they disagree the discrepancies can sometimes be quite revealing. In October 1999, all three succeed in violating important down trendlines, and the joint break indicates a rally lies ahead. On the other hand, the Russell

Chart 18-18   Three Russell Indexes, 1999–2001. (*From www.pring.com.*)

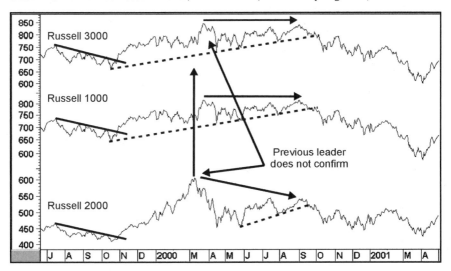

2000, which is often used as a proxy for the low cap sector, experienced a sharp rally going into February 2000. All three indexes then retreat, but the Russell 2000 was unable to rally to a new high, unlike the other two. Thus, we have what had previously been the leader, no longer leading. Such *leadership failures are often a sign that the prevailing trend is running out of steam and throws up a definite red flag.* In this case, the April rally proved to be the top of the bull market.

Finally, we see that the Russell 1000 rallied back to its Spring high in September 2000, but the Russell 2000 was unable to confirm. When all three violated their (dashed) up trendlines, a little later the divergences were confirmed, and a major decline followed.

The relationship between the Russell 2000 (low cap) and Russell 1000 (blue chip/high cap) can also be helpful because it can provide a clue as to which category investors should favor. Chart 18-19 shows that the relationship can be quite cyclical in nature. This can be seen from the four deliberate swings in the long-term KST. Sometimes it is possible to augment KST MA crossovers with trendline breaks in the ratio itself. This was the case in 1991 and 1995, but the drop was too steep in the late 1990s to construct a line. The next breakout, flagged by the dashed arrow, developed with the sharp rise in 2000 that turned out to be a whipsaw. The reason was the dramatic first quarter run up in the technology sector that temporarily domi-

Chart 18-19 Russell, 2000/1000 Ratio, 1988–2001, and long-term KST. (*From www.pring.com.*)

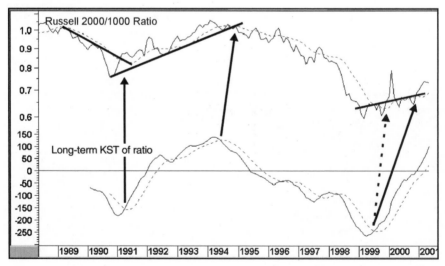

Major Technical Principle When several closely related securities are being led by one of the group and that leader fails to confirm a new high (or low in the case of a declining trend), this is usually a sign of exhaustion and is followed by a trend reversal.

nated the Russell 2000. Later, if one were prepared to ignore this whipsaw, it was possible to observe the breakout from the extended base at the end of 2000.

Summary

- No perfect index or average exists that consistently and truly represents "the market."
- There are basically two methods of calculating market averages, those that use capitalization and those incorporating an unweighted formula.
- The technical indicators described elsewhere in this book can be applied to the market averages.
- Most of the time, market indexes move in gear with each other. It is when discrepancies develop and are confirmed that reversals in trend are signaled.

19
Price: Group Rotation

Chapter 2 discussed the relationship between the three key financial markets—debt, equity, and commodities—and the business cycle. It was established that there are certain periods when they move in concert, but more often their trends diverge. The combination depends on the maturity of the business cycle. The most important point to remember is that deflationary forces predominate during the early stages of the cycle, whereas inflationary pressures come to the fore as the recovery matures. No business cycle ever repeats itself exactly, and the leads and lags between the peaks and troughs of the various financial markets differ from cycle to cycle. In spite of this drawback, the concept of the chronological development of the debt, equity, and commodity cycles works quite well in practice.

Industry Groups and the Business Cycle

This chapter takes the concept of chronological development of these cycles one step further by pointing out that specific industry groups are sensitive to different types of economic conditions. In effect, it categorizes them according to their sensitivity to deflationary or inflationary forces—that is, leading or lagging characteristics. Since the cycle itself is continually switching between a deflationary and inflationary environment, it follows that the various industry groups also undergo a rotation.

Unfortunately, this categorization is far from an exact process. First, many industries do not conveniently fall into an inflationary or a deflationary category. Second, equities rise and fall in reaction to the outlook for profits and also, what is more important, in response to investor attitudes to those profits. Because interest rates are a significant, but not necessarily dominant, influence on the profits of interest-sensitive stocks, it follows that the price performance of certain interest-sensitive issues may, from time to time, become unlatched from, or independent of, the price movements in the debt markets. For example, savings and loan stocks declined in 1989 because of a financial crisis in the industry. Normally, they would have been expected to rise because interest rates fell during most of that year.

In spite of such drawbacks, the theory of group rotation serves two useful functions. First, it can provide a framework within which to assess the maturity of a primary trend. For example, there may be technical evidence that the stock market is deeply oversold and other factors that suggest that the primary trend is reversing from bearish to bullish. At such times it would be useful to know that some of the groups that normally lead market turns have failed to confirm new lows made by the market averages or have established an uptrend in relative strength.

On the other hand, in a situation in which the technical picture is indicating the possibility of a market top, it would be helpful to know that industry groups that typically lead the averages up and down had made their highs some weeks or months earlier, and that stronger relative performance was concentrated in industry groups that typically lag the stock market cycle.

Second, the group rotation theory is helpful in determining which groups, and therefore which stocks, should be purchased or pared back. This aspect is discussed in greater detail in Chapter 31.

The comments in this chapter refer to the U.S. stock market, but the concept of group rotation can be extended in principle to other stock markets. Every country experiences business cycles, and Italian or Japanese utilities respond to changes in interest rates just as U.S. utilities do. Indeed, it is possible to take this concept one step further by saying that markets heavily weighted to the resource area, such as Canada, Australia, and South Africa, ought to perform best at the tail end of the global economic cycle, and in most cases they do.

Major Technical Principle A bull market is an extended period, usually lasting somewhere between 9 months and 2 years, in which most stocks move up most of the time. A bear market is an extended period, usually lasting somewhere between 9 months and 2 years, in which most stocks decline most of the time.

The Concept of Group Rotation

Since the majority of stocks are rallying most of the time during a bull market, it follows that most record their bear market lows about the same time as the averages. When utilities are described here as a leading group and steels as a lagging group, the implication is not necessarily that utilities reach their lows ahead of the low in the Dow Jones Industrial Average (DJIA), although they do in most instances. What is more likely to happen is that utilities, being interest-sensitive, will put on their best performance relative to the market on either side of the bear market low. Similarly, steels might advance with the averages during the early stages of the bull market, but their best relative performance has a tendency to occur during the later stages of a bull market or the early phases of a bear market. Notice that I have emphasized the word "tendency" because that is really what we are talking about—tendencies and probabilities, never certainties.

The sine curve in Fig. 19-1 represents growth and contraction of the economy during a typical business cycle. The dashed line reflects intermediate rallies and reactions of the stock market. The idealized peaks and troughs of the other financial markets are also shown (the letter G is for gold price). Bond prices typically make their lows (that is, interest rates reach their cyclical peaks) after the recession has been under way for some months. The stock market, which essentially discounts profits, makes its low about 3 to 6 months before the low in economic activity, whereas the commodity market usually comes to life only several months after the recovery has set in. *Because the leads and lags vary in each cycle, this approach should be used as a framework, not a mechanical extrapolation.*

The overall market consists of many stock groups that are a reflection of the companies making up the various segments of the economy. The economy, as defined by an aggregate measure, such as gross national product (GNP), is either rising or falling at any one time. However, there are very few periods in which all segments advance or decline simultaneously. This is because the economy is not one homogeneous unit, but is an aggregate of a number of different parts. Some industries respond better to deflationary conditions and the early stages of the productive cycle; others are more prosperous under inflationary conditions that predominate at the tail end of the business cycle.

Economic recoveries are typically led by consumer spending, which is spearheaded by the housing industry. As interest rates fall during a recession, demand for housing gradually picks up. Hence, homebuilding and some building and construction stocks can be considered leading groups.

Because they anticipate a consumer spending improvement, retail stores, restaurants, cosmetics, tobacco, and so forth also show leading tendencies, as do certain interest-sensitive areas such as telephone and electric utilities,

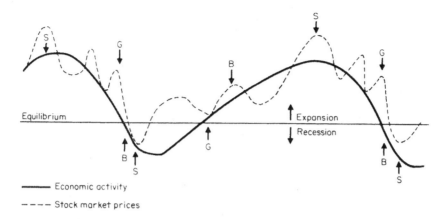

Figure 19-1 Economic activity and stock prices. (B = Bonds; S = Stocks; G = Gold)

insurance, savings and loans, and consumer finance companies. As the recovery continues, inventories that were cut dramatically during the recession become depleted. Manufacturing industry groups that might be classified as coincident respond by improving in price or relative strength (RS). Finally, as manufacturing productive capacity is used up during the last stages of the recovery, stock groups associated with capital spending, such as steels, some chemicals, and mines, have a tendency to emerge as market leaders.

Confidence is another influence on the group rotation cycle. During the initial stage of a bull market, emphasis is placed on prudence, because investors have lost a considerable amount of money and the news is usually bad. Stocks with good balance sheets and high yields begin a period of superior RS. As the cycle progresses, stock prices rise, the news gets better, and confidence improves. Eventually, the rotation turns to more speculative issues of little intrinsic value. Even though the peak in speculative issues usually leads that of the major averages, their most rapid and volatile period of advance typically occurs in the final or third leg of a bull market.

Some groups are not readily classifiable in terms of the productive process. Air transport, which goes through sharp cyclical swings, is a case in point. This industry average either coincides with or lags slightly at bear market lows, but is almost always one of the first groups to turn down before a peak. This could be because these companies are sensitive to interest rates and energy prices, both of which have a tendency to rise at the end of the business cycle. Drug stocks as a group, on the other hand, have a distinct tendency to present their best relative performance at the tail end of the bull market and in this respect should be regarded as a lagging group. They are likely also to lag (in terms of RS) at market bottoms, although this tendency is far less pronounced than that at market tops.

It is also worth noting that the group rotation process has a tendency to work during intermediate-term rallies and reactions as well as cyclical ones.

Splitting the Cycle into Inflationary and Deflationary Parts

Putting the group rotation theory into practice is not an easy matter because the character of each cycle is different. In a rough sense, the business cycle can be split into a deflationary part and an inflationary part. A useful starting point is to obtain an inflation/deflation indicator in order to determine that a falling trend in this indicator is deflationary and a rising one is inflationary.

One way would be to compare the price of a specific deflation-sensitive stock, such as a utility, with an inflation-sensitive one, such as a mining company. The problem with this approach is that one of the stocks may be affected by internal conditions totally unrelated to the business cycle. The same drawback might be true of a comparison of two industry groups, such as utilities versus gold. For instance, the utility group could be suffering from aggressive government regulation, whereas the gold group may be unduly stimulated because of a mining strike in South Africa, a major gold producer. Neither event would be associated with the business cycle, but both would strongly influence the trend and level of an inflation/deflation ratio.

A better solution is obtained by constructing an inflation indicator from several inflation-sensitive groups and a deflation indicator from deflation-sensitive industry indexes. Thus, if one particular industry is influenced by noncyclical forces, it will not unduly distort the total result.

These indicators are shown in Chart 19-1. The Inflation Group Index was constructed from a simple average of the Standard & Poor's (S&P) Gold, Miscellaneous Metals Domestic Oil, and Aluminum, and the Deflation Group Index from Electric Utilities, Savings and Loans, and Property and Casualty Companies indexes.

The series in the top panel is a ratio of the inflation/deflation indexes. Reversals in the trend of this indicator reflect the market's view of whether the cycle is in its inflationary or its deflationary stage. When the line is rising, it indicates that the rotational phase has moved to the inflationary side, and vice versa.

Chart 19-2 takes this a step further by comparing trends in the inflation/deflation ratio to those of bond yields and industrial commodity prices. These series do not move in exactly the same direction all the time but definitely correlate. The solid vertical lines on the chart show those periods when the 18-month rate of change (ROC) of the ratio in the bottom

Chart 19-1 Inflation- versus deflation-sensitive groups, 1950–2001. The ratio of the two is shown in the top panel and the two components underneath. When they are in a rising mode, inflation-sensitive equities outperform their deflation-sensitive counterparts, and vice versa. (*From www.pring.com.*)

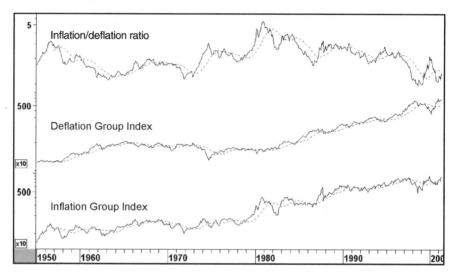

Chart 19-2 Inflation/deflation ratio, bond yields, and commodity prices, 1966–2001, Bottoms. (*From www.pring.com.*)

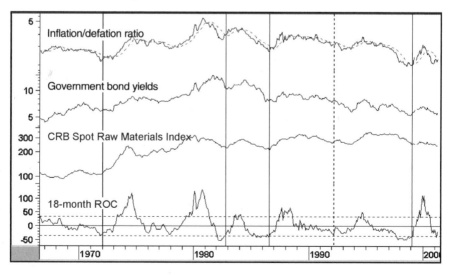

panel reverses direction from below its oversold level. In most instances this corresponds reasonably closely with the commodity low. Since bond yields lag commodity prices, they bottom some time after the ROC has started to rise. Chart 19-3 shows the exact same data, but this time the vertical lines flag the overbought crossovers. These signals work out better for tops in the government bond yield series.

Relative Paths of Leading and Lagging Groups Are Usually Diverging

Chart 19-4 features some smoothed momentum calculated from the RS lines of the S&P Energy and Financial Indexes. It is also possible to substitute groups calculated from other organizations such as Dow Jones, Investors Business Daily, and so forth. The principles remain the same. The striking thing is that for most of the time both series are moving in opposite directions, indicating that they are at opposing ends of the group rotation process. Thus, one might consider emphasizing interest-sensitive and other issues with leading tendencies when the Financial Index RS momentum bottoms. A switch to inflation-sensitive areas would be made when the Energy Index bottoms and the Financial Index peaks.

Chart 19-3   Inflation/deflation ratio, bond yields, and commodity prices, 1966–2001, tops. (*From www.pring.com.*)

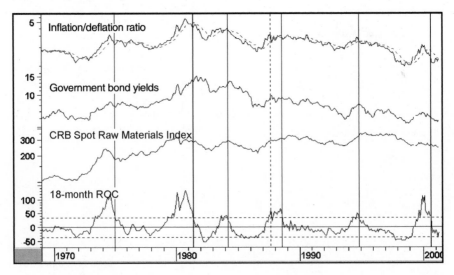

Chart 19-4 Financial versus energy relative momentum, 1985–2001. (*From www.pring.com.*)

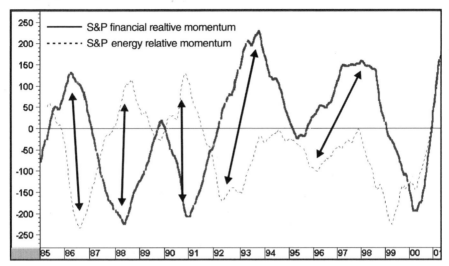

It is, of course, important to make sure that the RS momentum of the groups being purchased or liquidated is consistent with the pattern established by the Energy Index and the Financial Index. For example, it would make no sense to buy gold shares if energy RS was bottoming and gold RS was overbought and peaking. Remember that the momentum series shown in Chart 19-4 are indicators of RS. Rises and declines in these indicators indicate improving or deteriorating *relative* strength. They say nothing about the *absolute* price performance, although in most cases it is moving in the same direction as the relative trend.

Chart 19-5 shows a similar arrangement, but this time the financial progress is being compared to technology. Some people believe that technology is a leading sector. However, this chart shows that this is not the case because the dashed technology RS momentum has a tendency to lag, as both series diverge in their trajectories. Thus, each is offering different opportunities at different times.

Using the Ratio of a Leading versus Lagging Group

Most people would find it quite tedious to update the inflation/deflation indicator described earlier, although it is possible in the real-time version

Chart 19-5 Financial versus computer relative momentum, 1980–2001. (*From www.pring.com.*)

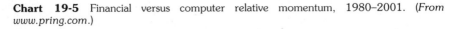
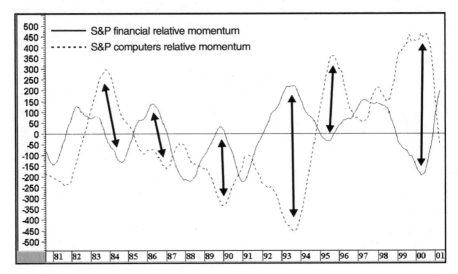

of MetaStock with my companion CD.[1] A useful shortcut is to calculate a ratio of the S&P Aluminum (lagging) and Banking (leading) Indexes (shown in Chart 19-6). The trajectory of this series is not identical to that of the Inflation/Deflation Ratio, but it does experience the same broad inflationary and deflationary swings. For a large amount of time, it moves sympathetically with trend changes in the thick line that represents the Commodity Research Board (CRB) Spot Raw Industrial Material Index. Underneath is a know sure thing (KST) of this relationship.

It is possible, of course, to substitute a different smoothed measure of momentum such as a price oscillator, variation of a moving average convergence divergence (MACD), stochastics, and so forth. Moving average (MA) crossovers by the KST can be used for signaling when a major rotational change is getting under way. For example, the two latest signals on the chart, in 1998 and 2000, at *A* and *B,* indicate a reversal to an inflationary and then deflationary environment, respectively.

Chart 19-7 shows the exact same spots for the S&P Oil and Gas Drilling group. It is fairly evident that the group rallied around the time of the infla-

---

[1]Martin Pring's How to Select Stocks MetaStock Comparison.

Chart 19-6 Aluminum/Bank ratio, 1972–2001. (From *www.pring.com.*)

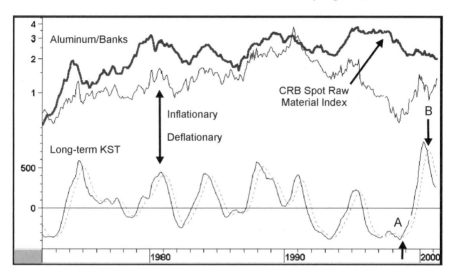

tionary signal in late 1998. The deflationary crossover was not as timely because the energy sector as a whole put in a strong performance during the deflationary part of the cycle. This demonstrates the fact that specific industry fundamentals can occasionally distort the performance of individual groups from their normal business cycle experience. This means that it *is important not to blindly follow a ratio reflecting a rotational change, but to examine the technical position of the individual groups before taking any action.*

Chart 19-8 shows the same time periods, but this time for a leading group, the Tobaccos. This time both signals are quite timely.

Leading, Middle, and Lagging Groups Categorized

Table 19-1 offers a rough approximation of where a particular industry group falls within the cycle. It is important to bear in mind that not all groups fit neatly into these categories.

Chart 19-7 S&P Drillers, 1996–2001, and relative strength. (*From www.pring.com.*)

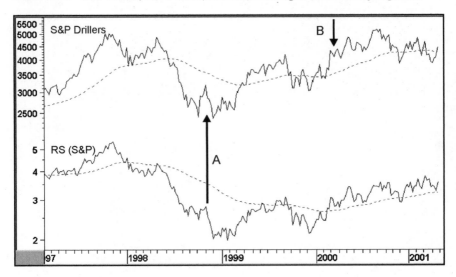

Chart 19-8 S&P Tobaccos, 1996–2001 and relative strength. (*From www.pring.com.*)

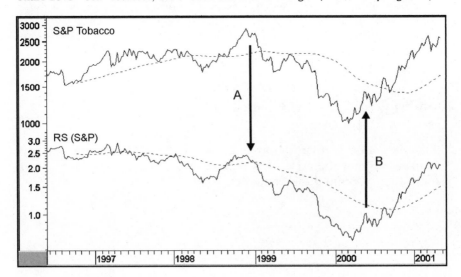

Table 19-1 Industry Group Categories

Leading (Liquidity Driven)	Middle Groups
Utilities	Retailers
Electric	Manufacturers
Telephone	Health Care
Natural Gas	Consumer Durables
Financials	Autos and Parts
Brokers	Furniture and Appliances
Banks	Building Materials
Insurance Cos	Containers Metal and Glass
S&Ls	Leisure and Entertainment
Reits	Hotels
Homebuilders	Waste Management
Containers and Packaging	
Consumer Nondurables	**Lagging Leaders (Earnings Driven)**
Beverages	Mining
Household Goods and Housewares	Oil
Tobacco	Coal
Personal Care	Oil Drillers
Foods	*Basic Industry*
Restaurants	Papers
Footware	Chemicals
Textile Manufacturers	Steels
Transports	Heavy Machinery
Airlines	Most Technology
Truckers	Computer Manufacturers
Railroads	Electronics
Air Freight	Semiconductors

Summary

- The stock market cycle experiences a distinct pattern of industry group rotation because of the chronological nature of the business cycle. Interest-sensitive groups have a tendency to lead at peaks and troughs, whereas corporations with profits that are enhanced by increases in capital spending or commodity price inflation generally lag in the overall market.
- Sometimes significant changes in the fundamentals of an industry cause a group to be uncharacteristically strong or weak during a specific cycle. It is therefore better to monitor a spectrum of groups rather than a specific one as a proxy for the rotation process.
- An understanding of the industry group rotation cycle is helpful both in assessing the maturity of a primary trend and for the purpose of stock selection.

20
Time: Longer-Term Cycles

The Importance of Time

Time is represented on the horizontal axis of most technical charts. It is normally used in conjunction with price, volume, and breadth—the other three dimensions of psychology that are involved in determining trends in the stock market. These are measured on the vertical axis. Time can also be assessed independently through the analysis of cycles.

> **Major Technical Principle** Time is concerned with *adjustment*, because the longer a trend takes to complete, the greater its psychological acceptance and the greater the necessity for prices to move in the opposite direction and adjust accordingly.

Discussions of the importance of time have, so far, been limited to the idea that the significance of a reversal in trend depends upon the length of time needed for the completion of distribution or accumulation. The longer the period, the greater the magnitude and duration of the next move are likely to be. Removing the speculative excesses of a trend requires a commensurately large corrective movement, just as the discipline of a long period of accumulation provides a sound base from which a substantial and lengthy advance can take place. The very long (8-year) bull market between

1921 and 1929 was interrupted by corrective reactions, but the substantial increase in stock prices during this period resulted in a considerable amount of excesses, confidence, and speculation, which were only erased by a sharp and lengthy decline.

Similarly, the 1966 stock market peak was preceded by 24 years of basically rising prices followed by a long period of consolidation involving widely swinging stock prices. When adjusted for inflation, stock prices peaked in 1965 and then went through an extremely severe bear market, which was comparable to the 1929–1932 debacle.

Another example comes from the bull market in gold, which started in 1968 at $32 and ran up to $850 in January of 1980. Although the price decline was not as severe as the 1929 crash, the next 20 years were spent in a frustrating sideways trading range at prices well under half their peak value.

Investors become accustomed to rising prices in a bull market, each reaction being viewed as temporary. When the trend finally has reversed and the first bear market rally takes place, the majority are still convinced that this, too, is a temporary reaction and that the bull trend is being renewed. The initial response is always disbelief as reflected in the attitude, "It's bound to come back" or, "It's a good company—I am in it for the long term." As prices work their way lower in a bear market, the adjustment takes a less optimistic form because the majority of investors forsake expectations of a rising market and look to move sideways for a time. The psychological pendulum finally swings completely to the other (bearish) side, as investors watch prices slip even further and become overly pessimistic. At this point, *sufficient time and downside price action have elapsed to complete the adjustment process, and the market in question is then in a position to embark on a new bull cycle.*

Time has been viewed here in an emotional context, since it is required for investors to adjust to unrealized expectations. Both traders and investors need to realize that time is deeply bound with the business cycle. This is because a strong and lengthy recovery, like that between 1921 and 1929 or between 1990 and 2001, breeds confidence among investors and business-people, who tend to become inefficient, careless, and overextended as a result of a long period of prosperity. The subsequent contraction in business conditions needed to eliminate these distortions is thus more severe. Equity prices therefore suffer the double influence of (1) losing their intrinsic value due to the decline in business conditions and (2) being revalued

---

Major Technical Principle   The idea of a reaction commensurate with the previous action is known as the principle of *proportionality.*

downward from the unrealistically high levels that prevailed during the period of prosperity. The reverse set of circumstances applies following a long market decline.

Some Basic Principles of Cycles

Measuring time as an independent variable is a complicated process, since prices move in periodic fluctuations known as *cycles*. Cycles can operate for periods ranging from a few days to many decades. At any given moment a number of cycles are operating simultaneously, and since they are exerting different forces at different times, the interaction of their changing relationships often has the effect of distorting the timing of a particular cycle.

The most dominant of the longer ones is the so-called 4-year cycle, in which there is a nominal or average length between troughs of 41 months. Since several other cycles are operating at the same time but with different influences, the length of the 4-year cycle can vary either way by 6 months or so.

Cycles are shown on a chart in the form of a sine wave, as in Fig. 20-1. These curves are usually based on a rate of change (ROC) or trend-deviation calculation, which is then smoothed to eliminate misleading fluctuations.

In Fig. 20-2, this idealized cycle is represented by the dashed line and the actual cycle by the solid one. The arrows indicate the peaks and troughs of

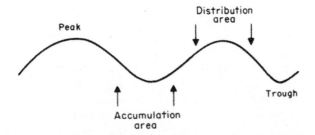

Figure 20-1   Typical cycle.

Major Technical Principle   Only rarely are two cycles of identical length, so an average or *nominal* period is calculated. This theoretical time span is used as a basis for forecasting.

the idealized cycle: In actual fact, price trends rarely reverse exactly at theoretical points, and especially not at peaks, where there is often a long leadtime. Nevertheless, the theoretical points provide a useful guide.

This means that a 4-year cycle exists not only for the U.S. stock, bond, and commodity markets, but also for each individual stock and for international markets as well.

For example, if two food stocks are experiencing breakouts, the trend for food stocks is likely to be less significant than if, say, 10 stocks are experiencing breakouts.

In other words, all stocks, indexes, and markets go through a similar cycle, but the timing of their peaks and their troughs differs as does the size of their price fluctuations. For example, the interest-sensitive and cyclical (basic industry) stocks go through a similar cycle, but because interest-sensitive stocks such as utilities lead the market, cyclicals such as steel groups generally lag behind them. This is shown in Fig. 20-3. Similarly, interest-sensitive issues may rise by 80 percent from the trough to the peak of their cycle, while cyclicals might advance by only 20 percent, and vice versa.

Chart 20-1 also illustrates this principle and shows the interaction of a financial series during a typical business cycle. The rising part of each cycle usually consists of three stages, which correspond to the three phases described in the Dow theory. It is normal for prices to reach a new high as each stage unfolds, but sometimes this does not happen. This is known as a *magnitude failure* and is a distinct sign of weakness. A magnitude failure occurs because of very poor underlying fundamentals. In effect, the cycle misses a beat.

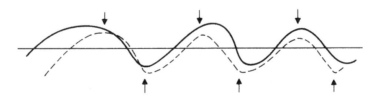

Figure 20-2 Typical cycle.

Major Technical Principle The principle of *commonality* states that a cycle of similar duration exists in the price action of all stocks, indexes, and markets.

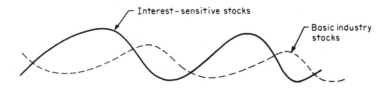

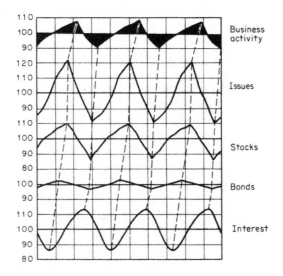

Figure 20-3   Leading versus lagging sectors.

Chart 20-1   Typical cycles with financial series in percentages of their averages: A mechanistic approach to business conditions. (*From L. Ayres, Cleveland Trust Co. 1939.*)

Major Technical Principle   The greater the number of securities moving in the same direction, the stronger (other things being equal) the trend.

Major Technical Principle   The principle of *variation* states that while stocks go through similar cycles, the price magnitudes and durations of these nominal cycles will be different because of fundamental and psychological considerations.

The opposite can also occur; exceptionally strong fundamentals (or the perception of them) can give rise to a fourth stage, in which prices undergo an additional upward leg. For equity markets, this final upward surge is often associated with an extended period of declining interest rates. Such strong underlying conditions normally develop when the 4-year cycle occurs in conjunction with the peak of longer-term cycles, such as the Kondratieff (50- to 54-year) and Juglar (9.2-year) cycles, which are discussed later.

In cases in which the cyclic turning points of a number of components of a particular market converge, the magnitude of the next move will be much greater. For example, the turning points of individual stock markets around the world can occur at different times. However, in the summer of 1982 most of their cyclical lows coincided. The resulting rally in virtually all markets was explosive.

This is the concept behind the know sure thing (KST) market cycle model discussed in Chapter 12. If the result were plotted as one idealized cycle, it would be represented by a curve similar to that approximated in Fig. 20-4.

There are four influences affecting a time series trend at any one time: secular, cyclical, seasonal, and random. The cyclical trend is the starting point for the purpose of analyzing primary bull and bear markets. Specifically, this is the 4-year or *Kitchin cycle*. The secular influence is very long term and embraces several 4-year cycles. From the point of view of a stock, bond, or commodity market, the most dominant "secular cycle" is the 50- to 54-year cycle known as the *Kondratieff wave* (after the Russian economist Nicolai Kondratieff). Two other important cycles in excess of 4 years have also been noted, namely the 9.2- and 18 and one-third-year cycles.

Major Technical Principle The principle of summation occurs when several cycles are combined in the calculation of a specific indicator.

Figure 20-4 Summed cycles.

Charts 20-2(*a*) and (*b*), adapted from *Business Cycles* by Joseph Schumpeter,[1] combine the effect of three observable business cycles into one curve. In effect, it shows the summation principle using three longer-term cycles: the 50- to 54-year (Kondratieff), the 9.2-year, and the 41-month (Kitchin) cycles. The model is not intended to be an exact prediction of business conditions and stock prices, but rather indicates the interaction of the shorter cycles with the longer ones. Even so, it is worth noting that the

Chart 20-2(*a*) Schumpeter's model of nineteenth-century business cycles. (*From Joseph Schumpeter,* Business Cycles, *McGraw-Hill, New York, 1939.*)

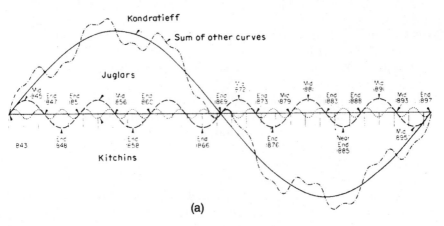

(a)

Chart 20-2(*b*) Twentieth-century business cycle and crisis points (calculated path).

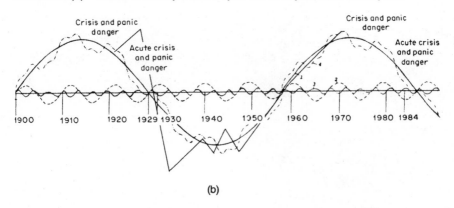

(b)

[1]McGraw-Hill, New York, 1939.

long-term curve crossed below the zero line in 1987, that is, the year of the stock market crash. This model was originally constructed in the early part of the 1920s. Comparing this model with Chart 20-3 reveals that the long upward move dating from about 1942 to about 1966 was associated with rising stock prices interrupted by relatively mild cyclical corrections.

Because the underlying force of this model is the 54-year Kondratieff wave, this will be a good starting point for discussion.

The Long (Kondratieff) Wave

The 54-year wave is named after a little-known Russian economist who observed in 1926 that the United States had undergone three long economic waves, each lasting between 50 and 54 years.[2] It is worth mentioning

Chart 20-3 U.S. stock prices, 1790–1976, showing Kondratieff bull markets (annual mean monthly averages). The Foundation for the Study of Cycles spliced together the following series: 1790–1831, bank and insurance companies; 1831–1854, Cleveland Trust Rail Stocks; 1854–1871, Clement Burgess Composite Index; 1871–1897 Cowles Commission Index of Industrial Stocks; 1897–1976, DJIA. The shaded areas represent the plateau period in the Kondratieff cycle. (*From www.pring.com.*)

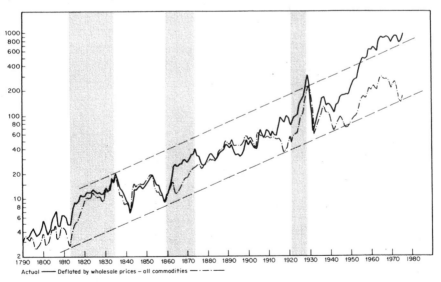

Actual ——— Deflated by wholesale prices – all commodities — · — · —

[2]The cycle was also noted by Professor William Stanley Jevons, an English economist, in the second half of the nineteenth century.

that while only three such cycles have been recorded for the United States, E. H. Phelps Brown and Sheila Hopkins of the London School of Economics have noted a regular recurrence of 50- to 52-year cycles of prices in the United Kingdom between 1271 and 1954. The crest for the most recent cycle was projected for the 1974–1978 period. In terms of global commodity prices and bond yields, this was a pretty close call because bond yields and gold peaked in 1981. The same cycle has been observed in interest rates, as shown in Chart 20-4.

Kondratieff used wholesale prices as the focal point of his observations, as shown in Chart 20-5. My own view is that this cycle reflects the balance between long-term inflationary and deflationary forces as they affect the financial markets. For example, there is little doubt that there were serious deflationary pressures in the 1980s, and yet the Consumer Price Index (CPI) rose during this period. This anomaly can be explained by the fact that the antideflationary activity of governments has been much greater in previous years. This has had the effect of offsetting the deflationary symptoms of lower prices. Kondratieff noted that each wave had three phases: an upwave lasting about 20 years, a transition or plateau period of 7 to 10 years, and a downwave of about 20 years. He observed that each upwave was associated with rising prices, the plateau with stable prices, and the downwave with declining prices. He also noted that a war was associated with both the beginning and the end of each upwave.

At the start of a cycle, business conditions are very depressed. Because of a considerable excess capacity of plant and machinery, there is really no incentive to invest in capital projects. Most people prefer to save money rather than invest it because of extreme uncertainty. The war at the bottom

Chart 20-4 Interest rates for the U.K. and France, 1815–1925. (*From N.D. Kondratieff, The Long Wave of Economic Life.*)

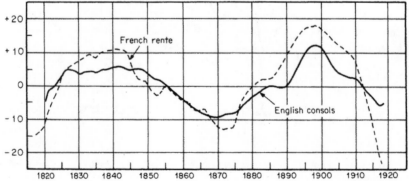

Chart 20-5 The Kondratieff wave, 1789–2000.

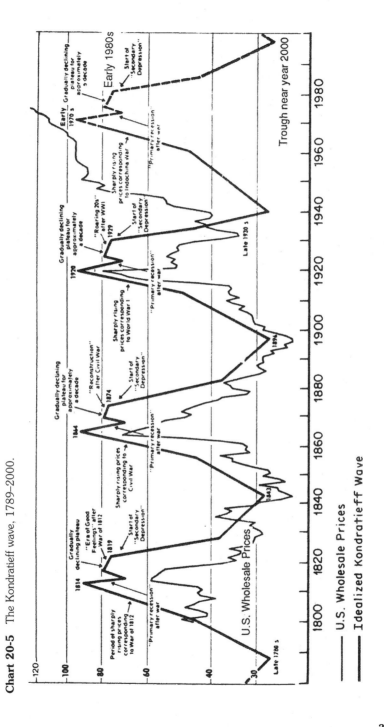

U.S. Wholesale Prices

——— U.S. Wholesale Prices

▬▬▬ Idealized Kondratieff Wave

Trough near year 2000

of the downwave, known as the *trough war* (see Chart 20-5), acts as a cata-lyst to get the economy moving again. In view of the tremendous economic slack in the system, this war is not associated with inflation. As time pro-gresses, each cyclical upwave becomes stronger and stronger; confidence returns and business once again reaches full productive capacity. Because price inflation is almost absent, interest rates are very low. Credit, a neces-sary fuel for any recovery, is both abundant and cheap. During this phase, businesses replace old plant and equipment and also invest in new capac-ity, which improves productivity and creates wealth. This rising phase is usu-ally associated with widespread exploitation of a previously developed technology, such as canals in the 1820s and 1830s, railroads in the mid-nineteenth century, automobiles in the 1920s, and electronics in the 1960s. As the rising phase progresses, inflationary distortions caused by overin-vestment start to develop. This development has a tendency to cause social tensions and economic instability. A common characteristic around this period is another war, known as the *peak war.* Unlike the trough war, which acts as a catalyst to the economic recovery, the peak war places undue pres-sure on a system that is already close to full capacity. As a result, commod-ity prices and bond yields move to very significant 20- to 25-year new highs. This was true of the peaks of 1814, 1864, 1914, and the late 1970s.

This long-term background is important because it influences the cycli-cal movements of the financial markets. For example, during the up phase and the associated shallow recessions, it would be reasonable to expect mild and brief bear phases for equity markets. The relatively stable plateau period has always been associated with a very powerful bull market (such as 1820, 1860, 1920, and 1982). Finally, if a sharp and devastating bear market is to develop, it usually occurs during the down phase.

In a similar vein, commodity bull markets are long and bear trends are short during the up phase. Trends in bond prices are the opposite. The tables are turned during the down phase since commodity bear markets tend to be prolonged, but cyclical advances in bonds are quite strong. The interpretation of the technical indicators should be adjusted accordingly. For example, the time span for a cyclical bear market in stocks might be 12 months during the up phase, with the annual rate of monthly price change limited to a −20 percent reading, but the standards would be different dur-ing the Kondratieff downwave when each business cycle becomes weaker and weaker. Under these conditions, bear markets would be expected to last considerably longer and to be far more devastating. The same sort of per-spective should be applied to cyclical trends of commodities and bonds for which the Kondratieff cycle is far more reliable.

A study and appreciation of the Kondratieff cycle are fine examples of why any market predictions based on the experience of only the two or three previous cycles are likely to prove unfounded. The Kondratieff wave has occurred only three times in the United States, and on each occasion the conditions have been different. *It should therefore be used as a framework on which to base a better understanding of the very long term trends of inflationary and deflationary forces, rather than as a basis for mechanistic prediction.*

The 18-Year Cycle

Normally, the amplitude of a cycle is a function of its duration; that is, the longer the cycle, the larger the swing. The 18-year or, more accurately, the 18 and one-third-year cycle has occurred fairly reliably in stock market prices since the beginning of the nineteenth century. This cycle gains credibility because it operates in other areas, such as real estate activity, loans and discounts, and financial panics.

Chart 20-6 shows a 3-year centered moving average (MA) of common-stock prices from 1840 to 1974. This average helps to smooth the trend and isolate the long-term picture more clearly. The beginning of the 18-year cycle at major market bottoms is self-evident.

Chart 20-6 The 18 and one-third year cycle in stock prices, 1840–1974 (3-year centered MA). *(From www.pring.com.)*

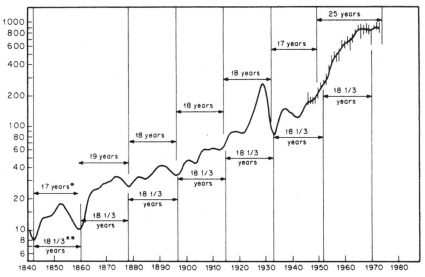

* Actual cycles spanning 17–25 years marked above

** Idealized cycles averaging 18 1/3 years marked below

Although the average cycle lasts 18 and one-third years, actual cyclical lows can vary 2 or 3 years either way. These troughs are marked on the chart above the 3-year MA. The increase in government interference in the economy resulting from the Keynesian revolution and the post-World War II commitment to full employment appears to have had two effects on the cycle that spanned 1952–1970. First, it was stretched out from 18 to 25 years (1949–1974), and second, it prolonged the up phase. This is especially noticeable for the 1949 low, which on a 3-year MA hardly shows as a trough.

There is a question of whether this cycle is still operating since the conceptual low last bottomed out in the spring of 1988, which did not coincide with a bottom associated with a business cycle. Also, 18 years from the actual low recorded in 1974–1975 would place the cyclical low in the 1992–1993 period, which was not a major bottom. The next two conceptual lows develop in 2006 and 2024.

The 18-year cycle fits in well with the Kondratieff picture, since three such cycles form one Kondratieff wave. In the last two Kondratieff waves, when the upwave part of the 18-year cycle coincided with the plateau period, an explosive bull market and only a mild correction took place. This was also true for the 1980s.

Since 1840, the 18-year cycle has operated fairly consistently. However, the prolonged nature of the last two cycles casts doubt on whether it is still continuing to operate.

The 9.2-Year Cycle

Chart 20-7 shows the 9.2-year cycle in stock prices from 1830 to 1946. The dashed lines represent the ideal cycle in which stock prices reversed exactly on schedule, and the solid line shows the actual annual average as a percentage of its 9-year MA trend.

The cycle occurred 14 times during the 1930–1946 period, and according to the Bartels test of probability, it could not occur by chance more than once in 5000 times. Further evidence of the significance of this cycle is given by observation of the 9.2-year periodicity in other phenomena as unrelated as pig iron prices and the thickness of tree rings.

One problem with using the technique illustrated in the chart is that the annual average is expressed as a percentage of a centered 9-year MA. This means that the trend is not known until 4 years after the fact, so that there is always a 4-year lag in learning whether the 9.2-year cycle is still operating. Nevertheless, if the theoretical crest in 1965[3] is used as a base and the 9.2

[3]Macmillan, New York, 1939 (available in reprint from Fraser Publishing, Burlington, VT, 1989).

years are subtracted back to 1919, the peaks of the 9.2-year cycle correspond fairly closely to major stock market tops.

Chart 20-8 shows that the cycle has worked reasonably well since the start of the last century. The vertical lines represent the 9-year cyclical lows. The arrows show where the actual low was off the mark as far as the 55-month (approximately half the 9.2-year time span) ROC was concerned. The major exception was the August 1987 top, but the cycle soon made up for it by October.

One interesting characteristic of the 9-year cycle that is probably of greater forecasting significance is the so-called decennial pattern.

Chart 20-7 The 9.2-year cycle in stock prices, 1830–1946. (*From Edward R. Dewey, Cycles: The Mysterious Forces That Trigger Events, Hawthorne Books, New York 1971, p. 119.*)

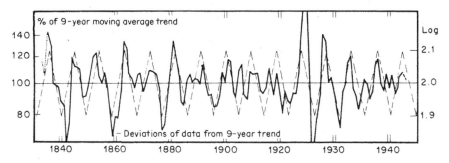

Chart 20-8 S&P Composite, 1900–2001, and the 9-year stock cycle. (*From www.pring.com.*)

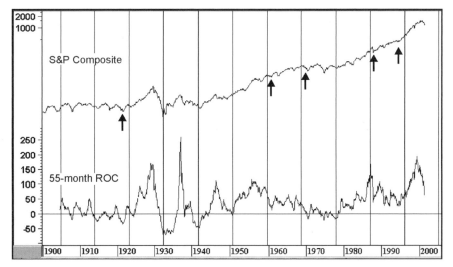

The Decennial Pattern

This pattern was first noted by Edgar Lawrence Smith, who in 1939 published a book called *Tides and the Affairs of Men.*[4] His previous book, *Common Stocks as a Long-Term Investment,* had been a bestseller in the late 1920s.[4] Smith researched equity prices back to 1880 and came to the conclusion that a 10-year pattern or cycle of stock price movements had more or less reproduced itself over that 58-year period. He professed no knowledge as to why the 10-year pattern seemed to recur, although he was later able to correlate the decennial stock patterns with rainfall and temperature differentials. Even though the cycle is relatively reliable, there has been to date no rational explanation as to why it works.

Smith used the final digit of each year's date to identify the year in his calculations. The years 1881, 1891, 1901, and so on are the first years; 1882, 1892, and so on are the second; and so forth. Inspired by the research of Dr. Elsworth Huntington and Stanley Jevons, who both emphasized the 9- to 10-year periods of recurrence in *natural* phenomena, Smith experimented by cutting a stock market chart into 10-year segments and placing them above each other for comparison, as shown in Chart 20-9. He concluded from these data that a typical decade consists of three cycles, each lasting approximately 40 months.

The late Edson Gould, who came into prominence in the mid-1970s because of his uncannily accurate stock forecasts, used the decennial cycle as a cornerstone for his research. In his 1974 stock market forecast, Gould wrote, "In the 35 years that have passed since Mr. Smith's book was published, 35 years of wars, inflation and vast changes in our economic monetary set-up and background the action of the stock market has, much of the time, fitted unusually well with the 10-year pattern." Smith's discovery has stood the test of time.

The 1980s and 1990s versus the Average Decennial Pattern

The stock series in Chart 20-10 represents a simple average of the decennial pattern from 1900 to 1996, giving equal weight to the proportional movements of each period. The swings in the 12-month ROC indicator show three distinct cycles troughing in the first, fourth, and eighth years. I have calculated this average for other time spans and find that the first cycle low of the decade has more of a tendency to fall between the end of year 1 and the middle of year 2. In a similar vein, the final cycle low for the decade often comes at the tail end of the seventh year rather than in the middle of

---

[4]From Smith, *Tides and the Affairs of Men.*

Chart 20-9   The decenniel pattern of industrial stock prices (adapted from Edson Gould's 1974 *Stock Market Forecast*. The years 1974–1980 represent our own approximations for major waveforms in the DJIA.).

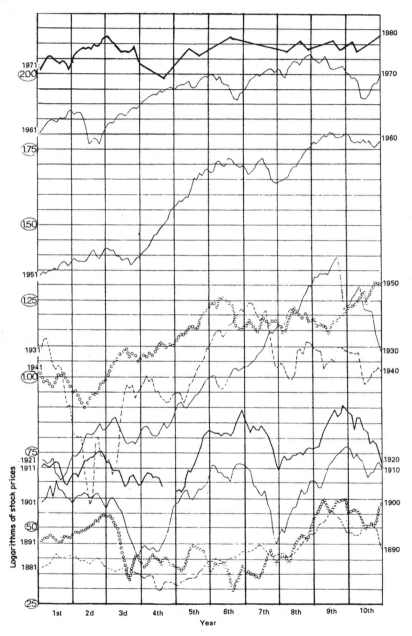

the eighth. Since this series represents an average, it is highly unlikely that a typical decade will duplicate it exactly.

The decennial pattern can be of greater value if it is used to identify where the strong and weak points usually occur, and then to see whether other technical phenomena are consistent. For example, in the middle of year 9, the 12-month ROC indicator for the average cycle is very overbought, which is consistent with a decline or consolidation starting at the end of that year and following through to the tenth, that is, the year ending in zero. In 1949, the 12-month ROC was very oversold and was inconsistent with its normal position in the decennial pattern. Instead of declining into 1950, the market actually rose. This experience is a good example of why *the decennial approach should be used with other technical indicators and not in isolation.*

Bearing this in mind, note that Chart 20-11 shows the decade beginning in 1981. The swings in the 6-month MA of the 12-month ROC are very close to the decennial average shown in Chart 20-10, with lows in 1982, 1984, and 1988. The strong bull market of the 1990s in Chart 20-12 does not fit the pattern so well because of its upward bias. Even so, it is still possible to observe weakness in the ROC going into 1994 with subsequent strength in 1995. The cycle calls for a sharp rally into years 8 and 9. In the case of the 1990s, the MA of the ROC was already overbought, but there is still a definite rally during this period. However, by the end of 2000 the smoothed ROC begins its descent right on cue and by 2001 (not shown) it falls below the zero reference line, which is again consistent with the cycle.

Chart 20-10   Decennial pattern, 1900–1996. (*From www.pring.com.*)

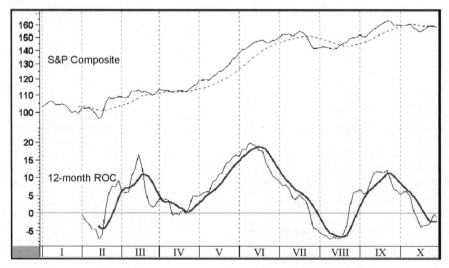

Chart 20-11   Decennial pattern, 1981–1990. (*From www.pring.com.*)

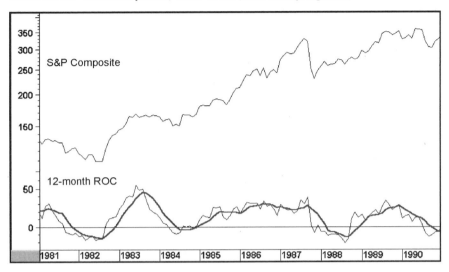

Chart 20-12   Decennial pattern, 1991–2000. (*From www.pring.com.*)

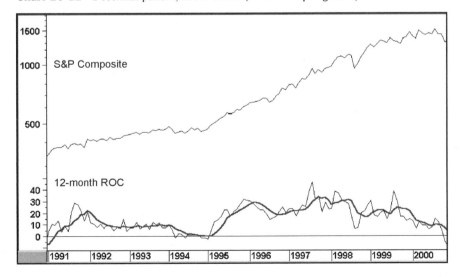

Important Years

The decennial average shows that there is a distinct upward bias beginning at the tail end of the seventh or the middle of the eighth year, which runs through to the third quarter of the ninth. Table 20-1 shows data between 1881 and 2000; 73 percent of these years were bullish. The best years for equities have been those ending with a 5. The other strong years appear to be those ending with 2, 4, and 8.

Weakness is most pronounced in the years ending with 1, 3, 6, 7, and 0. Only the seventh year has declined on more occasions than it has advanced, and it is therefore the weakest. The optimum periods for investment appear to be during the second, fourth, late seventh, and early eighth years. Since these comments relate to "average" years, they only indicate a bias. Investment decisions should take other indicators, such as the position of the 12-month ROC, into consideration. For example, if the market is extremely over-bought at the end of the ninth year, the chances are that its "peaking" characteristic will result in weakness. On the other hand, if the market is oversold, as it was in 1949, this is likely to outweigh the normal decennial weakness.

Table 20-1   The 10-Year Stock Market Cycle

	Annual percent change in Dow Jones Industrial Average Year of decade									
Decades	1st	2nd	3rd	4th	5th	6th	7th	8th	9th	10th
1881–1890*	3.0	−2.9	−8.5	−18.8	20.1	12.4	−8.4	4.8	5.5	−14.1
1891–1900	17.6	−6.6	−24.6	−0.6	2.3	−1.7	21.3	22.5	9.2	7.0
1901–1910	−8.7	−0.4	−23.6	41.7	38.2	−1.9	−37.7	46.6	15.0	−18.0
1911–1920	0.5	7.6	−10.3	−5.1	81.7	−4.2	−21.7	10.5	30.5	−32.9
1921–1930	12.7	21.7	−3.3	26.2	30.0	0.3	28.8	48.2	−17.2	−33.8
1931–1940	−52.7	−23.1	66.7	4.1	38.5	24.8	−32.8	28.1	−2.9	−12.7
1941–1950	−15.4	7.6	13.8	12.1	26.6	−8.1	2.2	−2.1	12.9	17.6
1951–1960	14.4	8.4	−3.8	44.0	20.8	2.3	−12.8	34.0	16.4	−9.3
1961–1970	18.7	−10.8	17.0	14.6	10.9	−18.9	15.2	4.3	−15.2	4.8
1971–1980	6.1	14.6	−16.6	−27.6	38.3	17.9	−17.3	−3.1	4.2	14.9
1981–1990	−9.2	19.6	20.3	−3.7	27.7	22.6	2.3	11.8	27.0	−4.3
1991–2000	20.3	4.2	13.7	2.1	33.5	26.0	22.6	16.1	25.2	
Total %										
Change	**7%**	**40%**	**41%**	**89%**	**369%**	**74%**	**−38%**	**222%**	**111%**	**−81%**
Up years	8	7	5	7	12	7	6	10	9	4
Down years	4	5	7	5	0	5	6	2	3	7

*Based on annual close
Cowles Indices 1881–1885

The 41-Month (4-Year) Cycle

One perceptive observation made by Smith was that the decennial pattern appeared to "contain three separate cycles in a decade, each one lasting for approximately forty months,"[5] which is also apparent from the rhythmic action of the 12-month ROC, shown on Chart 20-10. This is most interesting, as it ties in with the so-called 4-year cycle of stock prices. More precisely, the 4-year cycle is a 40.68-month (41-month) cycle. It has been observed to operate in stock prices since 1871. Around 1923, Professor Joseph Kitchin was also able to show a cycle of 41 months in bank clearings, wholesale prices, and interest rates in the United States and United Kingdom. This cycle has since carried his name.

The Kitchin cycle, applied to stock prices, is illustrated in Charts 20-13(*a*) and (*b*). Between 1871 and 1946, it has occurred 22 times with almost uncanny consistency. Then in 1946, as Edward Dewey describes it, "Almost as if some giant hand had reached down and pushed it, the cycle stumbled, and by the time it had regained its equilibrium it was marching completely out of step from the ideal cadence it had maintained for so many years."[6]

The 4-year cycle can also be observed by looking for a major buying opportunity every 4 years and in this way is arguably the most reliable of the cycles described here. Chart 20-14 shows that this usually develops after a decline such as 1962, 1966, 1970, 1974, 1978, 1982, 1990, 1994, and 1998. Sometimes, as in 1986, the market is very strong and the buying opportunity develops after a sideways consolidation. As the new century opens, the years to watch out for are 2002, 2006, 2010, and 2112.

The reversal in the Kitchin 4-year cycle in the 1940s is a fine example of how a cycle that has appeared for a long time to be working consistently can suddenly, for no apparent reason, become totally distorted. Once again, the fact that a particular indicator or cycle has operated successfully in the past is no guarantee that it will continue to do so in the future.

Seasonal Pattern

There is a distinct seasonal pattern of stock prices that tends to repeat year after year. Stocks seem to have a spring rise, a late-second-quarter decline, a summer rally, and a fall decline. The year end witnesses a rally that usually extends into January. Stocks purchased in October have a high probability of appreciating if held for a 3- or 6-month period.

[5]Smith, *Tides and the Affairs of Men,* pp. 55ff.
[6]Edward R. Dewey, *Cycles: The Mysterious Forces That Trigger Events,* Hawthorne Books, New York, 1971, p. 121.

Chart 20-13(a)   The 41-month rhythm in stock prices, 1868–1945. (*From Edward R. Dewey*, Cycles: The Mysterious Forces That Trigger Events, *Hawthorne Books, New York, 1971.*)

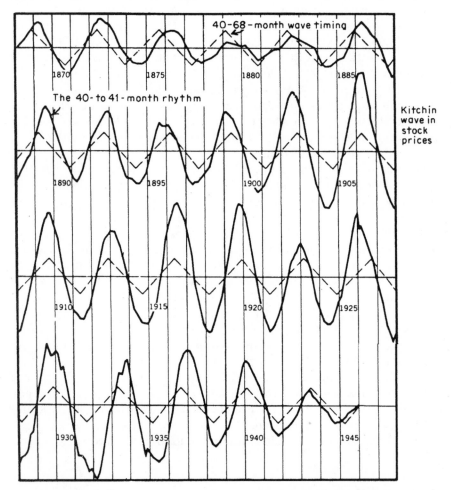

Chart 20-13(b)   The 41-month rhythm in stock prices reversed, 1946–1968. (*From Edward R. Dewey*, Cycles: The Mysterious Forces That Trigger Events, *Hawthorne Books, New York, 1971.*)

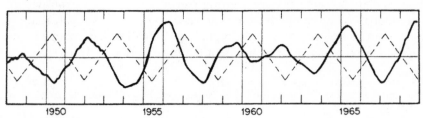

Chart 20-14 S&P Composite, 1959–2001, the 4-year cycle in stock prices. (*From www.pring.com.*)

Apart from seasonal changes in the weather that affect economic activity and investor psychology, there are also some seasonal patterns in financial activities. For example, July and January are heavy months for dividend disbursement, and for the retail trade the year-end (Christmas) period is the strongest of the year.

Chart 20-15 represents the seasonal tendency of the stock market to rise in any given month. The probabilities were calculated over the twentieth century by Ned Davis Research. All movements are relative, since a month with a strong tendency will be accentuated in a bull market, and vice versa. It is also important to note that the direction of the trend is more important than the level.

Table 20-2 shows the average monthly performance of the DJIA for the twentieth century. The source is Ned Davis Research, but the data have been reproduced from Tim Hay's *The Research Driven Investor*,[7] arguably one of the best investment books ever written.

Generally, if the market rises in the first 5 days of January, it is likely to extend for a rise for the whole year. This rule worked almost perfectly between 1950 and 2000, with exceptions in 1994, 1966, 1973, and 1991. The latter three were associated with wars. A more consistent indicator is the

[7]DJIA monthly performance since 1900. (Source: Tim Hayes, *The Research Driven Investor*, McGraw-Hill, 2000.)

Chart 20-15   The seasonal pattern in the stock market. [*From* The Research Driven Investor, *Timothy Hayes (McGraw-Hill, New York, 2000)*.]

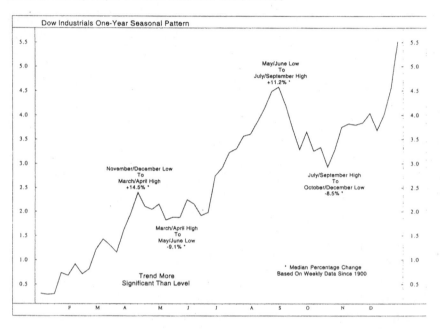

Table 20-2   DJIA Average Monthly Performance, 1900–2000

Jan.	Feb.	March	April	May	June	July	Aug.	Sept.	Oct.	Nov.	Dec.
Average rise/fall											
1.1%	−.1%	.7%	1.1%	−.1%	.5%	1.4%	1.1%	−1%	0%	.9%	1.5%
Percentage of months in which the market gained											
64	50	61	55	52	52	61	65	42	55	62	73

Source: Ned Davis Research

January barometer. Between 1950 and 2000, it has been an excellent indicator for market performance for the whole year. If prices rise in January, they are likely to do so for the whole year. The rule has a 90 percent track record.

Small-capitalized stocks have a tendency to outperform large-capitalized issues at the turn of the year. This may be because October is the weakest month and small-capitalized stocks, lacking the quality of their blue-chip brethren, get hit the worst. This makes them ideal tax-loss candidates, which adds to the downside pressure. When tax-loss selling abates, they are natural candidates to experience a strong year-end rally and strength into the opening months of the new year.

In most years, the November–January period tends to be the best 3-month holding period for the market as a whole. This year-end effect of superior returns also seems to apply to the month end.

End of the Month

Data covering the 89-year period ending in 1986 show that returns from the last trading day of a month are consistently good. The rationale for this effect may well come from higher month-end cash flows, such as salaries.

The 4 trading days ending in the third trading day of the new month have also proved to be profitable. Figure 20-5 shows that these 4 trading days average 0.118 percent versus 0.015 percent for all trading days. Turn-of-the-month returns can be said to account for all the positive capital gain returns generated by the market. Other research suggests that the period lasts from the penultimate day of the month to the third day of the new month. Whatever the length of the holding pattern or its exact entry and exit points, there is no doubt that there is a strong seasonal end-of-the-month tendency.

As a note of caution, in an article entitled "Calendar Anomalies,"[8] Bruce Jacobs and Kenneth Levy point out that this effect was less prevalent in the

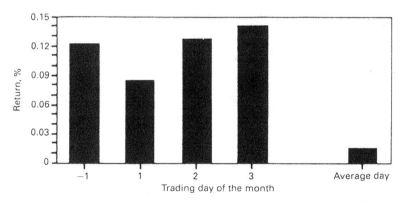

Figure 20-5 The turn-of-the-month effect (average daily returns). (*Data from J. Lakonishok and S. Smidt; "Are Seasonal Anomalies Real? A Ninety Year Perspective," Johnson working paper 80-07, Cornell University, Ithaca, 1987.*)

[8]*MTA Journal*, winter 1989-1990.

1980s, which shows that it is not a wise policy to follow one indicator exclusively. In the 2001 edition of the *Stock Traders Almanac*, a must read for the seasonally oriented trader, Yale Hirsch points out that the seasonal indicator shifted between 1981 and 2000 to the last 4 and first 5 trading days of the new month.

For a practical application, it makes sense to integrate this reliable long-term seasonal effect with short-term oscillators. Clearly, the potential for the market to advance at this time will be much greater if it is oversold going into the last (presumably) bullish days of the month.

Days of the Week

The term "blue Monday" is very much justified. The influence of weak Mondays originated during the 1929–1932 crash. During the Depression, the market advanced, on average, every day of the week except Mondays. It could be said that the entire market decline took place over weekends, during the periods from Saturdays to closings on Mondays.

Figure 20-6 shows the average return for each day from 1928 to 1982. Monday is the only down day. Remember that this takes account of "black Thursday" in 1929, but does not include the 500-point drop that occurred on "black Monday" in 1987. The strong markets of the 1990s resulted in a different outcome in that Mondays, by a small margin, actually turned out to be the *strongest* day of the week. Thursday turned out to be the villain in

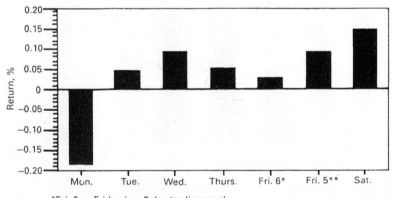

*Fri. 6 = Friday in a 6 day trading week.
**Fri. 5 = Friday in a 5 day trading week.

Figure 20-6   The day-of-the-week effect (average daily returns). (*Data from D. Klein and R. Stambaugh, "A Further Investigation of the Weekend Effect in Stock Returns,"* Journal of Finance, *July 1984, pp. 819–837.*)

that 48.9 percent turned out to be winners. It remains to be seen whether this is a permanent shift.

There does not appear to be any acceptable rationale for this effect, which also reportedly occurs in non-U.S. equity markets, debt instruments, and even orange juice.

Preholiday Advances

The day preceding holidays is statistically a bullish period. This is indicated in Fig. 20-7, which covers the period between 1963 and 1982. With the exception of Presidents' day, all these (average) preholiday trading sessions handsomely beat the average day.

Time of Day

Recent studies[9] have indicated that there is a definite time-of-day effect, as shown in Fig. 20-8. There is little difference in the activity from day to day, except for Monday mornings. All days, however, show an upward bias going into the last half-hour. The study showed that this rallying effect was empha-

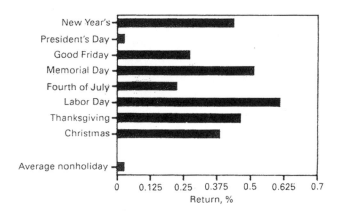

Figure 20-7 The holiday effect (average preholiday returns). (Data from R. Ariel, *"High Stock Returns Before Holidays,"* Sloan working paper, Massachusetts Institute of Technology, Cambridge, MA, 1984.)

[9]Jarris, "How to Profit from Intradaily Stock Returns," *Journal of Portfolio Management,* winter 1986.

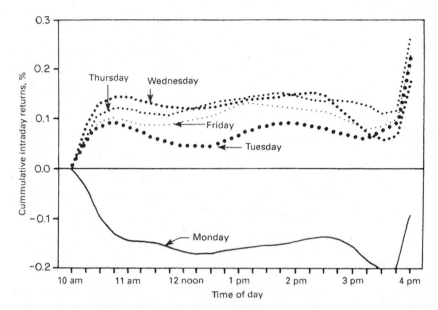

Figure 20-8 The time-of-day effect. (*Data from L. Harris, "A Transaction Data Study of Weekly and Intradaily Patterns in Stock Returns,"* Journal of Financial Economics, *vol. 16, 1986, pp. 99–117.*)

sized even to the closing bell, with the average return of the last trade equal to 0.05 percent or 0.6 cents per share. The nearer the return took place to the closing bell, the higher it was. Trades after 3:55 P.M. averaged 0.12 percent returns or 1.75 cents per share. That upbeat note is a good place to close this chapter.

21

Practical Identification of Cycles

This chapter discusses some of the basic principles of cyclic analysis and uses examples to illustrate some simple techniques that help in their identification.

Cycles Defined

A cycle is a recognizable price pattern or movement that occurs with some degree of regularity in a specific time period. A market, stock, or indicator that has a relatively consistent price low at 6-week intervals is said to have a 6-week cycle. That successive lows are higher or lower than their predecessor is of no importance in identifying the cycle. What is significant is that there is a clearly definable "low" point every 6 weeks, separated from its predecessor by a high point known as the cycle high. Figure 21-1 shows some possible examples.

Figure 21-1 also shows that although cycle lows occur at approximately 6-week intervals, cycle highs can vary. Occasionally, they arrive early, as at point *A*; sometimes they occur in the middle of the cycle, as at point *B*; but they may also appear late, as at point *C*. Generally, when the cycle high develops shortly after the cycle low, the implications are that the upward part of the cycle is weak and that its overall strength lies on the downside. In this situation, each cycle low is normally below that of its predecessor. Similarly, a

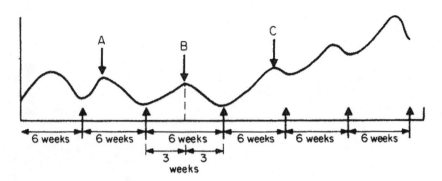

Figure 21-1   Cycle highs and lows.

cycle high that is "late" in arriving, that is, it arrives well after the halfway period, usually indicates a strong cycle, with the implication that the cycle low will be above the low of the previous cycle. A number of different cycles can be observed for any market or stock, some long and some short in duration. The task of the technician is not to identify as many as possible, but to isolate the most dominant and reliable.

Principles

- The longer the cycle, the greater the amplitude in price; for example, a 10-week cycle will have far greater trading significance than a 10-hour cycle.
- It follows from item 1 that the larger the cycle, the greater the significance of the low.
- The larger the number of cycles reaching a low at around the same time, the stronger the ensuing price movement.
- In a rising trend, the cycle high has a tendency to "translate to the right," that is, to occur after the halfway point of the cycle. The same principle holds in reverse for bear markets; that is, there is a tendency for the cycle high to translate to the left.
- It is possible to observe cyclic highs that occur at regular time intervals.
- A projected cyclic high or low may develop in the opposite way to that anticipated. In such cases, the cycle is said to be "inverted."

Methods of Detection

Many mathematical techniques have been used to identify cycles. Fourier analysis, for example, isolates the existence of various cycles by length, amplitude, phases, and so on. Systematic reconnaissance is a technique that tests for periods requested. The result is a periodgram that shows the most dominant cycles. Although such techniques can be useful, they tend to make technical analysis look as if it is an exact science, which it very definitely is not. These approaches fall outside the scope of this book, but materials listed in the Bibliography will give more information. This chapter will be confined to three methods of cycle identification: deviation from trend, momentum, and simple observation.

Deviation from Trend

This method takes a series of data and divides each item by a moving average (MA). The period under observation represents the deviation, and the MA represents the trend.

Chapter 9 explained that since an MA is designed to reflect the underlying price trend, ideally it should be plotted halfway along its span. This is because the "average" price occurs halfway through the time span, such as in the seventh week for a 13-week MA. However, changes in the direction of the MA usually occur far too late to offer timely signals for the purpose of identifying trend reversals. For this reason, technicians normally use an MA crossover for generating signals. Since only historical data are used in cycle identification, this disadvantage is not important. The MA deviation is therefore calculated by dividing the period in question by the midpoint of the MA. The price observation for February 27 is divided by a 13-week MA, as calculated on April 18; that is, the MA is "moved" back 7 weeks. The result is then plotted as an oscillator, which isolates the cyclical high and low points.

It is then a relatively simple task to see whether any consistent time periods separate these points. One method is to note the time differences between all the cycle lows and highs in order to determine which ones come up most frequently. Since MAs smooth out all cycles within their time span, it is important to experiment with several averages in order to identify as many cycles as possible. The more reliable ones should then be used in the analysis.

Momentum

A simpler method is to calculate a momentum oscillator and smooth it by an appropriate MA, as determined by trial and error. This approach will bring out the underlying rhythm in the price movement, just as a deviation-from-trend calculation does. It is doubtful whether the momentum approach alone can be successfully used for cycle identification, but it can prove to be an invaluable confirmation of cyclic reliability when used in conjunction with the technique of simple price observation discussed later.

The position of a momentum index can also be useful in warning of potential cyclic inversions, that is, when a projected cyclic low might turn out to be a cyclic high, and vice versa. For example, a cyclic inversion may occur when the observed data project that a cyclic low is likely to develop around a specific date, while the momentum indicator used in conjunction with this study is at, or coming down from, an overbought level. A good example is shown in Chart 20-8 of the S&P Composite. In 1987 the 9.2-year cycle appeared to reach its peak, as measured by the 55-month rate of change (ROC) at exactly the time when a low should have been recorded.

Simple Observation

Chart 21-1 shows the Philadelphia Gold and Silver Share Index. The solid vertical line represents an 82-week cycle of lows and the dashed vertical line a 126-week cycle of highs. The ROC has a time span of 41 weeks, half the 82-week cycle. Neither of these cycles is perfect, but they do, for the most part, explain most of the turning points in the period under consideration. These two cycles were isolated on a trial-and-error basis using the cycle line tool in the MetaStock program.

If you do not have access to a package such as this and wish to accomplish this task manually, the easiest method of identifying cycles is to start by observing on a price chart two or three major lows that appear to be relatively equidistant. The next step is to pencil in the projections for that particular cycle. If a substantial proportion of those projections result in either highs or lows, it is a good idea to mark them with a colored pencil. If most projections result in failure, the cycle should be abandoned and a new one sought. A cycle high occurring at any of these points should be treated as a successful projection, since the first objective of cycle analysis is to determine potential turning points.

Once a reliable cycle has been established, the analyst should look at all the important cycle lows that are unexplained by the first cycle and try to explain them by discovering another cycle. The chances are that the second cycle will not only fit some of the unexplained lows, but also will occur

Chart 21-1 Philadelphia Gold and Silver Share Index and a 41-Week ROC, 1985–2001. (*From www.pring.com.*)

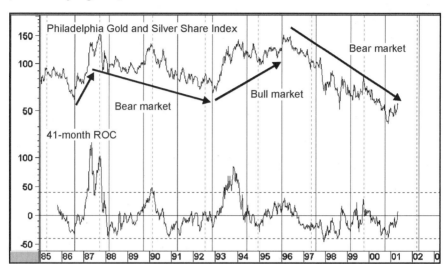

at or near some of the cycle lows previously established. This is very important, because a basic principle of cycle analysis is that the greater the number of cycles making a low around a certain time, the stronger the ensuing move is likely to be. Such knowledge must be used in conjunction with other technical evidence, but if that too offers a green light, the odds that a significant upwave will occur are increased. The next step in the method is discussed in the following section.

Combining Cycle Highs and Lows

The vertical lines in Chart 21-1 point out a fairly reliable pattern for both cycle highs and lows. One of the most important principles coming out of this exercise is that the various turning points derive their significance from the direction of the main or primary trend. In this respect, the arrows on the chart flag the various bull and bear market environments. Note how the cycle tops tend to have greater magnitude in a bear market, such as the 1987 and 1990 tops. Conversely, the 1986 and late 1992 lows developed at the start of a bull market and experienced far greater magnitude than the 1997 and 1999 signals, which developed in a bear market.

One of the advantages of combining high and low cycles is that this approach makes it possible to obtain some idea of how long a rally or reaction might last. This arises from the proximity of the high and low. For example, the late 1992 low developed just after the high. The ensuing decline was quite brief. The reverse was true at the end of 1989, where the low was very close to the early 1990 high. The rally in this instance was short. The position of the ROC can often provide a clue as to whether a particular cyclical turning point will work. For example, the strong peaks in 1987, 1990, and late 1999 all developed when the ROC was at or close to an overbought condition. Similarly, the 1986 and 1988 lows were associated when moderately oversold conditions failed to materialize.

Not all examples work out quite as accurately as that shown in Chart 21-1. Readers are cautioned not to try to make a cycle work. If it does not fit naturally and easily, chances are that it either does not exist or is likely to be highly unreliable, and therefore should not be used. In any event, such analysis should always be used in conjunction with other indicators.

Summary

- Recurring cycles, both of low points and high points, can be observed from charts of financial markets.
- A cycle turning point is significant both for the time interval between cycles and for the number of cycles that are turning at the same time.
- Cyclic analysis should always be used in conjunction with other indicators.
- Suspected cycles that do not easily fall into a consistently recurring pattern should not be made to work and should be discarded.

22

Volume: General Principles

Advantages of Volume Analysis

Pretty much all of the indicators covered so far, with the notable exception of cycles, have been concerned with price or a statistical manipulation of it. This means that each of these indicators represents a variation on a theme.

As a result, the study of volume patterns gives greater depth to the weight of the evidence approach described earlier. In this chapter we will explore some basic volume principles, and in Chapter 23 we will expand the discussion to include volume indicators that are suitable for analyzing individual securities and the stock market.

There are three principal benefits from monitoring volume. First, when we look at indicators that measure both price and volume momentum, it is possible to see if they are in agreement. If so, the probabilities favor an extension of the prevailing trend. Second, if they disagree, it tells us that the underlying trend is not as strong as it might appear on the surface. Finally, volume often throws up characteristics of its own that literally shout the message of an impending trend reversal.

> **Major Technical Principle** Volume not only measures the enthusiasm of buyers and sellers, but it is also a totally independent variable from price.

397

Volume is usually featured in a chart in histogram format under the price series, as in Fig. 22-1. This arrangement is usually acceptable since it highlights significant expansions and contractions in trading activity. These, in turn, confirm or question the sustainability of the price trend itself. Volume may also be expressed in a momentum format, which has the effect of accentuating fluctuations in activity in a more graphic way.

Principles of Volume Interpretation

1. The most important principle is that *volume typically goes with the trend.* It is normal for activity to expand in a rising market and contract in a declining one. In this sense volume is always interpreted in relation to the recent past. It's no good comparing current 1 *billion* plus share days on the NYSE with 5 or 6 *million* 70 years ago. This expansion is a result of institutional changes, a larger market, derivatives, and so forth. However, a 2-billion share day compared to a recent 1.5-billion share day is relevant. Prices move in trends, but do not generally rise and fall in straight lines, as reactions to the prevailing trend set in. The same principle applies to volume. On the left side of Fig. 22-1, for instance, the arrow shows that the volume trend is up. By the same token, it is apparent that the level of activity does not expand every day. There are quiet ones and active ones, but the general thrust is up. The right-hand part of the diagram features a downtrend in volume, but it too is irreg-

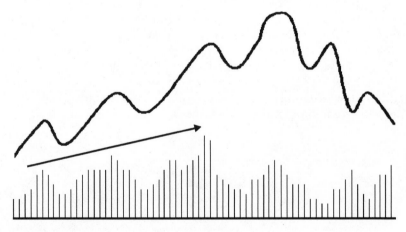

Figure 22-1 Volume histogram.

ular. When we talk about volume rising or falling, then we are usually referring to its trend. Volume trends, like price, can be intraday, short, intermediate, or long, depending on the nature of the chart.

2. One important aspect to consider is the fact that volume reflects an exchange between buyers and sellers. By definition the amount of money flowing into a security must always equal the amount flowing out. This is true regardless of the level of volume.

3. If buyers get greedy, they will push up the bid until they obtain as much quantity as they want. If sellers react to bad news, they might panic, pushing prices down sharply, but at all times the amount of a security being sold is always equal to that being purchased.

4. Rising volume and rising prices are normal. This combination indicates that the market is in "gear" and has no forecasting value. If this is the case, it is reasonable to expect at least one more rally that reaches a new price high when volume does not.

5. Volume normally leads price during a bull move. A new high in price that is not confirmed by volume should be regarded as a red flag, warning that the prevailing trend may be about to reverse. In Fig. 22-2, the price peaks at point *C*, yet volume reached its maximum at point *A*. Such action is normal; the declining volume peaks warn of underlying technical weakness. As with momentum divergences, there are no hard and fast rules about how many divergences precede a peak. Generally speaking, though, the greater the number of negative divergences, the weaker the underlying technical picture. Also, the lower the peaks relative to each other, the less enthusiasm that is generated and the more susceptible the technical position becomes once buying dries up or selling enthusiasm intensifies. A new high accompanied by virtually no volume is just as bearish as a new price high with virtually no upside momentum.

6. Rising prices and falling volume (see Fig. 22-3) are abnormal and indicate a weak and suspect rally. This type of activity is also associated with a primary bear market environment and can be used as an indicator in this respect. Just remember, volume measures the relative enthusiasm

Major Technical Principle It is the level of enthusiasm of buyers or sellers that determines the course of prices.

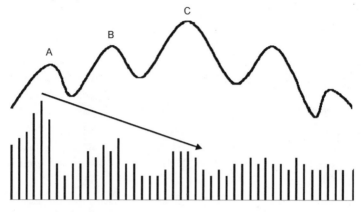

Figure 22-2   Volume leads price.

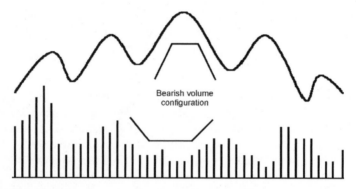

Figure 22-3   Bearish volume configuration.

of buyers and sellers. A market that rallies on a trend of lower volume indicates that prices are rising because of a lack of sellers rather than the enthusiasm of buyers. Sooner or later the market will reach a point where sellers become more motivated. After that, prices will start to pick up on the downside. One tip-off is to watch for volume to increase noticeably as the price starts to decline. This is shown in Fig. 22-4.

7. Sometimes both price and volume expand slowly, gradually working into an exponential rise with a final blowoff stage. Following this develop-ment, both volume and price fall off equally sharply. This represents an exhaustion move and is characteristic of a trend reversal. The signifi-

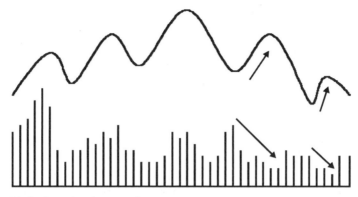

Figure 22-4 Bearish volume configuration.

cance of the reversal will depend upon the extent of the previous advance and the degree of volume expansion. Obviously, an exhaustion move that takes 4–6 days will be nowhere near as significant as one that develops over a matter of weeks. This phenomenon is termed a parabolic blowoff and is featured in Fig. 22-5. Unfortunately, exhaustion or blowoff moves such as this are not easy to define in the sense that it is possible to construct clearly definable trendlines, price patterns, and so on. For this reason it is not usually possible to spot the terminal phase until a day or so after volume and price have reached their crescendos.

8. The opposite of a parabolic blowoff is a selling climax. A selling climax occurs when prices fall for a considerable time at an accelerating pace, accompanied by expanding volume. Following a selling climax, prices may be expected to rise, and the low established at the time of the climax is unlikely to be violated for a considerable time. A price rise from a selling climax is by definition accompanied by declining volume. This is the only time when contracting volume and a rising price may be regarded as normal. Even so, it is important to make sure that volume expands on subsequent rallies, as indicated in Fig. 22-6. Termination of a bear market is often, but not always, accompanied by a selling climax.

9. When prices advance following a long decline and then react to a level at slightly above, or marginally below, the previous trough, it is a bullish sign if the volume on the second trough is significantly lower than the volume on the first. There is an old saying on Wall Street: "Never short a dull market." It applies very much to this type of situation in which a previous low is being tested with very low volume. This indicates a complete lack of selling pressure (see Fig. 22-7).

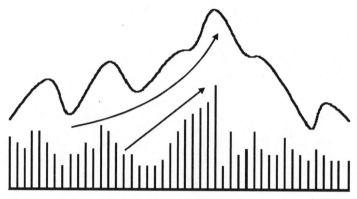

Figure 22-5   Parabolic blowoff.

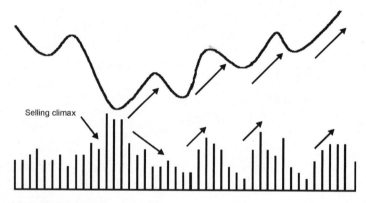

Figure 22-6   Selling climax.

10. A downside breakout from a price pattern, trendline, or moving aver-
    age (MA) that occurs on heavy volume is abnormal and is a bearish sign,
    confirming the reversal in trend (see Fig. 22-8). When prices decline,
    it is usually because of a lack of bids, so volume contracts. This is nor-
    mal activity and is not giving us much information. However, when vol-
    ume expands on the downside, it is because sellers are more motivated;
    the decline, other things being equal, is likely to be more severe.

11. When the market has been rising for many months, an anemic price
    rise (see Fig. 22-9) accompanied by high volume indicates churning
    action and is a bearish factor.

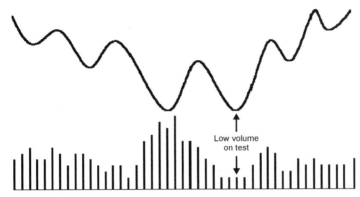

Figure 22-7   Low volume on test.

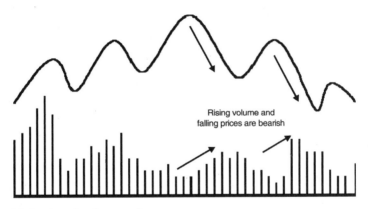

Figure 22-8   Bearish volume configuration.

12. Following a decline, heavy volume with little price change is indicative of accumulation and is normally a bullish factor (see Fig. 22-10).

13. Record volume coming off a major low is usually a very reliable signal that a very significant bottom has been seen because it indicates that an underlying change in psychology has taken place. Such reversals in sentiment are usually of a primary-trend magnitude. Examples in the U.S. stock market developed in March 1978, August 1982 and 1984, and October 1998. It also developed at the 1987 low in bonds and eurodollars. It is not an infallible indicator though, because record volume was achieved in January 2001 for both the NYSE and NASDAQ, yet this did not turn out to be the final low for the move.

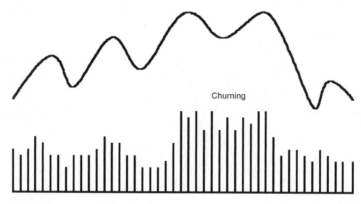

Figure 22-9   Churning.

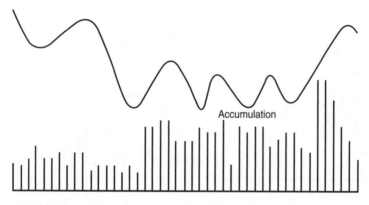

Figure 22-10   Accumulation.

14. When volume and price expand at a sharp pace, short of a parabolic blowoff, and then contract slightly, this usually indicates a change in trend. Sometimes this is an actual reversal, and at other times, it is a consolidation. This phenomenon is featured in Fig. 22-11 and represents a temporary exhaustion of buying power.

15. When price experiences a small rounding top and volume a rounding bottom, this is a double abnormal situation since price is rising and volume falling as the peak is reached. During the decline, price declines and volume expands, which is also abnormal and bearish. An example is shown in Fig. 22-12.

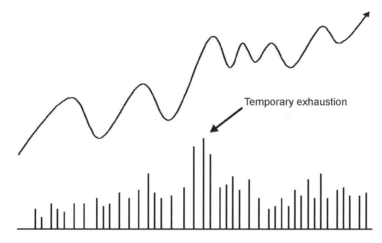

Figure 22-11   Temporary exhaustion.

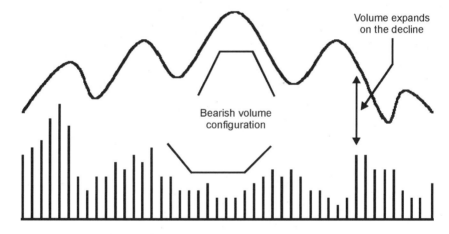

Figure 22-12   Bearish top configuration.

Marketplace Examples

Chart 22-1 features RadioShack. The volume price configuration at *A* is indicative of bull market activity, where price and volume are expanding simultaneously. The character of the technical position changes quite dramatically by the time we reach *B*. Here, the price is rallying, but volume is declining. This is a tip-off that a bear market has begun, because such a relationship is abnormal. Note how volume picks up again in early February as

Chart 22-1   RadioShack, 2000–2001. (*From www.pring.com.*)

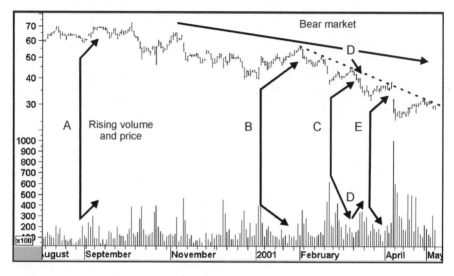

Chart 22-2   Coors, 2000–2001, volume divergence. (*From www.pring.com.*)

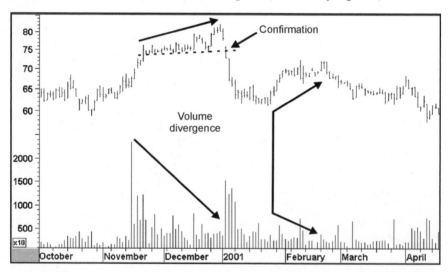

the price begins its decline. This again is abnormal behavior and is bearish. As the price bottoms at *C*, this could be construed as a selling climax. If that had been the case, then the declining volume associated with the subsequent rally could be construed as normal. However, this was clearly not the case as volume started to pick up again at *D*. This was the tip-off that the bear market was still intact. A confirmation developed at *E*, because volume and price once again diverged negatively.

Finally, an explosion of volume occurred in early April, well above that seen previously, thereby hinting at a selling climax. The next rally was associated with a volume decline, which again would have been consistent with a climax. However, the chart leaves us in doubt as to what actually happened next. The requirement for a change in trend signal would be a violation of the dashed down trendline and expanding volume.

Chart 22-2 features Adolf Coors. Note the distinct divergence between the two tops and the extraordinary expansion of volume on the downside breakout. These negative signs were confirmed by a violation of the dashed trendline, which really marked the lower part of a small broadening formation with a flat bottom. This example also demonstrates the deadly power of these formations.

The subsequent January–February rally was associated with a trend of declining volume, so it was not surprising that the price went on to make a new 2001 low.

Chart 22-3 indicates a parabolic blowoff for Newmont Mining in 1987. Normally, the price fluctuations would be greater as it reaches its peak. However, there is no doubt that this situation reflected the flavor of a blowoff with the parabolic run-up in both the volume and the price trend.

Finally, Chart 22-4 shows Air Products with a double bottom formation in 1987. Note how the volume shrank at the second low registered in December. Generally speaking, the greater the volume contrast between the two

Chart 22-3 Newmont Mining, 1986–1987, parabolic blowoff. (*From www.pring.com.*)

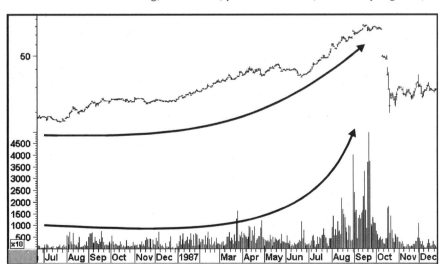

Chart 22-4   Air Products, 1987–1988. (*From www.pring.com.*)

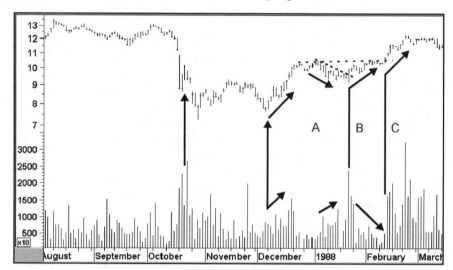

lows, the more positive the situation, once the price has confirmed with a breakout above the rally separating the two lows. Some doubt would have crept into the situation during the decline at *A*, since volume started to expand. However, it then exploded on the outside day (*B*) when the price rallied above the small dotted trendline. Once again volume fell off as the price reached the horizontal dashed trendline, but it would have been hard to top the huge increase in volume associated with the outside day and the sessions following it. This was actually the neckline of a reverse head-and-shoulders pattern. The volume decline was therefore associated with the initial rally off the head and the formation of that very narrow right shoulder. However, there was no doubt about the validity of the breakout, which once again developed on heavy volume.

Summary

- It is normal for volume to go with the trend.
- In a rising market volume usually leads price.
- When volume contracts as prices rally, it is bearish; when volume expands when prices fall, it is also bearish.
- Climactic volume, both on the upside and downside, usually indicates exhaustion and the likelihood that the prevailing trend will reverse.

23

Volume Oscillators

In this chapter we will explore several volume indicators that can be used for any form of security, finishing up this discussion on volume indicators used to analyze stock markets.

Rate of Change of Volume

Normally, volume is displayed as a histogram underneath the price. A quick glance at any chart usually reveals a noticeable increase in the size of the volume bars that are associated with breakouts, selling climaxes, and so forth. This is all well and good, but occasionally there are subtle shifts in the level of volume that are not easily detectable by this method. By massaging the volume data with a rate of change (ROC) calculation it is possible to get some new insights into the dynamics of volume interpretation.

Monitoring Short-Term Trends

Chart 23-1 shows a 10-day ROC of volume together with a regular volume histogram for Northern Trust. A 10-day ROC is being used in this example, but of course it is possible to use any time span you wish. The price peak at *A* looks quite normal under the histogram method, but the ROC technique indicates a dramatic surge commensurate with an exhaustion move.

Peaks in the ROC indicator, then, can often signal exhaustion moves in volume that are not readily apparent with the histogram. In Chart 23-2, featuring T. Rowe Price, the initial peak at *A* is dramatically signaled by the ROC, but not in the histogram in the bottom panel. The peak at *B* is indicated by an expansion in the histogram levels, but the rise is nowhere near that of the volume ROC, which was close to a record for the period covered in the chart. At *C*, the histogram rallies to a record level, but this is not

Chart 23-1   Northern Trust, 2000–2001. (*From www.pring.com.*)

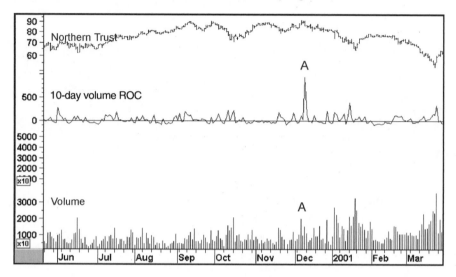

Chart 23-2   T. Rowe Price, 2000–2001. (*From www.pring.com.*)

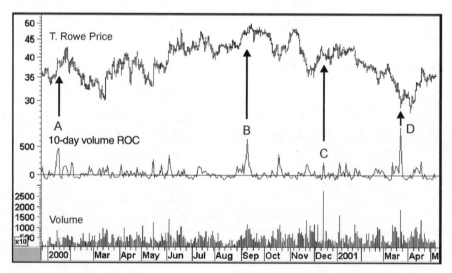

picked up by the ROC. In this instance, the day of the high volume followed the initial peak by 2 days and appears to be an isolated affair, totally unimportant from an analytical point of view. Finally, at *D* both series flag the selling climax at the first bottom, but the comparison is far more dramatic for the ROC.

The ROC sometimes flags divergences. In Chart 23-3, for instance, the two dashed arrows point up the series of declining volume momentum peaks and rising price highs. This indicated serious potential weakness, and sure enough, the price did experience a decline once it had been confirmed by violating its uptrendline at *C*.

In Chart 23-4, we see a breakout in volume at *A*. Since this was also confirmed by the price, a nice rally followed. Rising volume can also be a bearish factor. Later in Chart 23-4, the volume curve rallies above a small up trendline. This indicated a trend of rising volume, but told us nothing about the price. A couple of days later we get a vital clue since the price violated an up trendline. Whenever, after a rally, prices decline on expanding volume, this is a bearish sign. It was not surprising therefore that the sell-off continued until the right-hand part of the chart.

It is fairly evident by now that a simple ROC of volume can be a pretty jagged indicator suitable only for pointing up exhaustion moves and divergences, and, on a limited basis, for constructing trendlines. Sometimes, it makes sense to run a moving average (MA) through a volume ROC because it smoothes out the jagged nature of the raw data.

Chart 23-3 Stanley Works, 1999–2000, and a volume ROC. (*From www.pring.com.*)

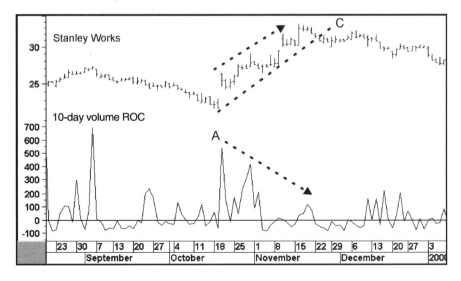

Chart 23-4   Stanley Works, 1999, and a volume ROC. (*From www.pring.com.*)

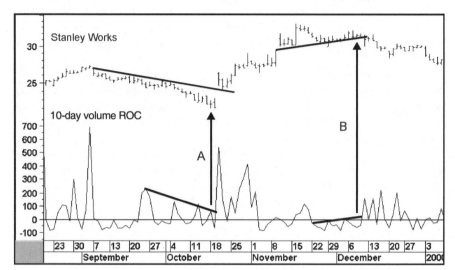

In Chart 23-5, this has been taken one step further by dividing a 10-day ROC of volume by a 25-day MA. This series is a lot smoother than the previous examples. It is fairly evident from the chart that this calculation lends itself more readily to price pattern and trendline analysis. First note that the overbought and oversold lines are not drawn on an equidistant basis. This is because this approach treats the ROC as a percentage. Volume can expand, even on a smoothed basis, by 200 or 300 percent quite easily, yet can only fall by a maximum of 100 percent. This means that downside action is far more limited than upside potential. Later we will look at an alternative form of calculating a smoothed ROC of volume. There are two principal events on the chart. The first is a head-and-shoulders (H&S) top. The head represented a buying crescendo, which indicated a change of trend. Once the neckline had been violated, this merely represented a confirmation that the volume trend was down. Since the price also violated an up trendline, both price and volume were now in gear on the downside and it was reasonable to anticipate an extended correction.

The end of the sell-off was signaled as both series violated important downtrend lines. Since they were now in gear on the upside, this provided a nice confirmation that the uptrend was healthy. In this instance, a down trendline for volume actually represents the neckline of a reverse H&S pat-

Chart 23-5 Snap-on Inc., 1993–1994, and a smoothed volume ROC. (*From www.pring.com.*)

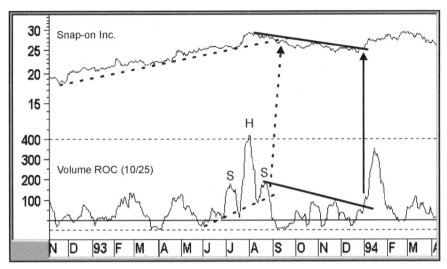

tern. I did not display the H and S letters because the left shoulder was also the right shoulder of the previous upward sloping H&S top and this would have complicated things.

We discovered earlier that the volume ROC indicator, when calculated with a percent method, does not indicate oversold volume conditions very well. A solution is to calculate the ROC using subtraction as a basis for the calculation in place of the division technique. This is represented in the lower panel of Chart 23-6. An oversold condition is signaled at *A* for the subtraction method, but not for the division calculation. The disadvantage of the subtraction calculation is that volume momentum cannot be compared over long periods of time if the security being monitored experiences a substantial increase in average daily volume. For charts covering less than 2 years, the subtraction technique is probably a better approach, though it's important to remember that because the volume level for individual stocks and markets can vary tremendously, the overbought and oversold lines will have to be adjusted accordingly. In Chart 23-6, the horizontal line represents an overbought reading in both volume indicators. Since the price had been declining, the high level at *B* was a selling climax. Since the subtraction-based momentum indicator was deeply oversold at *A*, the next slightly lower bottom indicated a classic double bottom characteristic.

Chart 23-6 Snap-on Inc., 1994–1995, and two-volume ROC calculations. (*From www.pring.com.*)

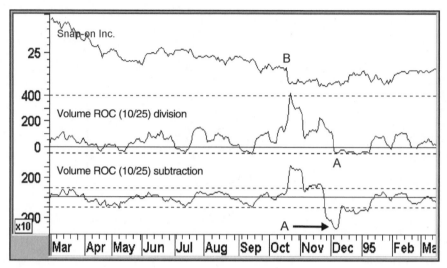

> **Major Technical Principle** A high overextended reading in a volume indicator does not necessarily mean that the price is overbought, merely that volume is overextended. A high reading in volume oscillators can mean a top or a bottom depending on the direction of the previous price trend. A reversal from a high level can also signify a *change* as opposed to a *reversal* in trend.

Monitoring Primary Trends

Annual (12-month) ROCs are a useful way of measuring primary-trend price momentum, but since volume trends are more random in nature, such indicators tend to be quite jagged in nature. Chart 23-7 shows the annual ROC price for the Standard & Poor's Composite and NYSE volume. However, in order to overcome the jagged nature of the volume data, both series have been smoothed with a 6-month MA. When used together, the two series can be extremely instructive.

Chart 23-7 Price versus volume momentum. (*From www.pring.com.*)

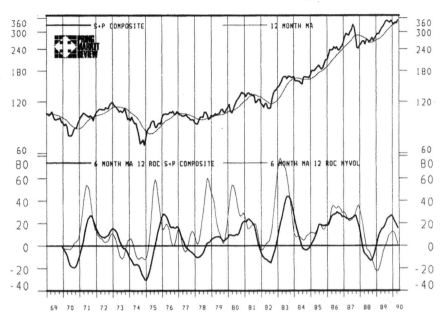

There are several observations that can be made:

- The volume curve has an almost consistent tendency to peak out ahead of price during both bull and bear phases.

- In most instances, fairly reliable indications of a *potential* trend reversal can be obtained when the volume momentum crosses price.

- When the price index is above its zero reference line and is falling, but volume is rising (such as late 1976, 1981, and late 1987), the expanding activity represents distribution and should be interpreted as a very bearish factor once the rally has terminated.

- A reversal in volume at a market bottom should be confirmed by a reversal in price momentum as well.

- Very high readings in the volume indicator are usually followed by strong bull markets.

- When volume crosses below zero, it is normally, but not always, a negative sign. The most bearish situations seem to arise when the price indicator is well above zero. In 1988, for instance, price momentum was well below zero when volume moved into negative territory, but the market rallied. On the other hand, in 1973 and 1977 volume crossed below zero

just after price momentum had started to roll over from an overbought level, and this was followed by a major decline.
• During the initial stages of a bull move, volume momentum is always above price. (The 1988–1989 rally represents the only exception.)

Chart 23-7 also shows that a reversal in one curve unaccompanied by a reversal in the other at market bottoms often gives a premature signal. For example, volume turned up ahead of price at the end of 1973 and 1977. Consequently, it is wiser to await a signal from both, even though it may occur at a slightly higher price level.

Volume Oscillator

The volume oscillator is an alternative method of presenting volume in a momentum format. It is calculated by dividing a short-term measure of the volume trend by a longer-term one and plotting the result as an oscillator. It is also possible to divide the close by a measure of trend. In effect, the calculation is identical as that for price under the trend deviation section in Chapter 11. The only difference is that volume is substituted for price. An example is shown in Fig. 23-1. The resulting indicator is an oscillator that revolves around a zero reference line. A zero reading in the indicator occurs when both MAs are at identical levels. Positive readings develop when the shorter-term (10-day in the figure) MA is above its longer-term (25-day) counterpart, and vice versa.

An example is shown in Chart 23-8 featuring Humana. Here we can see that the volume oscillator breaks above a small down trendline in March of 1999. This upside breakout merely indicated that the trend of volume momentum was up. It said nothing about the course of prices. In this instance, the price violated a horizontal trendline, signaling a bearish combination of declining prices and expanding volume. This was then followed by an overbought reading in the oscillator, which indicated a selling climax. That could have proved to be the final bottom. However, the oscillator broke above a trendline in July 2000, and the price violated one on the downside, indicating an almost exact replay of the 1999 price action. This just goes to show that a *selling climax often represents the final low, but this is certainly not the case every time.*

Chart 23-9 features a 15/45 volume oscillator for Columbia Energy. This longer-term relationship offers more deliberate and less jagged price action. The most obvious thing to note is the late 1999 summer reverse H&S in the oscillator. Once again an increase in volume was indicated, but this time the price broke to the upside. We see another example later in November. It is

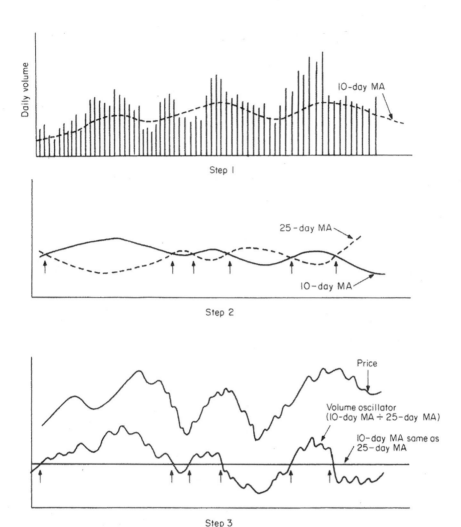

Figure 23-1 Calculating a volume oscillator.

rare when these oscillators are able to trace out price patterns, but when they do, the signals tend to be very reliable. The chart also shows a buying climax in early November, which was later confirmed by a trend break in the price itself. Finally, a selling climax developed in the following March.

It is fairly obvious by now that volume oscillators move between bands of extremes, just as price momentum does, but with one important difference. When a price oscillator is overextended on the upside, it usually indicates

Chart 23-8 Humana, 1998–1999, and a volume oscillator. (*From www.pring.com.*)

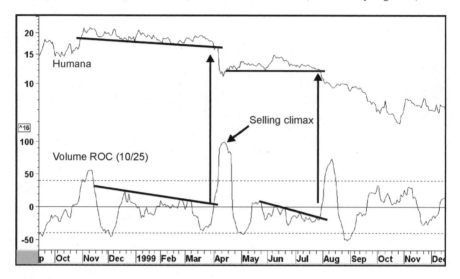

Chart 23-9 Columbia Energy, 1999–2000, and a volume oscillator. (*From www.pring.com.*)

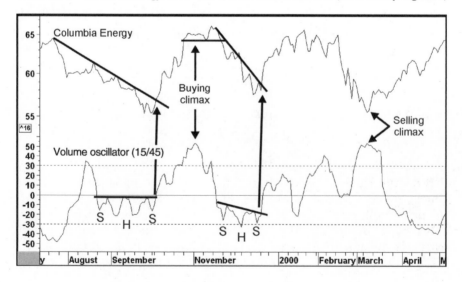

an overbought market, with the implication that a reversal to the downside is due. With a volume oscillator, an unusual rise in activity is also associated with an imminent trend reversal, but we only learn of the direction with reference to the price. Apart from this important difference, volume oscillators should be interpreted in the same way as price oscillators.

If an exhaustion reversal can be observed in a volume indicator, other indicators should then be consulted to make sure that the volume action is being confirmed. One possibility is the use of a volume with a price oscillator. This relationship is not always exact. If volume and price changes are not closely related for the security being followed, this approach should not be used.

Chart 23-10 of Compaq compares a price and volume oscillator of different time spans. At points *B* and *D* we see selling climaxes. Point *B* is

Chart 23-10   Compaq, 1999–2001, with a volume versus a price oscillator. (*From www.pring.com.*)

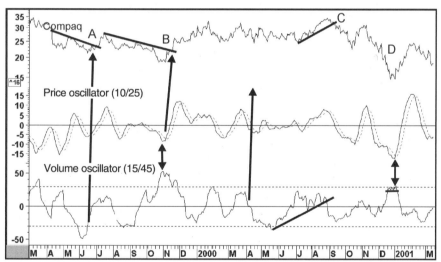

Major Technical Principle   Reversals from overbought readings in volume momentum indicators usually signal exhaustion, either from the buy or sell side. Exhaustion is usually a sign that the prevailing trend has reversed.

particularly interesting because both the price and the price oscillator violate down trendlines. Notice how both oscillators almost touch at *D*. This oversold reading in the price oscillator and overbought volume oscillator is what I term the *double whammy effect*, since each oscillator is telling us in its own way that a climax is in the air.

In July 1999 at *A*, we see a quite different effect. The volume oscillator becomes extremely oversold, thereby indicating a complete lack of interest. Then it rallies and crosses above the oversold level, indicating an expansion of volume. This could go either way, but the break in the two down trendlines for the moderately oversold price oscillator and the price itself indicated an upside resolution.

Finally, at *C* it's possible to observe a break in the volume oscillator's up trendline. This indicated that a declining trend of volume had begun. You can also see a small negative divergence between the volume oscillator and price. Under such circumstances it would be normal to expect the price to consolidate or decline. Of course, the price could also rise, but with declining volume the trend would be very suspect. As it turned out, the price confirmed with a small trendline break, and the price oscillator reversed to the downside from a moderately overbought condition.

The main rules for interpreting the volume oscillator are summarized here:

- When the oscillator reaches an extreme and starts to reverse, it is indicating the potential for a reversal of the prevailing trend.
- Volume oscillators occasionally lend themselves to trendline and pattern construction.
- Expansion in price, associated with a contraction in the volume oscillator, is bearish.
- An expansion in the oscillator, associated with a contraction in price, is bearish, except when volume reaches an extreme, in which case a selling climax is usually signaled.
- The volume oscillator usually leads the price oscillator.

Remember, this is by no means a perfect indicator; therefore, you should first make sure that it bears a resemblance to the price trend being measured, and subsequently look for corroborating evidence from other indicators.

The Demand Index

The Demand Index was developed by Jim Sibbet as a method of simulating upside and downside volume for markets and stocks where such data are not generally available. It combines price and volume into one indicator with the objective of leading market turning points. The Demand Index is based on the premise that volume leads price. It is included in many charting packages. Unlike the volume ROC and volume oscillator, the Demand Index always moves in the same direction as the price. High Demand Index readings always indicate overbought conditions, and vice versa. I find this to be a very useful indicator when applied in the following ways:

- Divergences between the indicator and the price indicate an underlying strength or weakness, depending on whether it is a positive or negative one.
- Overbought and oversold crossovers often generate good buy and sell signals in some markets. Since the level of the Demand Index is affected by the volatility of the security being monitored, optimum overbought and oversold levels will vary, and should be determined on a case-by-case approach. However, the + and −25 levels appear to be a good compromise for most securities.
- The index sometimes forms price patterns and experiences trendline violations. They normally represent a reliable advance warning of an impending price trend reversal.

Chart 23-11 shows some interesting features. First, at *A*, both the price and Demand Index break trendlines for a good sell signal. Later on the process

Chart 23-11   Citrix Systems, 2000–2001, and a Demand Index. (*From www.pring.com.*)

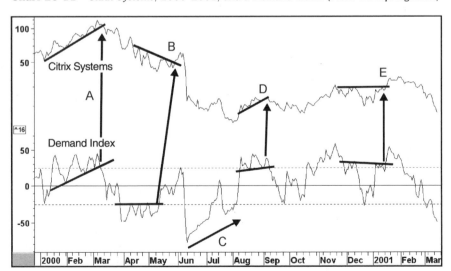

is reversed as the Demand Index completes a base along with the price. The subsequent rally can only be described as a whipsaw. Does this mean that the Demand Index is no good? No, this is a normal phenomenon in a bear market. What looks to be a very valid breakout turns out to be a whipsaw. This type of disappointing action can happen with any indicator. The remedy is to try to identify the direction of the main trend before doing any short-term analysis. Point C shows a positive divergence between the Demand Index and the price, and D a small double trendline break develops. Finally, at E, we see a breakout by the Demand Index from a reverse H&S pattern, but it fails. Once again we need to use some common sense, because in this case, the breakout came from an overbought condition. As we learned in the momentum section, breakouts from such high levels typically result in whipsaws.

Chaikin Money Flow

The Chaikin Money Flow (CMF) indicator, developed by Marc Chaikin, is based on the principle that rising prices should be accompanied by expanding volume, and vice versa. The formula emphasizes the fact that market strength is usually accompanied by prices closing in the upper half of their daily range with increasing volume. Likewise, market weakness is usually accompanied by prices closing in the lower half of their daily range with increasing volume. This indicator can be calculated with any time span; the longer the period, the more deliberate the swings. Money flow indicators calculated with a short-term time frame, such as 10 periods, are therefore much more volatile.

When prices consistently close in the upper half of their daily high/low range on increased volume for the period under consideration, the indicator will be positive (above the zero line). Conversely, if prices consistently close in the lower half of their daily high/low range on increased volume, the indicator will be negative (below the zero line).

It's possible to construct overbought and oversold lines, crossovers of which are used as buy and sell alerts, but the indicator really comes into its own with divergence analysis. In Chart 23-12 of National Semiconductor, we can see some good examples in practice. In early 1994, the Chaikin was falling sharply as the price ran up to its final peak. At the time of the actual high, it was barely above the equilibrium line. This showed that the quality of the last few weeks of the rally left a lot to be desired. At the end of 1995, the divergence was more blatant since the indicator was barely able to rise above the zero line at a time when the price was making a new high. Both these examples were followed by long downtrends.

Chart 23-12 National Semiconductor, 1993–1997, and CMF. (*From www.pring.com.*)

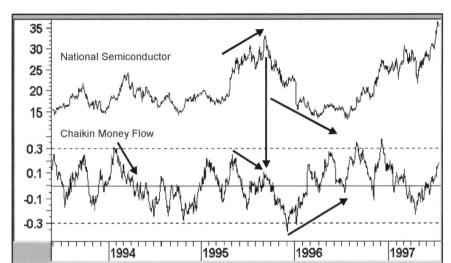

Positive divergences also work quite well, as we can see from the early 1996 bottom. See how the price makes a marginal new low, but the oscillator is hardly below zero. This compares to the late 1995 bottom, where it was at an extremely oversold condition. Of course, this is merely a positive momentum characteristic; we still need to witness some kind of trend reversal in price to confirm this event.

Divergences are not uncommon in momentum indicators. What sets the Chaikin Money Flow indicator apart from the rest is that the divergences are usually far more blatant than, say, the relative strength indicator (RSI) or ROC. As a result, it can provide clues of probable trend reversals that may not be apparent elsewhere.

One of the ways in which I like to use this indicator is to study trading ranges, and then compare the price action to the oscillator to see if it is giving a clue as to the direction of the eventual breakout. Chart 23-13 shows American Business Products with a 20-week CMF. The price was experiencing a sideways trading range in 1987. During the formation of the rectangle, the CMF indicator violated an up trendline and, later in the September–October period, diverged very negatively with the price. This combination indicated vulnerability, so it was not surprising that the price subsequently experienced a nasty decline. Later, the price traced out another trading range, but this time the CMF rallied the moment the trading range started, thereby suggesting that the sideways pattern would be resolved in a positive way.

Chart 23-13 American Business Products, 1986–1991, and CMF. (*From www.pring.com.*)

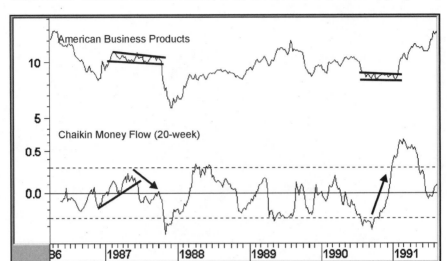

Volume in the Stock Market

Upside/Downside Volume

Measures of upside/downside volume try to separate the volume in advancing and declining stocks. The adoption of this technique makes it possible to determine in a subtle way whether distribution or accumulation is taking place. The concept sounds impressive, but in practice I find volume momentum based on ROC or trend-deviation data to be more reliable.

The upside/downside volume data are published daily in *The Wall Street Journal* and weekly in *Barron's,* and they are provided by many data services such as Reuters, CSI, and Dial data. Upside/downside volume is measured in two ways.

The Upside/Downside Volume Line The first is a cumulative indicator similar in construction to advance/decline lines. It is known as the *upside/downside volume line.* It is constructed by cumulating the difference between the daily plurality of the volume of advancing and declining stocks. Since an indicator of this type is always started from an arbitrary point, it is a good idea to begin with a fairly large number. Otherwise, there is the possibility that if the market declines sharply the line will move into negative territory. If a starting total of 500 million shares is assumed, the line will be constructed as shown in Table 23-1.

Table 23-1 Calculation for the Upside/Downside Volume Line

Date	Volume of advancing stocks, in millions	Volume of declining stocks, in millions	Difference	Upside/downside line
Jan. 1	101	51	+50	5050
2	120	60	+60	5110
3	155	155	0	5110
4	150	100	+50	5160
5	111	120	−9	5151

These statistics are not published on a weekly or monthly basis, so longer-term analysis should be undertaken by recording the value of the line at the end of each Friday, or taking an average of Friday readings for a monthly plot. The appropriate MA can then be constructed from these weekly and monthly observations. It is normal for the upside/downside line to rise during market advances and to fall during declines.

Major Technical Principle When the upside/downside line fails to confirm a new high (or low) in the price index, it warns of a potential trend reversal.

The basic principles of trend determination discussed in Part I may be applied to the upside/downside line. When a market is advancing in an irregular fashion, with successively higher rallies interrupted by a series of rising troughs, the upside/downside line should be doing the same. Such action indicates that the volume of advancing issues is expanding on rallies and contracting during declines. When this trend of the normal price/volume relationship is broken, a warning is given that one of two things is happening. Either upside volume is failing to expand sufficiently, or volume during the decline has begun to expand excessively on the downside. Both are bearish factors. The upside/downside line is particularly useful when prices are rising to new highs and overall volume is expanding. In such instances, if the volume of declining stocks is rising in relation to that of advancing stocks, it will show up either as a slower rate of advance in the upside/downside line or as an actual decline.

The upside/downside line from 1985 to 1987 is shown in Chart 23-14, together with its 200-day MA. For most of this period, the line remained above its MA despite some fairly large short-term corrections in the S&P

Chart 23-14   S&P Composite, 1985–1987, and an upside/downside volume line. (*From www.pring.com.*)

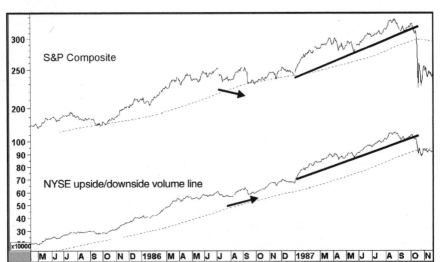

Composite, but in early October 1987 it fell below the MA, just before the crash. An important up trendline was violated simultaneously with the MA, which had the effect of emphasizing the bearish signal.

Also worth noting were the positive divergences that occurred in October 1986 when the S&P made a new short-term low, which was not confirmed by the cumulative upside/downside line.

Between 1988 and 1997 there were no major divergences since the line and the S&P moved more or less in gear. Chart 23-15 shows the same indicator between 1998 and 2001. Note the negative divergence at the 1998 summer peak, and the trendline break that signaled the subsequent rally. Between 1999 and the summer of 2000 some major negative divergences arose between the two series. This period was one of most confusing on record, since there were numerous discrepancies. First, one series would lead, and then the other.

Upside/Downside Volume Oscillators   Another method of measuring upside/downside volume is to plot an oscillator of up and down volume and overlay them. Possibilities include the volume oscillator, a smoothed RSI, and so forth. Chart 23-16 features such an exercise using two know sure things (KSTs) of volume. The idea is that when the KST constructed from up volume

Chart 23-15 S&P Composite, 1998–2001, and an upside/downside volume line. (*From www.pring.com.*)

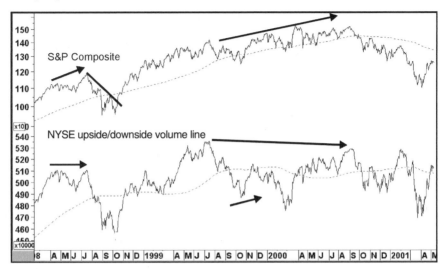

Chart 23-16 S&P Composite, 2000–2001, and upside/downside volume oscillators. (*From www.pring.com.*)

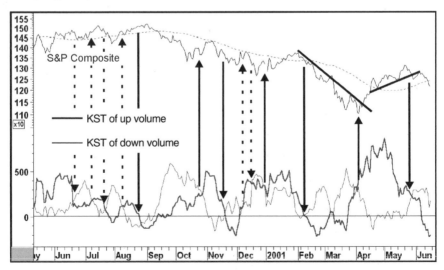

crosses the one constructed from down volume, this triggers a volume buy signal, and vice versa. The various signals are flagged in the chart by the up and down arrows. The dashed arrows indicate whipsaw signals. Unfortunately, there is no way of knowing from the indicator itself whether a signal will work or not. For this reason, it is important to monitor the price itself for trendline breaks, and so on. In this respect, a couple have been drawn on Chart 23-16.

Sometimes it helps to construct a ratio of upside to downside volume and study the overbought/oversold levels. In this respect, Chart 23-17 shows a ratio of a 10-day to a 45-day volume oscillator for the two series. The volume oscillator for the up volume data is calculated by dividing a 10-day by a 25-day simple MA of up volume. This is then divided by a similar measure for down volume. There is nothing special about these time spans. Shorter-term trend reversals would be spotted by using shorter time frames, and vice versa.

The arrows on the chart indicate when the ratio crosses its overbought and oversold zones on its way back to zero. By and large, these signals appear to work quite well, but they should always be integrated with trend-reversal signals in the price itself to reduce the risk of whipsaw signals. There is no reason why trendlines, price patterns, and even MA crossovers could not be used as a method of analysis using this ratio.

Chart 23-17   S&P Composite, 1999–2001, and an upside/downside volume ratio. (*From www.pring.com.*)

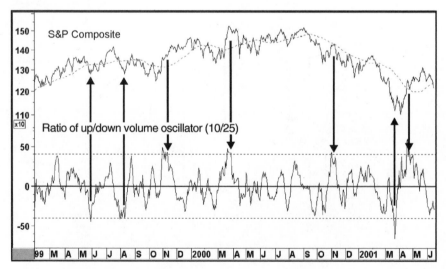

The Arms Index

This indicator was developed by Richard Arms (www.ArmsInsight.com) and is constructed from breadth and upside/downside volume data. It is sometimes referred to as the TRIN or MKDS. It is calculated by dividing the ratio of advancing and declining stocks by the ratio of volume in advancing issues over volume in declining issues as follows:

$$\frac{(advances/declines)}{(advancing\ volume/declining\ volume)}.$$

In almost all cases, daily data are used, but there is no reason why a weekly or even monthly series could not be constructed. Normally, the Arms Index is used in conjunction with NYSE data, but its principles can be applied to any market situation, such as the NASDAQ, where upside/downside volume and breadth data are available. There is one important thing to note, and that is that movements in the Arms Index move contrary to those of the market. This means that oversold conditions appear as peaks and overbought as valleys. Since this is contrary to virtually all other indicators described in this book, *the chart examples are presented inversely in order to be consistent with the other indicators.*

The concept behind this indicator is to monitor the relative power of the volume associated with advancing issues to that of declining ones. Ideally, it is important to see a healthy amount of volume moving into rising issues relative to that associated with declining stocks. If this is not the case, the indicator will diverge negatively with the market average. On the other hand, if a substantial amount of volume is moving into declining issues, this indicates tremendous selling pressure. At some point selling pressure reaches an extreme and prices are poised for a reversal.

This momentum series can be calculated for any period. For example, the quote services and the number appearing on the CNBC ticker represent an instant in time and are based on the volume and number of issues experiencing an up or down tick. Unless you are fortunate enough to be able to chart this indicator on a continuous basis through a real-time service, isolated quotes of this nature are limited to gauging whether the market is intraday overbought or oversold. In this respect, 120 or higher is regarded as oversold and 50 or below overbought (remember these numbers are inverse to the other momentum indicators).

The Arms Index can also be used with an MA, where the 10-day (open TRIN) time span is the most widely followed. It is interpreted in much the same way as the 10-day A/D ratio discussed earlier in this chapter. Most of the time these two series move in a consistent manner, but from time to time the Arms Index gives some subtle indications that the prevailing trend is about to reverse. Chart 23-18 shows three different versions of the Arms

Chart 23-18 S&P Composite, 1998–2001, and three Arms Indexes. (*From www.pring.com.*)

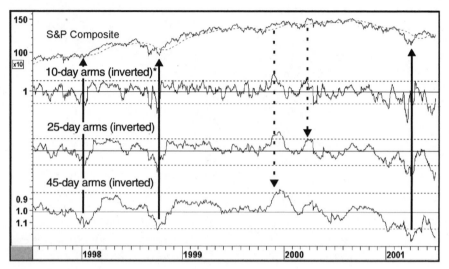

Index with a 10-, 25-, and 45-day time spans. The rationales for including three indicators on one chart were explained in Chapter 10. The arrows indicate those points when at least two of these inversely plotted series are at an extreme and have begun to reverse since tops tend to be rolling affairs where volume leads price. The Arms Index often reaches its extreme ahead of the market average, whereas the selling climax conditions often seen at bottoms mean that there is usually more of a coincident nature between the Arms and the market. Generally speaking, when the 10-day Arms rises above 150, this signals a major low. Sometimes this happens right away; at other times there is a delay of 10–20 days before the final bottom is seen. Between 1968 and 2001 there were no exceptions to this rule.

On-Balance Volume

On-balance volume (OBV) was discovered by Joe Granville and published in his book *Granville's New Key to Stock Market Profits.* The indicator is plotted as a continuous, cumulative line. The line is started with an arbitrary number, which rises and falls depending on what the price does. The volume for the day is added in when the price rises and is subtracted when it falls. If intraday charts are being used, volume units would be added and subtracted based on the time frame of the bars; for weekly charts, the basis would be the week, and so forth. OBV therefore offers a rough approximation for buying and selling pressure and has become a very popular indicator. It is interpreted by comparing the line to the price, using divergences, trendline breaks, price patterns, and MA crossovers to point up underlying strength or weakness.

Chart 23-19 shows how this should happen. The price makes a lower low in November, but the OBV, indicating a lack of selling pressure, does not. This is a bullish sign and the price rises. Earlier in September, the OBV makes a marginal new high, and the price makes a more significant one. This indicated that volume was not as strong as price and was a bearish sign. You can also see that both examples were then confirmed with trend breaks in the price and OBV lines. Note also in late July that the price broke below its 200-day MA and OBV did not, another sign that selling pressure was not as strong as it appeared on the surface. This example represents a pretty perfect analytical picture. Unfortunately, I do not find OBV to normally be as accurate as this. Indeed, its warnings are often as misleading as the valid signals. Chart 23-20 featuring Alergan, for example, shows a situation at the end of 1999 when OBV was pointing to higher prices and they went down; in early 2000, weakness in the OBV pointed to lower prices, but they went up! Note that in both charts the joint trendline technique worked, which is probably the best way to interpret OBV.

Chart 23-19 Amerada Hess, 2000–2001, and OBV. (*From www.pring.com.*)

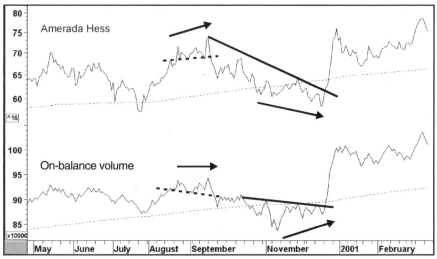

Chart 23-20   Alergan, 1998–2000, and OBV. (*From www.pring.com.*)

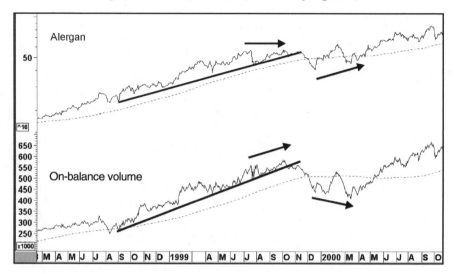

Equivolume

Equivolume is a plotting concept that was developed by Dick Arms (www.ArmsInsight.com). It is similar to the candlestick volume discussed in Chapter 13. Bars are plotted equally for each period, day, week, and so on. With equivolume, the bars are plotted in different widths depending on the level of volume for that particular period. The greater the volume, the wider the bar. The top and bottom of each bar are the high and low for that particular period. This is a very useful approach because it shows graphically in one series whether prices are rising or falling on light or heavy volume. Because of this technique, dates on the X axis are not equidistant from each other as they normally would be, but depend on volume patterns instead.

Chart 23-21 shows MMM Company. At *A*, the price breaks out with a couple of thick bars, indicating very heavy volume. In effect, this is a classic buy signal. At *B*, the rally is associated with very narrow equivolume bars, which tells us that there is a distinct lack of upside volume. Thus, a warning of an impending trend reversal is given.

Chart 23-22 shows an equivolume chart for Johnson and Johnson. The decline at *A* is associated with very thin bars, which indicates a total disinterest in the stock. This is the type of characteristic that is often associated with a short-term bottom. Other indicators are, of course, required to confirm. Another rally on shrinking volume is signaled at *B*. *C* points up the

Chart 23-21 MMM, 2000–2001, and equivolume. (*From www.pring.com.*)

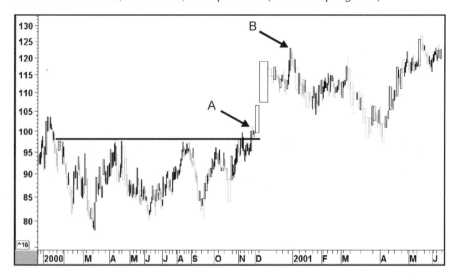

Chart 23-22 Johnson and Johnson, 2000–2001, and equivolume. (*From www.pring.com.*)

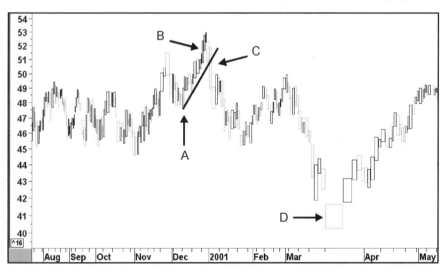

fact that volume is expanding on the decline, which is bearish. The trend-line break in the price then acts as a confirmation. Finally, the extremely wide bar at *D* indicates the possibility of a selling climax.

Summary

- The ROC of volume often gives signs of subtle changes in the level of volume that are not apparent from volume histograms.
- The ROC of volume can be expressed as a percentage or in a subtraction format.
- Volume ROCs and oscillators can be used with overbought/oversold crossovers, trendline analysis, and price patterns.
- Overbought readings in the volume ROC and the volume oscillator can be followed by declining or rising prices, depending on the nature of the previous trend.
- The Demand Index is constructed from volume and price, moves in the same direction as a regular price oscillator, and is best used with divergence and overbought/oversold analysis, trendline, and price pattern construction.
- The CMF is constructed from volume and price data and moves in the same direction as a regular price oscillator. It is best used with divergence analysis.
- Upside/downside volume measures the volume in advancing and declining stocks. It can be used as a continuous line or in oscillator format.
- The Arms Index is constructed from advancing and declining stocks and their respective volume. It is usually used as a 10-day MA. Readings in excess of 150 signal major bottoms.
- OBV is constructed as a continuous line and used with divergence analysis. Joint trendline breaks between the OBV line and the price offer a more accurate method of interpretation.

24
Breadth

Basic Concepts

Breadth indicators measure the degree to which the vast majority of issues are participating in a market move. It therefore monitors the extent of a market trend. Generally speaking, the fewer the number of issues moving in the direction of the major averages, the greater the probability of an imminent reversal in trend. Breadth indicators were originally developed to monitor trends in the stock market. Even though most of the comments in this chapter refer to U.S. equities, it should be remembered that breadth can just as validly be applied to other markets around the world. It can also be applied to any sector or market that can be broken down into components. An example might include a basket of commodities being compared to a commodity index, a series of currencies to an overall currency index (such as the Dollar Index), or a selection of stocks in an industry to an industry group index. The main thing to keep in mind is that the principles of interpretation remain constant.

The concept of breadth can probably be best explained using a military analogy. In Fig. 24-1, lines *AA* and *BB* indicate military lines of defense drawn during a battle. It might be possible for a few units to cross over from *AA* to *BB*, but the chances are that the *BB* line will hold unless an all-out effort is made. In Fig. 24-1(*a*), the two units represented by the arrows are quickly repulsed. In Fig. 24-1(*b*), on the other hand, the assault is successful since many units are taking part, and army *B* is forced to retreat to a new line of defense at B_1.

A narrowly advancing stock market can be compared to Fig. 24-1(*a*), where it looks initially as though the move through the line of defense (in stock market terms, a *resistance level*) is going to be successful, but because

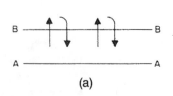
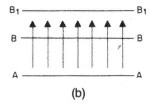

(a)   (b)

Figure 24-1 Trench warfare.

the move is accompanied by such little support, the overall price trend is soon reversed. In the military analogy, even if the two units had successfully assaulted the *BB* defense, it would not be long before army *B* would have overpowered them, for the farther they advanced without broad support, the more vulnerable they would have become to a counter offensive by army *B*.

The same is true of the stock market, for the longer a price trend is maintained without a follow-up by the broad market, the more vulnerable is the advance.

At market bottoms, breadth is not such a useful concept for determining reversals because the majority of stocks usually coincide with or lag behind the major indexes. On the few occasions when breadth reverses its downtrend before the averages, it is actually a more reliable indicator than the one at the top. I will begin this discussion with a rationale as to why the broad market normally leads the averages at market tops. The word *normally* is used because, in the vast majority of cases, the broad list of stocks does peak out ahead of a market average such as the Dow Jones Industrial Average (DJIA) or the S&P Composite. This rule is not invariable, however, and it should not be assumed that the technical structure is necessarily sound just because market breadth is strong.

Advance/Decline Line

The Concept

The most widely used indicator of market breadth is an *advance/decline* (A/D) *line*. It is constructed by taking a cumulative total of the difference (plurality) between the number of New York Stock Exchange (NYSE) issues that are advancing over those that are declining in a particular period (usually a day or a week). Similar indexes may be constructed for the American Exchange (AMEX) or NASDAQ issues. Because the number of issues listed on the NYSE has expanded since breadth records were first kept, an A/D line constructed from a simple plurality of advancing over declining issues gives a greater weighting to more recent years. For the purpose of long-term comparisons, it is better to take a ratio of advances versus declines, or a ratio of advances and declines divided by the number of unchanged issues, rather than limiting the calculation to a simple plurality.

The late Hamilton Bolton devised one of the most useful measurements of breadth. It is calculated from a cumulative running total of the following formula:

$$\sqrt{A/U - D/U}$$

where A = the number of stocks advancing, D = the number declining, and U = the number unchanged.

Because it is not mathematically possible to calculate the square root of a negative number (that is, when the number of declining stocks is greater than the number of those advancing), the D and A are reversed in such cases, so that the formula becomes the square root of $D/U - A/U$. The resulting term is then subtracted from the cumulative total, as opposed to the term in the earlier formula, which is added. Table 24-1 illustrates this calculation using weekly data.

Inclusion of the number of unchanged issues is useful because the more dynamic the move in either direction, the greater the tendency for the number of unchanged stocks to diminish. Consequently, by giving some weight to the number of unchanged stocks in the formula, it is possible to assess a slowdown in momentum of the A/D line at an earlier date, since an expanding number of unchanged issues will have the tendency to restrain extreme movements.

The A/D line normally rises and falls in tandem with the major market averages, but it usually peaks well ahead of them. There appear to be three basic reasons why this is so:

1. The market, as a whole, discounts the business cycle and normally reaches its bull market peak 6 to 9 months before the economy reaches its peak. Since the peak in business activity is itself preceded by a deterioration of certain leading sectors such as financial, consumer spending, and construction, it is logical to expect that the stocks representing these sectors will also peak ahead of the general market.

2. Many of the stocks listed on the NYSE, such as preferred and utility, are sensitive to changes in interest rates. Since interest rates usually start to rise before the market peaks, it is natural for the interest-sensitive issues to move in tandem with rising rates.

Table 24-1 Weekly A/D Line Calculation (Bolton Formula)

Date	Issues traded (1)	Advances (2)	Declines (3)	Unchanged (4)	Advances + unchanged (5)	Declines + unchanged (6)	Col. 5 − col. 6 (7)	$\sqrt{\text{Col. 7}}$ (8)	Cumulative A/D line (9)
Jan. 7	2129	989	919	221	448	416	32	5.7	2475.6
14	2103	782	1073	248	315	433	−118	−10.9	2464.7
21	2120	966	901	253	382	356	26	5.1	2469.8
28	2103	835	1036	232	360	447	−87	−9.3	2460.5
Feb. 4	2089	910	905	274	332	330	2	1.4	2461.9
11	2090	702	1145	243	289	471	−18.2	−13.5	2448.4
18	2093	938	886	269	349	329	20	4.5	2452.9
25	2080	593	1227	260	228	472	244	−15.6	2437.3

3. Poorer-quality stocks offer the largest upside potential, but they are also representative of smaller, underfinanced, and badly managed companies that are more vulnerable to reduced earnings (and even bankruptcy) during a recession. Blue-chip stocks normally have good credit ratings, reasonable yields, and sound underlying assets; thus, they are typically the last stocks to be sold by investors during a bull market.

The DJIA and other market averages are almost wholly composed of larger companies, which are normally in better financial shape. These popular averages therefore continue to advance well after the broad market has peaked.

Interpretation of A/D Lines

The following are some key points for interpreting A/D data:

1. Some A/D lines appear to have a permanent downward bias. It is therefore important to observe the relationship between an A/D line and an index over a very long period to see whether this bias exists. Examples include breadth data for the AMEX market, the U.S. OTC market, and the Japanese market.

2. Divergences between a market average and an A/D line at market tops are almost always cleared up by a decline in the average. However, it is mandatory to await some kind of trend-reversal signal in the average as confirmation before concluding that the average will also decline.

3. It is normal for the A/D line to coincide or lag at market bottoms. Such action is of no forecasting value. When the A/D line refuses to confirm a new low in the index, the signal is unusual and very positive, but only when confirmed by a reversal in the average itself.

4. Breadth data may diverge negatively from the averages, but an important rally is often signaled when a down trendline violation is signaled, along with a breakout in the market average itself.

5. In most cases, daily A/D lines have more of a downward bias than lines constructed from weekly data.

6. A/D lines may be used with MA crossovers, trendline breaks, and price pattern analysis. For longer periods the 200-day MA appears to work reasonably well.

7. When the A/D line is in a positive trend, for example, above its 200-day MA, it indicates that the environment for equities in general is a positive one *regardless of what the major averages such as the DJIA or S&P Composite*

may be doing. A positive A/D line is therefore a better bellweather for the market as a whole than a narrowly based blue-chip index. The opposite is true when the A/D line is in a declining trend.

Major Technical Principle   The longer and greater the negative divergence between the A/D line and the market average it is monitoring, the deeper and more substantial the implied decline is likely to be.

For this reason, divergences between the A/D line and the major market averages at primary peaks are more significant than those that occur at intermediate peaks. For example, Chart 24-1 shows that the weekly A/D line peaked in March 1971, almost 2 years ahead of the DJIA, a very long period by historical standards. The ensuing bear market was the most severe since the Depression. On the other hand, *the absence of a divergence does not necessarily mean that a steep bear market cannot take place,* as the experience of the December 1968 peak indicates. This is also shown in Chart 24-1.

Chart 24-1   The DJIA and the weekly NYSE A/D Line, 1966–1977. (*From www.pring.com.*)

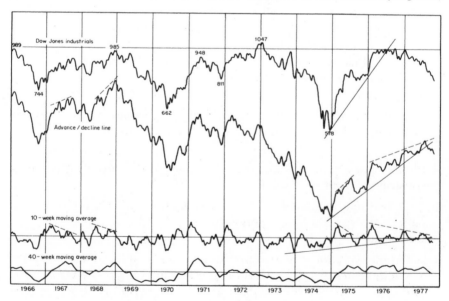

Positive divergences develop at market bottoms, where the A/D line refuses to confirm a new low in the Dow. The most significant one occurred in the 1939–1942 period. The DJIA (shown in Chart 24-2) made a series of lower peaks and troughs between 1939 and 1941, while the A/D line refused to confirm. Finally, in the middle of 1941, the A/D line made a post-1932 recovery high unaccompanied by the DJIA. The immediate result of this discrepancy was a sharp sell-off into the spring of 1942 by both indicators, but even then the A/D line held well above its 1938 bottom, unlike the DJIA. The final low in April 1942 was followed by one of the best (in terms of breadth) bull markets on record. This positive action by the broad market is unusual. Typically, at market bottoms the A/D line either coincides with or lags behind the low in the DJIA and has no forecasting significance until a reversal in its downtrend is signaled by a breakout from a price pattern, a trendline, or an MA crossover.

A/D Lines Using Daily Data

Because daily A/D lines have a tendency toward a downward bias, some care should be used in comparing recent highs with those achieved 2 to 3 years ago. Daily A/D lines come into their own when they fail to confirm new highs in the market average that have occurred within an 18-month period. An example is shown in Chart 24-3(*a*), where the A/D line peaks in April 1987, but the S&P Composite does not top out until late August. The S&P did not fall right away, but eventually followed the leadership of the A/D line. Quite often, a number of divergences will be set up. Initially, these might be well publicized, but since the widely expected decline fails to materialize, many technicians give up, stating that the divergence won't work this time. Invariably, it does work, though much later than most would anticipate. This was very much the case at the market peak in January 1973, which was preceded by a 2-year divergence.

Because bottoms in the daily line usually coincide with or lag behind bottoms in the average, they are not very useful at this point for the purpose of identifying a trend reversal.

A more practical approach is to construct a trendline for both the A/D line and the market average. Violation of both lines usually signals that an important rally is underway. Some examples are shown in Chart 24-3(*b*). Two resistance lines are violated at the end of 1992. Later, the two dashed up trendlines are violated for a joint sell signal. Note that in this case, the lines are penetrated at approximately the same time that both series cross below their respective 200-day MAs. This action adds to our weight of the evidence approach and increases the odds of a valid breakout. Finally, both series violate down trendlines at the beginning of 1995.

Chart 24-2 The DJIA and the long-term A/D ;ine, 1931–1983. (*From www.pring.com.*)

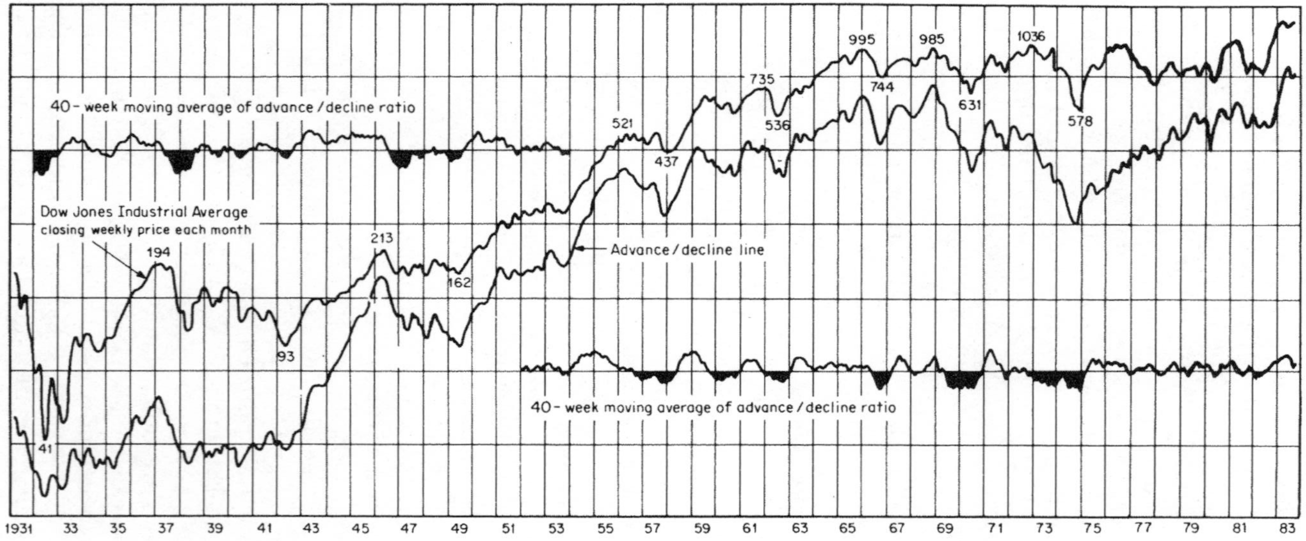

Chart 24-3(a) The S&P Composite versus the daily NYSE A/D line, 1986–1988. (*From www.pring.com.*)

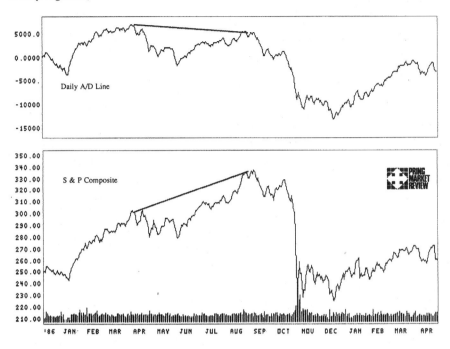

Chart 24-3(b) The S&P Composite versus the daily NYSE A/D line, 1991–1995. (*From www.pring.com.*)

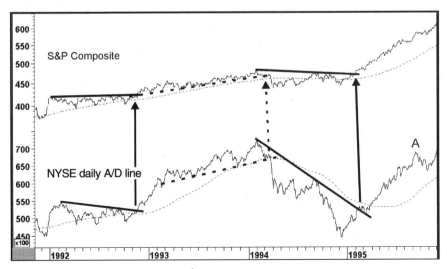

When considering potential divergences or nonconfirmations, it is always important to give these relationships some room. For example, at point *A* it may have appeared that the A/D line was going to experience a major negative divergence, since it had yet to beat its early 1994 high. It would have been easy to jump to a bearish conclusion. However, it would not have been supported by the facts since the A/D line was well above its 200-day MA at this point. Moreover, there was no sign of a trend break in the S&P Composite that would confirm the negative divergence, had it even existed. As it turned out, both series went on to make significant new highs, thereby pointing out the importance of giving the prevailing trend and this relationship the benefit of the doubt.

Breadth Oscillators (Internal Strength)

For historical comparative purposes, the rate-of-change (ROC) method of determining momentum is useful in measuring price indexes because it reflects moves of similar proportion in an identical way. This method, however, is not suitable for gauging the vitality of indicators constructed from cumulative data monitoring internal market structure, such as those that measure volume or breadth. This is because the calculation of such indicators is often started from a purely arbitrary number. Consequently, increases or decreases in such series are not proportionate in nature. Under certain circumstances, this might require an ROC to be calculated between a negative and a positive number, which would obviously give a completely false impression of the prevailing trend of momentum. The following sections provide a brief summary of some oscillators constructed from breadth data using a more suitable method of calculation.

10-Week A/D Oscillator

Chart 24-4 shows the A/D line and its 10-week oscillator. The oscillator is constructed by taking a 10-week MA of the square root of *A/U–D/U* (the formula discussed previously). A comparison of the A/D line and the oscillator illustrates the principle of divergence, as evidenced by declining peaks of momentum and rising peaks in the A/D line itself. These discrepancies are shown by the dashed lines just above the two indexes. It is not possible to know at the time how high the A/D line will extend, only that the technical position (indicated by the declining peaks in the 10-week momentum) is deteriorating. The best method of determining when the A/D line has made its final advance is to wait for a downside trendline penetration or an

MA crossover to confirm the action of the momentum indicator. Normally, the A/D line will sell off quite sharply following a combination of such trend breaks, but sometimes an extended sideways fluctuation results as the line struggles to regain some momentum. The same principle can also be applied during bear markets, when signals are triggered as a series of higher troughs in the oscillator and lower lows in the A/D line are confirmed by a break in the negative trend of the A/D line itself.

10- and 30-Day A/D Oscillators

These indicators are calculated by taking a 10- or 30-day MA of the A/D or the A/D ratio. An alternative calculation can be made by dividing the total of advancing issues by the total of declining issues over a specific time span. Their interpretation is exactly the same as with other momentum indicators, bearing in mind their relatively short time span. An example of a 10-day breadth momentum series is shown in Chart 24-5.

Note that in this instance the oscillator is being compared to the A/D line itself rather than the S&P or DJIA. Both series experience a set of positive divergences between 1999 and March 2000. Then we see some negative divergences as the A/D line peaks out later that year. Note how the 10-day series is barely able to rally above the equilibrium point, indicating extreme weakness at the time of the actual rally high in September (at A). Finally,

Chart 24-4   The NYSE A/D line and a 10-week breadth oscillator. (*From www.pring.com.*)

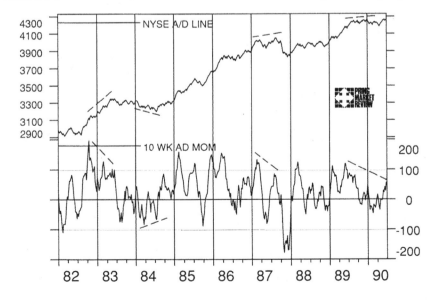

Chart 24-5 The NYSE A/D line and two breadth oscillators, 1999–2001. (*From www.pring.com.*)

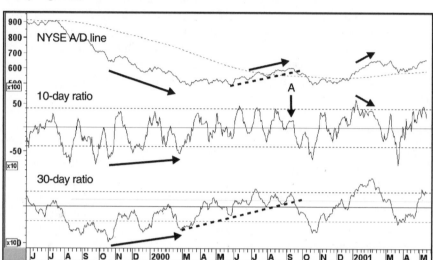

both the 30-day oscillator and the line itself violate up trendlines for a classic weight of the evidence sell signal. One final negative divergence develops in January 2001.

The McClellan Oscillator

The McClellan oscillator is a short-term breadth momentum indicator that measures the difference between a 19-day and a 39-day exponential moving average (EMA) of advancing minus declining issues. In this respect, it is based on the same principle as the moving average convergence divergence (MACD) indicator discussed in Chapter 11. The generally accepted rules are that buy signals are triggered when it falls to the oversold area of −70 to −100, and sell signals when it rises to the +70 to +100 area. My own experience suggests that its interpretation should be based on the same principles as those described in Chapter 10, using divergences, trendline analysis, and so forth. An example is shown in Chart 24-6 for the NASDAQ. The arrows show that good buy signals often arise when the oscillator peaks out from above the 175 level.[1] This is the McClellan version of the mega overbought described in Chapter 10. It is certainly not infallible, as the 2000–

---

[1] Note that the scale on the chart plots the oscillator as 1/10 of its real value; hence, 170 appears as 17 and so on.

Chart 24-6 The NASDAQ Composite, 1996–2001, and the McClellan oscillator. (*From www.pring.com.*)

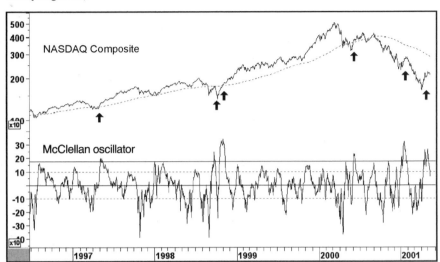

2001 bear market testifies. This again is a stark reminder that we should never rely soley on one indicator before coming to a conclusion.

Finally, the oscillator has been described here using two specific time frames for the EMAs used in the calculation, since these are the generally accepted default values. However, there is nothing to stop the innovative technician from experimenting with different combinations.

The McClellan Summation Index

The McClellan Summation Index is a derivation of the McClellan oscillator. It is calculated as a cumulative total of the daily readings of the oscillator itself. The result is plotted as a slow-moving curve that changes direction whenever the raw oscillator (described previously) crosses above or below its zero line. The slope of the summation curve is determined by the difference between the actual reading and the zero line. In other words, an overbought reading will cause the summation index to rise sharply, and vice versa. Many technicians use these changes in direction as buy and sell signals, but this can result in a lot of whipsaws. My own preference is to use an MA crossover. This is often less timely, but it filters out a significant number of false signals. A suggested time frame for this exercise is a 35-day simple MA. An example is featured in Chart 24-7. Even here, we see numerous whipsaw signals, indicating that this approach is far from perfect.

Chart 24-7   The S&P Composite and the McClellan Summation Index. (*From www.pring.com.*)

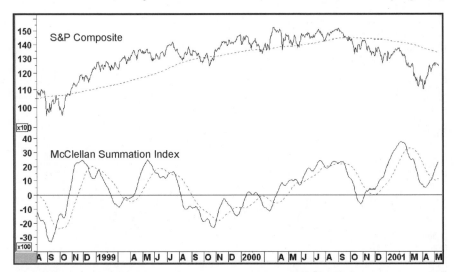

> **Major Technical Principle**   A rising market over a period of time
> should be accompanied by a healthy, but not necessarily rising, num-
> ber of net new highs.

High-Low Figures

The popular press and many online data providers publish daily and weekly
figures for stocks reaching new highs and lows. These statistics relate to the
number of issues making new highs or lows over a 52-week period. There
are various methods of measuring the high-low figures, but since the raw
data are very jagged, displaying this data in an MA format is usually better.
Some technicians prefer to plot an MA of the two series individually; others prefer an MA of the net difference between highs and lows.

   When the major averages trace out a series of higher peaks following a
long advance, but the net number of new highs forms a series of declining
peaks, it represents a warning of potential trouble. This is because successive peaks in the market average are accompanied by fewer stocks making
breakouts (new highs) from price patterns. The net number of new highs
also takes into consideration stocks registering new lows. In a bear market,
a new low in the S&P Composite, or other market average, that is not accompanied by a declining number of net new highs is a positive sign.

In this case, a declining number of stocks reaching new lows implies fewer downside breakouts, that is, a shrinkage in the number of stocks resisting the downtrend in the major averages. In Chart 24-8, for instance, the S&P falls to approximately the same level in December 1994 as it did earlier in the year, yet the number of new lows was far less. This indicated an improving technical position that was eventually confirmed when the index rallied above the solid trendline.

The bottom panel in Charts 24-9 and 24-10 shows a 10-day MA of the daily high/low differential. Note the negative divergence between this series and the average between 1989 and 1990 in Chart 24-9. Other evidence of a trend reversal came from the fact that it was possible to construct a couple of (dashed) trendlines for the ratio and the S&P that were violated in early 1991. The implied trend of expanding net new highs was signaling that once the index itself responded with a breakout, prices were likely to move higher.

The cumulative net new high series in the second panel is constructed by cumulating the daily difference between the new highs and lows, in a similar fashion to the daily A/D line. For example, if there are 100 new highs and 20 new lows, the difference, 80, would be added into the total, and vice versa. I have found that using 100-day MA crossovers offers reasonably good signals of when the overall environment is positive or negative for the general market. Signals of this nature generated between 1988 and 1993 are indicted by the vertical arrows in Chart 24-9. An alternative method of calculating high-low data is shown at the bottom of Chart 24-11, where a 6-week

Chart 24-8 The S&P Composite, 1993–1996, and 52-week new NYSE lows. (*From www.pring.com.*)

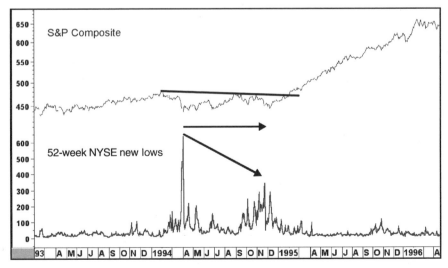

Chart 24-9 The S&P Composite, 1988–1993, and two net new high indicators. (*From www.pring.com.*)

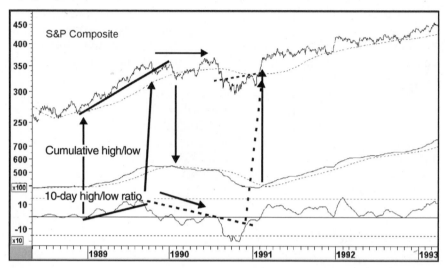

Chart 24-10 The S&P Composite, 1995–2001, and two net new high indicators. (*From www.pring.com.*)

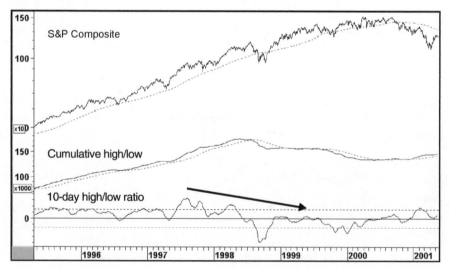

Chart 24-11   The S&P Composite, 1986–2001, and a 6-week MA of net new NYSE Highs. (*From www.pring.com.*)

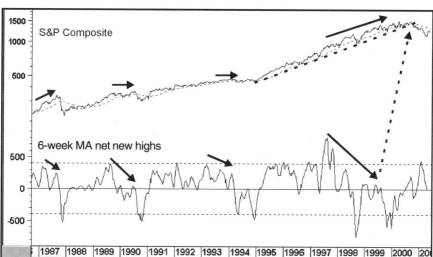

MA of net weekly new highs has been plotted against the S&P Composite. This is a particularly good indicator for identifying major turning points. For example, the 1987, 1990, 1994, and 1999 tops were all indicated by a negative divergence. Not shown are the 1978 and 1982 bottoms, both of which experienced positive divergences with this indicator.

In this discussion we have limited ourselves to 52-week periods for the new high/low calculations. However, there is no reason why such calculations cannot be made for any time period. In my experimentation, I have found that 30 days, 13 weeks, and 26 weeks have all worked reasonably well. The interpretation would be the same except that, as with all technical indicators, the shorter the time span, the greater the volatility and the less significant the signal.

Diffusion Indicators

The Concept

In technical analysis, a diffusion indicator is a form of oscillator constructed from a basket of securities that are often the components of an index. It typically measures the percentage of the universe that is in a positive trend. An example might be the percentage of the 30 stocks comprising the DJIA that are above their 30-day MAs. When all members are in a bullish mode, the picture is as positive as it can get. The implication is that the aggregate measure, the DJIA in our example, is vulnerable and therefore likely to peak out. The reverse set of conditions, in which none of the series is in a positive trend, produces the opposite effect; that is, the aggregate index may be reaching its low point and may therefore be a buy. This simple interpretation of diffusion indexes is a good starting point, but in practice it does not always work out, as we will see later. Since a diffusion measure is a form of momentum indicator, it is subject to the principles outlined in Chapter 10.

What Is a Positive Trend?

In technical analysis, a market or stock that forms a series of rising peaks and troughs, or is above a trendline, may be classified as being in a positive trend. However, the only way trends can be monitored through this interpretation is on the basis of individual judgment, which would make the construction of a diffusion index covering many series over many years a very laborious process. For this reason, and because of the need for greater objectivity, a statistical measure that can be easily calculated on a computer is normally used.

The most common measurements calculate the percentage of a series that is above a specific MA or that has a rising MA. Another popular alternative is to take the percentage of a universe of series that have a positive ROC—that is, a reading above 0 or 100. The choice of the time span for the MA or ROC is very important. The shorter the span, the more volatile the resulting oscillator.

In practice, it seems that the MAs and ROCs commonly used in other areas of technical analysis offer superior results. These are 10-, 20-, 30-, 45-, and 50-day for short-term trends; 13-, 26-, and 40 (39)-week for intermediate-term trends; and 9-, 12-, 18-, and 24-month for longer-term trends. The same exercise could also be accomplished with intraday data. One characteristic of using any raw series is that the resulting indicator is quite jagged and usually needs to be smoothed. For example, the group diffusion indicator series shown in Chart 24-12 is calculated from the percentage of S&P industry groups that are above a 12-month MA. These data in turn have been smoothed, and thus the solid line actually represents a 6-month MA of the percentage of groups above their respective 12-month MAs.

How Many Items Should Be Measured?

A natural tendency is to use as many items as possible to calculate a diffusion indicator, but this involves the maintenance of a very large database. My own experience shows that the same objective can be obtained from a relatively small universe of securities. The main thing to bear in mind is that

Chart 24-12 The S&P Composite, 1960–2001, and a group diffusion indicator. (*From www.pring.com.*)

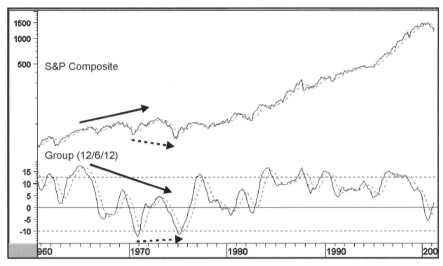

the basket of items used in the calculation reflects the diverse nature of the components of the aggregate index.

Interpretation

When a diffusion indicator moves to an extreme, it reflects an overbought or oversold condition. However, such readings do not in themselves constitute actual buy or sell signals. Obviously, the odds favor a profitable investment made at the time of a zero reading, and vice versa. However, it is usually much safer to wait for a reversal in the trend of the diffusion index, or better still for the confirmation of a trend break in the aggregate index being monitored.

Whenever the diffusion index in Chart 24-12 has risen to, or above, the 12.5 level and then reversed direction, it has usually been associated with a decline of at least intermediate-term proportions. The same is also true, in an opposite sense, for the trend reversals that have taken place when the index has fallen below zero.

In order to avoid premature or whipsaw signals, one solution is to combine a signal from the diffusion indicator with the aggregate index itself. In such instances, an extreme reading in the diffusion index is used as a pointer for a reversal in the intermediate or primary trend, which is confirmed when the index crosses a long-term MA or violates a significant trendline.

Divergences also play a part. Note how the 1973 peaks in the oscillator were well below the 1966 and 1968 tops, unlike the S&P, which was at a new high. Conversely, the 1974 low in the oscillator was higher than that set in 1970, even though the S&P was lower.

Seasonal Breadth Momentum[1]

The Seasons Defined

Every cycle effectively goes through four momentum stages before completion. This is shown conceptually in Fig. 24-2. The first occurs after downside momentum has reached its maximum. At this point the series turns up, but is still below its equilibrium level. The second is signaled when it crosses above its zero reference line. The third phase starts when it peaks out from above zero. Finally, phase four is triggered when the indicator crosses below the equilibrium point.

For simplicity's sake, the respective stages have been labeled as spring, summer, fall, and winter. From both an agricultural and an investment point of view, the best results occur when planting (investing) is done in the spring, and harvesting in late summer or fall.

In effect, spring represents accumulation, summer the markup phase, fall the distribution phase, and winter the markdown phase. In situations in which a market can be subdivided into components, it is possible to take this approach one step further by calculating a diffusion index based on the position of the seasonal momentum of its various components, for example, industry groups for a stock market average, commodity prices for a commodity index, and so on. This seasonal momentum approach has two merits. First, it helps to identify the prevailing stage in the cycle, that is, whether a high number of components are in an accumulation, markup, distribution, or markdown phase. Second, it also helps identify major buying and selling opportunities.

Choice of Time Span

The choice of time span is critical for all momentum indicators, including those used in the seasonal momentum studies. For example, a series based on a smoothed 13-week ROC will have far less significance in terms of long-term investment strategy than a series based on a 48-month time span. This

---

[1]This approach was first brought to my attention by Ian S. Notley, Notley Group, Yelton Fiscal Inc., Unit 211-Executive Pavilion, 90 Grove Street, Ridgefield, CT 06877.

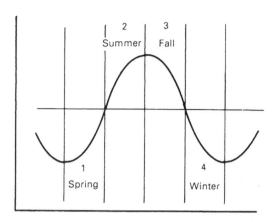

Figure 24-2 Seasonal momentum defined.

approach can be used for daily, weekly, and monthly data. I am sure you could expand this concept to include intraday data because the principle is the same. I have never done so, but encourage active traders to give it a try. Nevertheless, I have found that daily and weekly calculations, even when greatly smoothed, do not give as reliable a picture as the monthly series. Monthly seasonal momentum also works well for commodities and international markets. The indicators represented in the charts included in this chapter have been constructed by finding the number of a basket of ten S&P industry groups that are in their respective winter, spring, summer, or fall positions, and then smoothing that data with a 6-month MA.

Seasonal (Diffusion) Momentum for the Stock Market[2]

Chart 24-13 shows all four seasonal momentum curves, based on a basket of S&P industry groups, between 1963 and 1990. Chart 24-14 shows the same data for the 1990–2001 period. A high reading in the spring series, for example, indicates that the momentum of a significant proportion of the groups is in phase 1, that is, below zero and rising. This means that the market is in a strong position to begin a major advance.

---

[2]When I first introduced this concept in the third edition of this book, the ability of most of us to do the calculations was limited to professionals who had access to powerful computers and a large database. However, it is now more widely accessible since it can be formulated and plotted in any version of MetaStock that contains the security function. For details, go to www.pring.com.

Chart 24-13 The S&P Composite, 1963–1990, and seasonal momentum. (*From www.pring.com.*)

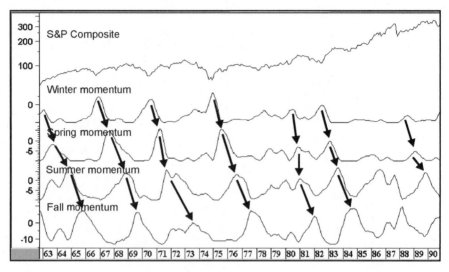

Chart 24-14 The S&P Composite, 1990–2001, and seasonal momentum. (*From www.pring.com.*)

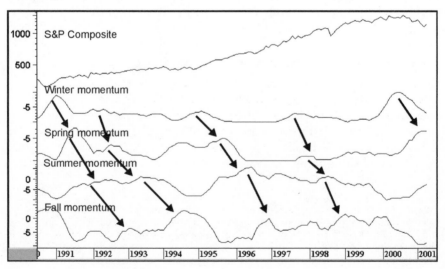

It is important to note that in most cycles there is a chronological sequence as the majority of groups move from spring to summer, fall, and finally winter, as shown by the arrows. Bear market lows typically occur around the time winter momentum peaks. As with all momentum series, confirmation should come from the price, which in this case would be the S&P Composite.

The peaking out of spring momentum is often associated with the first intermediate-term peak in the bull market, but it is *not* a bearish sign. It simply means that the majority of groups are moving from the spring (accumulation) to the summer (markup) phase. It is bearish only if a significant number of groups are moving from spring back to winter.

Potential market weakness is signaled when the summer momentum, the third series, starts to turn down. This is not an actual sell signal because the market often moves sideways or even higher after summer momentum peaks. It does, however, indicate that the environment has become much more selective as the smoothed momentum for more groups moves to the fall (distribution) phase.

The S&P Composite sometimes declines during the transition from the summer to the fall phase, but it is more normal for downside momentum to pick up as the cycle moves from fall to winter, that is, the point at which the momentum indicators for most groups cross below their zero reference lines.

Bear Market Bottoms

Major buying points occur when winter momentum reaches its peak and starts to turn down. Generally speaking, the higher the peak, the greater the potential for upside activity. This is because a movement out of winter momentum must flow into spring. A high and falling level in winter momentum, therefore, indicates that a significant number of groups have the potential to move into the spring position, that is, to move to the point from which they have the greatest potential to rise. This is shown more clearly in Chart 24-15.

Normally, the winter momentum series moves up steadily toward a peak and then reverses direction. Reversals that come from high readings are usually a reliable indication that the downtrend in the overall market has reversed. Occasionally, winter momentum temporarily peaks out, but the market itself does not bottom, as in late 1973. This is a very unusual state of affairs, but it does point out that no system is perfect. Intermixing the seasonal momentum analysis with other indicators is very important. In 1973, for example, bond yields were in a persistent rising trend. This is one of the reasons it is often important to make sure that other indicators are acting in sympathy before concluding that a trend has reversed.

New bull markets are sometimes signaled by a reversal in the downtrend in spring momentum, but since the lead times can also be extremely long,

Chart 24-15 The S&P Composite, 1956–2001, and winter momentum. (*From www.pring.com.*)

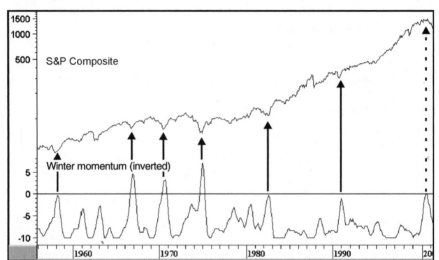

upward movement in spring momentum by itself is no guarantee that the market will rally.

A confirming signal of a major bottom is often given by a reversal in a trend of summer momentum occurring simultaneously with, or very close to, a peak in winter velocity. In other words, winter turns down and summer reverses to the upside. Generally speaking, the lower the level of summer velocity when a reversal occurs, the greater the potential for a market rise.

Signs of a Market Peak

Market tops are far more elusive than bottoms, but advance warning is usu-ally given by a reversal in the uptrend of spring momentum. Lead times can vary, but it is normally safe to assume that as long as summer and spring momentum are both rising, higher prices are in store. It is also generally true that the market will rise for at least a month or so following a peak in spring momentum, usually much longer.

Market tops normally occur at some point between the peak in summer and fall momentum. For example, the stock market peaked in 1983 at the time when summer momentum peaked. Even a topping out in the fall momentum is not always sufficient to trigger a full-fledged bear market. Declining fall momentum is usually associated with a distribution, or topping-out phase, as in 1973 and 1977. Occasionally, group momentum swings back to summer, thus averting a major market decline. It is only when a large and expanding number of groups fall below their zero reference lines, that is, move into winter, that a bear market picks up downside momentum.

Indian Summer

During periods such as 1984–1987, which are associated with a strong, persistent linear uptrend, the normal spring–summer–fall–winter sequence does not occur. Instead, a chronology of a different nature, alternating between summer and fall, enables the market to regain its internal strength without suffering a major decline. In a sense, the market undergoes an Indian summer rally.

As a result, it is not possible to conclude that a peak in summer momentum will always lead to a market decline. It is more important to watch the beginning of the decline in fall momentum to see whether the flow of groups moves into winter or back into summer.

How to Identify Indian Summers

The best way to determine whether fall momentum will flow back to summer or on to winter is to watch both winter and summer momentum. As long as the winter quadrant continues to rise, this is a bearish sign, and it indicates that an expanding number of groups are declining in price. This will clearly have a negative impact on the S&P Composite.

It is important to note that during the Indian Summer phase between 1985 and early 1987, the winter momentum series never succeeded in decisively crossing above its MA.

Short-Term Seasonal Momentum

Chart 24-16 shows the DJIA together with a spring momentum. This series is constructed from a basket of 20 stocks in the DJIA. The measurement of trend in this case is the daily KST. The oscillator has been inverted so that its movements correspond to the ups and downs in the DJIA. Buy signals are indicated when it first reaches an oversold condition. Signals between 1996 and 2001 are indicated by the dashed vertical lines. Since the data are short term in nature, so are the ensuing rallies. However, there is certainly a nice consistency to these trend-reversal signals.

Conclusion

The concept of progressive seasonal momentum is important to understand, even for those who cannot follow this approach on a regular basis. This is

Chart 24-16 DJIA and DJ spring momentum (inverted).

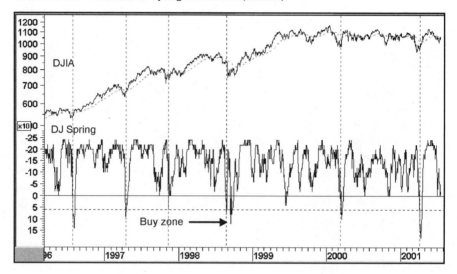

because it explains how a market goes through its various stages, and the kind of conditions required for major bull and bear moves.

Summary

- Market breadth measures the degree to which a market index is supported by a wide range of its components.
- It is useful from two aspects. First, it indicates whether the environment for most items in a universe (normally equities) is positive or negative. Second, market breadth indicators signal major turning points through positive and negative divergences.
- Indicators constructed from breadth data include A/D lines, breadth oscillators, diffusion indicators, and net new highs.
- Breadth divergences are a fine concept, but should be confirmed by a trend reversal in the market averages themselves.
- New highs and lows can be used to indicate the underlying strength or weakness of the prevailing trend. Indicators constructed from this data can be used to flag divergences or measure trends by cumulating the plurality of the highs and lows.
- Seasonal momentum signals major buying and selling opportunities and can often be used to identify the maturity of the prevailing primary trend.

PART III

Other Aspects of Market Behavior

25

Why Interest Rates Affect the Stock Market

In this chapter, we will examine why changes in the level of interest rates are an important influence on equity prices and apply technical analysis to credit market yields and prices.

Changes in interest rates affect the stock market for four basic reasons:

- Fluctuations in the price charged for credit have a major influence on the level of economic activity and therefore an indirect influence on corporate profits.
- Because interest charges affect the bottom line, changes in the level of rates have a direct influence on corporate profits and therefore the price investors are willing to pay for equities.
- Movements in interest rates alter the relationships between competing financial assets, of which the bond/equity market relationship is the most important.
- A substantial number of stocks are purchased on borrowed money (known as *margin debt*). Changes in the cost of carrying that debt (that is, the interest rate) influence the desire or ability of investors and speculators to maintain these margined positions. Because *changes in interest rates usually lead stock prices,* it is important to be able to identify primary trend reversals in the debt market.

The Indirect Effect of Interest-Rate Changes on Corporate Profits

Perhaps the most important effect of interest-rate changes on equity prices comes from the fact that tight monetary policy associated with rising rates adversely affects business conditions, whereas falling rates stimulate the economy.

Given time, most businesses can adjust to higher rates, but when they change quickly and unexpectedly most have to curtail expansion plans, cut inventories, and so on. This has a debilitating effect on the economy and therefore corporate profits. Higher rates and smaller profits mean lower price/earnings multiples and therefore lower stock prices.

When the authorities become concerned about the economy, they lower short-term rates and a reverse effect takes hold.

The Direct Effect of Interest-Rate Changes on Corporate Profits

Interest rates affect profits in two ways. First, almost all companies borrow money to finance capital equipment and inventory, so the cost of money, that is, the interest rate they pay, is of great importance. Second, a substantial number of sales are in turn financed by borrowing. The level of interest rates therefore has a great deal of influence on the ability and willingness of customers to make additional purchases. One of the most outstanding examples is the automobile industry, in which both producers and consumers are very heavily financed. The capital-intensive utility and transportation industries are also large borrowers, as are all the highly leveraged construction and housing industries.

Interest Rates and Competing Financial Assets

Interest-rate changes also have an impact upon the relative appeal of various investment sectors. The most significant relationship is that of stocks to bonds. For example, at any point there is a balance between bonds and stocks, in the judgment of investors. However, if interest rates rise faster than dividends can increase, bonds will become more attractive and, at the margin, money will flow out of stocks into bonds. Stocks will then fall in value

> **Major Technical Principle**   It is not the level of rates that is impor-
> tant, but their rate of change because this has the bigger influence on
> profits and equity prices.

until the relationship is perceived by investors to be more reflective of the
higher level of interest rates.

The effect of interest-rate changes on any particular stock group will
depend upon the yield obtained combined with the prospects for profit
growth. Most sensitive will be preferred shares, which are primarily held for
their dividends and which do not generally permit benefit from profit
growth. Utility stocks are also highly sensitive to interest-rate movements
since they are held as much for their current dividend yields as for potential growth. Changes in the level of interest rates therefore have a very direct
effect on utility stocks. On the other hand, companies in a dynamic stage
of growth are usually financed by corporate earnings and for this reason pay
smaller dividends. These stocks are less affected by fluctuations in the cost
of money, since they are purchased in anticipation of fast profit growth and
future yield rather than an immediate dividend return.

Interest Rates and Margin Debt

Margin debt is money loaned by brokers for which securities are pledged
as collateral. Normally, this money is used for the acquisition of equities, but
sometimes margin debt is used for purchases of consumer items, such as
automobiles. The effect of rising interest rates on both forms of margin debt
is similar, in that rising rates increase the carrying cost. There is, therefore,
a reluctance on the part of investors to take on additional debt as its cost
rises. When the service charges become excessive, stocks are liquidated and
the debt is paid off. Rising interest rates have the effect of increasing the
supply of stock put up for sale with consequent downward pressure on
prices.

Bond Yields Versus Bond Prices

When a bond is brought to market by a borrower, it is issued at a fixed interest rate (coupon), which is paid over a predetermined period. At the end

of this maturity period, the issuer agrees to repay the face amount. Since bonds are normally issued in denominations of $1000 (known as *par*), this figure usually represents the amount to be repaid at the end of the loan period. Because bond prices are quoted in percentage terms, par ($1000) is expressed as 100. Normally, bonds are issued and redeemed at par, but they are occasionally issued at a discount (at less than 100) or at a premium (at a price greater than 100).

While it is usual for a bond to be issued and redeemed at 100, the price can fluctuate quite widely over its life because interest-rate levels are continually changing. Assume that a 20-year bond is issued with an 8 percent interest rate (coupon) at par (that is, 100); if interest rates rise to 9 percent, the bond paying 8 percent will be difficult to sell because investors have the opportunity to earn a return of 9 percent. The only way in which the 8 percent bondholder can find a buyer is to reduce the price to a level that would compensate a prospective purchaser for the 1 percent differential in interest rates. The new owner would then earn 8 percent in interest together with some capital appreciation. When spread over the remaining life of the bond, this capital appreciation would be equivalent to the 1 percent loss in interest. This combination of coupon rate and averaged capital appreciation is known as the *yield*. If interest rates decline, the process is reversed, and the 8 percent bond becomes more attractive in relation to prevailing rates, so its price rises. The longer the maturity of the bond, the greater will be its price fluctuation for any given change in the general level of interest rates.

The Structure of the Credit Markets

The credit markets can be roughly divided into two main areas, known as the *short end* and the *long end*. The short end, more commonly known as the *money market*, relates to interest rates charged for loans up to 1 year in maturity. Normally, movements at the short end lead those at the longer end, since short rates are more sensitive to trends in business conditions and changes in Federal Reserve policy. Money-market instruments are issued by the federal, state, and local governments as well as corporations.

The long end of the market consists of bonds issued for a period of at least 10 years. Credit instruments are also issued for periods of between 1 and 10 years, and are known as *intermediate-term* bonds.

The bond market (that is, the long end) has three main sectors, which are classified as to issuer. These are the U.S. government, tax-exempt issuers (state and local governments), and corporate issuers.

The financial status of the tax-exempt and corporate sectors varies from issuer to issuer, and the practice of rating each one for quality of credit has therefore become widespread. The best possible credit rating is known as AAA; next in order are AA, A, BAA, BA, BB, and so on. The higher the quality, the lower the risk undertaken by investors, and, therefore, the lower the interest rate required to compensate them. Since the credit of the federal government is higher than that of any other issuer, it can sell bonds at a relatively low interest rate. The tax-exempt sector (bonds issued by state and local governments) is able to issue bonds with the lowest rates of all, in view of the favored tax treatment assigned to the holders of such issues.

Most of the time, price trends of the various sectors are similar, but at major cyclical turns, some will lag behind others because of differing demand and supply conditions in each sector.

Debt Versus Equity Prices

Bond and money market prices typically top out ahead of the equity market at cyclical peaks. The lead characteristics and degree of deterioration required to adversely affect equities differ from cycle to cycle. There are no hard-and-fast rules that relate the size of an equity decline to the time period separating the peaks of bond and equity prices. For example, short- and long-term prices peaked 18 and 17 months, respectively, ahead of the 1959 bull market high in the Dow. This compared with 11 months and 1 month for the 1973 bull market peak. While the deterioration in the bond and money markets was sharper and longer in the 1959 period, the Dow, on a monthly average basis, declined only 13 percent, as compared to 42 percent in the 1973–1974 bear market.

A further characteristic of cyclical peaks is that high-quality bonds (such as Treasury or AAA corporate bonds) decline in price ahead of poorer-quality issues (such as BAA-rated bonds). This has been true of nearly every cyclical turning point since 1919. This lead characteristic of high-quality bonds results from two factors. First, in the latter stages of an economic expansion, private-sector demand for financing accelerates. Commercial banks, the largest institutional holders of government securities, are the

Major Technical Principle Virtually every primary stock market peak in the last 100 years was preceded by, or has coincided with, a peak in both the long and the short ends of the credit markets.

lenders of last resort to private borrowers. As the demand for financing accelerates against a less accommodating central bank posture, banks step up their sales of these and other high-grade investments and reinvest the money in more profitable bank loans. This sets off a ripple effect, down the yield curve itself and also to lower-quality issues. At the same time these pressures are pushing yields on high-quality bonds upward and are also reflecting buoyant business conditions, which encourage investors to become less cautious. Consequently, investors are willing to overlook the relatively conservative yields on high-quality bonds in favor of the more rewarding lower-rated debt instruments; thus, for a temporary period, these bonds are rising while high-quality bonds are falling.

At bear market bottoms, these relationships are similar in that *good-quality* bonds lead both debt instruments and *poorer-quality* equities. The lead characteristics of the debt markets are not quite so pronounced as at primary peaks and, occasionally, bond and stock prices trough out simultaneously. The trend of interest rates is, therefore, a useful benchmark for identifying stock market bottoms.

Charts 25-1(*a*)–(*c*) show that primary stock market peaks and troughs between 1919 and 2001 were almost always preceded by a reversal in the trend of short-term interest rates. This is indicated by the solid lines for the peaks and dashed ones for the troughs, almost all of which slope to the right.

Chart 25-1(*a*)   The S&P Composite, 1914–1950, and short-term interest rates. (*From www.pring.com.*)

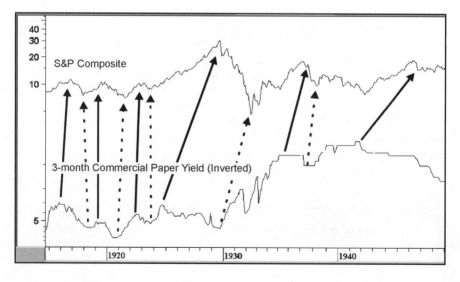

Chart 25-1(*b*) The S&P Composite, 1956–1976, and short-term interest rates. (*From www.pring.com.*)

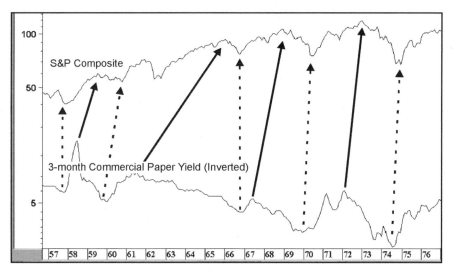

Chart 25-1(*c*) The S&P Composite, 1976–2001, and short-term interest rates. (*From www.pring.com.*)

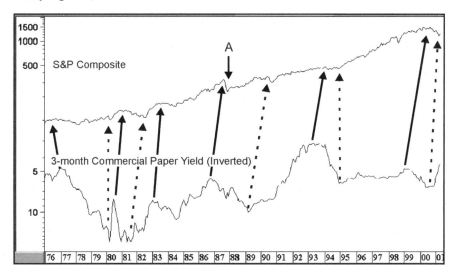

Note that the interest-rate series in the lower panels have been plotted inversely so that their movements are consistent with equity prices.

A declining phase in interest rates is not in itself a sufficient condition to justify the purchase of equities. For example, in the 1919–1921 bear market, money market prices reached their lowest point in June 1920, 14 months ahead of, or 27 percent above, the final stock market bottom in August 1921. An even more dramatic example occurred during the 1929–1932 debacle, when money-market yields reached their highs in October 1929. Over the next 3 years, the discount rate was cut in half, but stock prices lost 85 percent of their October 1929 value. The reason for such excessively long lead times was that these periods were associated with a great deal of debt liquidation and many bankruptcies. Even the sharp reduction in interest rates was not sufficient to encourage consumers and businesses to spend, which is the normal cyclical experience. Although falling interest rates alone do not constitute a sufficient basis for an expectation that stock prices will reverse their cyclical decline, they are a necessary part of that basis. On the other hand, a continued trend of rising rates has proved to be bearish.

There was one notable exception to the interest-rate leading equity price rule and that developed in 1977 when the peak in equities preceded that of money-market prices. The 1987 low in equities at point A in Chart 25-1(c) was also out of sequence.

The principles of trend determination apply to the credit markets as well as to the stock market. In fact, trends in yields and prices are in many ways easier to identify, since the bulk of the transactions in credit instruments are made on the basis of money flows caused by a need to finance and an ability to purchase. Consequently, while emotions are still important from the point of view of determining the short-term trends of bond prices, money flow is generally responsible for a far smoother cyclical trend than is the case with equities. This statement was true for most of the twentieth century, but with the advent of futures, bond and money-market participants have become more sophisticated in the discounting mechanism. Even so, cash or spot yields at the short end are still very much influenced by economic forces.

Relating Changes in Interest Rates to Equity Market Turning Points

We have already established that interest rates lead stock prices at virtually every primary turning point. However, the leads, lags, and level of interest rates required to affect equity prices differ in each cycle. For example, 1962 experienced a sharp market setback with short-term interest rates at 3 percent. On the other hand, stock prices were very strong in the latter part of 1980, yet rates never fell below 9 percent.

Earlier it was stated that it is not the level of interest rates that affects equity prices, but their rate of change (ROC). One method for determining when a change in rates is sufficient to influence equities is to overlay a smoothed ROC of short-term interest rates with a similar measure for equity prices. This is shown in Chart 25-2. Buy and sell signals are triggered when the interest-rate momentum crosses above and below that of the Standard & Poor's (S&P) Composite. These signals are indicated by the arrows on the chart, dashed for buy and solid for sell.

We know that the stock market can rally even in the face of rising rates, but this relationship tells us when the rise in rates is greater than that of equities, and vice versa. At times, this approach gives some very timely signals, as happened at the 1973 market peak. At other times, it is not so helpful. For example, it failed to signal the 1978–1980 rally. Even so, it is interesting to note that the total return on equities and cash during that 2-year period was approximately the same. This approach is far from perfect, as is clearly demonstrated by the confusing signals in the 1988–1990 period; but generally speaking, it is better to be cautious when the interest-rate momentum is above that of equities and to take on more risk when the reverse set of conditions holds true.

Chart 25-2 The S&P Composite, 1970–2001, and stock and interest-rate momentum. (*From www.pring.com.*)

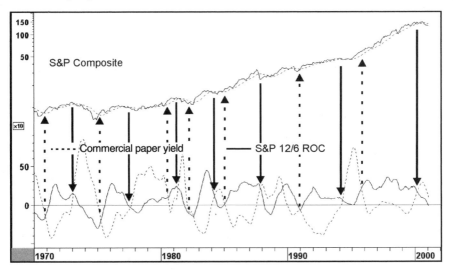

An alternative approach to the interest-rate/equity relationship recognizes that rallies in equity prices are normally much stronger when supported by falling rates, and vice versa. It follows that if a measure of the equity market, such as the S&P Composite, is divided by the yield on a money-market instrument, such as 3-month commercial paper, the series will either lead or fall less rapidly at bear market bottoms and peak out ahead or rise at a slower pace at market tops, if interest rates are experiencing their usual leading characteristics.

An indicator constructed in this way, called the Money Flow Index, is plotted underneath the S&P Composite in Chart 25-3. The arrows point out the lead characteristics.

Since the rate of change of money-flow movements is more important than the actual level, Chart 25-4 overlays the ROCs of the two series. They are both 12-month ROCs smoothed with a 6-month MA. Buy signals are generated when the money-flow momentum (the thicker line) crosses above that of the S&P, and vice versa. A couple of signals are flagged by the two dashed and solid arrows.

Chart 25-5 plots the S&P Composite together with an indicator constructed by subtracting the ROC of the S&P from the ROC of the Money Flow Index, as shown in the previous chart. The zero line represents the crossover points that are flagged by the arrows in Chart 25-4. This final format is a simple way of presenting this interest-rate/stock market relationship. Research back to the 1950s shows that every buy signal (zero crossover)

Chart 25-3 The S&P Composite, 1969–2001, and the Money Flow Index. (*From www.pring.com.*)

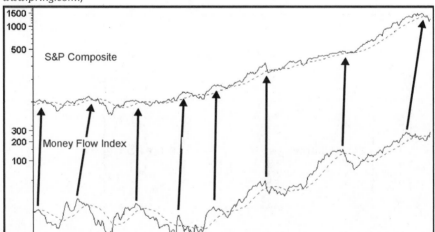

Chart 25-4 The S&P Composite, 1969–2001, and stock and money flow momentum. (*From www.pring.com.*)

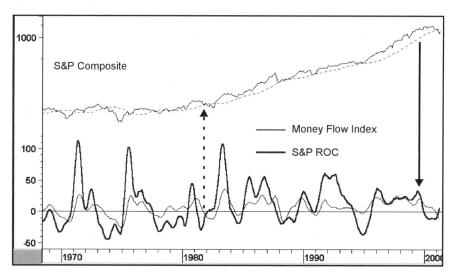

Chart 25-5 The S&P Composite, 1969–2001, and the money flow indicator. (*From www.pring.com.*)

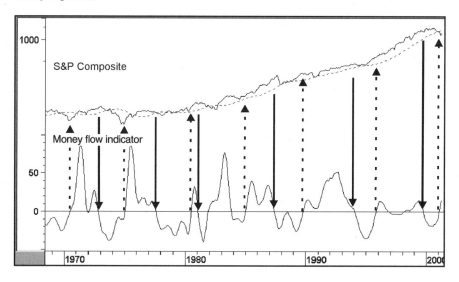

has been followed by a major stock rally. The only exception was 1989, but in this case the crossover took place when both momentum series (see Chart 25-4) were in an overbought condition. By the same token, when a crossover develops from below the zero reference line, it has normally represented an extremely powerful signal that a new bull market was underway. Sell signals have also been reasonably timely for the most part. Chart 25-5 reflects these buy and sell signals with the dashed and solid vertical arrows.

Applying Technical Analysis to Short-Term Rates

Short-term rates are much more sensitive to business conditions than long-term rates. This is because decisions to change the level of inventories, for which a substantial amount of short-term credit is required, are made much more quickly than decisions to purchase plants and equipment, which form the basis for long-term corporate credit demands. The Federal Reserve, in its management of monetary policy, is also better able to influence short-term rates than those at the longer end.

Short-term interest rates, when used with monthly data, generally lend themselves well to trend analysis. There are a number of series we could use, such as 13-week T-bills, certificates of deposit, 3-month eurodollars, and the federal funds. I usually use the 3-month commercial paper yield because the series has a greater history and is not that volatile. In any event, most of these series, with the occasional exception of T-bills, move closely together over the short run. T-bills sometimes temporarily diverge from other money-market rates because central banks often hold them as reserves and buy or sell them as part of currency intervention programs. Also, in times of crisis the so-called *flight to quality* results in a temporary safe-haven demand for short-term government paper.

Chart 25-6 shows the commercial paper yield together with the Growth Indicator. This series is constructed from four economic indicators: the Conference Board Leading Indicators and Help Wanted series, the CRB Spot Raw Industrial Material Index (www.crbtrader.com/crbindex/1450.txt), and the Commerce Department Capacity Utilization Index. All four are expressed as a 9-month ROC, and then combined and smoothed with a 6-month MA. This represents an example of how technical analysis can be applied to economic data. Positive zero crossovers indicate when the economy, as reflected by these indicators, is sufficiently strong to be consistent with rising short-term rates, and vice versa. The dashed vertical lines indicate sell signals for rates (buy signals for prices), and vice versa. The Growth Indicator is not perfect and has occasionally experienced some whipsaws, but does offer an independent variable (from the price itself)

Chart 25-6 The 3-month commercial paper yield, 1978–2001, and the Growth Indicator. (*From www.pring.com.*)

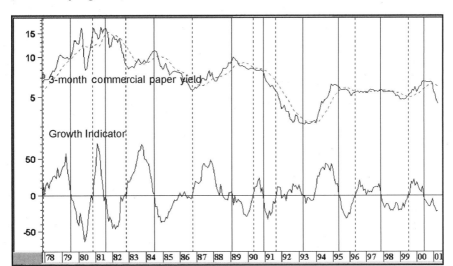

when considering potential trend reversals in rates. The yield itself has been plotted with a 12-month MA, crossovers of which have generally offered reliable signals of primary trend reversals.

Chart 25-7 shows the commercial paper yield with an 18-month EMA and a long-term KST. The KST MA crossovers are flagged with the arrows. By and large, a KST MA crossover, when confirmed with an 18-month EMA crossover, has been reasonably reliable. If the growth indicator is included in the approach, the results are even more impressive.

The Importance of Changes in the Discount Rate

Movements in the discount rate reflect changes in monetary policy, and are therefore of key importance to the trend of both short-term interest rates and equity prices.

Such action also has a strong psychological influence on both the debt and equity markets. This is because the Fed does not reverse policy on a day-to-day or even week-to-week basis, so a reversal in the trend of the discount rate implies that the trend in market interest rates is unlikely to be reversed for at least several months, and usually much longer. A corporation does

Chart 25-7   The 3-month commercial paper yield, 1980–2001, and a Long-Term KST. (*From www.pring.com.*)

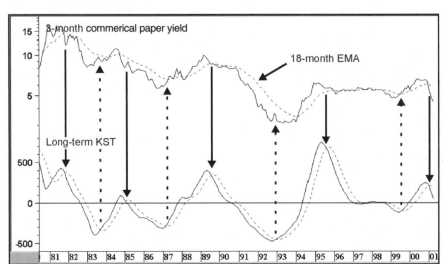

Major Technical Principle   Reversals in the direction of the discount rate offer reliable signals of primary trend reversals in short-term interest rates.

---

not like to cut dividends once they have been raised. In a similar vein, the central bank wishes to create a feeling of continuity and consistency. A change in the discount rate is therefore helpful in confirming trends in other rates, which, when taken by themselves, can sometimes give misleading signals because of temporary technical or psychological factors.

Effect on Short-Term Rates

Market rates usually lead the discount rate at cyclical turning points. Even so, a discount rate cut after a series of hikes acts as confirmation that a new trend of lower rates is underway. The same is true at cyclical or primary-trend bottoms. It is often a good idea to monitor the relationship between the discount rate and its 12-month MA (see Chart 25-8) because crossovers almost always signal a reversal in the prevailing trend at a relatively early stage.

Chart 25-8 The 3-month commercial paper yield, 1969–2001, and the discount rate. (*From www.pring.com.*)

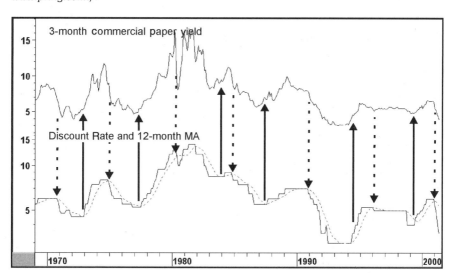

Effect on the Stock Market

Since the incorporation of the Federal Reserve System, every major bull market peak in equities has been preceded by a rise in the discount rate, with the exception of the Depression in 1937, the war year of 1939, and more recently 1976. The leads have varied. In 1973, the discount rate was raised on January 12, 3 days before the bull market high, whereas the 1956 peak was preceded by no fewer than five consecutive hikes.

There is a well-known rule on Wall Street: *Three steps and stumble!* It was developed by the late Edson Gould and implies that after three consecutive rate hikes the equity market is likely to stumble, that is, enter a bear market. The three-steps rule is therefore recognition that a significant rise in interest rates and tightening in monetary policy have already taken place. Table 25-1 shows the dates when the discount rate was raised for the third time, together with the duration and magnitude of the subsequent decline in equity prices following the third hike.

Cuts in the rate are equally as important. Generally speaking, as long as the declining trend of discount rate cuts continues, it is usually safe to assume that the primary bull market in stocks is intact. Even after the last cut, the market usually possesses enough momentum to extend its advance for a while. Quite often the last intermediate reaction in the bull market will get under way at the time of or just before the first hike.

Table 25-1 Discount Rate Highs and Subsequent Stock Market Lows, 1919–2001

Date of discount rate 3rd hike		Months between 3rd hike and market low	Magnitude of loss, %
November	1919	21	29.86
May	1928	49	77.45
August	1949	0	0
September	1955	27	9.04
March	1959	19	4.31
December	1965	10	15.92
April	1968	27	20.99
May	1973	16	36.47
January	1978	2	1.58
December	1980	19	18.06
February	1989	20	Gain of 4.7
November	1994	1	0
November	1999	16*	16*

*Until March 2001.

Most of the time the cyclical course of discount rate cuts resembles a series of declining steps, but occasionally it is interrupted by a temporary hike before the downtrend continues. The *discount rate low* is defined as a low that occurs after a series of declining steps has taken place, and that either remains unchanged at this low level for at least 15 months or is followed by two or more hikes in 2 different months. In other words, if the series of cuts is interrupted by one hike, the trend is still classified as downward unless the rise occurs after a period of 15 months has elapsed. Only when two hikes in the rate have taken place in a period of *less* than 15 months is a low considered to have been established. Since the data are available for almost 100 years, they cover both inflationary and deflationary periods and are therefore reflective of a number of different economic environments.

Table 25-2 shows that there have been 15 discount rate lows since 1924. On each occasion, except 1987, the market moved significantly higher from the time the rate was cut. The average increase from the date of the cut was 57%, while the average period between the final cut and the ultimate high was 31 months.

A discount rate cut is only one indicator, and while it is invariably bullish, the overall technical position is also important. For example, the low in the discount rate usually occurs just after the market has started a bull phase. If the market is long-term overbought, the odds that the ensuing rally will obtain the magnitude and the duration of the average are slim. It should also be noted that while each discount rate low has ultimately been followed

Table 25-2 Discount Rate Lows and Subsequent Stock Market Peaks, 1924–2000

Discount rate low	S&P Composite high	S&P Composite at time of cut	S&P Composite price peak	Time between last cut and market high (months)	Magnitude of % gain	Average % gain per month
August 1924	September 1929	10.4	31.3	61	200.1	3.3
June 1932	July 1933	4.7	10.9	13	132.0	3.3
January 1934	February 1937	10.3	18.1	125	75.7	10.1
August 1937	June 1946	16.7	18.6	94	11.3	0.1
April 1954	April 1959	27.6	48.1	25	74.3	3.0
April 1958	December 1959	42.3	59.1	20	39.7	2.0
August 1960	February 1966	56.5	92.7	65	64.1	1.0
April 1967*	December 1968	91.0	106.5	20	17.0	0.9
December 1971	January 1973	99.2	118.4	13	19.4	1.5
November 1976	February 1980	101.2	115.3	27	13.9	0.5
July 1980	November 1980	119.8	135.7	4	13.3	3.3
February 1982	July 1983	146.8	167.0	5	13.8	2.8
August 1986	August 1987	252	329	12	3.5	2.5
July 1992	January 1994	424	481	18	13.4	.7
October 1998	August 2000	1098	1517	22	38.2	1.7
Average				35	48.6	2.5

*The April 1967 cut did not occur after a series of declines, but was associated with the 1966 business slowdown. The exclusion of this cut would improve the average results.
Source: *www.pring.com.*

by a bull market high, this by no means excludes the risk of a major intermediate correction along the way. Such setbacks occurred in 1934 and 1962 and during 1977–1978 and 1998. In the 1977–1978 period, the market as measured by the NYSE A/D line did not correct, but moved irregularly higher. Chart 25-9 shows the relationship between the discount rate and the stock market for the second half of the twentieth century.

While cuts in the discount rate usually precede market bottoms, this relationship is far less precise than that observed at market tops. For example, the rate was lowered no fewer than seven times during the 1929–1932 debacle, whereas it was not changed at all during the 1946–1949 bear market.

Applying Technical Analysis at the Long End

It is often a useful exercise in technical analysis to use one market to forecast another. This is known as an intermarket relationship. Chart 25-10 compares long-term gold momentum to U.S. government bond yields (the dashed line). The concept relies on the assumption that gold prices discount (industrial commodity) inflation and that bond yields respond to this by rising. Gold momentum as expressed here is a 3-month MA divided by a 24-month MA. The idea is that when this series rallies above zero, it indicates

Chart 25-9 The S&P Composite, 1950–2001, and the discount rate. (*From www.pring.com.*)

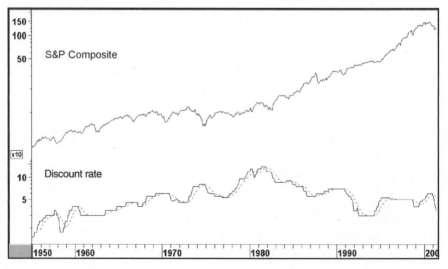

Chart 25-10 The 20-year government bond yield and gold momentum, 1972–2001. (*From www.pring.com.*)

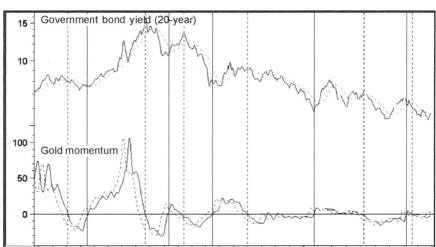

that the gold market is expecting inflation, which means that the clock has begun to tick for the bear market in yields (bull market in prices). The indicator has a reasonably good track record, but really needs to await confirmation from the bond yield series itself by a trend break, 12-month MA crossover, and so on. The solid line is the same momentum, advanced by 5 months. The vertical lines show that the zero crossovers have a better timing record. Also, because the dashed line moves ahead, crossovers of the advanced indicator are known ahead of time.

Bond yield series tend to be very cyclical. We can take advantage of this situation by comparing a yield series such as Moody's AAA corporate bonds to an ROC indicator. An example is shown in Chart 25-11, where the arrows show that overbought/oversold crossovers of the 12-month ROC have consistently flashed excellent buy and sell signals for the yield. They cannot be used as an actual system because offsetting signals may not be given. For example, during the 1940–1981 secular or very long term uptrend, no buy signals were given between the 1950s and 1981. This contrasts to the secular downtrend, where several were triggered. This represents a classic example of how oscillators tend to move and stay at overbought levels during a bull market and reverse the process during bear markets. In this case, the bull market was the secular trend and the overbought readings represented primary-trend peaks.

Chart 25-12 expresses a similar idea, except that this time the oscillator is a short-term one, an 8-day MA of a 9-day RSI. The arrows above the yield show the primary trend environment. You can see quite clearly that over-bought conditions are far more common in the bull phase, and oversold during the bear trends. Note also that the 200-day MA can serve as an additional arbitrator of the direction of the primary trend. At the tail end of the chart, the oscillator reaches an overbought condition and the yield crosses above its MA, suggesting the probability that a new bull market is under way.

Finally, Chart 25-13 compares a perpetual contract of the U.S. Treasury bond futures against two ROC indicators. Between the opening of the year 2000 and the end of the chart, the primary trend was bullish. The four arrows attached to the 10-day ROC indicate oversold or close to oversold conditions. Each was followed by a worthwhile rally. The ellipse in the very right-hand part of the chart indicates a failure to respond to an oversold condition and offers the first hint that a new bear market had begun. Several joint trendline breaks in the price and momentum are also indicated. The adoption of this combination is quite useful because the 10- and 45-day spans are separated by a considerable distance. In this way, characteristics not shown by the 10-day series may show up in the 45-day one, and vice versa. Of course, it's even better when all three are indicating a trend reversal, as was the case in April 2000.

Chart 25-11 Moody's AAA bond yield, 1950–2001, and a 12-month ROC. (*From www.pring.com.*)

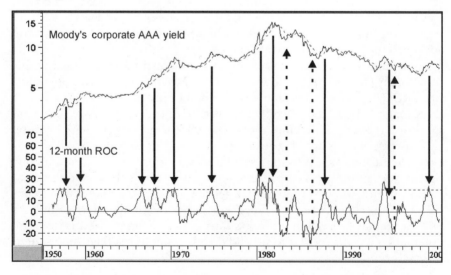

Chart 25-12 The 30-year government bond yield, 1997–2001, and a smoothed RSI. (*From www.pring.com.*)

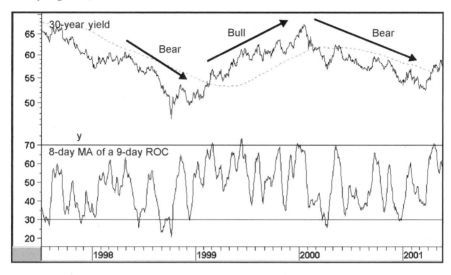

Chart 25-13 U.S. Treasury bond futures, 1999–2001, and two ROCs. (*From www.pring.com.*)

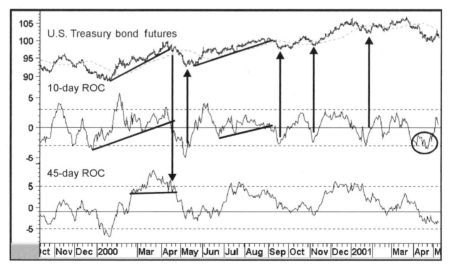

Summary

- Interest rates influence stock prices because they affect corporate profitability, alter valuation relationships, and influence margin transactions.
- Interest rates have led stock prices at major turning points in virtually every recorded business cycle.
- It is the ROC of interest rates, rather than their actual level, that affects equity prices.
- Short-term interest rates generally have a greater influence on stock prices than long-term rates.
- Changes in the discount rate offer strong confirmation that a primary-trend change in money-market prices has taken place.
- Reversals in the trend of the discount rate offer early-bird warnings of a change in the primary trend of stock prices.
- Intermarket relationships can be used to forecast or identify primary-trend reversals in bond prices and yields.

26
Sentiment Indicators

I find more and more that it is well to be on the right side of the minority since it is always the more intelligent.

Goethe

Some Basic Thoughts

During primary bull and bear markets, the psychology of all investors moves from pessimism and fear to hope, overconfidence, and greed. For the majority, the feeling of confidence is built up over a period of rising prices, so that optimism reaches its peak around the same point that the market is also reaching its high. Conversely, the majority are most pessimistic at market bottoms, at precisely the point when they should be buying. These observations are as valid for intermediate-term peaks and troughs as they are for primary ones. The difference is normally of degree. At an intermediate-term low, for example, significant problems are perceived, but at a primary market low, they often seem insurmountable. In some respects the worse the problem, the more significant the bottom.

The better-informed market participants, such as insiders and stock exchange members, tend to act in a manner contrary to that of the majority by selling at market tops and buying at market bottoms. Both groups go through a complete cycle of emotions, but in completely opposite phases. This is not to suggest that members of the public are always wrong at major market turns and that professionals are always correct; rather, the implication is that, in aggregate, the opinions of these groups are usually in direct conflict.

Historical data are available on many market participants, making it possible to derive parameters that indicate when a particular group has moved to an extreme historically associated with a major market turning point.

Unfortunately, several indexes that worked well prior to the 1980s have been partially distorted because of the advent of listed options trading in 1973 and the introduction of stock index futures in 1982. This is because the purchase and sale of options and index futures substitute for short selling and other speculative activity that had been used as a basis for the construction of sentiment indicators. For this reason, it is best to monitor several sentiment indicators simultaneously when attempting to assess the mood of market participants.

Momentum as a Substitute for Sentiment

Individual stocks and many markets do not have published sentiment data from which indicators can be derived. In such instances it is possible to substitute oscillators since there is a close correlation between overbought conditions and those of excessive bullishness, and vice versa.

In this respect, Chart 26-1 shows two series. Each week *Investors Intelligence*[1] classifies a huge number of market letters into bullish, bearish, and correction camps. The weekly percentage data of bearish market letter writers is featured in the upper panel. The actual plot is the weekly number divided by a 13-week moving average (MA), in effect, a simple trend deviation indicator. This indicator has also been plotted inversely so that its movements correspond to those of stock prices. The lower panel contains a similar oscillator constructed from the Friday closing price of the S&P Composite. The arrows connect the peaks and troughs of both series. It is fairly evident that there is an extremely close correlation. The principal differences relate to degree. For example, there were very few bears at the beginning of 1993 at *A*, yet the S&P oscillator never came close to an oversold reading. Then, in late 1995, at *B*, the S&P was close to an overbought condition, but the bears index was not.

Major Technical Principle The movement of oscillators and sentiment indicators is closely related.

---

[1]chartcraft.com

Chart 26-1 Sentiment versus S&P momentum, 1992–1997. (*From Investor's Intelligence.*)

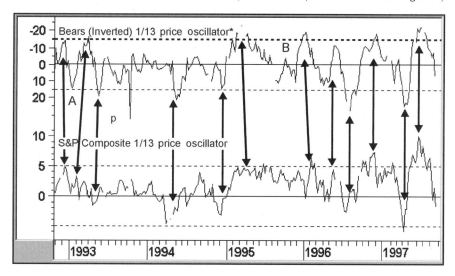

Chart 26-2 Government bond yields, bond bulls, and an RSI. (*From Market Vane.*)

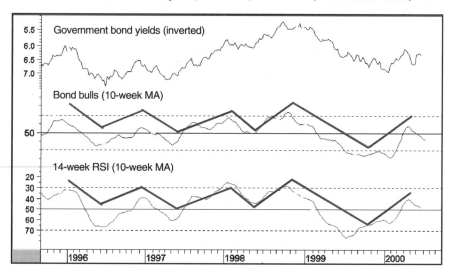

We can also see a similar relationship in the bond market. Chart 26-2, for instance, compares a 10-week MA of bullish traders as published by *Market Vane* against a 10-week MA of a 14-week relative strength indicator (RSI). The waves were constructed by approximating the rallies and reactions for the *Market Vane* bulls, and then copied and overlaid on the smoothed RSI. It is fairly evident that there is an almost perfect fit.

In Chapter 10 it was pointed out that protrend short-term momentum extremes often fail to signal significant contratrend moves; for example, oversold conditions in bear markets often fail to signal rallies. The same is true of sentiment indicators. For example, if there is a dearth of bulls after the price has declined in a bear market, the effect is nowhere near as powerful as the generation of a similar number would be in a bull market. It goes back to the rule that oversold readings in bull markets are far more powerful than oversold readings in bear markets, and vice versa.

The fact that sentiment and momentum indicators are closely related should come as no surprise, because rising prices attract more bulls and falling ones more bears. I am not suggesting that every sentiment indicator and oscillator have this close relationship. However, it does mean that *if sentiment indicators are not available, momentum series can become useful substitutes.*

The following sections will examine some of the more popular sentiment indicators.

A Few Words on Short Selling

Normal stock transactions involve a purchase in anticipation of higher prices in the future. In short selling the process is reversed. Stock is borrowed from a broker and sold in anticipation of lower prices. The position is closed out when the stock is bought and the borrowed stock returned to the broker. Whereas stock purchases are usually made on a buy-hold basis, the very nature of short selling implies a speculative bent in the person who is involved in such transactions. This means that short sellers make excellent candidates for indicators that monitor market sentiment.

Specialist/Public Ratio

Specialists are individuals and firms on the New York Stock Exchange who are charged with the responsibility of making markets in individual stocks in both quiet and volatile environments. They are therefore the trading experts on these equities. Chart 26-3 shows the ratio of short selling between specialists (smart money) and the public (not so smart money) on the NYSE.

Chart 26-3 DJIA 1978–2001 specialists and NYSE total short position. (*From Ned Davis Research.*)

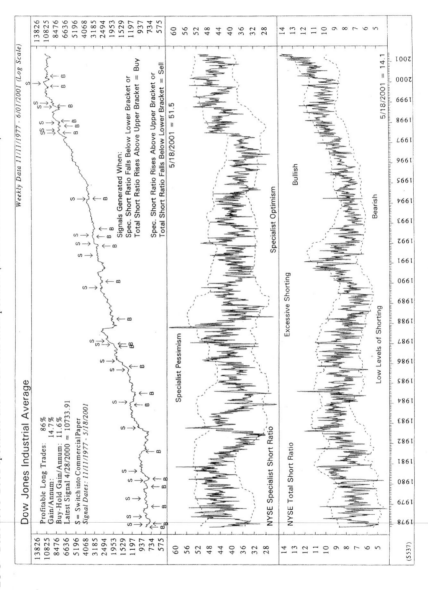

489

When the specialists are short selling at a high level relative to the public, this is bullish, and vice versa.

The ratio can be interpreted in a number of ways. Generally speaking, it seems to work better in signaling an advance. One might think that an extreme reading below 32 percent is bullish, but this is not usually the case. In some instances, such as late 1983, this type of signal was totally misleading because it occurred just as the market began a major decline. An alternative method is to construct brackets based on a deviation calculation and use crossovers in the bracket on the way back toward equilibrium as a buy signal. As the chart indicates, these envelopes are dynamic in nature and take into consideration changes in this relationship over time. Sell signals are not so reliable. Indeed, the ratio reached an extreme bearish level right after the 1987 crash, when logic would have indicated that it should have been at a bullish record extreme. Generally speaking, it would appear that a reading in excess of 52 percent tends to put a bit of a cap on prices.

Short-Interest Ratio

The short interest is a figure published around the end of the month that reports the number of shares that have been sold short on the NYSE. Similar data are also published by the other exchanges. The short interest is a flow-of-funds statistic, since every share sold short has to be repurchased (covered), but it is also a measure of sentiment. This is because a large number of shares sold short indicates a predominantly bearish attitude, and vice versa. Over the years, technicians have discovered that *the ratio of the short interest to the average daily volume of the preceding month offers more reliable signals than the short interest taken by itself.* Traditionally, the ratio has been considered bullish at a reading of 1.8 or higher. A short-interest ratio of less than 1 has normally reflected a very bullish consensus and from a contrary aspect is considered bearish. Also, if there are few shares being sold short, there is less potential demand since there are less shares to be covered.

Unfortunately, this indicator has shown a tremendous bullish bias since 1982, with consistent readings well in excess of 2.0. As a result, it failed to signal either the 1983–1984 bear market or the 1987 crash. This distortion has probably developed because of the widespread use of options and futures, which has increased the volume of short selling for hedging purposes and which has nothing to do with bullish or bearish sentiment. Consequently, the indicator is therefore unlikely to revert to its previously useful role. The upper panel of Chart 26-4 shows the ratio calculated with an average 12-month daily volume instead of with an average of monthly

Chart 26-4 S&P Composite, 1945–2001, and two short-interest ratios. *(From Ned Davis Research.)*

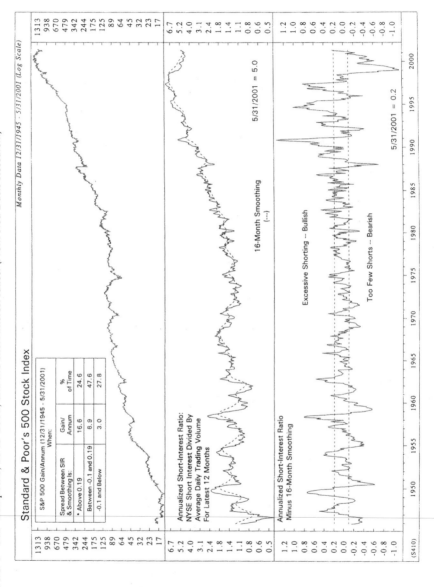

volume. Recent distortions are self-evident. The lower panel shows a better timing mechanism and is based on an annualized short-interest ratio minus a 16-month smoothing.

Insider Trading

Stockholders who hold in excess of 5 percent of the total voting stock of a company and corporate officers or other employees who have access to important corporate information are required to file with the Securities and Exchange Commission (SEC) any purchases or sales within 10 days. As a group, these "insiders" are generally correct in their decisions, having a tendency to sell proportionately more stock as the market rises, and vice versa. A 5-week MA of the weekly insider sell/buy ratio is shown at the bottom of Chart 26-5. The chart shows that as prices work their way higher, insiders accelerate their sales as a percentage of purchases. Market peaks are signaled when the ratio rises for a period of a few months or more and then reverses trend. In this respect, a rise above the 70 percent level and a subsequent reversal in the direction of the index are often enough to signal a decline. However, insiders can be uncomfortably early and the dashed lines on the chart show that quite often it is necessary for them to experience a couple of negative divergences before the market reacts to the downside. Because of this, the indicator should be used as a background factor rather than a precise timing device.

At major lows, a decline below the 60 level usually indicates that the market has found a floor and is relatively immune to further price erosion. However, reversals that take place from below the 40 percent level appear to offer the best warning of an impending advance.

Advisory Services

Since 1963, *Investors' Intelligence*[2] has been compiling data on the opinions of publishers of market letters. It might be expected that this group would be well informed and would offer advice of a contrary nature by recommending acquisition of equities at market bottoms and offering selling advice at market tops. The evidence suggests that the advisory services in aggregate act in a manner completely consistent with that of the majority and therefore represent a good contrary indicator.

---

[2]chartcraft.com

Chart 26-5 DJIA 1974–2001 and insider trading. *(From Ned Davis Research.)*

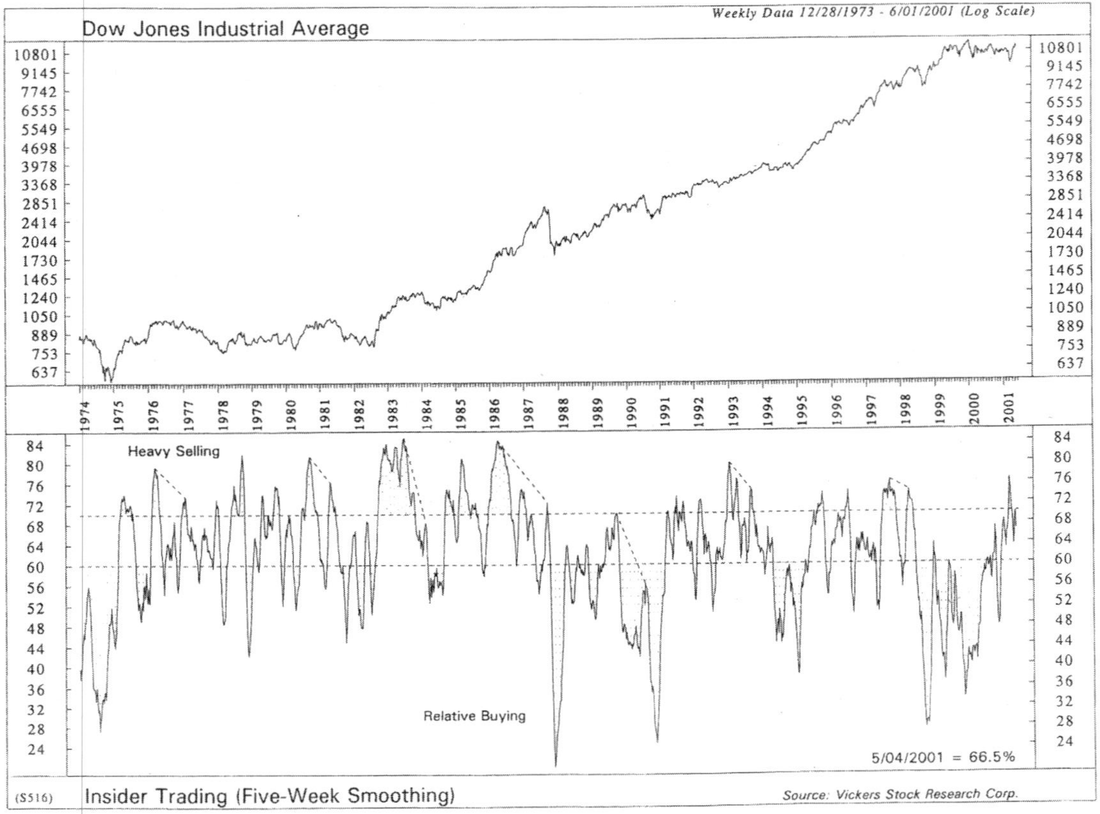

Weekly Data 12/28/1973 - 6/01/2001 (Log Scale)

Dow Jones Industrial Average

Insider Trading (Five-Week Smoothing)

5/04/2001 = 66.5%

Relative Buying

Heavy Selling

Source: Vickers Stock Research Corp.

(S516)

Chart 26-6 S&P Composite, 1968–2001, and newsletter writer sentiment. (*From Ned Davis Research/Investor's Intelligence.*)

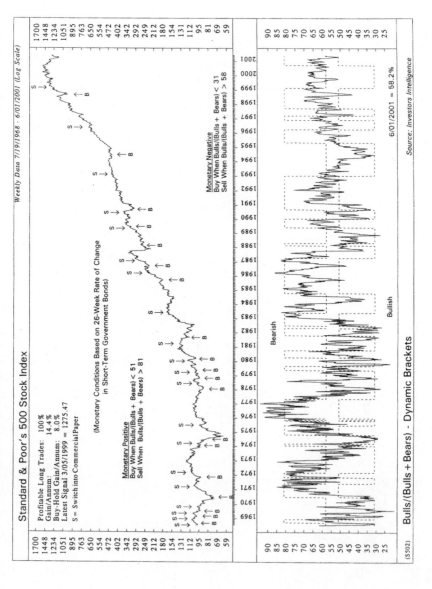

Chart 26-6 shows the percentage of bullish market letter writers in relation to the total of all those expressing an opinion. The resulting index shows that the advisory services follow the trend of equity prices by becoming most bullish near market tops and predominately pessimistic around market bottoms. *Investors would clearly find it more profitable, then, to take a position contrary to that of the advisory service industry.*

This index also gives a good indication of how market psychology can swing from outright pessimism to extreme overconfidence. In early 1968, for example, virtually all services were putting out bearish forecasts right at a major low. Then, as prices began to rise, their prognostications became more optimistic and turned to outright bullishness at the peak. This indicator would have been very useful during the 1973–1974 bear market. The averages experienced two substantial declines in 1973, but at no time did the index reach a 30 percent extreme level that would have been consistent with a market bottom.

Whenever the Advisory Services Sentiment Indicator has moved below the lower dashed line and then risen above it, important buy signals have usually resulted. At market tops, a decline below the upper line appears to offer a fairly consistent warning of impending trouble.

Chart 26-7 shows just the percentage of bears. Note that this has been plotted *inversely* to correspond with stock price movements. The principles of divergence can also be applied to the interpretation of this indicator. For

Chart 26-7 The S&P Composite, 1976–2001, and bearish newsletter writers. (*From Investors Intelligence.*)

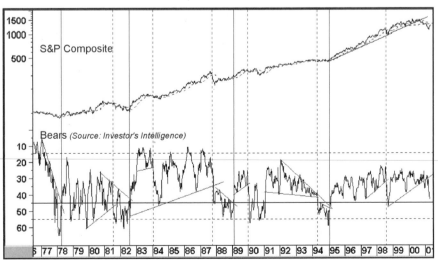

> **Major Technical Principle** Quite often the trend of sentiment can be as important as the level in identifying important market reversals. [The same observation can be made for fundamental indicators, such as price earnings (P/E) ratios and so on.]

example, the market low of 1982 and high of 1987 were both preceded by a divergence.

Chart 27-6 shows many examples in which it is possible to construct a trendline for the indicator. When the line is violated, a trend-reversal signal is given. The dashed vertical lines indicate sells, and the solid lines buy signals. Generally speaking, the buy signals tend to develop fairly closely to the lows, whereas the sell signals are less responsive in nature.

Market Vane and Bond Market Sentiment

Sentiment indicators are also published for the futures market. The most widely followed are data issued by *Market Vane,* which polls a sample of market participants on a regular basis. The results are published as the percentage of participants that are bullish. The theory is that when a significant number of traders are bullish on a particular market, they are already positioned on the long side and there is very little potential buying power left. The implication is that the price has only one way to go, and that is down. In a similar manner, if most participants are bearish, selling pressure has reached an extreme, and therefore prices will reverse to the upside.

One problem with these statistics is that they are based on the opinion of short-term traders, which makes them somewhat erratic and which therefore only has implications for near-term price movements. One way of surmounting this drawback is to calculate an MA of the raw data, thereby smoothing out the week-to-week fluctuations.

A 4-week MA of the *Market Vane* data and a long-term Treasury-bond (T-bond) index are plotted in Chart 26-8. The two dashed lines, at 70 percent and 30 percent, represent overbought and oversold levels, respectively.

Important sell signals often occur when the indicator crosses above the 70 percent level and then recrosses it on its way toward 50. Readings that have fallen below 30 percent and then risen above it (the lower dashed line) have often generated timely buy signals. The main drawback in interpret-

Chart 26-8 Government bond yields, 1980–2001, and bond sentiment and momentum. (*From www.pring.com/Market Vane.*)

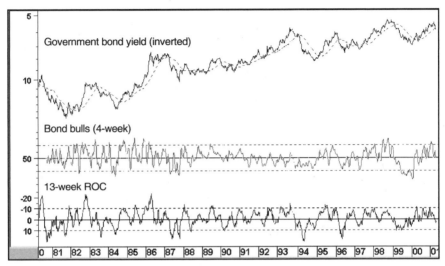

ing these data is that premature buy and sell signals often result when a persistent trend is under way. For example, in January 1986 a sell signal was triggered as it fell below the 70 percent level, but bond prices rallied sharply higher in what turned out to be the most explosive advance of the whole 1984–1986 period. Moreover, a buy signal was given in the spring of 1987. The bond price did experience a small rally, but this was soon followed by a very sharp decline. Other premature sell and buy signals were also given in late 1982 and early 1984. These flaws demonstrate the necessity of using this indicator in conjunction with others in order to obtain a more balanced picture.

The bullish consensus numbers appear to offer very timely signals when the indicator moves to an extreme during a contra trend move. For example, when the indicator reached a bullish extreme during a bear market in early 1984, the rally attracted a large number of bulls, pushing the index above the 70 percent level, but prices collapsed when it recrossed this level. By the same token, when the indicator moves to a bearish extreme in a bull market, a major buying opportunity is usually signaled. A classic example occurred in the spring of 1987, when the bulls moved to an extreme below the 30 percent level and then rallied above it. Some understanding of the prevailing nature of the main trend is therefore an important prerequisite for identifying such turning points.

Combining Sentiment and Momentum

One useful approach for identifying early reversals in trend is to combine sentiment and momentum into one series. Chart 26-9 shows an indicator that combines the smoothed bullish consensus numbers, described previously, with an 8-week MA, of a 13-week rate of change (ROC) of the Lehman Bond Index.

Buy and sell alerts occur when the bullish momentum index crosses through the oversold and overbought zones and then recrosses the zones on its way back to zero. With the exception of early 1986, every sell signal during the period covered by the chart was followed by a fairly lengthy correction, which took the form of a major sell-off or a long period of consolidation.

Sometimes important clues of a potential trend reversal occur as the bond bulls move to an extreme but are not confirmed by a similar move in momentum. Such action represents an exception to the rule that bulls are attracted only by sharply rising prices and bears only by sharply falling prices.

For example, Chart 26-8 shows that in mid-1982 the sentiment indicator moved to a bearish extreme, but momentum hardly declined at all. In 1986 the reverse set of conditions occurred: the sentiment indicator moved to a bullish extreme with virtually no upside price momentum. Such contradic-

Chart 26-9 Lehman Bond Index, 1984–1989, and bond sentiment. (*From www.pring.com/Market Vane.*)

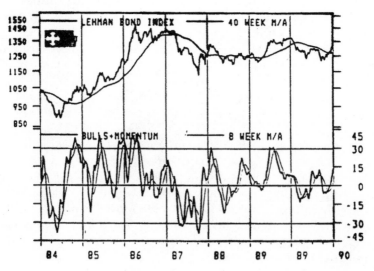

tions do not occur very often, but when they do, there is a high degree of probability that an important trend reversal is in the wind.

The rationale probably lies in the fact that rising prices (momentum) attract bulls, whereas falling prices (momentum) attract bears. However, when sentiment moves to an extreme and prices do not, the degree of optimism or pessimism is misplaced, and the price must adjust accordingly.

Mutual Funds

Data on mutual funds are published monthly by the Investment Company Institute. The statistics are useful because they monitor the actions of both the public and the institutions. Technical analysts usually calculate mutual fund cash as a percentage of assets. In a sense, these data should be treated as a flow-of-funds indicator, but they are discussed here as a measure of sentiment because they also reflect the attitudes of various market participants.

Cash/Assets Ratio

Mutual funds consistently hold a certain amount of their portfolios in the form of liquid assets in order to accommodate investors wishing to cash in or redeem their investments. A useful indicator is derived when this cash position is expressed as a percentage of the total value of mutual funds' portfolios (a figure known as *total asset value*) (see Chart 26-10). The index moves in the direction opposite to the stock market, because the proportion of cash held by mutual funds rises as prices fall, and vice versa. There are three reasons for this characteristic. First, as the value of a fund's portfolio falls in a declining market, the proportion of cash held will automatically rise even though no new cash is raised. Second, as prices decline, the funds become more cautious in their buying policy, because they see fewer opportunities for capital gains. Third, the decision is made to hold more cash reserves as insurance against a rush of redemptions by the public. In a rising market the opposite effect is felt, as advancing prices automatically reduce the proportion of cash, sales increase, and fund managers are under tremendous pressure to capitalize on the bull market by being fully invested.

One of the drawbacks of this approach is that mutual fund cash did, by and large, remain above the 9.5 percent level between 1978 and 1990 and lost a lot of validity as a timing device during this period. It is true that the market was in a rising trend, but one of the functions of an indicator of this nature is to warn of setbacks such as the 1980 and 1981–1982 bear markets, not to mention the 1987 crash.

Chart 26-10 The S&P Composite, 1966–2001, and mutual funds' cash/asset ratio. *(From Ned Davis Research.)*

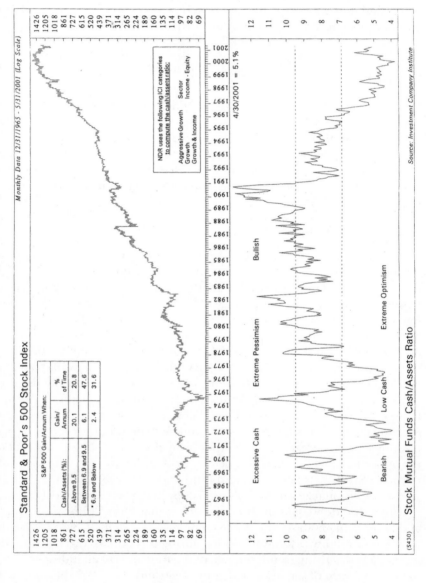

Standard & Poor's 500 Stock Index

Monthly Data 12/31/1965 - 5/31/2001 (Log Scale)

S&P 500 Gain/Annum When:		
Cash/Assets (%):	Gain/Annum	% of Time
Above 9.5	20.1	20.8
Between 6.9 and 9.5	6.1	47.6
* 6.9 and Below	2.4	31.6

NDR uses the following ICI categories to compute the cash/assets ratio:

Aggressive Growth   Sector
Growth   Income - Equity
Growth & Income

4/30/2001 = 5.1%

Excessive Cash

Extreme Pessimism

Bullish

Low Cash

Bearish

Extreme Optimism

Stock Mutual Funds Cash/Assets Ratio

(S430)

Source: Investment Company Institute

One way around this problem, originally devised by Norman Fosback of Market Logic, is to subtract the prevailing level of short-term interest rates from the cash percentage levels themselves. In this way the incentive for portfolio managers to hold cash due to high interest rates is neutralized. This adjustment to the cash/assets ratio is shown in the center panel of Chart 26-11. It is a definite improvement over the raw data, but unfortunately it too fails to explain the 1987 crash.

A final alternative, devised by Ned Davis Research, compares switch fund cash and mutual fund manager cash to total mutual fund assets. This series is also adjusted for interest rates and appears to offer the best results of all. The buy (B) and sell (S) signals in Chart 26-12 are generated when this series crosses below the lower dashed line; they remain in force until the adjusted switched cash crosses above the upper dashed (selling) line.

Margin Debt

Trends in margin debt are probably better classified as flow-of-funds indicators, but because the trend and level are also good indications of investor confidence (or lack of confidence), they are discussed in this section.

Margin debt is money borrowed from brokers and bankers using securities as collateral. The credit is normally used for the purchase of equities. At the beginning of a typical stock market cycle, margin debt is relatively low; it begins to rise very shortly after the final bottom in equity prices. As prices rise, margin traders as a group become more confident, taking on additional debt in order to leverage larger stock positions.

During a primary uptrend, margin debt is a valuable source of new funds for the stock market. The importance of this factor can be appreciated when it is noted that margin debt increased almost tenfold between 1974 and 1987. The difference between stock purchased for cash and stock bought on margin is that margined stock must at some point be sold in order to pay off the debt. On the other hand, stock purchased outright can theoretically be held indefinitely. During stock market declines, margin debt reverses its positive role and becomes an important source of stock supply.

This occurs for four reasons. First, the sophistication of margin-oriented investors is relatively superior to that of other market participants. When this group realizes that the potential for capital gains has greatly diminished, a trend of margin liquidation begins. Margin debt has flattened or declined within 3 months of most of the primary stock market peaks since 1932.

Second, primary stock market peaks are invariably preceded by rising interest rates, which in turn increase the carrying cost of margin debt, therefore making it less attractive to maintain.

502

Chart 26-11 DJIA, 1965–2001, and two mutual fund cash/asset ratios. *(From Ned Davis Research.)*

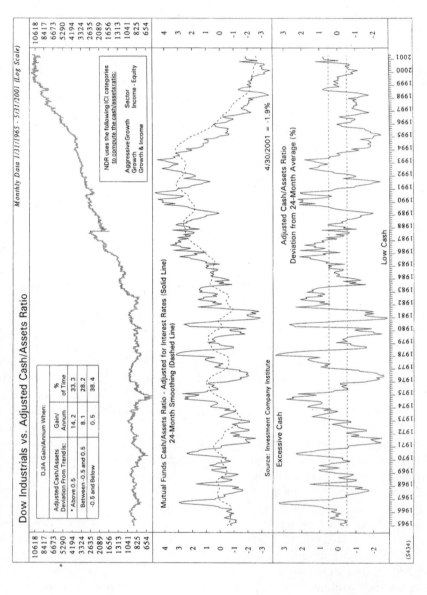

Dow Industrials vs. Adjusted Cash/Assets Ratio

Monthly Data 1/31/1965 - 5/31/2001 (Log Scale)

DJIA Gain/Annum When:		
Adjusted Cash/Assets Deviation From Trend Is:	Gain/ Annum	% of Time
* Above 0.5	14.2	33.3
Between -0.5 and 0.5	8.1	28.2
-0.5 and Below	0.5	38.4

NDR uses the following ICI categories to compute the cash/assets ratio:

Aggressive Growth   Sector
Growth   Income - Equity
Growth & Income

Mutual Funds Cash/Assets Ratio - Adjusted for Interest Rates (Solid Line)
24-Month Smoothing (Dashed Line)

4/30/2001 = -1.9%

Source: Investment Company Institute

Excessive Cash

Adjusted Cash/Assets Ratio
Deviation from 24-Month Average (%)

Low Cash

(S434)

Chart 26-12 S&P Composite, 1965–2001, and a switch fund cash/asset ratio. (*From Ned Davis Research.*)

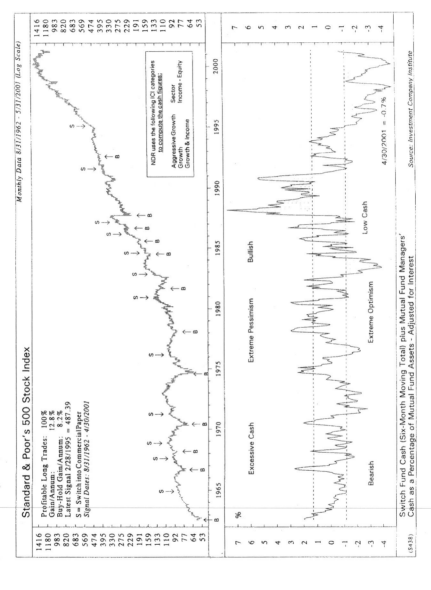

Third, since 1934 the Federal Reserve Board (the Fed) has been empowered to set and vary margin requirements, which specify the amount that can be lent by a broker or bank to customers for the purpose of holding securities. This measure was considered necessary in view of the substantial expansion of margin debt that occurred in the late 1920s. The liquidation of this debt pyramid contributed to the severity of the 1929–1932 bear market. When stock prices have been rising strongly for a period of time, speculation develops, often resulting in a sharp rise in margin debt. Sensing that things could get out of control at this stage, the Fed raises the margin requirement, which has the effect of reducing the buying power of the general public from what it might otherwise have been. Normally, it takes several margin-requirement changes to significantly reduce the buying power of these speculators. This is because the substantial advance in the price of stocks—which was initially responsible for the requirements being raised—normally creates additional collateral at a rate that is initially sufficient to offset the rise in reserve requirements.

Fourth, the collateral value of the securities used as a basis for the margin debt falls as stock prices decline. The margin speculator is faced with the option of putting up more money or selling stock in order to pay off the debt. At first, the margin call process is reasonably orderly, as most traders have a sufficient cushion of collateral to protect them from the initial drop in prices. Alternatively, those who are undermargined often choose to put up additional collateral or cash. Toward the end of a bear market, prices fall more rapidly, and this unnerving process, combined with the unwillingness or inability of margin customers to come up with additional collateral, triggers a rush of margin calls. This adds substantially to the supply of stock that must be sold regardless of price. The self-feeding downward spiral of forced liquidation continues until margin debt has contracted to a more manageable level.

Most people think that the level of margin debt is the most important way to interpret these data. It is true that the higher the level, the greater the market's vulnerability when the numbers begin to contract. Perhaps a better way to express this statistic is to express the level of debt as a percentage of outstanding market capitalization. Thus, the true vulnerability of the market would be represented in a more proportionate way. However, it is the trend of margin debt that is all-important, because trend reversals signal whether traders are confident (willing to take on more debt) or pessimistic (liquidating it). For this reason, margin debt is a useful indicator when expressed in relation to its 12-month EMA. This is shown in Chart 26-13. EMA crossovers then offer confirmation of major trend reversals.

Chart 26-13 DJIA, 1966–2001, and margin debt. *(From Ned Davis Research.)*

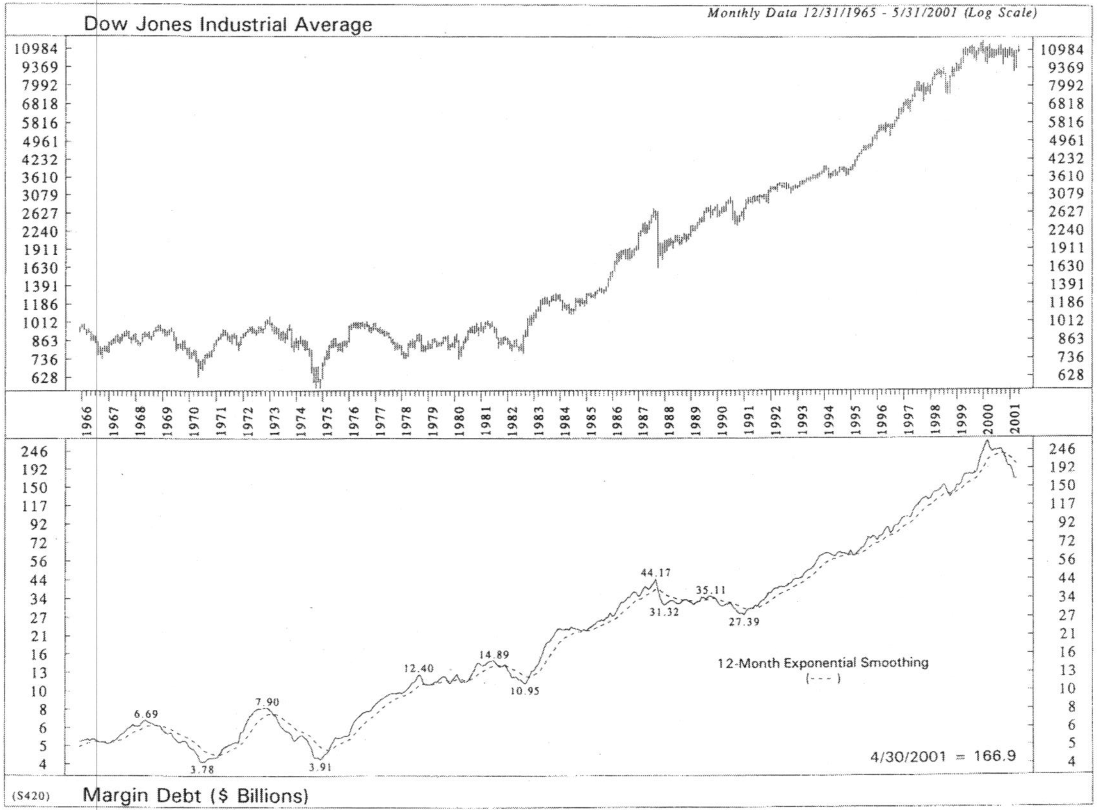

Dow Jones Industrial Average

Monthly Data 12/31/1965 - 5/31/2001 (Log Scale)

12-Month Exponential Smoothing
(- - -)

4/30/2001 = 166.9

Margin Debt ($ Billions)

(S420)

Put/Call Ratio

Sentiment indicators based on short-selling data appear to have been distorted in recent years, in part because of the introduction of listed options. On the other hand, options can themselves be used as a basis for the construction of sentiment indicators. Their performance is far from perfect but definitely worth consideration.

Perhaps the most widely followed option-derived indicator is one that measures the ratio of the volume of puts to the volume of calls. A *put* gives an investor or trader a theoretical option to *sell* a specific security at a predetermined price over specified period. In effect the purchaser of a put is betting that the price of the underlying asset will go down. This is a form of short sale in which the trader's risk is limited to the cost of the put. (The risk on a short sale is theoretically unlimited.)

A *call*, on the other hand, is a bet that the underlying asset will rise in price. It gives a purchaser the option to *buy* a security at a predetermined price over a specified period.

It is normal for call volume to outstrip that of puts, and so the put/call ratio invariably trades below the 1.0 or (100) level. This indicator measures the swings in sentiment between the bulls and the bears. In theory, the lower the ratio, the more bullish the crowd and the more likely the market is to decline, and vice versa. A low ratio means that very few people are buying puts relative to calls, whereas a high ratio indicates that a larger number of traders than normal are betting that the market will go down.

The put/call ratio is shown in Chart 26-14 as a 4-week MA of puts divided by a 4-week MA of calls. The 4-week MA of the ratio often signals a rally when it moves above the 69 level and then crosses below it. This approach had a good track record for the 1993–2000 period, but at the end of 2000 a false signal of strength was given. Its timing of market tops is not as reliable.

Inverted Yield Momentum

Historically, whenever the dividend yield on the S&P Composite fell below 3 percent, this indicated that investors were overpaying for stocks and that a bear market warning was being offered. In the mid-1990s, the yield began to slip, and eventually fell to just over 1 percent, well beyond the previous record around 2.7 percent. This experience completely overturned what had previously been a good measure of valuation and sentiment. It also demonstrated the point that *the trend of any indicator is often as important as its level.*

Chart 26-14 S&P Composite, 1993–2001, and a put/call ratio. *(From Ned Davis Research.)*

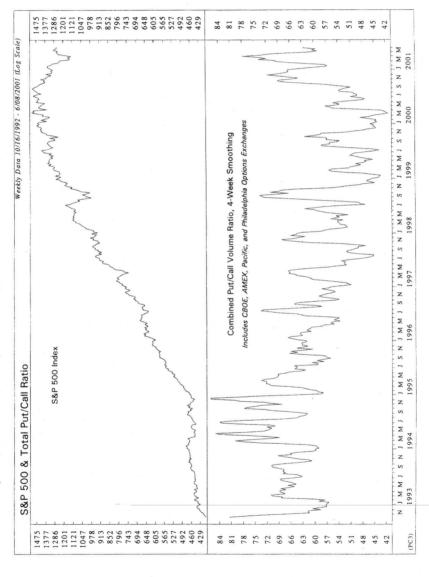

The idea is that swings in the dividend yield from a bullish extreme of around 3 percent to a bearish one of 5 to 6 percent reflect changes in psychology. If people are willing to accept a paltry 3 percent, they are quite confident, yet if they demand 5 or 6 percent, there is widespread fear because the high yield reflects investor pessimism and their requirement for a higher current return to compensate for the perceived escalation in risk. An alternative is to plot the yield in the form of a momentum indicator, as in Chart 26-15. In this instance the indicator, a 24-month ROC of the yield, has been plotted inversely so that it corresponds with price movements. Plotting a fundamental indicator such as the dividend yield in an oscillator format more accurately depicts these major psychological shifts in sentiment.

In Chart 26-15, the vertical lines show that when the oscillator reverses from an overbought condition and moves toward its equilibrium point, this is normally associated with a bear trend of some kind. When the opposite takes place, the indicator generally offers timely buy signals. The overbought and oversold levels are at +20 percent and −20 percent.

Chart 26-15   The S&P Composite, 1957–2001, and inverted dividend yield momentum. (*From www.pring.com.*)

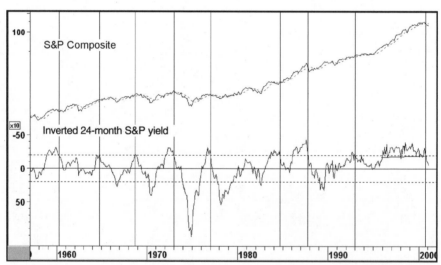

The Market's Reaction to News

Another extremely important, though imprecise, approach for assessing market sentiment is to observe the reaction of any market to news events, especially unexpected ones. This is a helpful exercise, since markets look ahead and factor all foreseeable events into the price structure. If a news event that would normally be expected to move the price does not do so, the likelihood is that all the news, good or bad, is already reflected in the price.

A classic example developed at the end of 1988 when the insider stock scandals began to appear, starting with the indictments of David Levine and Ivan Boesky. Under normal circumstances the market would have been expected to sell off. But in this instance it stalled for a while and then rallied sharply.

The discount rate was raised in the spring of 1978. This should have been a signal to sell, but the market rallied on record volume. In this instance, the fact that new highs quickly outpaced new lows just after a bear market low should have been the technical tip-off that the underlying structure was pretty sound.

Another example developed early in 2001. The Fed lowered the discount rate, the first in a series of rate cuts. However, within a few days bond prices were below the level they were trading at on the day of the cut. This was a terrible response to good news and prices continued to sell off for the next few months.

Very often excellent news develops and prices refuse to respond, yet the temptation is overwhelming to hang on until market participants "realize how bullish it is." Invariably though, the price will soon decline. In such situations when the price does not respond when it "should," the best tactic is to watch for a suitable stop point and exit the position if it is stopped. Remember, the more convincing the news and the more muted the response, beyond the initial few hours of trading after the news is published, the greater the potential vulnerability, and vice versa.

Countless examples could be cited for many stocks and markets, but the principle remains that if a price does not respond to news in the expected way, it is probably in the process of turning. Evaluation of this factor is very much a judgment call, but it can act as a very useful adjunct to an appraisal of the other technical indicators.

Summary

- Sentiment indicators are useful supplements to the trend-determining techniques described in other chapters. They should be used for the purpose of assessing the consensus view from which a contrary position can be taken.
- Since many sentiment indicators are subject to institutional changes, it is mandatory to consider them as a group rather than relying on one or two indicators alone.

Acknowledgments

I should like to thank Tim Hayes and Ned Davis of Ned Davis Research for providing the bulk of the charts for this chapter. Their innovative work is probably second to none in the field of sentiment and I am extremely grateful for permission to reproduce their excellent work.

27

Applying Technical Analysis to the Theory of Contrary Opinion

"The law of an organized, or psychological crowd is mental unity. The individuals composing the crowd lose their conscious personality under the influence of emotion and are ready to act as one, directed by the low crowd intelligence."
Thomas Templeton Hoyle

Contrary Opinion Defined

Humphrey Neil put together his own ideas and experience and joined them with the writings of Charles Mackay (*Popular Illusions*), Gustav Le Bon (*The Crowd*), and Gabriel Tarde to form the theory of contrary opinion. Today it is widely understood that since the "crowd" is wrong at major market turning points, the only game in town is to be a contrarian! Unfortunately, whenever a concept or theory becomes popular, the basic idea is often distorted. This means that those who have adapted the theory on its face value and not taken the trouble to study Neil and other writers are probably on shaky ground. Neil pointed out that the crowd is actually correct for substantial amounts of time. *It is at turning points that the majority get things wrong.* It is this last idea that is really central to Neil's thinking.

Once an opinion is formed, it is imitated by the majority until virtually everyone agrees that it is valid. As Neil (1980) put it:

> *When everyone thinks alike, everyone is likely to be wrong. When masses of people succumb to an idea, they often run off on a tangent because of their emotions. When people stop to think (emphasis added) things through, they are very similar in their decisions.*

The word *think* has been deliberately emphasized because the practice of contrary opinion is very much an art and not a science. To be a true contrarian, you need to study, be patient, be creative, and bring to the table widespread experience. Remember, no two market situations are ever identical because history may repeat, but it rarely repeats exactly. In effect, it's not as easy as saying, "Everyone else is bearish; therefore, I am bullish."

Perhaps the best definition of contrary opinion comes from the late John Schultz, who, in a timely article in *Barron's* just prior to the 1987 crash, wrote:

> *The guiding light of investment contrarianism is not that the majority view —the conventional, or received wisdom—is always wrong. Rather it's that the majority opinion tends to solidfy into a dogma while its basic premises begin to lose their original validity and so become progressively more mispriced in the marketplace.*

Three words must be emphasized because they encapsulate the three prerequisites of forming a contrary opinion. First, the original concept solidifies into a *dogma*. Second, it loses its *validity* and a new factor or series of factors comes into play. Finally, the crowd moves to an extreme, as reflected in a gross *overvaluation*. What he is saying is that at the start of a trend, a few far-seeing individuals anticipate an alternative scenario to that being promoted by the majority. Later, as prices rise, others are persuaded that the scenario is valid. Then, as the trend extends, more people join the camp, perhaps being persuaded as much by the rising prices as the concept itself. Eventually the concept or premise becomes a dogma with everyone accepting it as gospel. However, by now, it has been so well discounted or factored into the price that the security in question is way overvalued. Even if the price is not overvalued, the concept begins to lose its original premise and a new scenario emerges. All those betting on the old idea then lose money as the price reverses to the downside.

These trends occur because investors tend to move as crowds and are subject to herd instincts. If left to their own devices, individuals isolated from their peers would tend to act in a far more rational way. Say, for example, you see stock prices starting to move up sharply after they had already moved up a lot. Even though you might know from your own experience that they cannot continue to go up forever, it would be difficult not to become caught up in the excitement, especially after they had rallied significantly from the level at which you first thought them irrationally high.

Under such an environment it becomes very difficult to think independently from the accepted wisdom of the day.

Major Technical Principle A good contrarian should not go contrary for the sake of going contrary, but should learn to think in reverse, to creatively come up with alternative scenarios to those of the crowd. In other words, try to figure out why the crowd may be wrong.

Why Crowds Are Irrational

Neil wrote that there are several, what he terms as *social*, laws that determine crowd psychology. These are:

1. A crowd is subject to instincts that individuals acting independently would never do.

2. People involuntarily follow the impulses of the crowd. (See the section below on why it is difficult to be contrary.)

3. Contagion and imitation of the minority make individuals susceptible to suggestion, commands, customs, and emotional appeals.

4. When gathered as a group or crowd, people rarely reason or question, but follow blindly and emotionally to what is suggested or asserted.

Why then is the crowd wrong at turning points? The reason is that when everyone holds the same bullish opinion, there is very little potential buying power left, very few people left who can perpetuate the trend. By the same token, if the market is *mispriced*, to quote John Schulz, other investment alternatives are becoming more attractive. Little wonder that money soon flows from the overvalued to the more realistically priced alternative.

The opposite would, of course, be true in a declining trend. Take, for example, an economy deep in recession; business activity is declining rapidly, and layoffs and high unemployment are getting headlines in the nightly news. Stocks are extending the decline that began over a year ago, and the whole situation appears to be out of control in a self-feeding downward spiral. While everyone is looking down, it is the prerequisite of the contrarian to look up and ask the question, What could go right? This is where the alternative scenario comes in. Remember, people are rational. When they realize that hard times are coming, they adjust their plans accordingly. Businesses will cut excessive inventories, lay off workers, and pay off debts. Once this has been achieved, breakeven points drop, and they are in a great position to increase profits when the economy turns. All this economizing means that the demand for credit declines, and so does its price—interest rates. Falling rates encourage consumers to go out and buy houses, and a new recovery gets underway.

As Neil has described it, "In historic financial eras, it has been significant how, when conditions were slumping that, under the pall of discouragement, economics were righting themselves underneath to the ensuing revival and recovery."

The same is true in markets. No one is going to hold stocks if they think prices are in for a prolonged decline, so naturally they sell. When all the selling is over, there is only one direction in which prices can go, and that's up! At that point, true contrarians have decided that enough is enough, that an alternative, bullish outcome is likely, and that the underlying assumptions of the bear market are no longer valid.

Knowing *when* to go contrary is a key to the whole process because the crowd frequently moves to extremes, well ahead of a market turning point. Many professionals knew the situation was getting out of hand in 1928 and in 1999 (for Internet stocks). In both cases they had concluded that stocks were very overvalued and discounted the hereafter. They were correct, but their timing was early. Economic trends are often slow to reverse and manias take prices well beyond reasonable valuations, often to ridiculous and irrational ones. In a sense, crowd psychology can be reflected graphically as a long-term oscillator, such as a rate of change (ROC), moves to extraordinary levels not seen for decades. In normal times a market turns when the indicator reaches its overbought level, but on rare occasions the curve can run up to stratospheric levels. An example is shown in Chart 27-1 for the NASDAQ. The 18-month ROC in the lower panel moves up to a level dwarfing anything seen in the previous 20 years of trading history. Indeed, it was twice as high as the best reading for the S&P Composite in 200 years of history.

If crowd sentiment is reflected in oscillators constructed from the price, it follows that there are various levels or extremes to which crowds gravitate. The turn of the century peak in the NASDAQ, the 1980 top in gold, and the 1929 stock market peak are all examples of an extreme. However, since oscillators can be constructed from daily and weekly data, it follows that forming a contrary opinion is just as valid for shorter-term turning points. The difference is that the mood is not so all encompassing and intense as it is just prior to the bursting of a financial bubble.

Chart 27-1 The NADAQ Composite, 1974–2001, and an 18-month ROC. (*From www.pring.com.*)

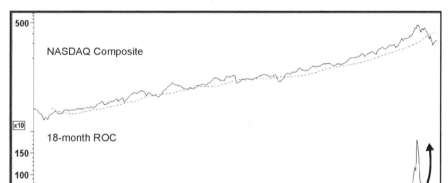

> **Major Technical Principle** Major turning points develop when the crowd moves to an overwhelming extreme. Short and intermediate turning points are associated with less intensive levels of crowd sentiment.

Bearing these comments in mind, it is now time to examine the signs that indicate when the crowd has moved to an extreme, either for small or large trends, and then to see how technical analysis can be applied to such situations.

Why It's Difficult to Go Contrary

Reading and learning about forming a contrary opinion are one thing, but actually applying it in the marketplace when your money is on the line is definitely another.

There are several reasons why it is difficult to take a position that is opposite to the majority:

1. It is very difficult for us to take an opposite view from those around us because of our need to conform.

2. If prices are rising sharply and we have already told friends of our reasons for being bearish, we are unlikely to continue in our contrarianism out of a fear of being ridiculed.

3. We often meet hostility when we go against the crowd.

4. We gain a sense of comfort by extrapolating the recent past.

5. A certain sense of security can be had from accepting the opinions of "experts," instead of having the confidence of thinking for ourselves. Chart 27-2 illustrates several quotations that three famous people probably wish they had never made. Never forget that most "experts" have a vested interest in the opinions they give publicly.

6. We tend to believe that the establishment has all the answers. The U.S. entry into Vietnam, the Soviets' into Afghanistan, and Neville Chamberlain's famous peace-in-our-time speech, just before the outbreak of World War II, should make us think twice about this assumption.

Chart 27-2 The S&P Composite, 1921–1935, and market comments. (*From www.pring.com.*)

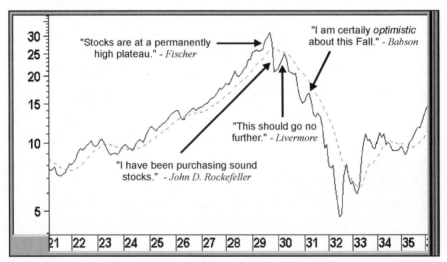

Three Steps to Forming a Contrary Opinion

1. Figuring Out What the Crowd Thinks

The first step is to try and get a fix on the consensus opinion of the market or individual security being monitored. If the crowd is not at an extreme, nothing can be done because we are only concerned with identifying potential trend reversals when crowd psychology has swung sharply in one direction or another. Bear in mind that the crowd is often correct during a trend; it is at the turning point that the herd is almost always wrong. One method of gauging where the majority of market participants lie in their opinion is to refer to the sentiment indicators discussed in the previous chapter, or even an oscillator. Most often these indicators are not telling us very much, but when they reach an extreme, a strong message is being given. Another possibility is to monitor valuations. If they are within the accepted norm, there is little to be learned, but if they are approaching an extreme, the crowd is giving us a valuable clue as to the way it is leaning.

Alternatively, a study of the media, particularly the financial media, can inform us of what people are thinking. If there is no clear-cut view, there is not likely to be an extreme, and there is no action we can legitimately take.

However, as it becomes clear that a general consensus is forming, and that consensus is approaching a dogma, it is then time to begin the creative process by thinking in reverse, and that involves the second step.

2. Forming Alternative Scenarios

At this point we know what the crowd thinks, so it is up to us as true contrarians to come up with *plausible* reasons why it is likely to be wrong. In effect, we have to remove ourselves from the crowd and think in reverse. Such a process will involve an understanding of the market we are watching. For example, Chart 27-3 shows the gold market at its secular peak in 1980. At that time, gold had risen from obscurity, when it first started to rise in 1968, to being quoted regularly on the nightly news. It seemed to the majority at the end of 1979 that inflation and gold prices would continue to rise forever. However, a realistic contrarian would have realized that the inflation would breed its own deflation as the rising trend of short-term interest rates would cause an economic recession and the high price would attract more mining activity and superior technology that would more efficiently mine higher-cost lodes. Once again technical analysis can come to our rescue, as Chart 27-3 shows that the 12-month ROC for gold hit a

Chart 27-3   Gold, 1970–1999. (*From www.pring.com.*)

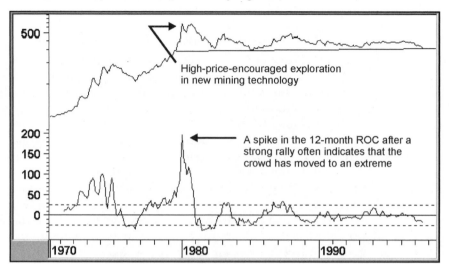

generational extreme. Silver also had a huge run-up in this period, from next to nothing to over $50. The talk was of a cornering of the market by Bunker Hunt and other operatives, so that the sky was the limit. In this instance the contrarian may have come up with the scenario that a lot of silver had already been mined and was available in the form of silverware, which could easily be melted down and sold as silver bullion. As it turned out the price was right, and the silver market was flooded, just at the time when high rates of interest caused margin liquidation in the silver pits.

Chart 27-4 shows bond yields and commodity prices. When yields are rising and it appears this trend will never end, an alternative scenario is to use the knowledge that peaks in yields are often preceded by peaks in commodity prices, which in turn precedes a slowdown in economic activity. This is shown in the chart by the rightward sloping arrows. Thus, if it is possible to spot a top in industrial commodity prices, the alternative scenario of weaker business activity may well come to pass.

3. Identifying When the Crowd Reaches an Extreme

When the crowd reaches an extreme, the question is not usually whether, but when and by how much? In other words, when the crowd truly reaches an extreme, it is a forgone conclusion that the trend will continue. It is not even questioned; only the *timing* and *amount* are in doubt. Such times are often asso-

Chart 27-4 Commodities and bond yields, 1970–1998. (*From www.pring.com.*)

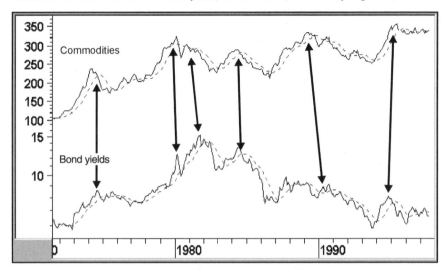

ciated with analysts making extreme forecasts that in the highly charged emotional atmosphere appear credible, but that would previously have been greeted with mirth or great doubt. The following represent some possibilities for identifying when the crowd is at an extreme.

Sentiment Indicators and Oscillators Sentiment indicators or long-term oscillators reaching an extreme represent one possibility for gauging that the crowd has as well.

The Media Sentiment indicators are not available for every market, so another useful exercise comes from a study of the popular and financial media. For most of the time, the media are silent on financial markets or individual stocks. It is when significant coverage appears that it is time to pay attention. Major peaks and troughs are often signaled by cover stories in the popular and financial press. *Time, Newsweek, BusinessWeek,* and *The Economist* are my particular favorites. The more these magazines give space to a particular market, the stronger the signal. It is not that the editors and writers of these magazines are idiots for publishing bear stories right at the low, or bullish ones close to the absolute high. It lies more in the fact that they are journalists keeping the pulse of market conditions. As good journalists, it is their duty to give more space to articles when the emotions in and around the floors of the exchanges come close to reaching a crescendo. Stories about quiet markets do not sell newspapers, but panic does. Generally speaking, cover stories are a fairly reliable indication of an impending turn, but they are not infallible and often lead turning points by a week or so. As with any form of analysis, it is important to use a good dose of common sense. For example, there is the famous "Birth of the Bull" cover story in *Time* magazine several weeks from the 1982 market bottom (see Chart 27-5). Just applying "contrary opinion" blindly would have led to the conclusion that the bull market was over in the course of a few weeks. However, it is important to remember that it takes time for crowds to reach an extreme, as the long trend of rising prices adds more careless bulls to the fold. Also, bear markets are usually preceded by rising interest rates. In the fall of 1982, the Fed was following an easy money policy, not a tight one.

The exact opposite was true in 1990 (see Chart 27-5) when a *BusinessWeek* cover featured the troubled brokerage industry. In this instance the prices of brokerage stocks had fallen sharply, but the Fed was engaged in an easy money policy, which is good for the equity market, and especially positive for brokers, who get more underwriting fees and commissions in a bull market. Moreover, the hard times they had just experienced would have resulted in a dramatic lowering of breakeven points. Increased revenue from the bull market would then go straight to the bottom line.

Chart 27-5 The S&P Composite and the discount rate, 1970–1999. (*From www.pring.com.*)

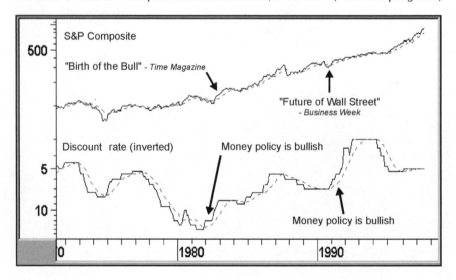

Another way in which the media can point to major turning points is when we can observe what I call a *misfit story*, where a heretofore invisible market is given the prominence it rarely if ever achieves. For example, the financial media are always featuring stories on the stock or bond markets. That is a normal state of affairs and is offering us no contrary bones. On the other hand, when we see a story in the popular press about an otherwise obscure market, we have something to gnaw on. For example, in 1980 the sugar price reversed from a long and strong bull market. Close to the day of the high the CBS Evening News led with a story on how traders were forecasting higher sugar prices. To my knowledge, sugar has never before or since been featured so prominently in the news. It was unusual and highly significant for the sugar market. Prominent stories in the U.S. press concerning specific foreign stock markets, currencies, and so on can also be valuable clues that these markets have reached an extreme.

Best-Selling Books Another area to monitor is that of best-selling non-fiction books. If a financial book appears on the list, it is usually a sign that that particular market has attracted the attention of the majority and that the good or bad news has been fully discounted. Thus, Ravi Batra's book on the coming depression became a bestseller just after the 1987 crash, a classic sign of a bottom. Adam Smith's *The Money Game* reached the same list just as the mutual fund boom was ending in late 1968. Perhaps the most unlikely of all was a book on money markets by William Donahue, just as short-term interest rates were making a secular peak in 1981.

Politicians A classic contrary indicator is the attitude of politicians, especially to bad news that is likely to adversely affect their election possibilities. Since they react to poll numbers and other trends in what we might term constituent psychology, *politicians are an excellent lagging indicator.* They are the last to take action, and when they do, the next trend has usually started. For instance, Gerry Ford, at the end of 1974, introduced the famous W(in)I(nflation)N(ow) buttons, but consumer price inflation had, for all intents and purposes, peaked for that cycle. I remember watching the network news in the fall of 1981, when the secular peaks of interest rates were occurring. The news was full of stories of congressmen returning to Washington "determined to do something about high interest rates." They had had earfuls of complaints from their constituents and were determined to do something about it. The problem was that the economy was already weakening and rates had peaked. When politicians promote price controls, you can be fairly certain that the specific commodity is in the process of peaking. When cries of corporate gouging arise because of high prices, this is also a sign of a top. Several case studies on the oil market bear this out.

Unrealistic Valuations　A final pointer that the crowd has reached an extreme arises when a particular market reaches a historic level of over- or undervaluation (progressively more *mispriced* in John Schultz's definition). For example, at the height of the Japanese real estate boom, it was reported that the real estate value of the Emperor's palace in Tokyo was worth as much as all the land in California. In *Psychology and the Stock Market*, David Dreman noted that during the 1920s real estate boom in Florida, it was reported that there were 25,000 brokers in Miami, an equivalent of one third of the population. This was not a valuation measure, but the statistic showed that things had clearly gotten out of hand. At one point during the 1990s tech boom, priceline.com, an online travel service, had a capitalization greater than the combined value of several of the airlines it represented. At its peak, the stock stood at around $160, but a year later it had fallen to just over $1.

Applying Technical Analysis

Since the crowd can and does move to an extreme, well beyond normal experience, being early can be particularly harmful to one's financial health. This is where the integration of technical analysis and the theory of contrary opinion can be quite helpful. Let us consider a couple of examples. The Japanese bull market of the 1980s represents a classic mania where price/earnings ratios and other valuation methods reached incredible extremes. The top had been called many times in the 1980s, but it never came. The crowd had clearly reached an extreme, but records continued to fall. In the end, the bubble was burst with the alternative scenario most likely to undo stock market bubbles: rising rates. Chart 27-6 shows that just after the 1990 top both the Nikkei and Japanese short rates crossed their 12-month MAs for the first time in many years. Both series also violated trendlines, thereby offering substantial technical evidence that the bubble had burst. Eleven years later, the Nikkei was still struggling at just over one-third of its 1990 high.

Chart 27-7 shows two *BusinessWeek* cover stories in 1982 and 1984 concerning the bond market. The fact that the bond market was featured so prominently after prices had fallen significantly was a sign that the crowd was at or close to an extreme. The next step was to appraise the technical position to see if there were any signs of a reversal. In the 1982 case, the 18-month ROC, in Chart 27-8, had already completed and broken out of a massive 4-year base. Later, the price broke out as well. This secondary breakout

Chart 27-6   The Nikkei and Japanese short-term rates, 1982–1997. (*From www.pring.com.*)

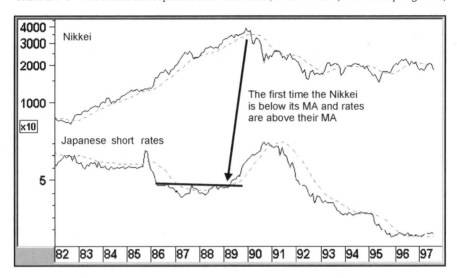

Chart 27-7   U.S. government bond prices 1977–1990, and an 18-Month ROC. (*From www.pring.com.*)

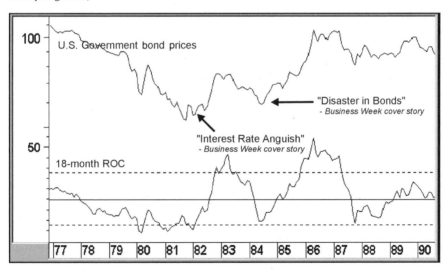

took place several months later, but it is important to remember that we are looking at the reversal of an extremely long trend and those sorts of things take time.

Chart 27-8   U.S. government bond prices 1977–1990, and an 18-Month ROC. (*From www.pring.com.*)

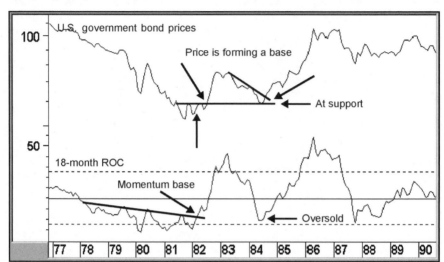

In 1984, the "Disaster in Bonds" cover story cumulated a 2-year decline. In this instance, the ROC was close to an extreme oversold condition and the price had reached support in the form of the extended trendline marking the previous breakout. The bear market trendline break was the triggering mechanism that indicated the crowd had now moved away from the bearish extreme and was now moving in the opposite direction. In both situations, the cover stories would have indicated that the bearish arguments were now well understood and discounted, and the trendline breaks the signals that it was time to play the contrary "card."

Distinguishing Between a Short- or Long-Term Turning Point

Before we close our discussion on contrary opinion, it is important to understand that the crowd can move to a smaller, less intense level of extreme. This type of sentiment is associated with a price reversal of a short- or intermediate-term nature. An example might be a 2 to 3 week run-up in the corn price, cumulating in a lead article in the commodities section in *The Wall Street Journal.* Such features are not uncommon; after all, some commodity is featured every day. The idea here is that when a commodity is written about, it usually comes after it has experienced a significant rally or reaction. The story develops because of excitement on the floor for that particular commodity and is reflective of the crowd reaching a short-term extreme. When confirmed by a technical indicator such as a 1- or 2-day price pattern, a trendline break, or a reliable MA crossover, this contrary position is usually well rewarded.

Another example might come from a recently released government employment report, which indicates that the economy is stronger than most traders expected. Because bond prices react unfavorably to good economic news, they could sell off sharply. Speculators now reverse sentiment from positive to a state of discouragement. Not only are bond prices declining, but rumors of a pickup in inflation cause prices to fall even further and sentiment to become even more bearish. The consensus mood amongst traders is now quite negative. The chances are, though, that this is only a small top. The alternative scenario in this case is to look through the gloom and examine the trend of employment and other economic numbers to see if the recent report was likely to be an aberration.

Summary

- During the unfolding of a trend, the crowd is usually right. It is at the turning points that it is wrong.
- Three prerequisites for justifying a contrary position are the original premise becomes a dogma, the premise loses its validity, and the market becomes progressively more mispriced.
- Three steps to forming a contrary opinion are figuring out what the crowd is thinking, coming up with alternative scenarios, and determining when the crowd reaches an extreme.
- It is difficult to go contrary in practice because of competing forces around us.
- When the crowd reaches an extreme the question is not whether, but when and how much?
- Signs that the crowd is at an extreme include cover stories, best-selling books, reactions by politicians, extremes in sentiment indicators, and gross over- or undervaluations.
- Because mass psychology can move well beyond the norm, technical analysis should be used as a triggering device for signaling when the crowd is backing off from a bullish or bearish extreme.
- Contrary opinion analysis should be used as one more indicator in the weight of the evidence approach.

28

Checkpoints for Identifying Primary Stock Market Peaks and Troughs

Primary bull market tops and bottoms are elusive affaires, largely because the points at which we expect them to develop are the ones that appear to be the most unlikely at the time. When most people are lucky enough to identify a bull market peak, they assume that prices will immediately decline. This is not normally the case because of the numerous and confusing crosscurrents necessary for the development of true distribution. This topping-out process usually requires a trading range environment, which reflects the tremendous battle between bulls and bears. First one comes out on top and then the other. By the time the distribution has been completed, both sides are exhausted. Even though the bears eventually win, most lose their original conviction because of the numerous false rallies that they did not anticipate. These rallies develop under an environment of extreme optimism, which also make them all the more convincing to those caught short or who have already sold out.

We know that the news is good at market peaks, but when a typical top is staring us in the face, the widespread contagion of optimism deludes market participants to expect conditions to get even better. The opposite is true of bottoms: The news is bad, but we expect it to get worse before prices hit their low. Alternatively, we expect the other shoe to drop, just like traumatized earthquake victims anticipating a killer aftershock.

The Mechanics of a Peak

Typical market peaks, and we need to use the word "typical" very carefully, should involve a battle between early- and late-cycle leaders. As the top begins, liquidity-driven issues peak out and begin their bear market (see Fig. 28-1). On the other hand, late-cycle leaders are still in the terminal stages of a bull market and are helping to push the averages higher. If strength in the earnings-driven sectors outweighs weakness elsewhere, the averages move to new bull market highs. This is the principal reason why breadth divergences are so prevalent at market peaks. In 1973, the commodity boom had the effect of prolonging the bull market, as far as the averages were concerned, but the NYSE A/D line had peaked 9 months earlier. In 2000, it was the unprecedented strength in technology stocks, another lagging sector, that propelled the averages higher, but under the surface the average stock peaked 2 years earlier in 1998.

What Is a Peak?

The objective of this chapter is to offer a checklist of characteristics present at a typical market top or bottom. In reality, there are no "typical" turning

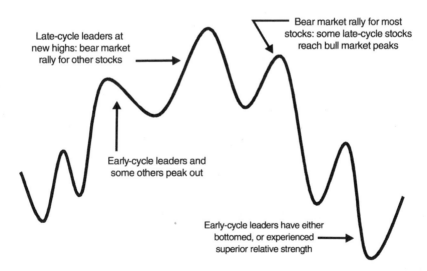

Figure 28-1 Sector rotation in the cycle.

points because no two situations are exactly the same. However, there are enough characteristics to enable us to identify the intricate tapestry of a market top or bottom.

There are really three types of market peak. The most important are those that develop after a prolonged bull market, extending over several business cycles. Around the time of the peak, it is possible to point to some kind of speculative bubble, often concentrated in a few sectors. At such times old rules are thrown out and virtually everyone becomes an overnight investment genius. Such peaks are very hard to pinpoint at the time because they have defied virtually every traditional rule. Eventually, new rules or rationalizations are developed to justify the final ascent to the equity summit. In this way traditional valuations are surpassed by several degrees. Normal extreme technical benchmarks are also exceeded, and divergences are so plentiful that they are ignored because they no longer work. Finally, contrarian positions based on observation of normal crowd behavior prove futile, as the majority march on to new extremes of irrationality. Old rules are thrust aside and ridiculed as new-era thinking predominates. The rallying cry of the bulls is almost always inculcated in the mantra that "this time it is different." In all cases, the leveling factor that brought investors back to reality was a good dose of rising short-term interest rates. Two such peaks possessing at least some of these characteristics developed in 1929 and 1966. The 1990 peak in Japanese equities also qualifies. In 1929, stocks lost close to 90 percent of their value in 3 years. The bear market that followed the 1966 peak lasted a lot longer and consisted of several minibull and minibear markets. When stocks are adjusted for inflation, the bottom, as measured by the major averages, did not take place until 16 years later in 1982. The top established in 2000, at least as far as technology stocks are concerned, could turn out to be one of similar importance to the 1929 and 1966 experiences, since many of the valuation, sentiment, and technical characteristics cited previously were present.

There are really two factors that cause the ensuing bear market to be so devastating or lengthy. The first is a direct result of the long and persistent bull trend and falls under the title "careless investment decisions." It is the function of the bear to cleanse the system of these poorly thought-out and precariously financed positions. Such is true of every market peak. It is just far more prevalent at these supercycle turning points. Second, it appears that the pendulum of human emotions, the ultimate arbitrator of prices, moves to an extreme of extremes. If such a level is reached on one side, an extreme of an extreme is likely to develop on the other. It almost appears as if a prerequisite for a huge bear market is a huge speculative bull market. These enormous changes in sentiment either come relatively quickly as prices are dramatically cut or take many years as the bulls, exhausted, finally give up.

The second level of peak is what we might term a *recession-associated top* (RAT). It is the most common and best fits the primary trend description described in Chapter 1. In such situations, the unwinding of distortions in the economy brought about by the recovery are sufficient to trigger an actual recession where profits in general are under attack. In each cycle, the sector responsible for the distortion will be different. In the early 1970s, it tended to be real estate; in 1974, bloated inventories from the commodity boom were the primary culprit. In 1990, the financial sector was under pressure, and so forth. Since these RAT-type bear markets are associated with economic contraction and recovery, which tend to take time to accomplish, they usually last 1 to 2 years, are broadly based and can be quite sharp.

The third kind of peak precedes so-called growth recessions or double-cycle peaks as described in Chapter 2. They are usually followed by shallower and shorter bear trends. Growth recessions involve the slowing down of the economy but not an actual contraction. In this process, several industrial sectors will experience recessionary conditions, but strength elsewhere will offset this weak activity so that the overall economy escapes the indignity of the "R" word. These weak sectors, therefore, experience a true 1- to 2-year bear market, whereas others merely experience a major trading range.

Examples of double-cycle bears are 1984 and 1994. Other bear trends are associated with a slowing in some of the economic indicators and are preceded by an unhealthy level of speculation. They take the form of severe technical corrections, but are so dramatic that the change in psychology is sufficient to correct much of the speculative juice. The 1962 and 1987 declines come to mind as good examples.

All the characteristics listed in the following section do not appear at every market peak, and neither is their intensity of the same magnitude. They are presented solely as a guide for things to watch out for at major highs.

Characteristics of Primary Market Peaks

1. In order for a bull market top to form, it must be preceded by a bull market. Thus, it must be possible to look back and identify a rally of at least 9 months' duration.

Monetary and Sector Rotation Factors

2. Almost all market peaks are preceded by a trend in rising short-term interest rates. The lead times vary from a couple of months to many years. If interest rates have not begun their ascent, the odds of a top are greatly reduced. For examples, refer to Charts 25-1(*a*) and (*b*) in Chapter 25.

3. Watch out for hikes in the discount rate. Has the three-step-and-stumble rule, discussed in Chapter 25, been triggered? If so, the distribution process may well be under way, and the reward of owning stocks is now usually outweighed by the risk.

4. In many instances, market tops are preceded by a peak in the DJ Utility Average. This is because this is a very interest-rate-sensitive market sector.

5. Observation of the long-term relative momentum for a selection of early- and late-cycle leaders often points up a bull market peak. This will be true if the long-term smoothed relative momentum for financials, utilities, and consumer nondurables peaked out some time ago. By the same token, a characteristic of a market peak is either continued strength in late-cycle leaders, such as basic industry and resource stocks, or an actual peaking of their smoothed momentum.

Technical Factors

6. When interest rates start to rise, this adversely affects financials and preferreds. Consequently, it is normal for the NYSE A/D line to peak out ahead of the DJIA and S&P Composite. The length of the divergence often has a related effect on the size of the ensuing bear market.

7. If the NYSE daily A/D line and or the Value Line Arithmetic Index are below their 200-day MAs, this indicates that the broad market is probably in a bear market. Even if the DJIA and S&P Composite are at new highs, this weak breadth position is telling us that the market has become very selective. Under such an environment, it is more difficult to find stocks that are advancing. Cutting back on equity exposure, therefore, makes excellent sense because your odds of success are less. The opposite would be true in a declining market, but where the A/D line is advancing.

8. An alternative way of looking at the technical position of market breadth is net new high data. Has the number of net new highs diverged negatively with the major averages? If it has not, this may not be a top. If they

it has, then fewer stocks are driving the market higher, and this is a sign of weakness. If the number of new highs has shrunk considerably, it means that it is very difficult to make money because the selection process is becoming progressively more difficult.

9. Momentum typically leads price, especially at market tops. Occasionally, it is possible to identify multiyear tops or trendline violations in several long-term ROC indicators. For example, if you can spot trendline breaks in the 12-, 18-, and 24-month ROCs, this indicates that the cycles they reflect are all starting to turn. Sometimes an individual ROC moves between specific benchmarks, and these have traditionally offered good timing points for major tops or bottoms. In Chapter 18 Charts 18-5(*a*) and (*b*) offer some useful benchmarks for a 9-month ROC of the S&P Composite.

10. Another way in which momentum can signal a maturing bull trend is with the use of a long-term smoothed oscillator such as the KST. Market tops are typically signaled by the indicator reversing to the downside from an overbought condition. This is represented in Chart 28-1 by the vertical lines, where the KST crosses below its 9-month MA. The chart shows that this approach works well when a normal cyclical bull market is experienced. However, during a secular bull market, such as that which developed in the 1990s, this indicator will give premature sell signals. All the more reason to make sure that such signals are confirmed by a trend break in the price. Alternatively, short-term oscillators may be registering mega-oversold or extreme swing conditions.

11. If the DJIA and the S&P Composite have just crossed below their 12-month MAs, there is a good chance that a bear market is under way, provided, of course, that other indicators are in agreement. Quite often a negative 7-month MA crossover will work as well as a 12-month time span. Also, in the trend-reversal department, monitor the current position of the Industrials and Transports as called for in Dow theory.

Psychological Factors

12. If key companies report excellent earnings and the stocks decline, this adverse response to good news indicates extreme technical weakness. Whenever a stock or market index fails to respond to good news, this is a sign of technical weakness. Remember, if good news cannot send a security higher, what will?

Chart 28-1 The S&P Composite, 1950–2001, and a long-term KST. (*From www.pring.com.*)

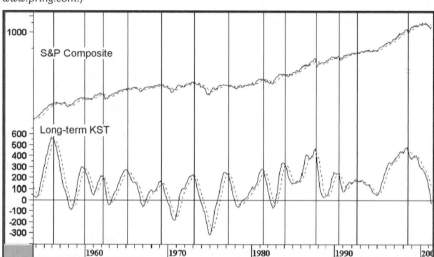

13. On the sentiment side, a reading in the *Investor's Intelligence* percentage of bears would be in the 10-20% range. Also, a public short ratio in excess of 52 and a 5-week insiders buy/sell ratio of 70 offer a flag of a market top, especially if the insiders have already diverged negatively with the price. Finally, in the sentiment area, if the level of margin debt has recently crossed below its 12-month EMA, this tells us two things. First, it indicates that traders are losing confidence. Second, it indicates that an expansion in margin debt will no longer support higher prices, but its contraction will put downward pressure on stock prices. A 12-month downward EMA cross is usually an excellent long-term sell signal.

14. If the media are full of optimistic news and stories of huge returns are being publicized, this is the type of atmosphere associated with a top. Additional signs might be cover stories on the market itself, especially ones citing a new paradigm, or concerning companies or groups that have been leaders in the bull market.

15. As the market is rallying, there is always a substantial amount of doubt. However, as equities approach a peak, the question of whether stocks are a good investment is not even debated. Instead, the debate revolves around which sectors will do well or how high the market will go. In

such an environment, forecasts that would previously have been ridiculed for their excessive optimism are given widespread publicity and credibility.[1]

16. Since brokerage companies thrive on bull markets, they become very prosperous. If you see reports of any of these companies moving into larger and more expensive office accommodations, this is often a sign that the uptrend is in a very mature stage. Alternatively, this could show up in the exchange or the back office of brokers being overwhelmed with backlogged orders.

Chronological and Cycle Factors

17. A quick review of the three markets in relation to their 12-month MAs will offer a quick reference for the current stage of the cycle. A market top should see the 3-month commercial paper yield above its 12-month MA. The three-step-and-stumble rule (Chapter 25) will probably have been triggered as well. Bond yields in the corporate and governmental sectors should be in a similar position. The S&P Composite should be above its average, and the CRB Spot Raw Industrials should be above its average as well. In cases where stocks have fallen quite some way from their peak, it is possible that the S&P would already be below its 12-month MA. If the CRB Spot RM Index has also recently crossed below its average, then little support from commodity-based equities is likely, and at the tail end of the cycle, this usually means a bear market.

18. Since the 4-year stock cycle has been extremely reliable by offering a buying opportunity once every 4 years, it follows that if the current year is 2 or 3 years from the previous 4-year low, the odds favor a bull market peak. If some of the other signs discussed here are present, this will obviously increase the probability of a top.

19. Is it possible to observe three identifiable intermediate advances that have already taken place? If this is the top of the third, it may be a primary peak. This is by no means infallible, because some bull markets consist of two advances and some more than three. However, when combined with others, these signs can be quite a useful benchmark.

---

[1]For one of the best discussion centers on the Web for automated systems and system designing software, go to wealth-lab.com.

Primary Market Bottoms

Bear market bottoms develop under exactly the opposite conditions as tops. The news is bad, sentiment is extremely bearish, and the long-term momentum indicators are usually extremely oversold. Perhaps the key difference between a major low and a major high is that in almost all cases, bear markets are shorter than bull markets. We have to say in almost all cases because the 1929–1932 bear market lasted for 3 long years, whereas the average primary decline has mercifully been much shorter. Characteristics of a major low are as follows.

Monetary and Sector Rotation Factors

1. Almost all bear market lows are preceded by a peak in short-term interest rates. I say "short-term rates," but in almost all cases, a peak in long-term rates also precedes an equity low. It is just that changes in the level of short-term rates have a much larger influence on equities than yields at the long end. The lead time varies from cycle to cycle, but generally speaking, the longer the lead, the greater the ensuing bull market. In 1966, for instance, interest rates and equity prices reversed almost simultaneously, whereas the lead was almost a year in 1920 and 1982. The 1967–1968 bull market was tame in comparison to the bull markets of the 1920s and 1980s. This is not the same thing as saying that every time the lead is a year or more the market will experience a mega-rally, merely that there is a rough tendency for that to be the case.

2. The industry group structure at market bottoms should reveal an improving trend of relative strength and relative smoothed long-term momentum favoring early-cycle leaders, such as utilities, most financials, and most consumer nondurables. At the same time there should be a pattern of deteriorating relative strength and relative smooth momentum in several lagging groups, such as resources, basic industry, and technology. Quite often when the long-term smoothed relative momentum of the S&P Financial Index bottoms, this is quite close to a market bottom. The weakness in earnings-driven stocks is used more as a confirmation.

Technical Factors

3. Positive divergences between the A/D line and the major averages are much rarer than negative ones at market tops. Indeed, the line often

lags at most bear market lows. However, when divergences do develop, they are usually followed by an above-average bull market. That was true of the divergence between the (Bolton) weekly A/D lines at the 1942 and 1982 lows (see Charts 24-1 and 24-2).

4. Net new highs also rarely diverge with the averages, but on a 6-week MA basis, this was the case again in 1982 and on a 5-day basis at the 1974 bottom.

5. Other confirming signs would be record volume coming off the low, as in 1978, 1982, and 1984. Also, most bottoms involve a rally and subsequent test of the low. When the second rally surpasses the first, a series of rising peaks and troughs is signaled. This approach was one of the few in the 1929–1932 bear market that had not previously experienced a whipsaw. It is generally a reliable signal, especially when combined with Dow theory buy signals. Another confirming but *extremely important* signal is the ability of the S&P Composite to rally above its 12-month MA.

6. In extended bear markets, the final low is usually confirmed by a bottoming in smoothed long-term momentum. In this instance, the Coppock Index, described in Chapter 10 and featured in Chart 10-8, is probably the most reliable, as it appears to work with amazing reliability on a number of different markets. During shallow bear markets not associated with recessions, smoothed long-term momentum can often prove to be agonizingly slow. Long-term ROCs will occasionally prove to be better substitutes when it is possible to observe momentum price pattern breakouts or upside penetrations of down trendlines.

7. If short-term oscillators are signaling mega-overbought or extreme swing conditions, as described in Chapter 10, this is also a sign that psychology has changed for the better.

Economic Factors

8. Normally, it is a prerequisite of a bottom for the economic news to be at or close to its worst. Charts 28-2(*a*) and 28-2(*b*) show that the 9-month trend deviation indicator for the coincident indicators is usually negative and close to its low at the time of a stock market bottom. Note that the major exceptions, flagged by the dashed arrows, develop during double-cycle lows such as 1984 and 1994. This is not surprising since these were not classic bear markets.

Chart 28-2(a) The S&P Composite, 1956–1980, and the coincident indicator (deviation from trend.) (*From www.pring.com.*)

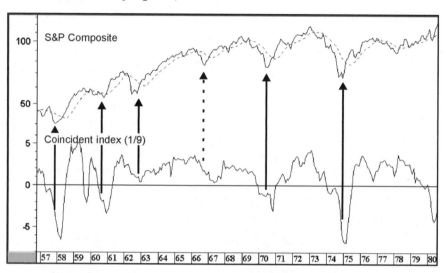

Chart 28-2(b) The S&P Composite, 1978–2000, and the coincident indicator (deviation from trend.) (*From www.pring.com.*)

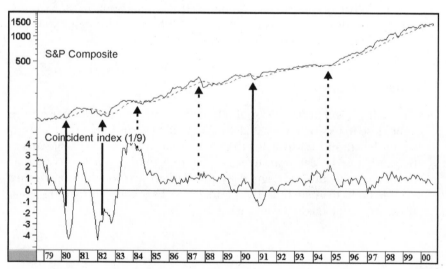

Chronological and Cyclical Factors

9. In terms of the financial market chronological sequence, it is normal for a stock market bottom to be preceded by the 3-month commercial paper yield crossing below its 12-month MA. At the actual bottom, the S&P will be below its 12-month MA, but so too will the CRB Spot Raw Material Index. If the yield and Commodity Index are below their average and the S&P is above its, then the S&P crossover confirms that a bottom is in place, and the markets are in the correct sequence for a Stage II, as described in Chapter 2.

10. Is it possible to observe three discernable intermediate declines during recession-associated bear markets? This is by no means infallible, but often a good sign.

11. Does the market meet most of the characteristics cited previously in a year in which the 4-year stock market cycle is due to bottom? If so, the odds of a major bottom are greatly increased. If the year ends in the number 4, this is also a positive sign since years ending in a 5 are the most bullish of the decade. Hence, 1954, 1974, 1984, and 1994 were major bottoms (the first bottom developed at the end of 1953), all of which were followed by 5 strong years. With the exception of 1984, all were also 4-year cycle lows.

Psychological Fctors

12. Sentiment is typically very bearish at a major bottom. This can show up in extreme readings in advisory sentiment, public short ratios, or the put/call ratio reversing from its overbought level.

13. Sentiment is also reflected in the media, and here cover stories are a great place to build a contrary case. Occasionally, brokers use the buying opportunity derived from the bear market as the basis for an ad campaign. Such ads do not necessarily indicate the wisdom of brokerage houses, although they are certainly courageous for taking a bullish stance. Rather, it is a recognition of the fact that the decline in equity prices has caught the attention of the public. Remember, when everyone thinks alike, it is time to expect a market turn.

14. How does the market respond to bad news? During the decline, it would be normal for it to sell off on bad news, such as an unexpectedly poor earnings report, huge layoffs, a major bankruptcy, and so on. However, if it starts to shrug off such news and actually rises, the psychology has probably changed.

Summary

If it were necessary to summarize these characteristics for peaks and troughs into a few vital points, they would probably be as follows:

- Crowd psychology has moved to a measurable extreme.
- Interest rates have already reversed their trend.
- Long-term momentum is at an extreme or has already reversed from one.
- The technical position of leading versus lagging groups is consistent with the direction of the turning point in question.
- These conditions have been confirmed with the completion of a price pattern and the penetration of a long-term MA, for example, 12-month, 200-day, and so on.

29
Automated Trading Systems

In recent years, there has been a substantial increase in the use of personal computers for the purposes of technical analysis. Not surprisingly, this has encouraged many traders and investors to use their own mechanical, or automated, trading systems. These systems can be very helpful as long as they are not adopted as a substitute for judgment and thinking. Throughout this book I have emphasized that technical analysis is an art, the art of interpreting a number of different and reliable, scientifically derived indicators.

I believe that mechanical trading systems should be used in one of two ways. The preferred method is to incorporate a well thought-out mechanical trading system to alert the trader or investor that a trend reversal has probably taken place. In this method the mechanical trading system is an important filter, but represents just one more indicator in the overall decision-making process.

The other way in which a mechanical trading system can be used is to take action on *every* signal. If the system is well thought out, it should generate profits over the long term. However, if you pick and choose which signal to follow without other independently based technical criteria, you run the risk of making emotional decisions, thereby losing the principal benefit of the mechanical approach.

Unfortunately, most mechanical trading systems are based on historical data and are constructed from a more or less perfect fit with past, in the expectation that history will be repeated in the future. This expectation will not necessarily be fulfilled, because market conditions change. A well thought-out and designed mechanical system, however, should do the job reasonably well. In this respect, it is better to design a system that gives a less-than-perfect fit, but more accurately reflects normal market conditions.

Remember that you are interested in future profits, not perfect historical simulations. If special rules have to be invented to improve results, the chances are that the system will not operate successfully when extrapolated to future market conditions.

Advantages of Mechanical Systems

One of the great difficulties of putting theory into practice is that a new factor, emotion, enters the scene as soon as money is committed to the market. The following advantages therefore assume that the investor or trader will follow the buy and sell signals consistently:

- A major advantage of a mechanical system is that it automatically decides when to take action; this has the effect of removing emotion and prejudice. The news may be atrocious, but when the system moves into a positive mode, a purchase is automatically made. In a similar vein, when it appears that nothing can stop the market from going through the floor, the system will override all possible emotions and biases and quietly take you out.
- Most traders and investors lose in the marketplace because they lack discipline. Mechanical trading requires only one aspect of discipline: the commitment to follow the system.
- A well-defined mechanical system will give greater consistency of profits than a system in which buying and selling decisions are left to the individual.
- A mechanical system will let profits run in the event that there is a strong uptrend, but will automatically limit losses if a whipsaw signal occurs.
- A well-designed model will enable the trader or investor to participate in the direction of every important trend.

Disadvantages of Mechanical Systems

- No system will work all the time, and there may well be long periods when it will fail to work.
- Using past data to predict the future isn't necessarily a valid approach because the character of the market often changes.
- Most people try to get the best or optimum fit when devising a system, but experience and research tell us that a historical best fit doesn't usually translate into the future.

- Random events can easily jeopardize a badly conceived system. A classic example occurred in Hong Kong during the 1987 crash, when the market was closed for 7 days. There would have been no opportunity to get out, even if a sell signal had been triggered. True, this was an unusual event, but it's surprising how often special situations upset the best rules.
- Most successful mechanical systems are trend following by nature. However, there are often extended periods during which markets are in a nontrending mode, which renders the system unprofitable.
- "Back-testing" won't necessarily simulate what actually would have happened. It is not always possible to get an execution at the price indicated by the system, because of illiquidity, failure of your broker to execute orders on time, and so forth.

Design of a Successful System

A well-designed system should try to capitalize on the advantages of the mechanical approach, but should also be designed to overcome some of the pitfalls and disadvantages discussed. In this respect there are eight important rules that should be followed:

- Back-test over a sufficiently long period with several markets or stocks. The more data that can be tested, the more reliable the future results are likely to be.
- Evaluate performance by extrapolating the results over an earlier period. In this case, the first step would involve the design of a system based on data for a specific time span, such as 1977 to 1985 for the bond market. The next step would be to test the results from 1985 to 1990 to see whether or not your approach would have worked in the subsequent period. In this way, rather than "flying blindly" into the future, the system is given a simulated but thorough testing using actual market data.
- Define the system precisely. This is important for two reasons. First, if the rules occasionally leave you in doubt about their correct interpretation, some degree of subjectivity will permeate the approach. Second, for every buy signal there should be a sell signal, and vice versa. If a system has been devised using an overbought crossover as a sell and an oversold crossover as a buy, it might work quite well for a time. An example is shown in Fig. 29-1(a). On the other hand, there could be long periods during which a countervailing signal is not generated, simply because the indicator does not move to these extremes. Failure to define the system precisely can therefore result in significant losses, as shown in Fig. 29-1(b).

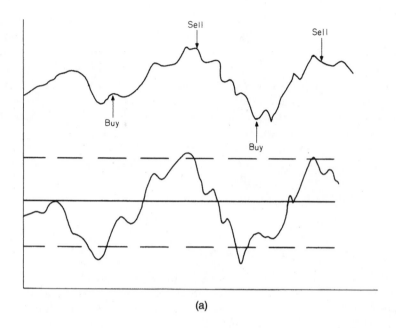

(a)

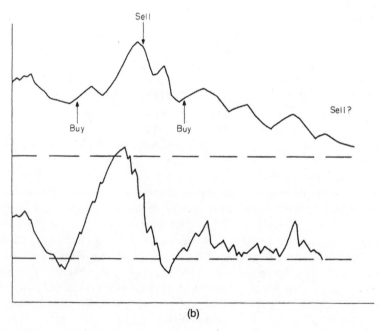

(b)

Figure 29-1 Overbought/oversold crossovers.

- Make sure that you have enough capital to survive the worst losing streak. When you are devising a system, it is always a good idea to assume the worst possible scenario and to make sure that you start off with enough capital to survive such a period. In this respect, it is worth noting that the most profitable moves usually occur after a prolonged period of whip-sawing.
- Follow every signal without question. If you have confidence in your system, do not second-guess it. Otherwise, unnecessary emotion and undisciplined action will creep back into the decision-making process.
- Use a diversified portfolio. Risks are limited if you place your bets over a number of different markets. If a specific market performs far worse than it ever has in the past, the overall results will not be catastrophic.
- Trade only markets that show good trending characteristics. Chart 29-1 shows the lumber market between 1985 and 1989. During this period the price fluctuated in a volatile, almost haphazard fashion and clearly would not have lent itself to a mechanical trend-following system. On the other hand, the Commodity Research Bureau (CRB) Spot Raw Industrial

Chart 29-1   Lumber, 1985–1989, CRB weekly charts.

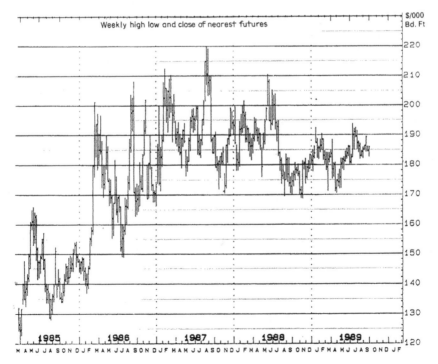

Materials Index (shown in Chart 29-2), although it is subject to the odd confusing trading range, has by and large moved in consistent trends.

- Keep it simple. It is always possible to invent special rules to make back-testing more profitable. Overcome this temptation. Keep the rules simple, few in number, and logical. The results are more likely to be profitable in the future, when profitability counts.

Trading Range and Trending Markets

There are basically two types of market conditions: trending and trading range. A trending market, as shown in Figure 29-2, is clearly suitable for moving average (MA) crossovers and other types of trend-following systems. In this kind of situation, it is very important to define the risk since an MA is a trade-off between volatility and sensitivity. In Figure 29-2, the maximum distance between the short-term MA, shown as the dashed line, and the series, shown as the solid line, is the maximum risk. Unfortunately, the short-term

Chart 29-2   CRB Spot Raw Industrial Materials Index, 1985–1989, and CRB weekly charts.

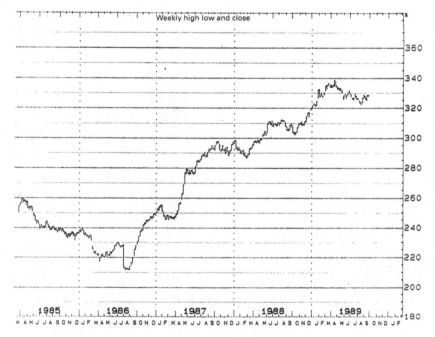

MA whips around and gives several false signals. Although the risk of the individual trade defined by the crossover of this MA is small, the chances of unprofitable signals are much greater. On the other hand, a longer-term MA, shown by the X's, offers larger maximum risk but fewer whipsaws.

MAs, as shown in Figure 29-3, are virtually useless in a trading range market since they move right through the middle of the price fluctuations, and almost always result in unprofitable signals. Oscillators, on the other hand, come into their own in a trading range market. They are continually moving from overbought to oversold extremes, which trigger timely buy and sell signals. During a persistent uptrend or downtrend, the oscillator is of relatively little use because it gives premature buy and sell signals, often taking the trader out at the beginning of a major move. The ideal automated system therefore should include a combination of an oscillator and a trend-following indicator.

The risk and reward for oscillator-type signals generated from overbought and oversold extremes are shown in diagrammatic form in Figure 29-4. The number of potential trading opportunities is represented on the horizontal axis and the risk on the vertical axis. There are very few times when an oscillator is extremely overbought or extremely oversold, but these are the occasions when the profit per trade is at its greatest and the risk the smallest. Moderately overbought conditions are much more plentiful, but the profits are lower and the risk higher. Taken to the final extreme, slightly overbought or oversold conditions are extremely plentiful, but the risk per

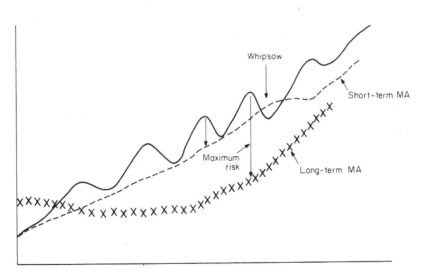

Figure 29-2 Trade-off between timeliness and sensitivity.

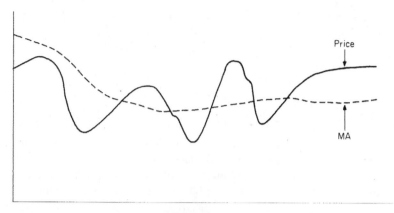

Figure 29-3 MA crossovers in trendless markets.

trade is much higher, and profits are significantly lower. Ideally, a mechanical trading system should be designed to take advantage of a situation in which profits per trade are high and risk is low. Execution of a good system therefore requires some degree of patience because these types of opportunities are limited.

Turning points in price trends are often preceded by a divergence in the oscillator, so it is a good idea to combine signals from extreme oscillator readings with some kind of MA crossover. This won't result in a perfect indicator, but it might help to filter out some of the whipsaws.

Guidelines for Appraising Results

When the simulated results of a mechanical system are being reviewed, there is a natural tendency to look at the bottom line to see which system would have generated the most profits. However, top results do not always indicate the best system. There reasons for this are as follows:

• It is possible that most, or all, of the profit was generated by one signal. If so, this would place lower odds on the system's generating good profits in the future since it would lack consistency. An example of an inconsistent system is shown in Table 29-1, which represents signals generated by a 10-day MA crossover of an oscillator that was constructed by dividing a 30-day MA by a 40-day MA (a form of moving average convergence divergence, or MACD). The market being monitored was Hong Kong during the 1987–1988 period. The system would have gained nearly 1200 points,

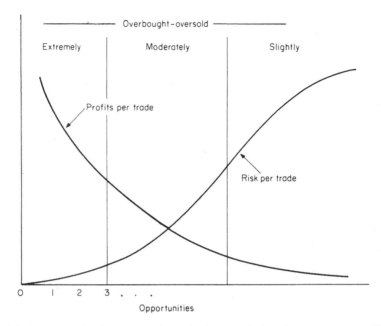

Figure 29-4 Relationship between profits and risk per trade, based on opportunities. (*From Perry Kaufman,* New Commodity Trading Systems, *John Wiley and Sons, Inc., New York, 1987.*)

compared to a buy-hold approach, which would have lost 800 points. However, this excellent gain would have actually resulted in a loss had it not been for the fact that a prescient short sell signal occurred just before the 1987 crash.

- Another consideration involves the identification of the worst string of losses (the largest drawdown). After all, it is no good having a system that generates a large profit over the long term if you don't have sufficient capital to ride out the worst period. There are two things to look for in this respect: the string of losing signals and the maximum amount lost during these adverse periods.
- A system that generates huge profits but requires a significant number of trades is less likely to be successful in the real world than is a system based on a moderate number of trades. This is true because the more trades that are executed, the greater the potential for slippage through illiquidity and so on. More transactions also require more time and involve greater commission costs and so forth.

Table 29-1 Hang Seng 3-Month Perpetual 30/40 Oscillator Performance, 1987–1988

| | | | Profit or loss | | | | |
| | | | Current trade | | Cumulative | | |
Date	Trade	Price	Points	Percent	Points	Percent	Dollars
08/19/87	Sell	3559.900	0.000	0.000	0.000	0.000	0.000
09/30/87	Buy	3843.900	−284.000	−7.978	−284.000	−7.978	−79.78
09/09/87	Sell	3696.900	−147.000	−3.824	−431.000	−11.802	−114.97
09/25/87	Buy	3918.900	−222.000	−6.005	−653.000	−17.807	−168.12
10/14/87	Sell	3999.000	80.100	2.044	−572.900	−15.763	−151.11
12/15/87	Buy	2099.900	1899.100	47.489	1326.200	31.726	252.02
02/04/88	Sell	2269.900	170.000	8.096	1496.200	39.822	353.38
02/22/88	Buy	2374.900	−105.000	−4.626	1391.200	35.196	290.77
03/28/88	Sell	2459.900	85.000	3.579	1476.200	38.775	336.97
04/08/88	Buy	2639.900	−180.000	−7.317	1296.200	31.458	239.14
04/19/88	Sell	2584.900	−55.000	−2.083	1241.200	29.374	213.32
06/06/88	Buy	2612.900	−28.000	−1.083	1213.200	28.291	200.18
07/05/88	Sell	2702.900	90.000	3.444	1303.200	31.736	241.52
07/06/88	Buy	2774.900	−72.000	−2.664	1231.200	29.072	208.45
07/18/88	Sell	2722.900	−52.000	−1.874	1179.200	27.198	185.80

Total long trades	7	
Profitable longs	4 (57.1%)	
Total buy stops	0	
Biggest gain	1899.100	
Successive gains	3	
Total gain or loss	$1179.200	

Total short trades	7
Profitable shorts	1 (14.3%)
Total sell stops	0
Biggest loss	−284.000
Successive losses	3
Average gain or loss	84.229
Total gain or loss	18.58%

Source: *Pring Market Review*/MetaStock.

The Best Signals Go
with the Trend

In virtually every situation the best signals invariably occur in the direction of the main trend. It is easy to pick out the direction of the primary trend in hindsight, of course, but in the real world we have to use some kind of objective approach to determine the direction of the main trend.

One idea might be to calculate a 12-month MA and to use the position of the price relative to the average as a basis for determining the primary trend. The trading system would be based on daily and weekly data and would be acted upon on the long side only when the index was above the average; short signals would be instigated when it was below.

There are two drawbacks to this approach. First, the market itself may be in a long-term trading range in which MA crossovers do not correctly identify the main trend. Second, the first bear market rally quite often occurs while the price is above its 12-month MA. In effect, the buy signal associated with that rally would be operating against the main trend. By and large, though, most markets trend, and this approach will filter out a lot of the countercyclical moves.

An alternative is to use a long-term momentum series, such as the monthly know sure thing (KST), calculated along the lines discussed in Chapter 12. When the KST is rising and the price is above its 12-month MA, a bull market environment is indicated, and all trades would be made from the long side. When the KST is falling and the price is above its 12-month MA, the chances are that the primary trend is in the process of peaking; no positions would be instigated. If you already had some exposure, the topping-out action of the KST would indicate that some profits should be taken, but total liquidation of the position would probably be better achieved at the time of a negative MA crossover. A trade would be activated only when the KST and the price, vis-à-vis its MA, were in a consistent mode. For example, when the KST peaks out and the market itself falls below its 12-month MA, a bear market environment is indicated and only trades on the short side should be initiated. If you do not have access to the KST the MACD, using an 18/20/9 combination on monthly data, is a close substitute.

A Simple Technique Combining
an Oscillator with an MA

A technique that enables investors to take advantage of both trending and trading range markets is to combine an MA and an oscillator in such a way that buy signals are triggered when the oscillator has fallen to a predetermined oversold level and the price itself subsequently crosses above an MA. The position is liquidated if the price crosses below the MA. On the other hand, if the oscillator crosses to an overbought level prior to an MA crossover, part of the position will be sold in recognition of the possibility that the market might be experiencing a trading range. The other part of the position will continue to ride until an MA sell signal is triggered.

This approach will make it possible to capitalize on the potential of a trending market, but some profits will be taken in case subsequent market action turns out to be part of a volatile trading range.

Recognizing that oscillators often diverge at important market turning points, an alternative might be to wait for the oscillator to move to an extreme for a second time before buying on an MA crossover. The same rules as previously described would be used for selling.

Marketplace Example

Now it is time to take an actual example of a system by combining these two techniques. The security I chose is a continuous contract for U.S. T-bonds, an MA, and a price oscillator, as shown in Chart 29-3. A price oscillator is calculated by dividing a short-term MA by a longer-term one. In this case, I used a one-period MA, that is, the close as the shorter average and the 10-day simple MA as the longer-term one. The 10-day average is plotted in the upper panel with the oscillator underneath.

Chart 29-3 shows the way the system works. It is really very simple: Buy when the price crosses above a MA (as it does in late July at point *A*). Then sell either when it crosses below the average or when the price oscillator reaches a specific predetermined level. The oscillator reaches the designated overbought level a few days later (*B*). In this case, I selected the + and −2 percent. This means the overbought and oversold lines are the equivalent of the price being 2 percent above and below the 10-day MA. Then, in early August, the price crosses below the average and this initiates a short signal (*C*). The position is covered at the end of the month fairly close to the actual low as the oscillator touches its oversold zone (*D*). The next buy signal comes on a MA crossover in early September (*E*). The oscillator never has a chance to move to the +2% level because the MA crossover comes first. The next short signal is a whipsaw, followed by the final buy that resulted in a small profit (*F*).

I optimized (optimization is the systematic search for the best indicator formula) this system by using one variable for the MA and the oscillator, and another for each of the overbought and oversold conditions. The best overall returns were given by the 26/2/−4 combination, as you can see in Table 29-2. This was not the one I finally chose, because I like to see identical levels for the overbought and oversold triggering points. The rationale for this

Chart 29-3 Treasury bonds and a 1/10 price oscillator. (*From Martin Pring*, Breaking the Black Box, *McGraw-Hill, New York, 2002.*)

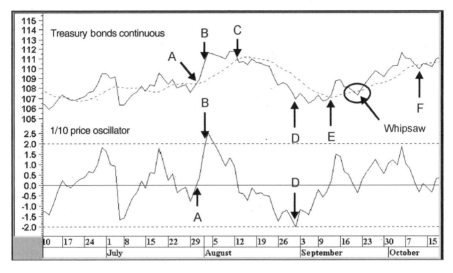

Table 29-2 Treasury Bonds

| | | U.S. Treasury Bonds 200003 Continuous | | | | | | |
Profit	Percent	Total	Win	Lost	Average	OP1	OP2	OP3
6039	160.39	387	126	261	2.6001	26	2	−4
5680	156.80	388	137	251	2.2558	26	2	−2
5573	155.73	365	131	234	2.2056	28	2	−2
5362	153.62	425	133	292	2.7005	24	2	−4
4968	149.68	426	145	281	2.3202	24	2	−2
4452	144.52	365	119	246	2.6470	28	5	−2
4389	143.89	365	119	246	2.6598	28	6	−2
3052	130.52	387	127	260	2.4372	26	2	−3
2980	129.80	353	110	243	2.7424	30	5	−2
2833	128.33	365	118	246	2.4860	28	2	−3

arises from the fact that oscillator sensitivity to overbought and oversold conditions depends on the direction of the primary trend. In a bull market, oscillators move to higher overbought levels and rallies are generated from moderate oversold levels. If you know you are in a bull market, you could skew the triggering points to the upside, and vice versa. Unfortunately, we never learn that the primary trend has reversed until sometime later. Also, if we go with numbers skewed to a bull market environment, the system is definitely going to be under pressure when a bear market begins. It makes sense to evenly balance the overboughts and oversolds. That is why I chose the 28/2/−2 combination. I could have chosen the 26/2/−2 combo, but the profit was only slightly better. The 28-day MA generated fewer signals, and fewer signals mean fewer chances for mistakes.

On the face of it, the number of losing signals of 234 to 131 winners looks pretty grim. However, when you look at the more detailed report of Table 29-3, the average win was 2.2 times greater than the average loss, which shows this system does a reasonable job of cutting losses short. The top panel of Chart 29-4 shows the equity line. The starting amount of $1 was increased to $2.55. Even though the system trailed the buy-hold approach, there were no major drawdowns in terms of peak-to-trough equity. The one in 1994 of 10 percent was the worst. Not bad, considering the 150 percent gain was achieved at a 9.4 percent annualized rate.

Other tests on many closed-end mutual funds covering the 1980s and 1990s have shown that the a 28/5/−5 combination of a 28-day MA and a close divided by a 28-day MA using + and − 5 as the overbought/oversold triggering points worked consistently well.

A 10/10/−10 combination for the Russell 2000 has worked magnificently since 1978, offering a return by 2001 of an equity in excess of $20 starting from $1 in 1978. The equity line for this system in Chart 29-5 shows no periods of serious drawdown.

All these systems assumed a 0.01 percent commission and an interest rate of 5 percent when not exposed to the market. No shorts were initiated, only long positions.

Table 29-3 Treasury Bonds

Current position	Short	Date position entered	10/19/98
Buy/Hold profit	1.12	Days in test	6291
Buy/Hold pct gain/loss	111.83	Annual B/H pct gain/loss	6.49
Total closed trades	365	Commission paid	0.20
Avg profit per trade	0.00	Avg Win/Avg Loss ratio	2.21
Total long trades	183	Total short trades	182
Winning long trades	70	Winning short trades	61
Total winning trades	131	Total losing trades	234
Amount of winning trades	4.15	Amount of losing trades	−3.36
Average win	0.03	Average loss	−0.01
Largest win	0.10	Largest loss	−0.06
Average length of win	8.05	Average length of loss	4.52
Longest winning trade	21	Longest losing trade	18

Chart 29-4 Treasury bonds, 1981–1998, and a 1/28 price oscillator. (*From Martin Pring, Breaking the Black Box, McGraw Hill, New York, 2002.*)

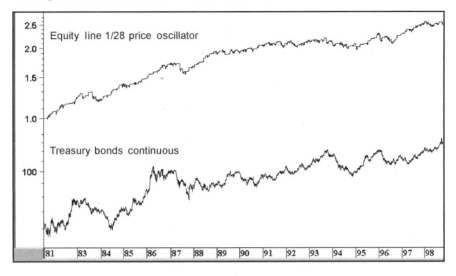

Chart 29-5 Russell 2000 Index, 1978–2001. (*From Martin Pring, Breaking the Black Box, McGraw-Hill, New York, 2002.*)

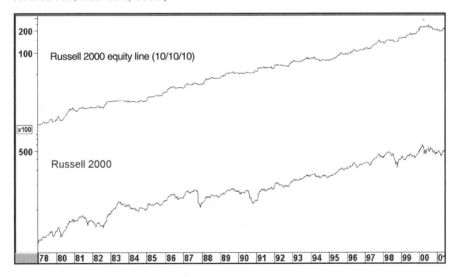

The Triple Indicator System

One important principle that should be followed when designing a system incorporating several triggering mechanisms is to make sure it incorporates different indicators based on different time frames. The contrasted time frames are important because prices at any one time are determined by the interaction of many different time cycles. We cannot make provisions for all of them, of course. If we can ensure there is a good time difference that separates the indicator construction, we will at least have made an attempt to monitor more than one cycle.

A system I devised in the late 1970s combines an MA crossover with a signal from two rate of exchange (ROC) indicators. These are a 10-week simple MA, a 6-week ROC, and a 13-week ROC. Thus, we have two different types of indicators: a trend-following MA and two oscillator types. The system also consists of three different time frames. The buy and sell rules are very simple. Buy when the price is above the 10-week MA and both ROCs are above zero. Sell when all three go negative, that is, when the ROCs cross below zero and the price crosses its MA. Signals cannot be generated unless all three agree. This is because we want to make sure the various cycles reflected in the three different time frames are all in gear. Originally, when I introduced this system, it was applied to the pound/dollar relationship because it was one that trended very consistently.

Let's take a close look at Chart 29-6 to see how it works by starting off with a simple 10-week MA crossover between mid-1974 and 1976. Buy signals are once again indicated by the upward-pointing arrows and short positions by the downward-pointing ones. There were 13 signals for a total profit of $0.19 on an initial $1 investment, from both the long and the short side. This compares to the buy-hold approach, with a loss of almost $0.70. Taken on its own, this was a fairly commendable performance, but let's remember that for a significant portion of the time, that is, most of 1975 and 1976, the British pound was in a sustained downtrend. It is true there were a number of whipsaws in late 1975 and early 1976. These are shown in the two ellipses, but they were of minor consequence as it turned out.

The next step is to introduce a 13-week ROC. Buy and sell signals are triggered when the 13-week ROC crosses above and below its zero reference line. This approach, shown in Chart 29-7, nets a gain of $0.23 with six signals. This was better than the results with the MA crossover, especially since fewer signals dramatically reduced the potential for whipsaws. Even so, there were a couple of nasty whipsaws in 1976.

The next step is to introduce a second ROC indicator to filter out some of the whipsaws. A 6-week ROC was chosen mainly because it spans approximately half the time span of the 13-week series. The result was an improved $0.24, but the number of signals increased to 12. The 6-week ROC is shown in the middle panel of Chart 29-8.

Chart 29-6 British pound system and a 10-week MA. (*From Martin Pring*, Breaking the Black Box, *McGraw-Hill, New York, 2002.*)

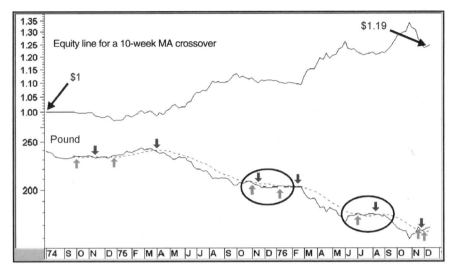

Chart 29-7 British pound system and a 13-wseek ROC. (*From Martin Pring*, Breaking the Black Box, *McGraw-Hill, New York, 2002.*)

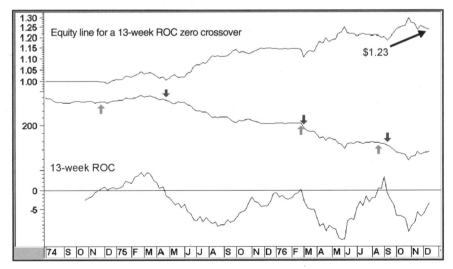

Chart 29-8   British pound system using three indicators. (*From Martin Pring*, Breaking the Black Box, *McGraw-Hill, New York, 2002.*)

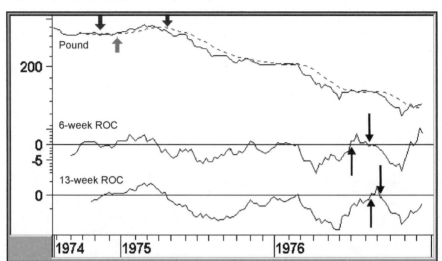

Putting the Indicators Together

I put all three indicators together in Chart 29-8 so you can see how their integration improves things. The actual result was a slight increase in profit over the previous 6-week ROC test. However, the important thing was that the signals were reduced to only three. A closer look at Chart 29-8 shows that the first sell comes in October 1974, as the 6-week ROC follows the others into negative territory. Then, in December, the 13-week ROC crosses above zero and this is closely followed by an MA crossover. Finally, the 6-week series moves above zero for a buy signal. All three then move into negative territory in April 1975. The MA and 6-week ROC go bearish simultaneously, and this is then followed by the 13-week series. The system stays bearish all the way through late 1976. It almost goes bullish when the price crosses its average and the 6-week ROC goes positive in February 1976. However, the 13-week series, which had been bearish, now goes bullish, but by this time, the currency had slipped below its MA and the 6-week series fell below zero. As a result, all three indicators were never in agreement. The same is true in the July–August period of 1976 when the two ROC indicators take turns in being bullish and bearish. Students of my momentum course will recognize this as a form of a negative complex divergence. The combination of all three indicators works extremely well in this environment. This is about as good as it gets.

Appraising the System

I introduced this approach in my book *International Investing Made Easy*[1] in 1981 with some hesitancy, because there was obviously no guarantee it would continue to operate profitably. It was subsequently reintroduced in the third edition of this book in 1992 with the same proviso. What I said was, "It is important to understand this approach will not necessarily offer such large rewards in the future. The example of the British pound must be treated as the exception rather than the rule, but it is introduced to give you an incentive to experiment along these lines."

The system continued to work extremely well, as you can see by looking back at the equity line in the upper panel in Chart 29-9. However, I am glad I used the cautionary statement, because once we move past 1993, the system falls apart. Just look at the declining equity line between 1993 and 1998 in Chart 29-10. This was due to the many whipsaws arising from the trading range that followed the drop from $2.00 in 1993. This goes to show that even if a system works well for 20 years, as this one had, market conditions can and do change, so you must be prepared for such instances. Obviously, we do not know until some time after the fact that the market environment has

Chart 29-9 British pound system results, 1983–1998. (*From Martin Pring*, Breaking the Black Box, *McGraw-Hill, New York, 2002.*)

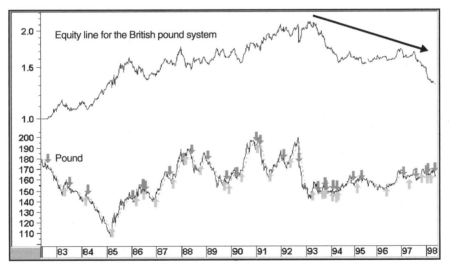

[1]McGraw-Hill, 1980.

Chart 29-10   British pound system using a 300-day MA. (*From Martin Pring*, Breaking the Black Box, *McGraw-Hill, New York, 2002.*)

changed. Is there anything we can do to avoid such situations? One possibility is to run a very long term MA or trendline through the equity line.

In Chart 29-10, I have plotted a 300-week simple MA. I used 300 weeks because I felt it necessary for the system to undergo a fairly long period before it can be considered out of touch. After all, with the pound system, the history goes back to the early 1970s, so 6 years is not a particularly long time. The idea is when the equity line crosses below the MA something is seriously wrong with the system, and it should be at least temporarily abandoned. At this point, it would make sense to reappraise it and see if it could be improved, and I do not mean by introducing special rules to block out a bad period. You could also wait until the equity line crosses back above the MA again.

The Advantages of Diversification

The second possibility is to use the same system on different markets, that is, diversify. Once again, we need to make sure the system tests well on any of the markets that are to be traded. Chart 29-11 features the same system for the Nikkei. It has a very profitable, but more consistent, feel to it. There are a few drawdowns in the early 1990s. The initial one in 1992 was just over 20 percent, but by and large it operated very successfully over this 12-year period. This system has also been successfully applied to individual stocks

Chart 29-11   British pound system applied to the Nikkei. (*From Martin Pring*, Breaking the Black Box, *McGraw-Hill, New York, 2002.*)

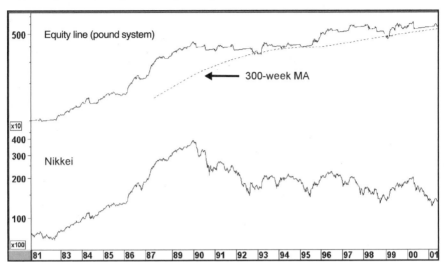

and the S&P Composite, AAA bond yields, and the DM when it was actively traded.

Introducing an Intermarket System

The Relationship

So far, we have just considered particular securities or markets in isolation, using statistically derived data from that security alone. An alternative approach is to adopt a tried and tested intermarket relationship as a cross-reference. Better results are often obtained in this way. An intermarket relationship develops when one market consistently influences another. The first step is to rationalize why such a relationship exists in the first place. Perhaps the most basic relationship is between equity prices and short-term interest rates. This was described in Chapter 25 where it was established that changes in the trend of short-term interest rates lead equity prices.

What we do not know is the lead time or the magnitude of the ensuing stock rally. The answer is to classify the trend of money-market prices, which is what the inverted short rate actually is, with an MA crossover. When a rising trend of money-market prices has been established, it is then time to look at the trend of equities to see when they respond. The rationale is that a rising trend of money-market prices sets the scene for an equity bull market. However, this is not confirmed until the S&P Composite crosses above its MA. Just think of this as something akin to an unconscious swimmer receiving mouth-to-mouth resuscitation. You know the treatment is good for the patient, just as falling rates are good for equity prices. However, we do not know how much treatment is required and whether the patient will recover until he or she is able to breathe by him- or herself. In our analogy, the stock market is shown to respond to the interest-rate treatment when it crosses its MA.

Here is how it works. Look at Chart 29-12 . In October 1981, the inverted commercial paper yield crosses above its 12-month MA (shown in the ellipse), indicating the environment is now bullish for equities. However, the equity market does not respond by bottoming out until August 1982. When the S&P rallies above its 12-month MA (*A*), it indicates that the market is responding to the positive interest-rate environment. In this case, the crossover comes in August 1982. At that time, both trends are bullish and so is the system. It remains positive until either series moves back below its average, which, in this case, developed in June 1983 (*B*). It then goes bullish again in January 1985 (*C*).

Finally, the inverted yield falls below its average in early 1987 (*D*). The market continues to rally, but the system is no longer bullish. In most instances, it would be better to generate the sell signals after the S&P crosses below its average. In this instance, though, the 1987 crash was over before the average was penetrated. Since the risk increases as the money-market series crosses below its average, it is probably best to act on the signal in two parts. This

Chart 29-12 S&P Composite versus 3-month commercial paper yield. (*From Martin Pring*, Breaking the Black Box, *McGraw-Hill, New York, 2002.*)

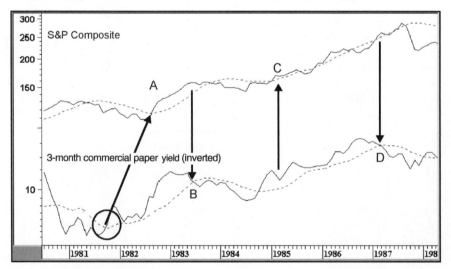

would involve taking off half the position as the money-market series goes negative and then liquidating the rest when the S&P crosses its average.

Figure 29-5 shows the risk and reward for the system between 1948 and 1991. The vertical axis measures the reward on an annualized basis and the risk is measured on the horizontal axis. In this sense, risk is measured as volatility. The best place for any system to be is in the top left-hand corner, often referred to as the northwest quadrant. This is where the reward is high and the risk, or volatility, is low. In the case of this system, the star labeled "positive environment" reflects the risk and reward of our stock/interest-rate system. At close to 25 percent annualized return, with about 5 percent volatility, it is clearly a superior system. The star labeled "entire period" reflects the buy-hold approach where the return is just under 10 percent with a bit over 12 percent volatility. Finally, the "negative environment" represents those periods when the system is not positive. It could be a bear market or there could be times when the interest-rate side of the equation is negative, but the S&P is still above its average. At any rate, you can certainly appreciate the difference of a 25 percent low-risk return when the system is bullish and the high-risk/low-reward period when it is not. In conclusion, not only was the reward from the system excellent, but the way in which it was earned, with low risk, was tremendous too.

The system says nothing about periods when the market is above its average and rates are not, since those are obviously bullish periods as well. However, once rates move above their 12-month MA, there is a real danger that the next correction could be the first downleg in a bear market. It is true that sooner or later the S&P Composite will cross below its MA, thereby stopping us out, but why run the risk when good returns and little volatility can be had under more favorable conditions?

Figure 25-5 Risk/reward ratio for the S&P composite versus 3-month commercial paper yield. (*From Martin Pring*, Breaking the Black Box, *McGraw-Hill, New York, 2002.*)

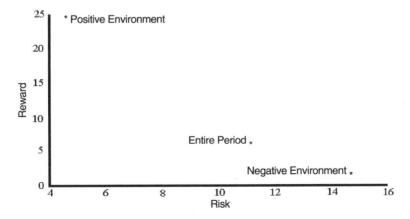

If you are a short-term trader, you probably feel this approach is worse than useless. However, it can be put to very good use if you realize that when the system is bullish, short sell signals are likely to result in losses. They are not just going against the main trend, but are occurring in one of the most bullish equity environments you can get. By the same token, you can use this knowledge to position yourself from the long side when a short-term buy signal is triggered. I am not going to say that sharp corrections will never happen when this system is positive, because there have been periods such as 1971 when a fairly large retracing move did materialize. It is merely that when the system is positive, the odds favor strong short-term rallies and whipsaw reactions.

Using Margin

All the systems described here were tested on a cash basis with no margin. You might think that it makes sense to go out and apply a system using lots of margin. That way the gains would multiply. In actual fact, this is not necessarily the case. Chart 29-13 shows a simple 10-day MA crossover system using no margin and Chart 29-14 shows it using a 10 percent margin requirement. Since the initial trades were losers, the account was wiped out in just over a year. Remember—leverage works both ways.

Chart 29-13 American Century Gold Fund, 1989–1998. (*From Martin Pring*, Breaking the Black Box, *McGraw-Hill, New York, 2002.*)

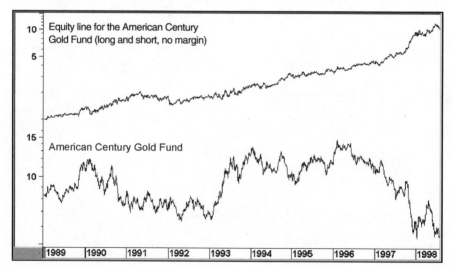

Chart 29-14 American Century Gold Fund, 1989–1998, with Margin. (*From Martin Pring*, Breaking the Black Box, *McGraw-Hill, New York, 2002.*)

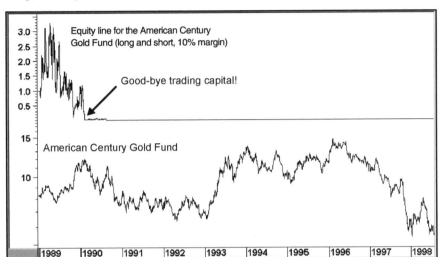

Summary

- There are two ways in which systems can be used: act on each signal without question or use the signals as a filter so the system becomes *one more indicator* in the weight of the evidence approach.
- The principal advantage of a mechanical system is that it removes subjectivity and encourages the adoption of discipline.
- No system will ever work all the time. It is important to understand the pitfalls of automated systems so that they can be programmed out.
- Systems should be designed to take into account the fact that there are two different types of market environments: trading range and trending.
- Because no system works perfectly, it should be exhaustively tested before being applied in the marketplace.
- The use of any system should involve diversification to spread the risk for any periods where it does not operate successfully for a specific security.
- The use of margin exaggerates the results, both on the upside and downside. The actual performance will depend on the chronological sequence of the good and bad signals.

30
Technical Analysis of Global Stock Markets

Since equities are bought and sold throughout the world for essentially the same reasons, the principles of technical analysis can be applied to any stock market. Unfortunately, the degree of sophistication in statistical reporting of many countries does not permit the kind of detailed analysis that is available in the United States, although things are improving rapidly. Even so, it is possible to obtain data on price, breadth, and volume for most countries. Information on industry groups and interest rates is also becoming more widely available.

In this chapter we will be concentrating on longer-term trends for the purpose of gaining perspective, but the analysis can just as easily be used to identify intermediate and short-term trends.

Identifying Primary Global Trends

Charts 30-1(a) and (b) show the Morgan Stanley Capital International (MSCI) World Stock Index, which is constructed from a selection of blue-chip stocks from many different countries weighted by capitalization. This series has been adjusted to U.S. dollars and is widely published in the financial press. Other world indexes published by *Dow Jones* and the *Financial Times* can be adopted into the analysis, but MSCI has been chosen because of its extensive history going back to the 1960s. The World Index is a good starting point from which to analyze the cyclical trends of the various stock

Chart 30-1(a)   MSCI World Stock Index, 1964–1985, and the 4-year cycle lows margin. (*From www.pring.com.*)

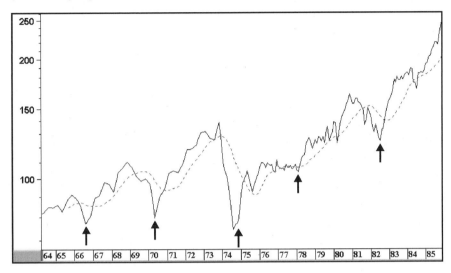

Chart 30-1(b)   MSCI World Stock Index, 1985–2001, and the 4-year cycle lows margin. (*From www.pring.com.*)

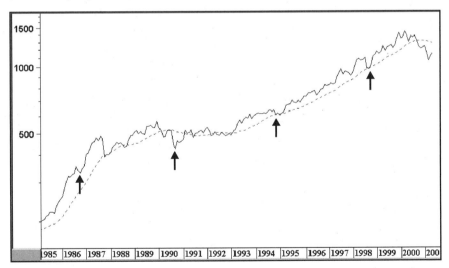

markets, just as the S&P Composite might be used as a starting point for the U.S. market. This is because the stock markets around the globe tend to move in the same direction, just as the majority of U.S. stocks reflect the primary trend of the S&P most of the time. Generally speaking, improvements in technology and communications have broken down geographical and trading patterns, and countries have become more interdependent, with the result that their stock market and business cycles are now more closely related than they once were. A giant leap in this direction appeared to take place after the 1987 crash, in which all markets participated on a synchronized basis. This was later reinforced almost 10 years later when the so-called Asian Meltdown reverberated around the world. The introduction of international and specific country closed and open-ended mutual funds in the 1980s and 1990s in the United States is a striking example of this growing sense of international awareness. There are exceptions, though, because different economies can be in a different state of expansion at any one point in time, or because some countries are experiencing a greater spurt of growth (or contraction) than others. As a result of the variations in the long-term economic, financial, and political situations between countries, a good world bull market in equities may be brief or almost nonexistent for a country undergoing financial distortions, such as Hong Kong between 1986 and 1990. In addition, country performance can also differ because of the makeup of specific markets. For example, the Swedish and Finish indexes performed superbly in the latter part of the 1990s because they were dominated by technology companies. Countries with substantial natural resources tend to outperform when commodity prices are rising and so forth. As a result, the U.K. market has a tendency to lead, while Canada, Australia, and South Africa are often late in turning down.

The MSCI charts show the existence of the international 4-year cycle, as indicated by the arrows. The troughs in 1962, 1966, 1970, 1974, 1978, 1982, 1986, 1990, 1994, and 1998 are all separated by approximately 4 years. I say "approximately" since the actual bottoms do not fall in the same month. Also, the 1986 bottom was more or less nonexistent and was essentially a 6-month trading range. This demonstrates that in a secular bull market, such as the 1980s, the cycle low is not so much a bottom as a buying point prior to further gains. The same sort of thing happened in 1994, where the sideways correction was more obvious.

Chart 30-2 shows the MSCI together with an 18-month rate of change (ROC). The solid arrows indicate those points where the ROC, having crossed above its overbought zone at +30 percent, then recrosses it on is way back to zero. The two dashed lines represent buy signals using the same approach for the oversold zone. Such signals often indicate that psychology has moved too much in a bullish direction and that the global equity cycle is due for a correction. During the 40-year period covered by the chart, there were numerous timely signals. However, there were also some failures, such as the late signal in 1984 and 1987 and the nonexistent declines that followed two signals in the late 1990s.

New Highs and Diffusion Indexes

The World Index can also be used with net new high data. Chart 30-3 was constructed using the popular MetaStock program. In this instance new highs and lows are calculated for a basket of individual stock markets. Instead of the normal time span of 52 weeks, I chose a 13-week period and smoothed the data with a 6-week simple moving average (MA). Thirteen weeks is, of course, a quarter of a year and appears to work quite well. The arrows indicate overbought/oversold crossovers as well as those periods when it was possible to construct trendlines for the net new high series. Most of the time the +7.5 percent overbought crossovers are followed by intermediate corrections. However, when the indicator reached +10 percent and reversed, such as during 1998 and 2000, a more severe decline appears to follow.

Chart 30-2 MSCI World Stock Index, 1960–2001, and an 18-month ROC. (*From www.pring.com.*)

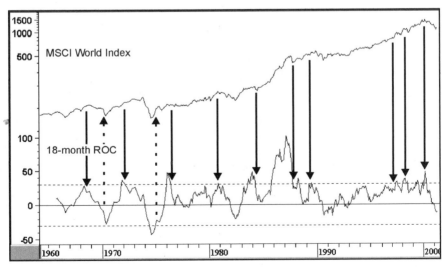

Chart 30-3 MSCI World Stock Index, 1993–2001, and a World Net New High Indicator. (*From www.pring.com.*)

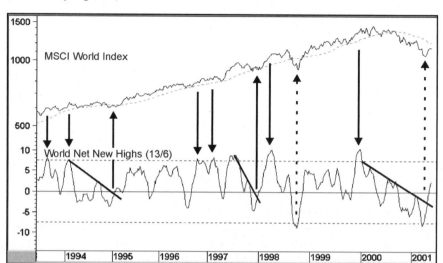

Chart 30-4 shows a different representation. In this case it is two diffusion indicators. The one in the center panel is constructed from a basket of individual country indexes that are above their 6-month MAs and the lower one for a 12-month span. Both series were then smoothed with a 6-month MA to iron out unnecessary fluctuations. The vertical arrows show when both series rally from an oversold condition, which is usually indicative of a major advance in the World Index. Diffusion indexes really come into their own when it is possible to spot some really glaring divergences. In this instance we do not see very many, but one in particular stands out. This is at the 1973 top, where both series are actually below zero when the MSCI is experiencing its bull market high. Such action tells us that the World Index is being supported by very few countries, yet at the same time many country indexes have already started to break down because they have violated their 6- and 12-month MAs. At that point it is reasonable to conclude that the weight of the bearish markets will adversely affect the World Index itself.

Chart 30-5 features another diffusion index. This time it is based on the percentage of country indexes that are above their 40-day MAs. The plotted series is a 10-day smoothing of the raw data. Once again, we can see one glaring divergence at the early 1998 bottom, where the diffusion index barely fell below zero as the MSCI was testing its low. Note also that it was possible to construct two trendlines, one for the diffusion indicator and

Chart 30-4 MSCI World Stock Index, 1968–2001, and two diffusion indicators. (*From www.pring.com.*)

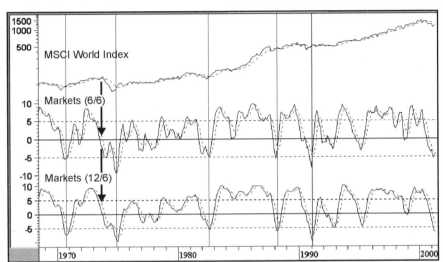

another for the index itself. Not surprisingly, a spirited rally followed the divergence and trendline violations. The diffusion index was also quite useful in signaling small tops and bottoms as it recrossed its overbought and oversold zones.

Individual Country Selection

Today there are a variety of ways in which investments or trades can be executed in specific markets. Individual stocks can be purchased through brokers with an international presence, through American depositary receipts (ADRs) and so on. In recent years the exchanges of most countries have established futures markets on key indexes. Exposure can also be achieved through closed and open-ended mutual funds that specialize in individual countries or regions. Baskets of stocks reflecting the principal indexes of many countries, known as webs, are also traded on the AMEX. Similar vehicles are also available on the NYSE.

The key to selecting better performing stock markets is the adoption of relative strength (RS) analysis using the principles outlined in Chapter 16. Chart 30-6 shows the S&P Composite and its RS line against the MSCI World Stock Index together with two KSTs of the same series. During the period

Chart 30-5 MSCI World Stock Index, 1997–1998, and a short-term diffusion indicator. (*From www.pring.com.*)

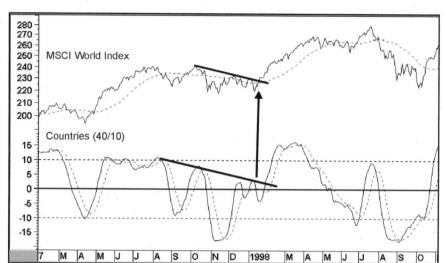

covered by the chart, there were three major changes in the RS action as flagged by trendline violations. The first was a sell signal in 1985. Note how the relative KST was barely able to rally above zero at the time, and later gave a sell signal by crossing below its MA. The S&P itself rallied quite nicely over the coming years, but the persistent drop in the RS line indicated that there were far better countries to invest in.

The next reversal came as an upside trendline break for the RS line at the end of 1988. Note that both KSTs were also positive. Finally, two KST sell signals and an RS up trendline violation in early 1993 signal a 2-year period of underperformance.

Chart 30-7 shows the same arrangement for the Nikkei. Here, the story is very different because Japanese equities were in a secular RS decline between 1990 and 2001. There was only one instance of a clear-cut buy or sell signal and that developed at the end of 1999 when both series violated down trendlines and each KST went positive. Even so, the RS trend remained relatively weak since the line was unable to rally above its secular down trendline. At the very end of the chart, the technical position appeared to be improving because the RS KST had not only diverged positively with the RS line, but the line itself had violated an up trendline.

Chart 30-6   The S&P Composite versus the MSCI World Stock Index, 1978–1995. (*From www.pring.com.*)

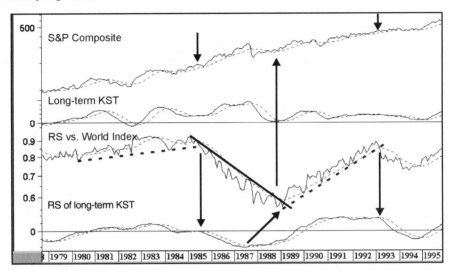

Chart 30-7   The Nikkei versus the MSCI World Stock Index, 1991–2001. (*From www.pring.com.*)

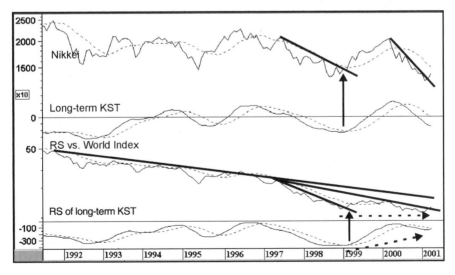

Sometimes it's possible to isolate a characteristic for a specific market. In this respect Chart 30-8 shows the German DAX Index together with its 18-month ROC. Overbought recrossovers have a 40-year history of offering reasonable primary trend sell signals. They are certainly not perfect, but a downside penetration of the +50 percent level is reasonably consistent.

Chart 30-9 features the RS line for the Sydney All Ordinaries Index. The series in the upper panel is the Commodity Research Board (CRB) Spot Raw Materials Index and the vertical lines mark the commodity peaks and troughs. The Australian market has a very high natural resource weighting, and it is fairly evident from the chart that most of the time when commodities are in a bull market, the All Ords are experiencing superior RS, and vice versa. There are exceptions, such as the 1986–1989 commodity rally, when the All Ords underperformed, but by and large this relationship has worked pretty well.

Chart 30-8 The DAX, 1950–2001, and an 18-month ROC. (*From www.pring.com.*)

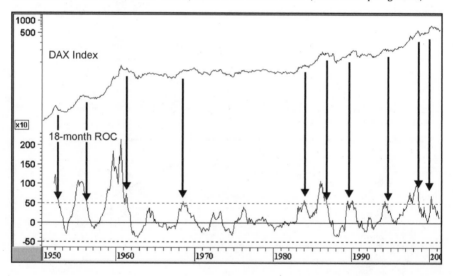

Chart 30-9 CRB Spot Raw Materials versus the Sydney All Ordinaries Index, 1974–2001.

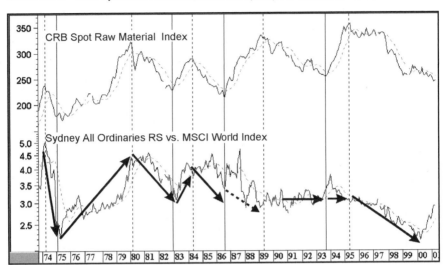

Summary

- There is a definite 4-year global equity cycle.
- Recent technological innovation and other factors have lead to a much closer relationship between equity markets around the world.
- Diffusion indexes, net new highs, and other breadth-based indicators incorporating individual country indexes can be used for identifying trend reversals in the World Index.
- Relative strength is the best tool for identifying markets that are likely to out- or underperform the World Index.

31
Technical Analysis of Individual Stocks

A useful systematic approach for stock selection is known as the *top down approach.* In this case the "top" represents an analysis of whether equities in general are experiencing a primary bull or bear market. Since most equities rise during a bull market and decline during a bear trend, the first step establishes whether the overall environment is likely to be positive or negative.

The next step involves an appraisal of the various industry groups, since equities in the same industry generally move together. Once an attractive group has been isolated, the final stage involves the selection of individual stocks. This approach is discussed later, but first here are some general observations.

All investors and traders would like their selections to appreciate rapidly in price, but stocks that satisfy this wish tend to be accompanied by a substantially greater amount of risk than most of us are willing to accept. Stocks that usually move up sharply in price typically have a high beta (that is, they are very sensitive to market movements), a very small float (that is, they are illiquid and very price sensitive to a small increase in volume), or a very strong earnings momentum resulting in constant upward revisions in the price/earnings multiple. Others may be experiencing a turnaround situation in which the price has fallen to unrealistically low levels, so that the slightest good news has an explosive effect on the price.

These are all fundamental factors and really fall outside the scope of this book. However, it is important to understand that investors can be very fashion conscious when it comes to stock ownership. When prices have been bid up to unrealistically high levels and the media are covering positive developments in cover stories, major articles, and so on, the chances are that the bullish arguments are understood by virtually all market participants. At this point virtually everyone who wants to buy has already done so and the stock is said to be *overowned*. This happened to the pollution control group (waste management) in the late 1960s, the so-called glamor growth stocks in 1973, the oil stocks in 1980, and the technology stocks in the spring of 2000. When the news is so bad that it appears that profits will never recover, or that the company might file for bankruptcy, the opposite condition sets in and the stock is said to be *underowned*. Real estate investment trusts in 1974 and tire stocks in 1980 are examples of underownership. Not all companies move to such extremes, but it is important to recognize that the psychological process exists.

A position of overownership usually takes several business cycles to develop, creating what is called a *secular rise*. Similarly, a position of underownership, in which a stock becomes totally out of fashion, usually takes many years to materialize.

Stock Selection from a Secular Point of View

General

It makes sense to start off from a very long term or secular point of view, gradually working down to the short-term aspects. Ideally, the selection process should begin by determining whether the stock in question is in a secular advance or decline in order to gain some idea of where the stock might be in its ownership cycle. Chart 31-1 shows Cominco, a Canadian mining company, which went through many cycles between the 1970s and the turn of the century. Stocks in resource and basic industries, such as Cominco, are called *cyclical* stocks since they offer great profit opportunities over one or two business cycles but are rarely profitable using the buy-hold approach.

Because of the long-term growth characteristics of the global economy, most stocks exhibit characteristics of a long-term secular advance interrupted by mild cyclical corrections or multiyear trading ranges. An example is shown in Chart 31-2, featuring Alberto Culver. Several secular trends are evident. The termination of the first is signaled by a joint trendline break in the price and the relative strength (RS) line in 1991. You may notice that the trendline for the RS is penetrated very briefly in 1985. Some might regard this as sacrilege, but I prefer to construct trendlines that best reflect the trend in a commonsense way, rather than one that joins the low with the initial corrective bottom. If it is possible to do that, and the line

Chart 31-1   Cominco, 1970–2001. (*From Telescan.*)

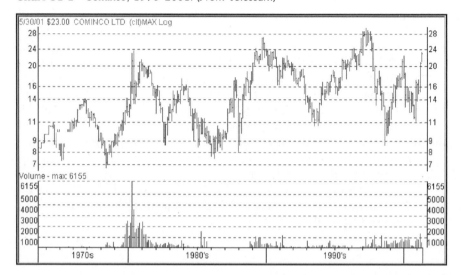

can also be touched on more occasions, that is fine. However, if it is not, as would have been the result in this case, then it makes more sense to make an exception and construct the line through one of the bottoms instead of just touching it.

Later we see a couple of 4-year down trendlines violated and in 1998 the penetration of two up trendlines. Both moving averages (MAs) have a 104-week (24-month) time span and are penetrated at around the same time as the trendlines.

I have incorporated the RS line into most of the charts in this chapter for two reasons. First, RS trends and divergences can be very helpful in understanding the strength or weakness in the underlying technical structure. Second, when a stock is purchased, it is far better for it to be in a trend that is outperforming than underperforming the market. Chart 31-3 offers a classic example of this. During the 20-year period covered by the chart, Reliant Energy was in a secular uptrend. This looked good on the surface, but a quick glance at the RS line indicates that it was in a secular downtrend in terms of relative performance. Note that it was possible to construct two trendlines for the price. The dashed one is an extremely good example of why it is a good idea to extend a trendline once it has been violated. Note how the extended line became formidable resistance several times in the mid- to late 1990s. Even when the price broke above the line at the turn of the century, the retracement move found support there.

Chart 31-2   Alberto Culver, 1982–2001. (*From www.pring.com.*)

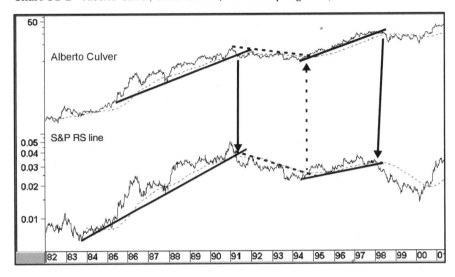

Chart 31-3   Reliant Energy, 1980–2001. (*From www.pring.com.*)

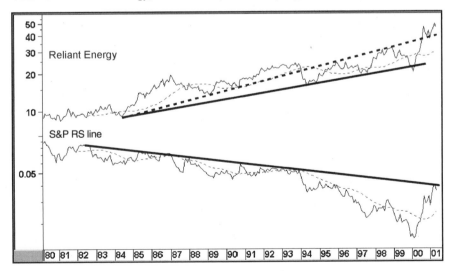

Finally, ADM experiences a secular break to the downside in 1998 (Chart 31-4). Its RS line also completed a downward head-and-shoulders top. Note that in ADM's case advance warning of potential weakness was given first by the failure of the RS line to confirm the new high in the price in 1995 (at the tip of the horizontal arrow) and then to diverge negatively with the late-1997 high.

These examples point up the differing life cycles and characteristics of individual stocks. Investors who are able to identify secular trend reversals in price and relative action are in a position to profit from extremes in the ownership cycle. Consequently, a very long term chart can provide a useful starting point for stock selection.

Major Price Patterns (Long Bases)

In Chapter 5, the relationship between the size of the formation and the ensuing price move in terms of both magnitude and duration was established. The larger the base, the farther they can race! Or the greater the top, the more they will drop! One of the best methods of stock selection for those with a patient long-term horizon is to search through long-term chart books (such as the SRC Green Book at www.babson. com/charts/

Chart 31-4 ADM, 1980–2001. (*From www.pring.com.*)

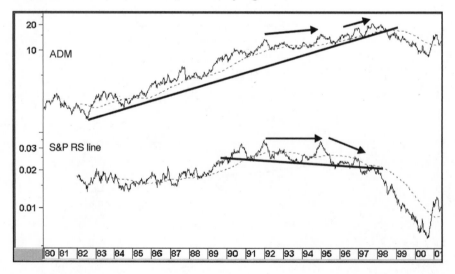

longterm.html) or your own downloaded database for issues that are emerging from or pulling back to long-term bases. By definition, there are few points in a stock's lifetime at which condition is prevalent, but when it can be spotted it is well worthwhile. At any one time there are usually at least a few of these situations developing. When it is possible to spot a lot of candidates simultaneously forming large bases, this usually means that the market as a whole or the stock group or groups in question are on the verge of a secular advance. In the late 1940s and the late 1970s, for example, there were numerous stocks breaking out from multiyear bases. Not surprisingly, the market itself experienced a strong secular advance in both instances.

Chart 31-5 shows an example for Andrew Corp. breaking out from a 6-year base in 1991; a good rally, more than meeting the objective of the pattern followed. Later the joint penetration of a 6-year up trendline indicated that the strong uptrend was unlikely to continue. In the case of the price, this was followed by a consolidation and for the RS line an actual trend reversal.

Applied Materials experienced a breakout from a 10-year base (Chart 31-6) in late 1992. The uptrend in the price continued until at least the spring of 2001, but the RS up trendline was temporarily violated in 1998 and 2000.

Chart 31-5   Andrew Corp. 1980–2001. (*From www.pring.com.*)

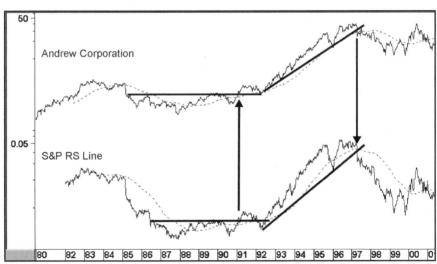

Chart 31-6   Applied Materials, 1980–2001. (*From www.pring.com.*)

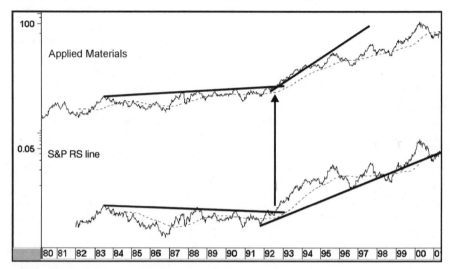

Some Basic Principles of Stock Selection During a Primary Bull Market

General

A bull market has been defined as an environment when most stocks are moving up most of the time for an extended period. In this case the extended period should be expected to last between 9 months and possibly as long as 2 to 3 years. A bear market is exactly the opposite, except that the average bear market typically unfolds over a shorter period. When exposure to the stock market is contemplated, it is clearly better for both investors and short-term traders with a 2- to 3-week horizon to be buying when the primary trend is positive. It is true that some stocks experience primary bull trends when the overall market is in a primary bear trend, but the law of probability indicates that it is much more difficult to make money when swimming against an overall bearish environment. We must also remember that because of the group rotation process, different stock groups are experiencing different phases of their bull and bear cycles simultaneously[1]. Thus, while the S&P, for instance, may have just embarked on the first downleg of a new bear market, lagging groups, such as mines, may still be experiencing the final leg of their bull market. The selection

[1]Table 14-1 offers a rough approximation of where various industry groups fall into the market cycle.

process at this stage of the cycle is much more difficult, but there are still opportunities offering substantial upside magnitude at this juncture.

The performance of specific issues can differ widely, not only over the course of the total market bull move, but during its various stages. This concept was described in Chapter 19, which outlined the group rotation process.

The first step is to decide whether the market is in a primary bull or bear trend using the principles outlined earlier. If it is fairly evident that a bull market began some time ago and there are few signs of a bear market, then intermediate lows are a good place to begin the analysis. I'll have more to say on that one later, but for now, let's assume that there is ample evidence that a new bull market is just beginning. Signs would include the observation that the A/D line had been falling for a year or more. We would also probably see a confirmed new trend of declining interest rates, an oversold condition in the long-term momentum indicators, lots of media coverage on weakness in the stock market and the economy, layoffs at major brokerage firms, and so on.

If all of these conditions were present, it would be an odds-on probability that the market was either at or very close to a bear market low.

Selecting Stocks Close to a Bear Market Low

The next step would be an examination of the technical position of the various industry groups, especially the early cycle leaders, to make sure that they are technically sound on both an absolute and relative basis. Finally, an examination of the stocks within the groups found to be the most attractive should be undertaken.

In this respect the obvious starting points would be an analysis of the relative positions of the various industry groups in terms of the group rotation process described in Chapter 19. Not all groups fit into the cycle. Of the groups that do fit, not all respond in the way expected in each cycle. However, an analysis of the energy and financial sectors or the banks and aluminums would be a good point to determine whether the cycle is in an inflationary or deflationary phase. The next step would be to analyze the groups that were akin to the sector that looked more promising. We will do that later, but for now let us assume that we have been lucky enough to identify a bear market low.

The 1990 bottom met these requirements. The S&P Composite actually fell for a relatively short period of time, yet the NYSE daily A/D line had been declining for over a year by the time the market bottomed in late 1990. One of the good-looking groups falling into the early leader category at the end of 1990 was the brokerage industry. What made them especially appealing as a contrary player was the *BusinessWeek* cover story, cited in Chapter 27, questioning the future of the industry.

Technically, Chart 31-7 shows that the KSTs completed a base in early 1991. The RS line was ahead of the game because it experienced an 8-year down trendline break a couple of months earlier, right at the turn of the year. As the RS line was breaking out, the KSTs had simultaneously violated a smaller down trendline and crossed above its 24-month MA. The RS line also crossed above its 24-month MA. Both KSTs triggered bullish signals as well. Note how the RS line made a slightly lower low in 1990 than in 1987, but the RS KST did not.[2] This positive divergence added icing to the bullish case, indicating the odds of an emerging bull market to be quite high. The dotted vertical line on this chart indicates the approximate point where the initial trend breaks took place. They are replicated on Charts 31-8 to 31-13, which feature individual stocks.

Merrill Lynch (MER), the largest broker, is featured in Charts 31-8 and 31-9. MER violated a 2-year down trendline for the absolute price and an 8-year down trendline for the RS line against the S&P. Since both KSTs were turning bullish and the absolute one was actually completing a reverse head-and-shoulders pattern, MER would have qualified as a buy. Later, the bullish picture was completed as the 8-year down trendline for the absolute price was penetrated on the upside. Chart 31-9 shows the price together with a 4-week MA of the RS line against the Brokerage Index itself. A rising line means that the stock is outperforming the Brokerage Index, and vice versa. It is fairly evident at the opening of 1991 that the stock's RS line had broken its downtrend and was therefore likely to outperform both the S&P and the Brokerage Index.

Legg Mason (Chart 31-10) was also in a bullish position since both the absolute and relative prices had broken out from bases, and their respective KSTs had gone bullish. Indeed, the relative KST was actually diverging positively from the RS line. This sideways action actually contained more bullish potential than the technical position of MER, which was reversing from a downtrend. As it turned out, Chart 31-10 shows us that the RS line against the Brokerage Index was actually tracing out a top. Unfortunately, that was not known at the time of the breakout (that is, at the dotted vertical line). There was little doubt by the early spring of 1991 that a switch to another broker would have made sense since the RS line completed the top and dropped below its 65-week EMA.

Finally, Raymond James (Charts 31-12 and 31-13) came away virtually unscathed from the 1989–1990 bear market. At the time of the broker

---

[2]Please note that if you are unable to plot the KST substitute using various combinations of MACD, parameters are perfectly acceptable provided the resultant indicator retains a smooth rather than jagged characteristic.

Chart 31-7 S&P Brokerage Index, 1982–1993, and three indicators. (*From www.pring.com.*)

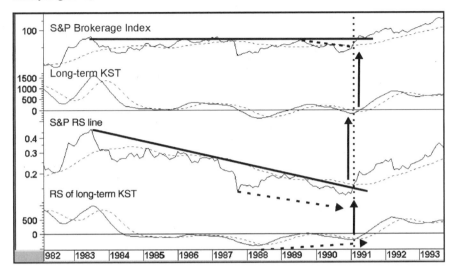

Chart 31-8 Merrill Lynch, 1983–1993, and three indicators. (*From www.pring.com.*)

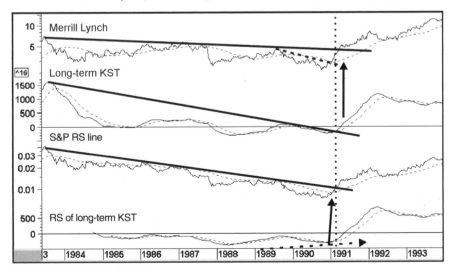

Chart 31-9 Merrill Lynch, 1986–1991, relative to the Brokerage Index. (*From www.pring.com.*)

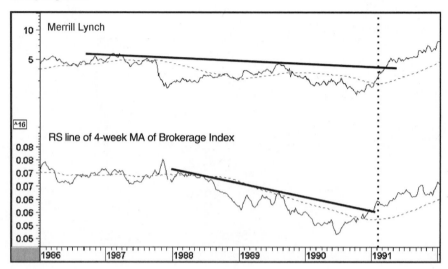

Chart 31-10 Legg Mason, 1986–1993, and three indicators. (*From www.pring.com.*)

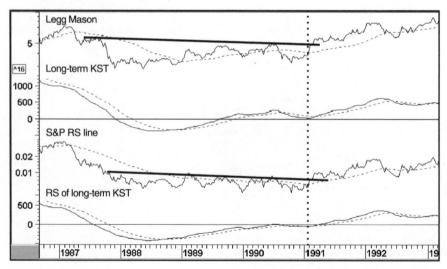

Chart 31-11 Legg Mason, 1986–1993, relative to the Brokerage Index. (*From www.pring.com.*)

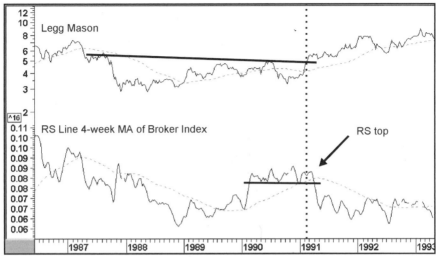

breakout, both the absolute and relative lines were completing large bases (see Chart 13-12). Unfortunately, this was not a low-risk situation like Merrill Lynch because the long-term KST for the absolute price was reversing from a moderately overbought condition that, on the one hand, made it less attractive. On the other hand, it often pays to go with the leader because strong stocks have a habit of getting stronger. This is because there are usually some good fundamentals that enabled them to be strong stocks in the first place. The arbiter in this case would have been the RS line against the Brokerage Index, as shown in Chart 31-13. Just after the breakout, it started to accelerate away from its 65-week EMA and up trendline and outperformed the Brokerage Index for the next year.

Using a Change in the Cycle to Select Stocks

Throughout the stock cycle, groups are continually changing leadership. One way of detecting this is to create a ratio of a leading and lagging group. Chart 31-14 shows such a series: property casualty insurers against Aluminum stocks. When the line is rising, it is bullish for insurance stocks relative to aluminums, and vice versa. The idea here is that changes in the direction of the ratio offer a proxy for a change in leadership from early-cycle, liquidity-driven issues to late-cycle, earnings-driven sectors. It is fairly evident from looking at the chart that this is a pretty jagged relationship subject to

Chart 31-12 Raymond James, 1985–1997, and three indicators. (*From www.pring.com.*)

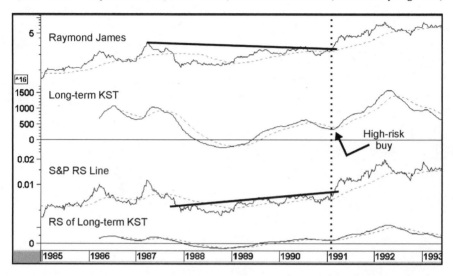

Chart 31-13 Raymond James, 1987–1993, relative to the Brokerage Index. (*From www.pring.com.*)

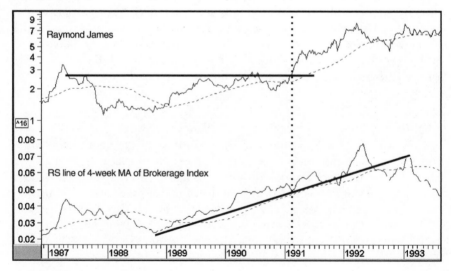

numerous whipsaws. One way around this is to construct a smoothed long-term momentum indicator, such as a KST. KST MA crossovers are then used as a proxy for when a change in leadership might be taking place. The arrows on the chart flag such reversals. The first arrow in December 1986 is the one we shall be focusing on. This downside reversal indicated a switch to lagging stocks. At the time it was possible to note breakouts in such groups as steels, aluminums, and so on. I decided to take a closer look at the semi-conductors, another lagging group, as represented in Chart 31-15. It looked pretty good going into 1987 as both the absolute and RS lines broke out, and the two KST's gave buy signals. Please remember that if you do not have access to the KST, another smoothed momentum indicator, such as a smoothed stochastic, trend deviation, and so on, can be substituted. In this instance the rally only lasted just over half a year. Normally, we would expect a more extended trend to follow such an exercise, say between 1 to 3 years.

Intel, featured in Chart 31-16, looked to be a good buy because it had broken out on both an absolute and RS basis just as the Index itself had. Moreover, the two KST's has also gone bullish. Intel would certainly have qualified as a buy.

Another stock in the group, AMD, did not look so exciting. It's true that the absolute price broke out and the two KSTs went bullish. However, as

Chart 31-14 Property Casualty/Aluminum ratio, 1985–2001, and a long-term KST. (*From www.pring.com.*)

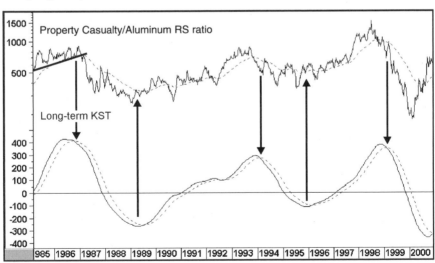

Chart 31-15 S&P Semiconductor Index, 1984–1988, and three indicators. (*From www.pring.com.*)

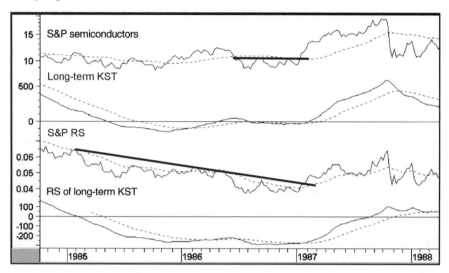

Chart 31-16 Intel, 1983–1988, and three indicators. (*From www.pring.com.*)

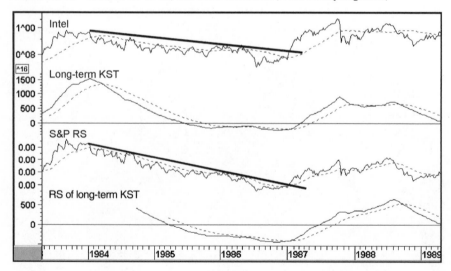

Chart 31-17 Advanced Micro, 1984–1990, and three indicators. (*From www.pring.com.*)

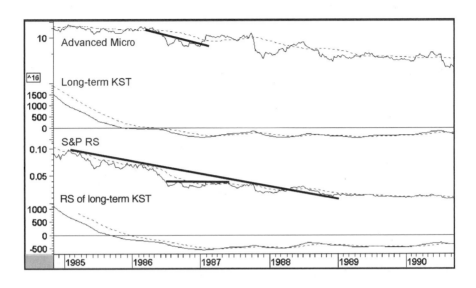

Chart 31-18 Advanced Micro, 1985–1991, relative to the Semiconductor Index. (*From www.pring.com.*)

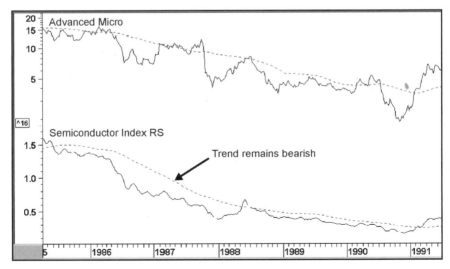

Chart 31-17 shows, the RS line never managed to break above its down trend-line. Conclusive evidence that there were better semiconductor candidates came from Chart 31-18, which indicated that the RS of the stock against the group index never broke its downtrend throughout 1987.

Short-Term Analysis

Short-term traders will need to adopt one more stage to the analysis, and that is to make sure that prior to a purchase the stock in question is in a technically strong short-term position as well as being in a constructive mode from a long-term point of view.

Chart 31-19 shows McKesson with a short- and long-term KST, both based on daily data. In this case the long-term KST uses the same time frames as the monthly formula, but it is multiplied by 21 to correspond to the approximate average trading days in a month. The vertical thick black line indicates the low point separating the bear market on the left from the primary bull trend on the right. The letters mark the short-term KST buy signals that developed close to or below zero. Other smoothed short-term oscillators, such as a stochastic, smoothed RSI, MACD, and so on, could, of course, be substituted for the KST. Note that none of the signals labeled *A* to *D* had any form of upside magnitude, with the exception of *C.* Even here, the nice

Chart 31-19   McKesson, 1999–2001, and two indicators. (*From www.pring.com.*)

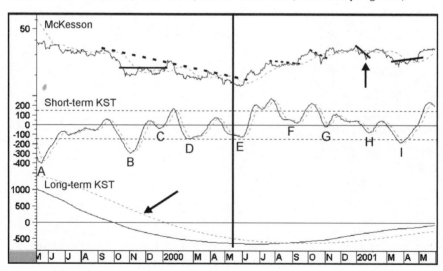

trendline break in the price was followed by a whipsaw breakout, simply because this was a bear market environment. This again emphasizes the point that the best signals generally go with the trend. This is not the same thing as saying that all short-term bear market buy signals result in whipsaws and all protrend moves will be successful. For example, the buy signal at *H* took place during the bull move but was essentially a false signal. Again, we could filter this one out, because it was not possible to construct a meaningful trendline as it was at *F*, *H*, and *I*.

The signal labeled *E*, of course, was the most successful, but at the time the long-term KST had not crossed above its MA. However, one of the principles of interpretation allows us to anticipate a reversal if the KST has flattened, and if a trendline break in the price or short-term KSTs is sufficient to anticipate a reversal. In this case an 8-month down trendline in the price had been violated, the short-term KST had gone bullish, and diverged positively with the price twice. Consequently, there would have been enough evidence to have concluded that the odds favored a long-term KST buy signal.

Sometimes, when a computer-scanning exercise returns a long-term smoothed momentum buy signal, the short-term situation is overbought. Chart 31-20 offers an example for IBM at arrow *A*. In such situations it doesn't matter too much for a long-term investor, but for a short-term trader entering when the price is overbought, it can prove disastrous. Chart 31-20 shows that the first opportunity to buy, once the long-term KST had crossed

Chart 31-20   IBM, 1993–1994, and two indicators. (*From www.pring.com.*)

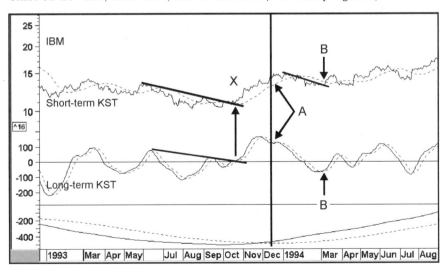

its MA, came under the cloud of a short-term overbought situation. The next one came at *B* when the price broke above a small trendline and the short-term KST triggered a buy signal. Even this was not the greatest of signals, but at least the entry price was lower than at the time of the bullish long-term KST signal. The best signal of all developed at *X* when the price violated a down trendline, and the short-term KST went bullish. Note also that the KST was barely below zero at the time, which was a tip-off for the sharp rally that followed. Since the long-term KST had reversed to the upside at this point, it would have been reasonable to use all this positive evidence to conclude that the probabilities strongly favored a long-term MA crossover.

I am not going to say that anticipating a long-term buy signal will work every time, but it is certainly true that on many occasions the first rally coming off a bear market low turns out to be very worthwhile.

Summary

- Most stocks go through ownership cycles, which normally take a long time to complete. It is important to identify whether a stock is in a secular uptrend or downtrend in order to better understand its position within its ownership cycle.
- Substantial profit potential is available to the long-term investor who can identify stocks that are breaking out from extended bases accompanied by expanding volume and an improving long-term trend in RS.
- A bull market generally carries most stocks with it, but the performance of individual issues can vary enormously, both over the course of the primary upmove and within it.
- Once a favorable market environment has been established, the process of selecting stocks should begin with the isolation of promising industry groups with a positive long-term technical position.
- Once attractive groups have been isolated, it is important to look for stocks that are outperforming the industry group index.

Epilogue

The suggestion was made at the outset that the keys to success in the stock market are knowledge and action. The knowledge part of the equation has been discussed as comprehensively as possible, but the final word has been reserved for investor action, since the way in which knowledge is used is just as important as understanding the process itself.

Indicated in the following are some common errors that all of us commit more often than we would like to admit. The most obvious of these can be avoided by applying the accompanying principles.

1. *Perspective.* The interpretation of any indicator should not be based on short-term trading patterns; the longer-term implications should always be considered.

2. *Objectivity.* A conclusion should not be drawn on the basis of one or two reliable or favorite indicators. The possibility that these indicators could give misleading signals demonstrates the need to form a balanced view derived from *all* available information. Objectivity also implies removing as much emotion from the trading and investing process as possible. If incorrect decisions are being made, they will almost always come from a position of mental imbalance. Every effort should therefore be made to reduce the emotional content of any decision on both the buy and sell sides.

3. *Humility.* One of the hardest lessons in life is learning to admit a mistake. The knowledge of all market participants in the aggregate is, and always will be, greater than that of any one individual or group of individuals. This knowledge is expressed in the action of the market itself, as reflected by the various indicators. Anyone who fights the tape or the verdict of the market will swiftly suffer the consequences. Under such circumstances, it is as well to become humble and let the market give its own verdict. A review of the indicators will frequently suggest the future direction of prices. Occasionally, the analysis proves to be wrong, and the market fails to act as anticipated. If this unexpected action changes the basis on which the original conclusion was drawn, it is wise to admit the mistake and alter the conclusion.

4. *Tenacity.* If the circumstances outlined previously develop, but it is considered that the technical position has *not* changed, the original opinion should not be changed either.

5. *Independent thought.* If a review of the indicators suggests a position that is not attuned to the majority view, that conclusion is probably well founded. On the other hand, a conclusion should never be drawn simply because it is opposed to the majority view. In other words contrariness for its own sake is not valid. Since the majority conclusion is usually based on false assumptions, it is prudent to examine such assumptions to determine their accuracy.

6. *Simplicity.* Most things done well are also done simply. Because the market operates on common sense, the best approaches to it are basically very simple. If an analyst must resort to complex computer programming and model building, the chances are that he or she has not mastered the basic techniques and therefore requires an analytical crutch.

7. *Discretion.* There is a persistent temptation to call every possible market turn, along with the duration of every move a security is likely to make. This deluded belief in one's power to pull off the impossible inevitably results in failure, a loss of confidence, and damage to one's reputation. For this reason, analysis should concentrate on identifying major turning points rather than predicting the duration of a move—there is no known formula on which consistent and accurate forecasts of this type can be based.

Appendix

The Elliott Wave

Introduction

The Elliott wave principle was established by R. N. Elliott and was first published in a series of articles in *Financial World* in 1939. The basis of the Elliott wave theory developed from the observation that rhythmic regularity has been the law of creation since the beginning of time. Elliott noted that all cycles in nature, whether of the tide, the heavenly bodies, the planets, day and night, or even life and death, had the capability for repeating themselves indefinitely. Those cyclical movements were characterized by two forces: one building up and the other tearing down.

The principal part of the theory is concerned with form or wave patterns, but other aspects include ratio and time. In this case, *pattern* does not refer to the types of formation covered in earlier chapters, but to a waveform. *Ratio* refers to the concept of price retracements and time to the period separating important peaks and troughs.

Chapter 15 described several techniques based on the Fibonacci number sequence. This same sequence forms the basis for retracement and time development in Elliott theory.

The Fibonacci Sequence

This concept of natural law also embraces an extraordinary numerical series discovered by a thirteenth-century mathematician named Fibonacci. The series that carries his name is derived by taking the number 2 and adding to it the previous number in the series. Thus, 2 + 1 = 3, then 3 + 2 = 5, 5 + 3 = 8, 8 + 5 = 13, 13 + 8 = 21, 21 + 13 = 34, and so on. The series becomes 1, 2, 3, 5, 8, 13, 21, 34, 55, 89, 144, 233, and so on. It has a number of fascinating properties, among which are the following:

1. The sum of any two consecutive numbers forms the number following them. Thus, 3 + 5 = 8 and 5 + 8 = 13, and so on.

2. The ratio of any number to its next higher is 61.8 to 100, and the ratio of any number to its next lower is 161.8 to 100.

3. The ratio 1.68 multiplied by the ratio 0.618 equals 1.

The connection between Elliott's observation of repeating cycles of nature and the Fibonacci summation series is that the Fibonacci numbers and proportions are found in many manifestations of nature. For example, a sunflower has 89 curves, of which 55 wind in one direction and 34 in the opposite direction. In music, an octave comprises 13 keys on a piano, with 5 black notes and 8 white. Trees always branch from the base in Fibonacci series, and so on.

The Wave Principle

Combining his observation of natural cycles with his knowledge of the Fibonacci series, Elliott noted that the market moves forward in a series of five waves and then declines in a series of three waves. He concluded that a single cycle comprised eight waves, as shown in Fig. A-1 (3, 5, and 8 are, of course, Fibonacci numbers).

The upper part of the cycle consists of five waves. Waves 1, 3, and 5 are protrend moves and are called impulse waves. Waves 2 and 4, on the other hand, are called corrective waves because they correct waves 1 and 3. The declining part of the cycle consists of three waves, known as a, b, and c.

The longest cycle in the Elliott concept is called the *grand supercycle*. In turn, each grand supercycle can be subdivided into eight supercycle waves, each of which is then divided into eight cycle waves. The process continues to embrace primary, intermediate, minute, minuette, and subminuette waves. The various details are highly intricate, but the general picture is represented in Figs. A-1 and A-2.

Figure A-2 shows a complete cycle with its subwaves. The determinant of whether a wave divides into five or three is the direction of the next largest wave. Corrections are always three-wave affairs.

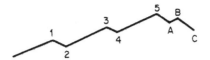

Figure A-1   Typical cycle.

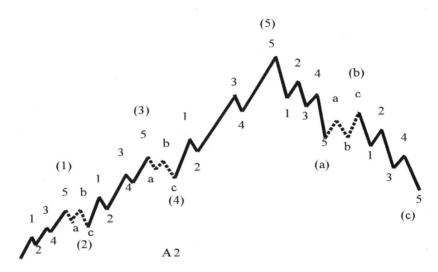

Figure A-2   Complete cycle with subwaves.

Figures A-3 and A-4 show Elliott in historical perspective. Figure A-3 illustrates the first five waves of the grand supercycle, which Elliott deemed to have begun in 1800. Some Elliott wave theoreticians believe that the grand supercycle peaked at the end of the twentieth century.

As the wave principle is one of form, there is no way to determine when the three corrective waves are likely to appear. However, the frequent recurrences of Fibonacci numbers representing time spans between peaks and troughs are probably beyond coincidence. These time spans are shown in Table A-1.

More recently, 8 years occurred between the 1966 and 1974 bottoms, the 1968 and 1976 tops, and the 1990 and 1998 bottoms. Also, there were 5 years between the 1968 and 1973 tops, for example. By the same token, there are many peaks and troughs that are not separated by numbers in this sequence.

It can readily be seen that the real problem with Elliott is interpretation. Indeed, every wave theorist (including Elliott himself) has at some time or another become entangled with the question of where one wave finished and another started. As far as the Fibonacci time spans are concerned, although these periods recur frequently, it is extremely difficult to use this principle as a basis for forecasting; there are no indications whether time spans based on these numbers will produce tops to tops or bottoms to tops, or something else, and the permutations are infinite.

We have hardly scratched the surface, and in some respects the old maxim "A little knowledge is a dangerous thing" applies probably more to Elliott than to any other market theorist. Its subjectivity in itself can be dangerous because the market is very subject to emotional influences. Consequently, the weight given to Elliott interpretations should probably be downplayed. Those wishing to pursue this theory in greater detail are referred to the classic text on the subject, by Frost and Prechter, called *Elliott Wave Principle*, Gainsville, GA, New Classics Library, 1978, since the theory has been described in this Appendix only in its barest outline.

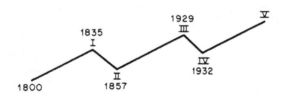

Figure A-3 The grand supercycle.

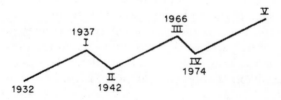

Figure A-4 Supercycle.

Table A-1 Time Spans Between Stock Market Peaks and Troughs

Year started	Position	Year ended	Position	Length of cycle (years)
1916	Top	1921	Bottom	5
1919	Top	1924	Bottom	5
1924	Bottom	1929	Top	5
1932	Bottom	1937	Top	5
1937	Top	1942	Btoom	5
1956	Top	1961	Top	5
1961	Top	1966	Top	5
1916	Top	1924	Bottom	8
1921	Bottom	1929	Top	8
1924	Bottom	1932	Bottom	8
1929	Top	1937	Top	8
1938	Bottom	1946	Top	8
1949	Bottom	1957	Bottom	8
1960	Bottom	1968	Top	8
1962	Bottom	1970	Bottom	8
1916	Top	1929	Top	13
1919	Top	1932	Bottom	13
1924	Bottom	1937	Top	13
1929	Top	1942	Bottom	13
1949	Bottom	1962	Bottom	13
1953	Bottom	1966	Bottom	13
1957	Bottom	1970	Bottom	13
1916	Top	1937	Top	21
1921	Bottom	1942	Bottom	21
1932	Bottom	1953	Bottom	21
1949	Bottom	1970	bottom	21
1953	Bottom	1974	Bottom	21
1919	Top	1953	Bottom	34
1932	Bottom	1966	Top	34
1942	Bottom	1976	Top	34
1919	Top	1974	Bottom	55
1921	Bottom	1976	Top	55

Glossary

Advance/Decline (A/D) line   An A/D line is constructed from a cumulative plurality of a set of data over a specified period (usually daily or weekly). The result is plotted as a continuous line. The A/D line and market averages usually move in the same direction. Failure of the A/D line to confirm a new high in the market average is a sign of weakness, whereas failure of the A/D line to confirm a new low by the market averages is a sign of technical strength.

Advisory services   Privately circulated publications that comment upon the future course of financial markets, and for which a subscription is usually required.

Bear trap   A signal that suggests that the rising trend of a security has reversed, but which soon proves to be false.

Breadth (in the market)   The term *breadth* relates to the number of issues participating in a move. A rally is considered suspect if the number of advancing issues is diminishing as the rally develops. Conversely, a decline that is associated with fewer stocks falling is considered to be a bullish sign.

Bull trap   A signal that suggests that the declining trend of a security has reversed, but which soon proves to be false.

Customer free balances   The total amount of unused money on deposit in brokerage accounts. These are "free" funds representing cash that may be employed in the purchase of securities.

Cyclical investing   The process of buying and selling stocks based on a longer-term or primary market move. The cycle approximates to the 4-year business cycle, to which such primary movements in stock prices are normally related.

Divergence   A nonconfirmation that is not cleared up. Negative divergences occur at market peaks, while positive divergences develop at market bottoms. The significance of a divergence is a direct function of its size—that is, over time and the number of divergences in a given situation.

Insider Any person who directly or indirectly owns more than 10 percent of any class of stock listed on a national exchange or who is an officer or director of the company in question.

Margin Occurs when an investor pays part of the purchase price of a security and borrows the balance, usually from a broker; the margin is the difference between the market value of the stock and the loan that is made against it. In the futures markets, margin is a good-faith deposit for a contract for future delivery.

Margin call The demand upon a customer to put up money or securities with a broker. The call is made if a customer's equity in a margin account declines below a minimum standard set by the exchange or brokerage firm. This happens when there is a drop in price of the securities being held as collateral.

Members Members of a stock exchange who are empowered to buy and sell securities on the floor of the exchange either for a client or for their own account.

Momentum The underlying power or thrust behind an upward or downward price movement. Momentum is represented on a graph as a line that is continually fluctuating above and below a horizontal equilibrium level, which represents the halfway point between extreme readings. Momentum is a generic term embracing many different indicators, such as rate of change (ROC), relative strength indicators (RSIs), and stochastics.

Moving average (MA) A simple MA is constructed by taking a mean average of a time series over a given period. When the price crosses above or below the MA, a buy or sell signal is given. MAs often serve as support or resistance points.

Moving average convergence divergence (MACD) An oscillator that measures the distance between two simple or exponentially smoothed MAs.

Nonconfirmation A market is said to be "in gear" when most averages and indicators that form a part of it confirm successive highs or lows. For example, when the Dow Jones Industrial Average (DJIA) makes new highs, but the A/D line does not, a nonconfirmation is said to occur. If other indicators or averages also fail to confirm, conditions are regarded as bearish until the nonconfirmations are cleared up, and vice versa.

Odd lots Units of stock of less than 100 shares; these do not customarily appear on the tape.

Odd-lot shorts   Odd lots that are sold short. Since odd lots are usually the vehicle of uninformed traders, a high level of odd-lot shorts in relation to total odd-lot sales often characterizes a major market bottom. A low level of odd-lot shorts compared with total odd-lot sales is a sign of a market top.

Option   The right to buy or sell specific securities at a specified price within a specified time. A *put* gives the holder the right to sell the stock, and a *call* gives the right to buy the stock.

Overbought   An opinion about the level of prices. It may refer to a specific indicator or to the market as a whole after a period of vigorous buying, after which it may be argued that prices are overextended for the time being and are in need of a period of downward or horizontal adjustment.

Oversold   An opinion about the level of prices. It is the opposite of overbought—that is, a price move that has overextended itself on the downside.

Price/earnings ratio   The ratio of the price of a stock to the earnings per share—that is, the total annual profit of a company divided by the number of shares outstanding.

Price patterns   When a trend reverses direction, the price action typically traces out a formation known as a *price pattern*. The larger and deeper the pattern, the greater is its significance. Patterns that are formed at market tops are called *distribution formations*; that is, the stock or market is assumed to be undergoing distribution from strong, informed hands to weak, uninformed buyers. Price patterns at market bottoms are known as *accumulation formations*. Price formations may also represent temporary interruptions of the prevailing trend, in which case they are called *continuation patterns*.

Rally   A brisk rise following a decline or consolidation of the general price level of a security price.

Reaction   A temporary contratrend price weakness or consolidation following an upswing.

Relative strength (RS) comparative   An RS line is calculated by dividing one security's price by another. Usually, the divisor is a measure of the market, such as the DJIA or the Commodity Research Bureau (CRB) Commodity Index. A rising line indicates that the index or stock is performing better than the market, and vice versa. Trends in RS can be monitored by MA crossovers, trendline breaks, and so on, in the same way as any other price trend.

Relative strength indicator (RSI)   An oscillator measuring the internal momentum of a price series. The RSI is designed to oscillate between 0 and 100. It can be calculated for any time span, but 14 days is the most commonly used period. It should not be confused with comparative RS, which measures relative performance between two different spans.

Secondary distribution or offering   The redistribution of a block of stock some time after it has been sold by the issuing company. The transaction is handled off the exchanges by a securities firm or group of firms. The shares are usually offered at a fixed price, which is related to the current market price of the stock.

Security   A generic term applied to any freely traded entity, such as a stock, bond, currency, commodity, or market index.

Short covering   The process of buying back stock that has been sold short.

Short-interest ratio   The ratio of the short position to the average daily trading volume of the month in question. A high short-interest ratio above 1.8 used to be considered bullish, but recent distortions due to the active trading of stock index futures and options have made this a less useful indicator than it once was.

Short position (interest)   The total amount of short sales outstanding on a specific exchange at a particular time. The short position is published monthly.

Short selling   Short selling is normally a speculative operation undertaken in the belief that the price of the shares will fall. The security is simply sold before it is bought. This process is accomplished in the stock market by borrowing stock from a broker in order to sell shares one does own. Most stock exchanges prohibit the short sale of a security below the price at which the last board lot was traded. This is not the case in the futures markets.

Specialist   A member of a stock exchange who acts as a specialist in a listed issue and who is registered with the exchange for that purpose. The member agrees to efficiently execute all orders and, insofar as reasonably practical, to maintain a fair and orderly market in the issue or issues for which he or she is a specialist.

Trendlines   Trendlines are constructed by joining a series of descending peaks or ascending troughs. Greater significance is attached to the trendline violation the more times it has been touched, the longer the line remains viable, and the less steep its angle. A trendline break does not necessarily signal a trend reversal, but can also result in a consolidation.

Yield curve   The structure of the level of interest rates through various maturities. Usually, the shorter the maturity, the lower the interest rate. Thus, 3-month T-bills usually yield less than 20-year government bonds. The slope of the yield curve relates to the speed, which rises as the maturity increases. In periods of tight money, short-term rates usually yield more than longer-term rates, and the curve is then called an *inverse yield curve*.

Bibliography

Achelis, Steven B. *Technical Analysis A to Z*, Probus, Homewood, Ill. 1995.

Appel, G. *Winning Stock Market Systems*, Signalert Corp., Great Neck, N.Y., 1974.

Arms, Richard W. *The Arms Index (TRIN)*, Dow Jones-Irwin, Homewood, Ill., 1989.

_____. *Volume Cycles in the Stock Market: Market Timing Through Equivolume-Charting*, Dow Jones-Irwin, Homewood, Ill., 1983.

Ayres, L. P. *Turning Points in Business Cycles*, August M. Kelly, New York, 1967.

Benner, S. *Benner's Prophecies of Future Ups and Downs in Prices*, Chase and Hall, Cincinnati, 1875; reprinted in *Journal of Cycle Research*, vol. 8, no. 1, January 1959.

Bernstein, J. *The Handbook of Commodity Cycles: A Window on Time*, John Wiley and Sons, Inc., New York, 1982.

Bressert, Walter *The Power of Oscillator Cycle Combinations*, Bressert and Associates, Tucson, Ariz. 1991.

Bretz, W. G. *Juncture Recognition in the Stock Market*, Vantage Press, New York, 1972.

Bulkowski, Thomas N. *Encyclopedia of Chart Patterns*, John Wiley and Sons, Inc., New York, 2000.

Colby, Robert W., and Thomas A. Meyers. *The Encyclopedia of Technical Market Indicators*, Dow Jones-Irwin, Homewood, Ill., 1988.

Coppock, E. S. C. *Practical Relative Strength Charting*, Trendex Corp., San Antonio, Tex. 1960.

De Villiers, Victor. *The Point and Figure Method of Anticipating Stock Price Movements*, 1933 (available from Traderslibrary.com).

Dewey, E. R. *Cycles: The Mysterious Forces That Trigger Events*, Hawthorne Books, New York, 1971.

Dewey, E.R., and E. F. Dakin. *Cycles: The Science of Prediction*, Henry Holt, New York, 1947.

Dorsey, Thomas J. *Point and Figure Charting*, John Wiley and Sons, Inc., New York, 1995.

Drew, G. *New Methods for Profit in the Stock Market*, Metcalfe Press, Boston, 1968.

Edwards, Robert D., and John Magee. *Technical Analysis of Stock Trends*, John Magee, Springfield, Mass., 1957.

Eiteman, W. J., C. A. Dice, and D. K. Eiteman. *The Stock Market*, McGraw-Hill, Inc., New York, 1966.

Elder, Alexander. *Trading for a Living*, John Wiley and Sons, Inc., New York, 1994.

Fosback, N. G. *Stock Market Logic: A Sophisticated Approach to Profits on Wall Street*, The Institute for Econometric Research, Fort Lauderdale, Fla., 1976.

Frost, A. J., and Robert R. Prechter. *The Elliott Wave Principle: Key to Stock Market Profits*, New Classics Library, Chappaqua, N.Y., 1978.

Gann, W. D. *Truth of the Stock Tape*, Financial Guardian, New York, 1932.

Gartley, H. M. *Profits in the Stock Market*, Lambert Gann Publishing, Pomeroy, Wash., 1981.

Gordon, William. *The Stock Market Indicators*, Investors Press, Palisades Park, N.J., 1968.

Granville, J. *Strategy of Daily Stock Market Timing*, Prentice Hall, Englewood Cliffs, N.J., 1960.

Greiner, P., and H. C. Whitcomb. *Dow Theory, Investors' Intelligence*, New York, 1969.

Hamilton, W. D. *The Stock Market Barometer*, Harper & Bros., New York, 1922.

Hayes, Timothy. *The Research Driven Investor*, McGraw-Hill, New York, 2001.

Hurst, J. M. *The Profit Magic of Stock Transaction Timing*, Prentice Hall, Englewood Cliffs, N.J., 1970.

Jiler, W. *How Charts Can Help You in the Stock Market*, Commodity Research Publishing Corp., New York, 1961.

Kaufmann, Perry. *New Commodity Trading Systems*, John Wiley and Sons, Inc., New York, 1987.

_____. *Smarter Trading*, McGraw-Hill, New York, 1995.

Krow, H. *Stock Market Behavior*, Random House, New York, 1969.

McMillan, Lawrence G. *McMillan on Options*, John Wiley and Sons, Inc., 1996.

Merrill, A. A. *Filtered Waves: Basic Theory*, Analysis Press, Chappaqua, N.Y., 1977.

Murphy John J. *Intermarket Technical Analysis*, John Wiley and Sons, Inc., New York, 1991.

_____. *Technical Analysis of the Financials Markets*, New York Institute of Finance, New York, 1999.

Nelson, S. *ABC of Stock Market Speculation,* Taylor, New York, 1934.

Nison, Steve. *Japanese Candlestick Charting Techniques,* New York Institute of Finance, New York, 1991.

Pring, Martin J. *The All Season Investor,* John Wiley and Sons, Inc., New York, 1991.

_____. *Breaking the Black Box* (book and CD-ROM tutorial combination), McGraw-Hill, New York, 2002.

_____. *How to Forecast Interest Rates,* McGraw-Hill, Inc., New York, 1981.

_____. *How to Select Stocks* (book and CD-ROM tutorial combination), McGraw-Hill, New York, 2002.

_____. *International Investing Made Easy,* McGraw-Hill, Inc., New York, 1981.

_____. *Introduction to Candlestick Charting* (book and CD-ROM tutorial combination), McGraw-Hill, New York, 2002.

_____. *Introduction to Technical Analysis* (book and CD-ROM tutorial combination), McGraw-Hill, New York, 1998.

_____. *Investment Psychology Explained.* John Wiley and Sons, Inc., New York, 1991.

_____. *Learning the KST: An Introductory CD-ROM Tutorial,* www.pring.com, 1997.

_____. *Martin Pring on Market Momentum,* McGraw-Hill, Inc., New York, 1995.

_____. *Technician's Guide to Daytrading* (book and CD-ROM tutorial combination), McGraw-Hill, New York, 2002.

_____. *Momentum Explained, vol. I* (book and CD-ROM tutorial combination), McGraw-Hill, New York, 2002.

_____. *Momentum Explained, vol. II* (book and CD-ROM tutorial combination), McGraw-Hill, New York, 2002.

Rhea, Robert. *Dow Theory,* Barrons, New York, 1932.

Shuman, J. B., and D. Rosenau. *The Kondratieff Wave,* World Publishing, New York, 1972.

Smith, E. L. *Common Stocks and Business Cycles,* William Frederick Press, New York, 1959.

_____. *Common Stocks as a Long-Term Investment,* Macmillan, New York, 1939 (now available in reprint from Fraser, Burlington, Vt., 1989).

_____. *Tides and the Affairs of Men,* Macmillan, New York, 1932.

Financial Book Dealers

James Fraser
Fraser Publishing Co.
P.O. Box 494
Burlington, VT 05402
(802) 658-0322
Traderslibrary.com
Traderspress.com

Technical Analysis Societies

International Federation of Technical Analysts (IFTA) [www.IFTA.org]
(From here links are available to major technical societies around the world.)

Useful Web Sites

Bigcharts.com   For commentary, charts and industry group information
Wealth-lab.com   For charting, discussion and rankings of automated systems plus unique system testing software.
Quote.com   For delayed real time and end-of-day charting
Quote.Yahoo.com   For charting for US stocks international indexes etc.
Investorlinks.com   For multiple links to financial sites

Index

O

About the Author

Martin J. Pring is the highly respected president of Pring Research (**www.pring.com**), editor of the newsletter *The Intermarket Review,* and one of today's most influential thought leaders in the world of technical analysis. The author of McGraw-Hill's *Martin Pring on Technical Analysis* series, Pring has written more than a dozen trading books and has contributed to *Barron's* and other national publications. He was awarded the Jack Frost Memorial Award from the Canadian Technical Analysts Society.